Essentials of Human Communication

SECOND EDITION

Joseph A. DeVito

Hunter College of the City University of New York

 HarperCollins*CollegePublishers*

If we are to achieve a richer culture, rich in contrasting values, we must recognize the whole gamut of human potentialities, and so weave a less arbitrary social fabric, one in which each diverse human gift will find a fitting place.

—MARGARET MEAD

Acquisition Editor: Cynthia Biron
Developmental Editor: Dawn Groundwater
Project Editorial Manager: Melonie Salvati
Senior Designer: John Callahan
Text Design: Circa 86, Inc.
Cover Illustration: Warren Linn
Art Studio: John Callahan
Electronic Production Manager: Su Levine
Desktop Administrator: Laura Leever
Manufacturing Manager: Willie Lane
Electronic Page Makeup: Circa 86, Inc.
Printer and Binder: R.R. Donnelley & Sons, Company
Cover Printer: The Lehigh Press, Inc.

For Permission to use copyrighted material, grateful acknowledgment is made to the copyright holders on pp. 419–420, which are herby made part of this copyright page.

Essentials of Human Communication, Second Edition

Copyright © 1996 by HarperCollins Publishers

Library of Congress Cataloging-in-Publication Data

DeVito, Joseph A.,
    Essentials of human communication / Joseph A. DeVito. — 2nd ed.
        p.   cm
    Includes bibliographical references and index.
    ISBN 0-673-99614-X
    1. Communication. I. Title
P90.D483   1995   95-4228
302.2—dc20   CIP

95 96 97 98   9 8 7 6 5 4 3 2 1

Contents

Specialized Table of Contents

Power Perspectives

Test Yourself

Preface

It is a pleasure to introduce the second edition of *Essentials of Human Communication* to those who used the first edition and to newcomers. *Essentials* is designed for the introductory course in human communication. It focuses on three contexts: interpersonal communication (including interviewing), small group communication, and public speaking. The book emphasizes the development and improvement of communication skills, but does not neglect the theoretical foundations for these skills.

Essentials is divided into two parts. Part One—"Foundations of Human Communication"—contains six chapters and focuses on the concepts and principles of human communication: the communication process, the self, perception, listening, and verbal and nonverbal messages. Part Two—"The Contexts of Human Communication"—contains nine chapters and covers interpersonal, interviewing, small group, and public speaking.

MAJOR THEMES

This book's uniqueness can best be appreciated by looking at its major themes and how they are presented.

Skills Development

This book provides the student with the essential skills of

- perceptual and listening effectiveness
- verbal and nonverbal message construction and reception
- interpersonal communication, including conversation, conflict, and interpersonal relationships
- interviewing, especially the information and the job interviews
- small group communication for idea generation, personal growth, information sharing, and problem solving, and their leadership
- public speaking for preparing and delivering informative and persuasive speeches

Cultural Awareness, Cultural Viewpoints

The topics in each chapter are presented with an awareness of (and clear reference to) the cultural diversity of the world in which we live. In addition, every chapter contains at least one Cultural Viewpoint box that focuses on an aspect of culture related to the topic of the chapter. A total of 22 Cultural Viewpoints are presented throughout the text and cover such topics as culture and competence, openness to intercultural communication, men and women as listeners, cultural and nonverbal communication, high- and low-context cultures, ethnocentrism, and fear in intercultural communication.

Critical Thinking

Critical thinking, a major component of the previous edition, is enlarged and enhanced here and the discussions are more closely tied to the topics of the text. Replacing the end of the part sections of the previous edition are specific sections—presented now at the end of each chapter—dealing with critical thinking in reference to the topics of the chapter. This position change—and the expansion of the material—gives even greater attention to the skills of critical thinking. The marginal quotations and probes likewise serve critical thinking functions.

Ethical Issues

Presented throughout this text in boxes are ethical issues such as gossiping, lying, public speaker ethics, censoring messages, and the like. Ten such boxes are spread throughout the text, juxtaposed to the content to which they are most clearly related.

Power

In each chapter, Power Perspectives are presented in the margins. These 22 sidebars identify the nature of power, how it works, and how it relates to the skills of human communication. Ranging from the traditional types of power (expert, reward, and legitimate, for example) to dealing with power plays, expressing confidence, using compliance-gaining and resisting strategies, and expressing power in speech and gesture, these sidebars relate the concepts of power and self-empowerment to the concepts and principles of human communication. Power Perspectives underscore the integral connection between power and effective communication and the very practical focus of this textbook.

THE PEDAGOGY

As in the first edition, the pedagogy is highly interactive but is improved in several important ways.

Self-tests

Twenty-one self-tests appear in this edition and include the thoroughly researched tests of apprehension, love, self-monitoring, time orientation, and argumentativeness, for example. Also included are tests designed to involve the reader in the concepts discussed in the chapter and which therefore serve a more purely pedagogical purpose—for example, confirmation, gender differences in language, giving effective criticism, and credibility.

Chapter Contents, Goals, and Skills

The contents of the chapter and their corresponding goals and skills are now presented in a table in the chapter opener. This table identifies the "goals" (cognitive learning objectives) the reader should be able to accomplish and the "skills" (behavioral learning objectives) the reader should master with each of the major topics in the chapter.

Feedback Summaries

The feedback summaries continue to include both a conceptual summary and a skills summary. The skills summary is presented as a checklist to allow the reader to determine his or her current level of mastery. In this way, those skills requiring further effort can be highlighted.

Skill Development Experiences

This edition contains 45 skill development experiences, approximately 3 per chapter. Many are new to this edition and many others have been streamlined. These exercises give primary emphasis to the learning of specific communication skills in an enjoyable way and in a supportive atmosphere.

Quotations and Probes

Quotations (philosophical, humorous, and practical observations on communication) and Probes (questions designed to stimulate critical thinking and discussion) continue to appear in the margin. A few changes were made here. First, the number of marginal items has been reduced to a more usable number; approximately 25 quotes and probes now appear in each chapter. This should help to emphasize the more important concepts and yet not interfere with the text itself. The quotations have been moved in the direction of the more literary and philosophical (rather than the purely definitional or academic). The number of probes built around specific research findings and theories have been increased, with the aim of presenting research findings in a provocative and in many instances in a practical context.

Culture, Ethics, and Power Boxes

These boxes pose a variety of important issues and may be read in connection with the text material to which they are juxtaposed or they may be read in sequence. Each of these items ends with a note identifying the page on which the next item appears. In this way they may constitute individual chapters—brief chapters in the case of ethics and power, and a fully developed chapter in the case of culture. Many of these boxes contain self-tests or exercises designed to promote active involvement with these discussions.

WHAT'S NEW?

A number of significant improvements have been made in this second edition. Here are a few of the major changes.

1. **Critical thinking** has been given greater importance. Each chapter now ends with a discussion of critical thinking as it applies to the chapter contents.

2. **Culture** has been given a much more important place in this edition; 22 Cultural Viewpoint boxes have been positioned throughout the text, coordinated to the content of the chapter.
3. **Ethics** is highlighted even more and is presented as part of the essentials of communication. Ten boxed items raise issues on the ethics of communication.
4. **Power** and its close connection with the skills of effective communication is highlighted in the 22 Power Perspectives appearing in the margins.
5. Numerous other **content improvements** have also been made; here are just a few examples:

   • The model of communication and the principles of communication have been clarified (Chapter 1).
   • Self-concept has been added (Chapter 2).
   • Perception and listening—formerly combined in one chapter—are each given a separate chapter and the content in each has been expanded.
   • Special attention is given to critical perception (strategies and guidelines), especially to perception checking (Chapter 3).
   • Effective listening has been reconceptualized as involving choices among modes of listening, for example, between empathic and objective listening, rather than as a simple (but potentially misleading) listing of dos and don'ts (Chapter 4).
   • Disconfirmation (and racism, sexism, and heterosexism) has been given greater attention (Chapter 5).
   • Added discussions on nonverbal communication include facial communication and cultural time (Chapter 6).
   • The process of conversation is used as a framework for interpersonal communication and its skills; the discussion of conflict has been greatly expanded (Chapter 7).
   • The coverage of interpersonal relationships has been completely reorganized; it is now presented in two parts: the stages in relationships and the theories of relationships (Chapter 8).
   • The interviewing chapter has been reorganized to give greater prominence to the information-gathering interview and the employment interview (Chapter 9).
   • New discussions on small group stages and focus groups have been added in the chapter on small groups (10). Approaches to leadership, a dialogue on member roles, and leadership qualities have been added to Chapter 11, "Small Group Members and Leaders."
   • The three public speaking chapters have been increased to four (Chapters 12–15) and totally reorganized. The first two chapters cover the ten steps a speaker should follow in preparing and delivering a speech. Chapters 14 and 15 then cover the informative speech and the persuasive speech. Additional organizational patterns, statistics as a means of support, reasoning fallacies, and sample speeches with critical thinking probes have been added to this edition.
   • New skill development experiences focus on, for example, applying communication principles to relationship problems, language accuracy, credibility, color in communication, small group roles, and public speaking audience attitudes.

- The text has been completely revised for language and style and a new design has been created for a more appealing and functional presentation of the material.

SUPPLEMENTARY MATERIALS

Essentials of Human Communication comes with a wide variety of supplementary materials to make this book an efficient and effective learning and teaching tool. Instructors should consult their local HarperCollins sales representative for further information on any of these materials.

1. **Instructor's Manual and Test Bank with Transparency Masters.** A detailed Instructor's Manual, prepared by Joseph Giordano of the University of Wisconsin, Eau Claire, contains Unit Planners for each chapter, sample syllabi, guidelines for using the Skill Development Experiences, suggestions for additional exercises, and 75 transparency masters. In addition, a test bank, containing over 600 test questions and organized by chapter, is included. The test bank is also available on the user-friendly TestMaster computer program.

2. **TestMaster.** A complete test bank is contained on diskette for IBM PCs and compatibles. TestMaster comes with a word-processing program that allows complete customizing capabilities. It will prepare up to four different versions of the same test (randomizing items and alternatives within items) and feedback sheets that give the correct answers and the text page reference.

3. **The Interpersonal Challenge 2.** Also available is a card game for use with such topics as perception, interpersonal relationships, ethics, self-disclosure, and (new to this second edition) cultural dimensions of communication. Constructed by the author, this game contains 200 questions designed to increase understanding of basic concepts, encourage self-analysis, and stimulate critical thinking.

4. **Brainstorms.** A brief creative thinking booklet, subtitled, *How to Think More Creatively about Communication or About Anything Else,* integrates creative thinking into the introductory communication course and complements the critical thinking emphasis in the text. **Brainstorms** introduces the creative thinking process (its nature, values, characteristics, and stages) and its relationship to communication and provides 20 specific tools for thinking more creatively about communication (or anything else). The discussion of each tool includes its purposes, the specific techniques to follow in using the tool, and at least one exercise or application to get started using the tool. Guides for coordinating the creative thinking tools with the topics of the text are provided as well.

5. **The HarperCollins Communication Video Library.** Numerous videos are available to users and cover such topics as effective listening, interpersonal relationships, speaker apprehension, interviewing, small group communication, and public speaking.

6. **Grades.** A grade-keeping and classroom management software program for IBM PC's and compatibles is also available. This program can maintain data for up to 200 students.

ACKNOWLEDGMENTS

I would like to thank the many reviewers who responded to elaborate questionnaires and critically analyzed every page of the manuscript. They gave graciously of their time and expertise and offered suggestions that resulted in numerous significant improvements. I want to again thank those who reviewed the first edition manuscript and to whose reviews I have turned repeatedly:

Edward M. Brown, Abilene Christian University
Kelly L. Burns, Indiana-Purdue University at Fort Wayne
Charles F. Cline, Tacoma Community College
Ray Collins, San Jose City College
Robert Dixon, St. Louis Community College
Mary C. Forestieri, Lane Community College
Laurie W. Hodge, Bergen Community College
Elaine S. Klein, Westchester Community College
Rachel Lauer, Pace University
Donald Loeffler, Western Carolina University
Weslynn Martin, Rockhurst College
William L. Robinson, Purdue University, Calumet
Patricia Rochelt, Western Wisconsin Technical Institute
Chris R. Sawyer, Tarrant County Junior College, Northwest
Robert J. Sternberg, Yale University
James S. Taylor, Houston Baptist University
Stella Ting-Toomey, California State University, Fullerton
Donald E. Williams, University of Florida

To those who reviewed the first edition of the text and the manuscript for this second edition, I am especially grateful. Their comments were extremely helpful; the effectiveness of this revision owes much to their insights. Thank you:

Samuel Andrews, Texas Southern University
Mary Bozik, University of Northern Iowa
Martin H. Brodey, Montgomery College
Cynthia E. Dewar, City College of San Francisco
Joseph Giordano, University of Wisconsin–Eau Claire
Marilyn J. Hoffs, Glendale Community College
Marcia Kelley-Canary, Daley College, Chicago City Colleges
Matt Martin, Mid Michigan Community College
Elizabeth O'Brien, Phoenix College
Richard F. Salamon, St. Louis Community College at Forest Park
Pan C. Shaannan, Bryant College
James S. Taylor, Houston Baptist University

I also owe a great debt to the people at HarperCollins who took such excellent care of this manuscript. I especially wish to thank Cynthia Biron, communication editor, Dawn Groundwater, developmental editor, John Callahan, designer, and Melonie Salvati, project editor. All helped tremendously in transforming the manuscript into the text you are now holding.

Joseph A. DeVito

ESSENTIALS OF HUMAN COMMUNICATION

Second Edition

Joseph A. DeVito
Hunter College of the City University of New York

ISBN 0-673-99614-X

Introducing the essential skills and applications of interpersonal, small group communication, and public speaking, the second edition of *Essentials of Human Communication* has been updated to place greater emphasis on five major themes: *skills development; intercultural perspectives; critical thinking; ethical issues; and self-empowerment.* Written for the introductory hybrid course in human communication, DeVito illustrates the importance of the fundamentals of communication, including the self, perception, listening, and verbal and nonverbal messages. The revised edition also features expanded coverage of public speaking, perception, and listening. Full-color photos, figures, tables, cartoons, captions, and marginal quotes and probes make-up the text's visually stimulating illustration program developed to further encourage students' critical thinking skills.

CULTURAL VIEWPOINT

Culture and Nonverbal Communication

Culture influences the way you communicate nonverbally, both as a sender of messages and as a receiver-interpreter of messages. Here are just a few examples.

Americans consider direct eye contact an expression of honesty and forthrightness, but the Japanese often view this as a lack of respect. The Japanese will glance at the other person's face rarely and then only for very short periods (Axtell, 1993).

In the United States, if you live next door to someone, you are almost automatically expected to be friendly and to interact with that person. It seems so natural that we probably don't even consider that this is a cultural expectation not shared by all cultures. In Japan, the fact that your house is next to another's does not imply that you should become close or visit each other. Consider, therefore, the situation in which a Japanese buys a house next to an American. The Japanese may well see the American as overly familiar and as taking friendship for granted. The American may see the Japanese as distant, unfriendly, and unneighborly. Yet, each person is merely fulfilling the expectations of his or her own culture (Hall & Hall, 1987).

Even the meanings you assign to different colors will depend on your culture (Dreyfuss, 1971). In China, for example, red is used for joyous and festive occasions, whereas in Japan it signifies anger and danger. Blue signifies defeat for the Cherokee Indian, but virtue and truth for the Egyptian. In the Japanese theater, blue is the color for villains. Yellow signifies happiness and prosperity in Egypt, but in tenth-century France yellow colored the doors of criminals. Green communicates femininity to certain American Indians, fertility and strength to Egyptians, and youth and energy to the Japanese. Purple signifies virtue and faith in Egypt, grace and nobility in Japan.

CULTURAL VIEWPOINT BOXES

Twenty-two *Cultural Viewpoint* boxes heighten students' awareness of diversity in the world around them and in their communication transactions. Topics covered include: culture and competence, openness to intercultural communication, men and women as listeners, culture and nonverbal communication, high and low context cultures, ethnocentrism, and fear in intercultural communication.

Twenty-two *Power Perspective* sidebars identify the nature of power, how it works, and how it relates to human communication skills. Topics range from the traditional types of power, to dealing with power plays, expressing confidence, using compliance-gaining and resisting strategies, and expressing power in speech and gesture.

POWER PERSPECTIVE

Power, Confidence, and Verbal Messages

The appearance of confidence gives the appearance of power. Here are some suggestions for communicating confidence with particular reference to the interview situation. The general principles, however, apply to all forms of human communication.

* Control your emotions. Once your emotions get the best of you, you will have lost your power and influence, and you will appear to lack confidence.
* Admit your mistakes. Only a confident person can openly admit mistakes and not worry about what others will think.
* Take the initiative in introducing yourself to others and in initiating specific topics of conversation. These behaviors communicate an ability to control the social situation.
* Generally, don't ask for agreement by using tag questions, for example, "That was appropriate, don't you think?" Don't turn normally declarative sentences into questions by a rising intonation, for example, "I'll arrive at nine?" Asking for agreement communicates a lack of confidence.
* Use open-ended questions to involve the other person in the interaction and follow these up with appropriate comments and/or questions.
* Use "you" statements ("What do you think? How do you feel about this?") to signal your personal attention to the other person. This one feature, incidentally, has been shown to increase men's attractiveness to women.

THE EMPLOYMENT INTERVIEW

Perhaps of most concern to college students is the **employment** or **selection interview.** In such an interview, a great deal of information and persuasion will be exchanged. The interviewer will learn about you, your interests, your talents—and, if he or she is clever enough, some of your weaknesses and liabilities. You will be informed about the nature of the company, its benefits, its advantages—and, if you are clever enough, some of its disadvantages and problems. Before reading about the employment interview, you may wish to take the accompanying test on your own apprehension in this situation.

TEST YOURSELF
How Apprehensive Are You in Employment Interviews?

Instructions This questionnaire is composed of five questions concerning your feelings about communicating in the job interview setting. Indicate in the spaces provided, the degree to which each statement adequately describes your feelings about the employment interview. Use the following scale: (1) = strongly agree, (2) = agree, (3) = are undecided, (4) = disagree, or (5) = strongly disagree.

_____ 1. While participating in a job interview with a potential employer, I am not nervous.
_____ 2. Ordinarily, I am very tense and nervous in job interviews.
_____ 3. I have no fear of speaking up in job interviews.
_____ 4. I'm afraid to speak up in job interviews.
_____ 5. Ordinarily, I am very calm and relaxed in job interviews.

Scoring: In computing your score, follow these steps:
1. Reverse your scores for items 2 and 4 as follows:

if you said	reverse it to
1	5
2	4
3	3
4	2
5	1

2. Add the scores from all five items; be sure to use the reverse scores for items 2 and 4 and the original scores for 1, 3, and 5.

Thinking Critically About Apprehension in the Job Interview

1. The higher your score, the greater your apprehension. Since this test is still under development, specific meanings for specific scores are not possible. A score of 25 (the highest possible score) would indicate a strongly apprehensive individual while a score of 5 (the lowest possible score) would indicate a strongly unapprehensive individual. How does your score compare with those of your peers? What score do you think would ensure optimum performance at the job interview?

INTERVIEWING

ETHICAL ISSUE

Speaker Ethics

Ethics is an essential aspect of all forms of communication. Here are four guidelines to stimulate you to start thinking about the ethical responsibilities of the public speaker. Which of these do you agree with? Which do you disagree with? What additional guides would you propose?

Truth
Present truth as you understand it. Be truthful also about the sources of your materials. Avoid defaming others—an act which is illegal as well as unethical. Defamation occurs when a speaker falsely attacks the reputation of another person that causes damage to this person. When this occurs in print or in pictures it is called *libel* and when it occurs in spoken form, it is called *slander.* So be careful of your facts, especially in speaking against another person.

Knowledge
As a speaker, you have the ethical responsibility to know what you are talking about, to have prepared yourself as thoroughly as possible.

Audience-Centered
An ethical speaker has the audience's interests in mind and avoids exploiting audiences for his or her own gain. This doesn't mean that the speaker cannot also gain—the politician seeking votes is seeking self-gain, but ideally is also concerned with the audience's interests. It is also unethical (and illegal) to present a "clear and present danger," for example, a speech that proves dangerous to the welfare of the people and the country, by causing people to riot.

Preparation
The audience has the right to expect that the speaker has done his or her best in preparing. This doesn't mean perfection; it means that reasonable preparation be made before engaging the attention of the audience.

The text's increased coverage of ethics in communication stresses the ethical responsibility of speakers and listeners. *Ethical Issue* boxes, found throughout the text, cover such topics as gossiping, lying, public speaking ethics, and censoring messages.

Where there is no difference,
there is only indifference.
—LOUIS NIZER

thoughts and feelings or directing him or her to go in any particular
direction. For example, "yes," "I see," or even "a-ha" or "hmm" are
minimal responses that tell the other person that you are interested in
his or her continued comments.
- Use positive affect statements to refer to the other person and to his or
her contributions to the interaction; for example, "I really enjoy talking with you" or "That was a clever way of looking at things" are
positive affect statements that are often felt but rarely expressed.

There are times when you may want to be more self-oriented and self-
focused. For example, in employment interview situations, the interviewee is expected to talk about himself or herself and to do more of the
speaking than the listening. On the other hand, if you are being interviewed because of something you accomplished, you obviously don't
want to focus the conversation on the interviewer; rather, you're expected
to focus the conversation on yourself. In this situation, you would obviously not ask the interviewer for suggestions or opinions or use minimal
responses to encourage the interviewer to express himself or herself. But,
you would be positive, use focused eye contact, lean toward the other
person, and so on.

INTERPERSONAL CONFLICT

Tom wants to go to the movies and Sara wants to stay home. Tom's insisting on going to the movies interferes with Sara's staying home and
Sara's determination to stay home interferes with Tom's going to the
movies. Randy and Grace have been dating. Randy wants to get married;
Grace wants to continue dating. Each has opposing goals and each interferes with the other's attaining these goals.

As experience shows, relational conflicts can be of various types: goals
to be pursued ("We want you to go to college and become a teacher or a
doctor, not a disco dancer"); allocation of resources such as money or
time ("I want to spend the tax refund on a car, not on new furniture");
decisions to be made ("I refuse to have the Jeffersons over for dinner");
or behaviors that are considered appropriate or desirable by one person
and inappropriate or undesirable by the other ("I hate it when you get
drunk, pinch me, ridicule me in front of others, flirt with others, dress
provocatively . . .").

Myths About Conflict

Never go to bed mad. Stay up
and fight.
—PHYLLIS DILLER

One of the problems in dealing with interpersonal conflict is that we may
be operating with false assumptions about what conflict is and what it
means. For example, do you think the following are true or false?

- If two people in a relationship fight, it means their relationship is a
bad one.
- Fighting hurts an interpersonal relationship.
- Fighting is bad because it reveals our negative selves—for example,
our pettiness, our need to be in control, our unreasonable expectations.

MARGINAL QUOTES AND PROBES

Over three hundred *Critical
Thinking Probes and Quotations*,
located in the margins throughout the text, stimulate critical
thinking on specific topics
covered in the text.

In one sentence, how would you
describe your style of conflict?

Remember that self-disclosure, like any communication, is irreversible
(see Chapter 1). You cannot self-disclose and then take it back. Nor can
you erase the conclusions and inferences listeners have made on the basis
of your disclosures.

THINKING CRITICALLY ABOUT THE SELF AND COMMUNICATION

Because the self is so crucial in every communication act, it is essential
that you carefully weigh the role of the self in your communication decisions. Your self-concept, self-awareness, and self-esteem will influence
how positively or negatively you communicate and how defensive or
supportive you will be. They will also influence how others communicate with you. Thus, when you want to figure out ways of improving
your own communications, consider the self-image that you are projecting. Attacking your self-destructive beliefs, engaging in self-affirmation—seeking out nourishing people, for example—will not only help
you to increase self-esteem but will also make you a more effective
communicator.

Similarly, think critically about the consequences of self-disclosing.
As we noted earlier, attitudes toward self-disclosure vary from culture
to culture and these must be considered in deciding whether to and
how to self-disclose. Moreover, decisions to self-disclose will be based
on several other factors. Among these is your concern for your relationship with the person or persons to whom you are self-disclosing
(Will this add tension to the relationship? Might it place an unfair
burden on the friendship?). You would also probably consider the

TABLE 2.1 A SUMMARY OF SELF-DISCLOSURE GUIDELINES

In Self-Disclosing:	In Responding to the Self-Disclosing of Others:
1. Is the motivation to improve the re-lationship?	1. Are you trying to feel what the other person is feeling?
2. Does the self-disclosure impose bur-dens on your listener?	2. Are you using effective and active listening skills?
3. Is the self-disclosure appropriate to the context and the relationship between yourself and your listener?	3. Are you communicating supportive-ness (verbally and nonverbally) to the discloser?
4. Is the other person disclosing also? If not, might this be a sign of disinterest?	4. Are you refraining from criticism and evaluation?
5. Might the self-disclosure place too heavy a burden on you?	5. Will you maintain confidentiality?

CRITICAL-THINKING SKILLS SECTIONS

An emphasis on critical-thinking
skills is expanded and enhanced
in this edition. The discussions
are located at the end of each
chapter and are closely tied to
the topics in the text.

CHAPTER ELEVEN

Members and Leaders in Group Communication

Chapter Concepts	Chapter Goals	Chapter Skills
	After completing this chapter, you should be able to	After completing this chapter, you should be able to
Members in Small Group Communication	identify the three major types of member roles and give examples of each	participate in a small group with a group orientation, serving group task and group building and maintenance roles and avoiding dysfunction (individual) roles
Leaders in Small Group Communication	describe the three leadership styles and when each of these would be most appropriate	adjust your leadership style to the task at hand and the needs of group members
	explain at least four functions of leaders in small group communication	serve the various leadership functions as appropriate
Factors That Work Against Small Group Effectiveness	identify those factors that work against small group effectiveness	recognize and avoid the major factors working against group effectiveness
Thinking Critically About Groupthink	define *groupthink* and identify its major symptoms	recognize and avoid the symptoms *groupthink*

SKILL DEVELOPMENT EXPERIENCES

Chapter-ending *Skill Development Experiences* promote active learning by providing students with opportunities to apply the theory and research they've learned to interpersonal and small group communication, interviewing, and public speaking situations.

Skill Development Experiences

4.1 Paraphrasing to Ensure Understanding

For each of the messages presented below, write an acceptable paraphrase. After you complete the paraphrases, ask another person if he or she would accept them as objective restatements of thoughts and feelings. Rework the paraphrases until the other person agrees that they are accurate. A sample paraphrase is provided in number 1.

1. I can't deal with my parents' constant fighting. I've seen it for the last ten years and I really can't stand it anymore.

   Paraphrase: You have trouble dealing with their fighting. You seem really upset by this last fight.

2. Did you hear I got engaged to Jerry? I'm the happiest person in the world.
3. I got a C on that paper. That's the worst grade I've ever received. I just can't believe that I got a C. This is my major. What am I going to do?
4. I really had a scare with the kids the other night. They went out to the night game at the high school. They didn't walk in till two A.M. I thought I'd die.
5. That rotten, inconsiderate pig just up and left. He never even said good-bye. We were together for six months and after one small argument he leaves without a word. And he even took my bathrobe—that expensive one he bought for my last birthday.
6. I'm just not sure what to do. I really love Chris. She's the sweetest kid I've ever known. I mean, she'd do anything for me. But she really wants to get married. I do too and yet I don't want to make such a commitment. I mean that's a long-term thing. And, much as I hate to admit it, I don't want the responsibility of a wife, a family, a house. I really don't need that kind of pressure.

4.2 Experiencing Active Listening

For each of the situations described below, supply at least one appropriate active listening response.

1. Your friend Phil has just broken up a love affair and is telling you about it. "I can't seem to get Chris out of my mind," he says. "All I do is daydream about what we used to do and all the fun we used to have."

DISCONFIRMATION

Before reading about disconfirmation, take the self-test to examine your own behavior.

TEST YOURSELF
How Confirming Are You?

Instructions: In your typical communications, how likely are you to display the following behaviors? Use the following scale in responding to each statement:

5 = always
4 = often
3 = sometimes
2 = rarely
1 = never

_____ 1. I acknowledge the presence of another person both verbally and nonverbally.
_____ 2. I acknowledge the contributions of the other person by, for example, supporting or taking issue with what the person says.
_____ 3. During the conversation, I make nonverbal contact by maintaining direct eye contact, touching, hugging, kissing, and otherwise demonstrating acknowledgment of the other person.
_____ 4. I communicate as both speaker and listener, with involvement, and with a concern and respect for the other person.
_____ 5. I signal my understanding of the other person both verbally and nonverbally.
_____ 6. I reflect back the other person's feelings as a way of showing that I understand these feelings.
_____ 7. I ask questions as appropriate concerning the other person's thoughts and feelings.
_____ 8. I respond to the other person's requests, by, for example, returning phone calls and answering letters within a reasonable time.
_____ 9. I encourage the other person to express his or her thought and feelings.
_____ 10. I respond directly and exclusively to what the other person says.

Thinking Critically About Confirmation and Disconfirmation All ten statements are phrased so that they express confirming behaviors. Therefore, high scores (say, above 35) reflect a strong tendency to engage in confirmation. Low scores (say, below 25) reflect a strong tendency to engage in disconfirmation. Don't assume, however, that all situations call for confirmation and that only insensitive people are disconfirming. You may wish to consider the situations in which disconfirmation would be, if not an effective response, at least a legitimate one.

A useful way to introduce disconfirmation and its alternatives, confirmation and rejection, is to consider a specific situation: Pat arrives home late one night. Chris is angry and complains about Pat's coming home so late. Consider some responses Pat might make:

SELF-TESTS

Twenty-one self-tests, appearing throughout the text, actively involve the reader by personalizing concepts and encouraging self-analysis.

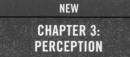

Formerly in one chapter, material in these two new chapters features expanded coverage on perception and listening.

NEW

**CHAPTER 3:
PERCEPTION**

Chapter 3 now gives special attention to the strategies and guidelines of critical perception, especially to perception checking, and a section on thinking critically about perception.

CHAPTER THREE

Perception

Chapter Concepts	Chapter Goals	Chapter Skills
	After completing this chapter, you should be able to	After completing this chapter, you should be able to
	define perception and describe its stages of sensation, organization, and evaluation	perceive others with a knowledge that perceptions are influenced by who you are and by the external stimulus
Processes Influencing Perception	explain the processes that influence interpersonal perception	perceive others while avoiding the common perceptual barriers
Critical Perception: Making Perceptions More Accurate	explain the suggestions for increasing accuracy in perception	perceive others with a variety of strategies and while following perceptual guidelines
Thinking Critically About Perception	explain the techniques for perception checking	use perception checking as appropriate

CHAPTER FOUR

Listening

Chapter Concepts	Chapter Goals	Chapter Skills
	After completing this chapter, you should be able to	After completing this chapter, you should be able to
The Listening Process	define *listening*	use listening to learn, relate, influence, play, and help as appropriate
	explain the five steps in the listening process	listen more effectively during each of the five listening stages
Effective Listening	explain the four dimensions of listening and the guidelines for regulating these characteristics	adjust your listening on the basis of the four dimensions of listening: participatory and passive, empathic and objective, nonjudgmental, and critical and surface and depth listening
Active Listening	define *active listening* and explain its functions and techniques	use active listening when appropriate
Thinking Critically About Listening	explain the guidelines for listening for truth and accuracy	listen critically for truth and accuracy

NEW

**CHAPTER 4:
LISTENING**

In Chapter 4, effective listening has been reconceptualized to involve choices among modes of listening. A section on thinking critically about listening is also included.

It's [success in the media] in the preparation—in those dreary pedestrian virtues they taught you in seventh grade and you didn't believe.
—DIANE SAWYER

The ultimate goal of all research is not objectivity, but truth.
—HELENE DEUTSCH

Today, more and more research is being conducted via computer. Data bases, containing vast amounts of information on just about any topic, can be easily and efficiently accessed in many college libraries. Which data bases will prove most useful in preparing your next speech? For what personal or professional interest might you access a computer data base? Which one(s) would you access?

STEP 3: RESEARCH YOUR TOPIC

Research is essential if your speech is to be worthwhile and if you and the audience are to profit from it. First read from a general source—an article in an encyclopedia or magazine. You might pursue some of the references in the article or seek books on the topic in the library catalog. You might also consult one or more of the guides to periodical literature for recent articles in journals, magazines, and newspapers. For some topics, you might want to consult individuals. Professors, politicians, physicians, or others with specialized information might prove useful.

Computer Searches

Many college libraries now provide access to computer searches, such as those on CD-ROM (Compact Disk Read-Only Memory), which make research both enjoyable and efficient. These systems enable you to access a wide variety of specialized data bases. For example, the ABI/INFORM data base covers more than 500 periodicals in business; ERIC indexes more than 775 major journals as well as convention papers, dissertations, and curriculum materials in education and communication; and PERIODICAL ABSTRACTS indexes more than 250 journals covered by the *Reader's Guide to Periodical Literature*. With such systems, you can access an annotated bibliography built around just about any topic.

One of the great advantages is that you can request references that deal with specific topics, for example, teenage drug abuse in schools, integrating multiculturalism into the college curriculum, or AIDS prevention programs in elementary schools. No longer do you have to look up, for example, drug abuse and then search each article to see if it deals with teenagers in school. The computer program will search the articles for you and indicate which of the articles deals with both drug abuse and teenagers in a school setting (as major topics). The program will not—unless you direct it to do so—access articles that merely contain the words *drug abuse* or *teenagers in school*. Most systems allow you to print out the bibliography or download it to your own computer disk.

Since these information retrieval systems vary so much from one library to another and since they are changing and expanding so rapidly, it is best to investigate the specific resources of your college or local library. Table 12.2 presents some helpful research sources.

STEP 4: FORMULATE YOUR THESIS AND IDENTIFY THE MAJOR PROPOSITIONS

The thesis is the main idea that you want to convey to the audience. The thesis of Lincoln's Second Inaugural Address was that Northerners and Southerners should work together for the good of the entire country. The thesis of the *Rocky* movies was that the underdog can win.

Let's say, for example, you are planning to deliver a persuasive speech in favor of Senator Winters. Your thesis statement might be: "Winters is the best candidate." This is what you want your audience to believe,

PUBLIC SPEAKING PREPARATION AND DELIVERY

STEP 5: SUPPORT THE MAJOR PROPOSITIONS

Now that you have identified your thesis and your major propositions, you need to support each. Tell the audience what it needs to know about color and style in clothing selection. Or, in the persuasive speech example, convince them that a college education will help them better get jobs.

In the informative speech, your support primarily amplifies—describes, illustrates, defines, exemplifies—the concepts you discuss. You want the "color in clothing" to come alive to the audience. Amplification accomplishes this. Specifically, you might use examples, illustrations, and the testimony of various authorities. Definitions especially help to breathe life into abstract or vague concepts. Statistics (summary figures) that explain various trends are essential for certain topics. Audiovisual aids—charts, maps, objects, slides, films, tapes, CDs, and so on—help clarify vague concepts. These forms of amplification are covered in detail in Chapter 14, "The Informative Speech."

In a persuasive speech your support is proof—material that offers evidence, argument, and motivational appeal and that establishes your credibility and reputation. To persuade your audience to buy Brand X, in part by demonstrating that it is cheaper, you must give proof that this is true. You might compare the price of Brand X to other brands. Or you might demonstrate that the same amount of Brand X will do twice the work of other brands selling at the same price.

You support your propositions with reasoning from specific instances, from general principles, from analogy, and from causes and effects. These may be thought of as logical support. Also, you support your position with motivational appeals. You might appeal to the audience's desire for status, financial gain, or increased self-esteem: "No one wants to be at the low end of the hierarchy. Our new management seminar will help you climb that corporate ladder faster and easier than you ever thought possible." You also add persuasive force through your personal reputation or credibility. If audience members see you as competent, highly moral, and charismatic, they are more likely to believe you. These forms of support are covered in depth in Chapter 15, "The Persuasive Speech."

STEP 6: ORGANIZE THE SPEECH MATERIALS

You must organize your material if the audience is to understand and remember it (Whitman & Timmis, 1975). Here are six patterns you might use to organize the body of a speech.

Time Pattern

Organizing major issues on the basis of some temporal relationship is a popular pattern for informative speeches. Generally, when this pattern is used, the speech is organized into two or three major parts. You might begin with the past and work up to the present or future, or begin with the present or future and work back to the past. You might organize a speech on a child's development of speech and language in a time or temporal pattern. Major propositions might look like this:

PUBLIC SPEAKING PREPARATION AND DELIVERY (STEPS 7–10)

Foundations of Human Communication

CHAPTER ONE

Introduction to Human Communication

Chapter Concepts	Chapter Goals After completing this chapter, you should be able to	Chapter Skills After completing this chapter, you should be able to
Communication Concepts	1. define *communication* and its essential components 2. diagram an original model of the essentials of human communication	communicate as speaker/listener with an awareness of the varied components involved in the communication act
Communication Principles	3. explain and give examples of the principles of human communication	communicate as speaker/listener with a recognition of the principles of human communication
Thinking Critically About Human Communication	4. explain the suggestions for approaching human communication and for transferring skills	follow the suggestions for approaching human communication and for transferring skills of critical thinking

Of all the knowledge and skills you have, those concerning communication are among your most important and useful. Whether in your personal, social, or work life, communication is and will continue to be your most vital asset. Through **intrapersonal communication** you talk with, learn about, and judge yourself. You persuade yourself of this or that, reason about possible decisions to make, and rehearse messages that you plan to send to others. Through **interpersonal communication** you interact with others, learn about them and yourself, and reveal yourself to others. Whether with new acquaintances, old friends, lovers, or family members, it is through interpersonal communication that you establish, maintain, sometimes destroy, and sometimes repair personal relationships. Interpersonal communication also occurs during interviews—in, for example, applying for a job, gathering information, and counseling.

Through **small group communication** you interact with others in groups. You solve problems, develop new ideas, and share knowledge and experiences. You live your work and social life largely in groups, from the employment interview to the executive board meeting, from the informal social group having coffee to the formal meeting discussing issues of international concern. Through **public communication,** others inform and persuade you. And you, in turn, inform and persuade others—to do, to buy, or to think in a particular way, or to change an attitude, opinion, or value.

This book focuses on these forms of communication and on you as both message sender and receiver. It has three major purposes. First, it explains the concepts and principles, the theory and research in human communication. Second, it explains the skills of human communication helpful in increasing your own communication competence and effectiveness in a multicultural world. Third, it enhances your ability to think critically in general and about communication in particular.

The differences between effective and ineffective communication are all around you. They are the differences between

- the self-confident and the self-conscious speaker
- the person who gets hired and the one who gets passed over because of a poor showing in a job interview
- the couple who argue constructively and the couple who argue by hurting each other and eventually destroying their relationship
- the group member who is too self-focused to listen openly and contribute to the group and the member who serves both the task and the interpersonal needs of the group
- the public speaker who lacks credibility and persuasive appeal and the speaker audiences believe and follow
- the culturally isolated person and the one who enjoys, profits from, and grows from effective and satisfying intercultural experiences

Communication is power. Those who have mastered its effective use can change their own experience of the world and the world's experience of them.
—ANTHONY ROBBINS

What do you think is the single most important benefit of learning the skills of communication?

TABLE 1.1 AREAS OF HUMAN COMMUNICATION

Areas of Human Communication	Some Purposes	Some Theory-related Concerns	Some Skill-related Concerns
Intrapersonal: communication with oneself	To think, reason, analyze, reflect	How does one's self-concept develop? How does one's self-concept influence communication? How can problem-solving and analyzing abilities be improved and taught? What is the relationship between personality and communication?	Enhancing self-esteem, increasing self-awareness, improving problem-solving and analyzing abilities; increasing self-control; reducing stress; managing interpersonal conflict
Interpersonal: communication between two persons	To learn, relate, influence, play, help	What is interpersonal effectiveness? Why do people develop relationships? What holds friends, lovers, and families together? What tears them apart? How can relationships be repaired?	Increasing effectiveness in one-to-one communication; developing and maintaining effective relationships (friendship, love, family); improving conflict resolution abilities
Small group: communication within a small group of persons, say 3–12	To share information, generate ideas, solve problems, help	What makes a leader? What type of leadership works best? What roles do members serve in groups? What do groups do well and what do they fail to do well? How can groups be made more effective?	Increasing effectiveness as a group member; improving leadership abilities; using groups to achieve specific purposes (for example, solving problems, generating ideas)
Public: communication of speaker to audience	To inform, persuade, entertain	What kinds of organizational structures work best in informative and persuasive speaking? How can audiences be effectively analyzed and adapted to? How can ideas be developed for communication to an audience?	Communicating information more effectively; increasing persuasive abilities; developing, organizing, styling, and delivering messages with greater effectiveness

Table 1.1 summarizes these areas of communication and the communication skills that you will focus on in this course.

A good way to begin your study of human communication is to examine your own beliefs about communication. The self-test provides a stimulus for such an examination.

TEST YOURSELF
What Do You Believe About Communication?

Instructions: Respond to each of the following statements with T (true) if you think the statement is always or usually true and F (false) if you think the statement is always or usually false.

_____ 1. Good communicators are born, not made.

_____ 2. The more you communicate, the better your communication will be.

_____ 3. Unlike effective speaking, effective listening really cannot be taught.
_____ 4. Opening lines such as "Hello, how are you?" or "Fine weather to-day" serve no useful communication purpose.
_____ 5. The best way to deal with *inter*cultural communication is in the same way that you deal with *intra*cultural communication.
_____ 6. When verbal and nonverbal messages contradict each other, people believe the verbal message.
_____ 7. Complete openness should be the goal of any meaningful interpersonal relationship.
_____ 8. Interpersonal conflict is a reliable sign that your relationship is in trouble.
_____ 9. Like good communicators, leaders are born, not made.
_____ 10. Fear of public speaking is detrimental and must be eliminated.

Those who believe in ghosts always see them
—CHARLES V. ROMAN

Thinking Critically About Communication Beliefs If you are like most people you have probably been told lots of things about communication—like the statements above—that are simply not true. In fact, none of the statements above are true, so hopefully you answered "false" to all or most. As you read this book, you'll discover not only why these statements are false but some of the problems that can arise when you act on the basis of such misconceptions. This is perhaps, then, a good place to start practicing the critical thinking skill of questioning commonly held assumptions about communication and about yourself as a communicator.

The self-tests in this book—often dealing with personal aspects of your communication behavior—are presented to stimulate you to think about your communications. Therefore, view your "scores"—even for those tests that have been thoroughly researched—as additional guides or signals for self-analysis and reflection.

Figure 1.1 The Essentials of Human Communication

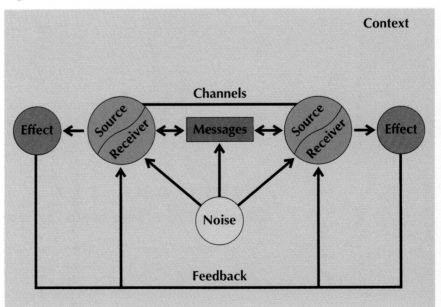

COMMUNICATION CONCEPTS

Communication occurs when you send or receive messages, and when you assign meaning to another person's signals. Human communication always is distorted by noise, occurs within a context, has some effect, and involves some opportunity for feedback (Figure 1.1). Let's look at each of these essential elements.

CULTURAL VIEWPOINT

The Importance of Intercultural Communication

Intercultural communication is more important today than at any other point in history. Consequently, it is given considerable importance in this text. Each chapter contains at least one Cultural Viewpoint box that relates the content of the chapter to some significant aspect of culture and intercultural communication. Each box ends with a note indicating the page on which the next Cultural Viewpoint box appears so you can read these in sequence—as a kind of separate chapter.

Several factors contribute to the importance of intercultural communication. The **mobility** of people throughout the world is at its height. Travel from one country to another is at an all-time high. People now frequently visit other cultures for the pleasure of exploring new lands and different people and for economic opportunities.

Another aspect of mobility is the **changing immigration patterns.** A walk through any major city in the United States will show that we are still a nation of immigrants (see figure on page 8, Ancestry of United States Residents). Whether you are a long-time resident or a newly arrived immigrant, you are living, going to school, and working with people very different from you. Your day-to-day experiences are becoming increasingly multicultural.

Today, most **countries are economically dependent on each other.** Our economic lives depend on our ability to communicate effectively across different cultures. Similarly, our political well-being depends in great part on that of other cultures. Political unrest in any part of the world—Latin America, Eastern Europe, or the Middle East, to take a few examples—affects our own security. Intercultural communication and understanding seem now more crucial than ever.

The rapid spread of **communication technology** has brought foreign and sometimes very different cultures right into your living rooms. News from foreign countries is commonplace. You see nightly—in vivid color—what is going on in remote countries. Technology has made intercultural communication easy, practical, and inevitable. Daily the media bombard you with evidence of racial tensions, religious disagreements, sexual bias, and, in general, the problems caused when intercultural communication fails.

[Next Cultural Viewpoint, page 10]

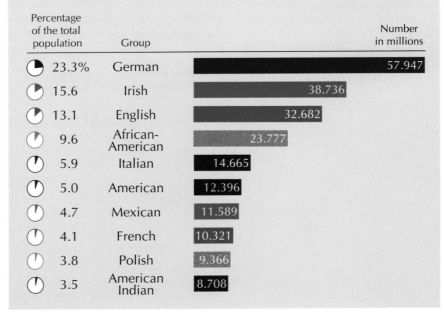

Ancestry of United States Residents

The top 10 categories that People claimed as their ancestry in the 1990 Census

Percentage of the total population	Group	Number in millions
23.3%	German	57.947
15.6	Irish	38.736
13.1	English	32.682
9.6	African-American	23.777
5.9	Italian	14.665
5.0	American	12.396
4.7	Mexican	11.589
4.1	French	10.321
3.8	Polish	9.366
3.5	American Indian	8.708

I am not an Athenian or a Greek, but a citizen of the world.
—SOCRATES

Communication Context

Communication always takes place in a specific setting or environment—a **context.** The context influences both what you say and how you say it. Contexts have at least four aspects: physical, cultural, social-psychological, and temporal or time:

How would you describe the communication context (physical, cultural, social-psychological, and temporal) in which you find yourself right now?

- *Physical context:* The tangible or concrete environment—the room, park, or auditorium; you don't talk the same way at a football game as at a funeral
- *Cultural context:* The lifestyles, beliefs, values, behavior, and communication of a group; the rules of a group for considering something right or wrong
- *Social-Psychological context:* The status relationships among speakers, the cultural rules of the society, the formality of the situation; you don't talk the same way in the cafeteria as you would at a formal dinner at your boss's house
- *Temporal context:* The position in which a message fits into a sequence of events; you don't talk the same way after someone tells of the death of a close relative as you do after someone tells of winning the lottery

These four aspects interact; each influences and is influenced by the others. For example, arriving late for a date (temporal context) may lead to changes in the degree of friendliness (social-psychological context) which would depend on the cultures of you and your date (cultural context) and which may lead to changes in where you go on the date (physical context).

In interpersonal and small group communication, it is relatively easy to appreciate the interconnectedness of source and receiver—of encoding and decoding. In public speaking, however, we often assume that the speaker is the only source and the audience is the receiver. In what ways does the public speaker receive messages from the audience? In what ways do audience members send messages to each other?

Sources-Receivers

The hyphenated term **sources-receivers** emphasizes that each person involved in communication is both a source (speaker) and a receiver (listener). You send messages when you speak, write, gesture, or smile. You receive messages in listening, reading, seeing, smelling, and so on. At the same time that you send messages, you are also receiving messages. You are receiving your own messages (you hear yourself, you feel your own movements, you see many of your own gestures) and you are receiving the messages of the other person—visually, auditorily, or even through touch or smell. As you speak, you look at the person for responses—for approval, understanding, sympathy, agreement, and so on. As you decipher these nonverbal signals, you are performing receiving functions.

Source-Receiver Encoding-Decoding

When you put your ideas into speech, you are putting them into a code, hence *en*coding. When you translate the sound waves (the speech signals) that impinge on your ears into ideas, you take them out of the code they are in, hence *de*coding. Thus speakers or writers are referred to as *encoders*, and listeners or readers as *decoders*.

As with source-receiver, the hyphenated term *encoding-decoding* emphasizes that you perform these functions *simultaneously*. As you speak (encoding), you are also deciphering the responses of the listener (decoding).

Source-Receiver Communicative Competence

Communicative competence is your knowledge of how communication works and your ability to use communication effectively (Spitzberg & Cupach, 1989). It includes such knowledge as the role the context plays in influencing the content and form of communication messages—for example, the knowledge that in certain contexts and with certain listeners one topic is appropriate and another is not. Knowledge about the rules of nonverbal behavior—for example, the appropriateness of touching, vocal volume, and physical closeness—is also part of communicative competence. One of the major goals of this text and this course is to spell out the nature of communicative competence and to increase your own communicative competence.

By increasing your competence—that is, your knowledge and skills of communication—the more choices you will have available for your day-to-day communications. The process is comparable to learning vocabulary. The more vocabulary you know, the more ways you have for expressing yourself. Thus, the aim of this book is to increase your communicative competence so you will have a broader range of options in performing your various communication activities. The process goes like this:

knowledge of communication

leads to

greater communication competence

leads to

greater number of choices or options for communicating

leads to

greater likelihood of communicating effectively in any situation

CULTURAL VIEWPOINT

Culture and Competence

Competence is specific to a given culture. The principles of effective communication vary from one culture to another; what proves effective in one culture may prove ineffective in another. For example, U.S. business executives will discuss business during the first several minutes of a meeting. However, Japanese business executives interact socially for an extended period of time in order to learn about each other. Thus, the small group communication principle influenced by U.S. culture would advise participants to attend to the meeting's agenda during the first 5 or 10 minutes. The principle influenced by Japanese culture would advise participants to avoid dealing with business until all have socialized sufficiently and feel they know each other well enough to begin business negotiations. Note that neither principle is right nor wrong. Each is effective within its own culture and ineffective outside its own culture.

[Next Cultural Viewpoint, page 33]

Messages and Channels

Communication **messages** take many forms and are transmitted or received through one or a combination of sensory organs. You communicate verbally (with words) and nonverbally (without words). Your meanings or intentions are conveyed with words (Chapter 5) and with the clothes you wear, the way you walk, and the way you smile (Chapter 6). Everything about you communicates.

The communication **channel** is the medium through which messages pass. Communication rarely takes place over only one channel. Rather, two, three, or four different channels are used simultaneously. In face-to-face conversations, for example, you speak and listen (vocal channel), but you also gesture and receive these signals visually (visual channel). You also emit and smell odors (olfactory channel) and often touch another person, this too is communication (tactile channel).

Metamessages

A **metamessage** is a message that refers to another message; it is communication about communication. Verbally, you can say, for example, "This statement is false" or "Do you understand what I am trying to tell you?" These refer to communication and are therefore **metacommunicational.**

Nonverbal behavior may also be metacommunicational. Obvious examples include crossing your fingers behind your back or winking when telling a lie. On a less obvious level, consider the frequent blind date. As you say "I had a really nice time," your nonverbal messages—the lack of a smile, the failure to maintain eye contact, the extra-long pauses—metacommunciate and contradict the verbal "really nice time" and tell your date that you did not enjoy the evening. Nonverbal messages may also metacommunicate about other nonverbal messages. The individual who, on meeting a stranger, both smiles and extends a totally lifeless hand shows how one nonverbal behavior may contradict another.

Usually when nonverbal behavior metacommunicates, it reinforces other verbal or nonverbal behavior. You may literally roll up your sleeves when talking about cleaning up the room, smile when greeting someone, or run to meet the person you say you are eager to see.

Feedback Messages

When you send a message—say, in speaking to another person—you also hear yourself. That is, you get **feedback** from your own messages; you hear what you say, you feel the way you move, you see what you write. In addition to this self-feedback, you get feedback from others. This feedback can take many forms. A frown or a smile, a yea or a nay, a pat on the back, or a punch in the mouth are all types of feedback.

Feedback tells the speaker what effect he or she is having on listeners. On the basis of this feedback—for example, boos or wild applause in public speaking—the speaker may adjust, modify, strengthen, deemphasize,

---

What kinds of feedforward messages did you hear today? What kinds of feedforward appears in this textbook?

Drawing by Handelsman, © 1994 The New Yorker Magazine, Inc.

or change the content or form of the messages. We return to this concept in the discussion of conversation (Chapter 7).

Feedforward Messages

Feedforward is information you provide before sending your primary messages (Richards, 1951). Feedforward, as illustrated in the accompanying cartoon, reveals something about the messages to come and includes, for example, the preface or table of contents to a book, the opening paragraph of a chapter, movie previews, magazine covers, and introductions in public speeches.

Feedforward may be verbal ("Wait until you hear this one") or nonverbal (a prolonged pause or hands motioning for silence to signal that an important message is about to be spoken). Or, as is most often the case, it is some combination of verbal and nonverbal. Feedforward may refer to the content of the message to follow ("I'll tell you exactly what they said to each other") or to the form ("I won't spare you the gory details"). As is feedback, feedforward is considered in the discussion of conversation (Chapter 7).

Noise

Noise interferes with your receiving a message someone is sending or with their receiving your message. Noise may be physical (others talking loudly, cars honking), psychological (preconceived ideas, wandering thoughts), or semantic (misunderstood meanings). Technically, noise is anything that distorts the message—anything that prevents the receiver from receiving the message.

Because messages may be visual as well as spoken, noise too may be visual. Thus, the sunglasses that prevent someone from seeing the messages from your eyes would be considered noise as would blurred type on a printed page. Table 1.2 identifies these three major types of noise in more detail.

All communications contain noise. It cannot be totally eliminated, but its effects can be reduced. Making your language more precise, sharpening your skills for sending and receiving nonverbal messages, and improving your listening and feedback skills are some ways to combat the influence of noise.

TABLE 1.2 THREE TYPES OF NOISE

Type	Definition	Example
Physical	Interferes with the physical transmission of the signal or message	Screeching of passing cars, hum of computer, sunglasses
Psychological	Cognitive or mental interference	Biases and prejudices in senders and receivers, closed-mindedness
Semantic	Speaker and listener assigning different meanings	People speaking different languages, use of jargon or overly complex terms not understood by listener

Effects

Communication always has some effect on those involved in the communication act. For every communication act, there is some consequence. For example, you may gain knowledge or learn how to analyze, synthesize, or evaluate something. These are intellectual or cognitive effects. Or you may acquire new attitudes or beliefs or change existing ones (affective consequences). Or, you may learn new bodily movements, such as how to throw a curve ball, paint a picture, give a compliment, or express surprise (psychomotor effects).

ETHICAL ISSUE

Ethics and Human Communication

Because communication has effects, it also involves questions of **ethics.** There is a right-versus-wrong aspect to any communication act (Bok, 1978; Jaksa & Pritchard, 1994; Johannesen, 1990). For example, although it may be effective to lie in selling a product, most would agree that it would not be ethical or right or morally justified.

Because of the central importance of ethics to all forms and functions of communication, Ethical Issue boxes are placed throughout this text. Here are just a few issues we will consider. As you read down the list, consider what you *would* do if confronted with this issue. What do you feel you *should* do (if this is different from what you *would* do)? What general principle of ethics are you using in making these *would* and *should* judgments?

- Would it be ethical to lie to your partner to avoid an argument and ill feelings?
- Would it be ethical to reveal another person's secrets?
- Would it be ethical to exaggerate your virtues and minimize your vices to win someone's approval? To get a job?
- Would it be ethical to assume leadership of a group to get members to do as you wish?
- Would it be ethical to persuade an audience to do something by scaring or threatening them?

[Next Ethical Issue, page 38]

PRINCIPLES OF COMMUNICATION

Several communication principles that are essential to understanding interpersonal, small group, and public communication will further clarify the nature of human communication. These principles, although signifi-

How many different communication signals can you identify in this photo?

cant in terms of explaining theory, also have very practical applications. These principles will provide insight into such practical issues as:

- why disagreements so often center on trivial issues and yet seem so difficult to resolve
- why you will never be able to mindread, to know just what another person is thinking
- how communication expresses power relationships
- why speaker and audience often see issues and arguments very differently

Communication Is a Package of Signals

Some researchers (for example, Beier, 1974) argue that the impulse to communicate two different feelings (for example, "I love you" and "I don't love you") creates messages in which the nonverbal contradicts the verbal message. Do you think this idea has validity? What other explanations might you offer to account for contradictory messages?

Communication normally occurs in "packages" of verbal and nonverbal behaviors or messages (Pittenger, Hockett, & Danehy, 1960). Usually, verbal and nonverbal behaviors reinforce or support each other. You do not usually express fear with words while the rest of your body relaxes. You do not normally express anger with your bodily posture while your face smiles. Your entire being works as a whole—verbally and nonverbally—to express your thoughts and feelings.

Usually, little attention is paid to the packaged nature of communication. It goes unnoticed. But when the messages contradict each other—when the weak handshake belies the verbal greeting, when the nervous posture belies the focused stare—you take notice. Invariably you begin to question the person's sincerity and honesty. Consider, for example, how you would react to mixed message situations such as these:

- Well, we've finally decided to break up after seven years. I think it's all for the best.
- Even if I do fail the course, so what? I don't need it for graduation.
- I haven't had a date in the last three years. People are jerks.

Is this cartoon an accurate depiction of the male's reluctance to talk about himself and the tendency to talk about things external to a relationship? Would the cartoon be humorous if the woman were the speaker?

Drawing by Drucker, © 1981
The New Yorker Magazine, Inc.

"If you want to talk, get a paper, and we'll talk about what's in the paper."

People don't care how much we know until they know how much we care.

—DUTCH BOLING

Communication Involves Content and Relationship Dimensions

Communication exists on at least two levels. Communication can refer to something external to both speaker and listener (for example, the weather) as well as to the relationships between speaker and listener (for example, who is in charge). These two aspects are referred to as **content and relationship dimensions** of communication (Watzlawick, Beavin, & Jackson, 1967).

The content aspect refers to the behavioral responses expected—namely, that the worker see the employer after the meeting. The relationship aspect refers to the relationship between the employer and the worker; it states how the communication is to be dealt with. For example, the use of the command indicates a status difference between the two

Recall a recent interpersonal, small group, or public communication situation. What were the major content messages communicated? What were the major relationship messages communicated? Can you think of a communication transaction in which only content messages are communicated? Only relationship messages?

parties: The employer can command the worker. If the worker commanded the employer, it would appear awkward and out of place simply because it would violate the normal relationship between employer and worker.

Problems often result from the failure to distinguish between the content and the relationship levels of communication. Consider a couple: Pat and Chris. Pat made plans to study with friends during the weekend without first asking Chris, and an argument ensued. Probably both would have agreed that to study was the right choice to make. Thus, the argument is not centered on the content level. The argument instead centers on the relationship level. Chris expected to be consulted about plans for the weekend. Pat, in not doing this, rejected this definition of the relationship.

Examine the following interchange and note how relationship considerations are ignored.

Pat: I'm going to the rally tomorrow. The people at the plant are all going to protest and I'm going with them. [Pat focuses on the content and ignores any relational implications of the message.]

Chris: Why can't we ever do anything together? [Chris responds primarily on a relational level and ignores the content implications of the message, expressing displeasure at being ignored in this decision.]

Pat: We can do something together anytime; tomorrow's the day of the rally. [Again, Pat focuses almost exclusively on the content.]

Here is essentially the same situation, but with an added sensitivity to relationship messages.

How would you describe the likely effects of these two dialogues?

Pat: The people at work are going to the rally tomorrow and I'd like to go with them. Would it be all right if I went to rally? [Although Pat focuses on content, there is always an awareness of the relational dimensions by asking if this would be a problem. Pat also shows this in expressing a desire rather than a decision to attend this rally.]

Chris: That sounds great but I'd really like to do something together tomorrow. [Chris focuses on the relational dimension but also acknowledges Pat's content orientation. Note too that Chris does not respond defensively, as if there were a necessity to defend oneself or the emphasis on relational aspects.]

Do you see this as a dialogue between a woman and a man? Two women? Two men?

Pat: How about your meeting me at Luigi's for dinner after the rally? [Pat responds to the relational aspect—without abandoning the desire to attend the rally. Pat tries to negotiate a solution that will meet the needs of both of them.]

Chris: That sounds great. I'm dying for spaghetti and meatballs. [Chris responds to both messages, approving of Pat's attending the rally but also of their dinner date.]

Communication Sequences Are Punctuated

Communication events are continuous transactions with no clear-cut beginning or ending. As a participant in or an observer of communication, you divide this continuous, circular process into causes and effects, or stimuli and responses. That is, you segment or **punctuate** this continuous stream of communication into smaller pieces (Watzlawick, Beavin, & Jackson, 1967). Some of these you label causes (or stimuli), and others effects (or responses).

Largely because of punctuation, it has been proposed (Duncan & Rock, 1991) that an unhealthy relationship cycle can be broken by either party, even without the knowledge and cooperation of the other person. Do you agree that you can change many relationship problems by yourself? What kinds of relationship problems can you change by yourself?

Consider this example: A manager lacks interest in the employees, seldom offering any suggestions for improvement or any praise for jobs well done. The employees are apathetic and morale is low. Each action (the manager's lack of involvement and the employees' low morale) stimulates the other. Each serves as the stimulus for the other but there is no identifiable initial stimulus. Each event may be seen as a stimulus or as a response.

If you are to understand what the other person means from his or her point of view, then you have to see the sequence of events as punctuated by the other person. Further, recognize that your punctuation does not reflect what exists in reality. Rather, it reflects your own unique, subjective, and fallible perception.

Communication Is Transactional

Communication is a transaction (Watzlawick, Beavin, & Jackson, 1967; Watzlawick, 1977, 1978; Barnlund, 1970; Wilmot, 1987). From a transactional viewpoint, each person is seen as both speaker and listener, as simultaneously communicating and receiving messages. Figure 1.2 illustrates this transactional view and compares it with earlier views of communication that may still influence the way in which you may see communication.

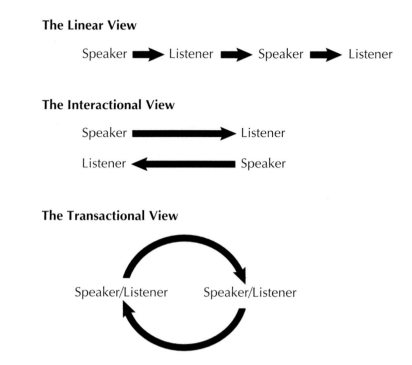

The Linear View

Speaker ➡ Listener ➡ Speaker ➡ Listener

The Interactional View

Speaker ➡ Listener

Listener ⬅ Speaker

The Transactional View

Speaker/Listener   Speaker/Listener

Figure 1.2 Three Views of Communication

The linear view of communication shows that the speaker speaks and the listener listens and that communication proceeds in a relatively straight line. In this linear view, speaking and listening are totally separate functions. The interactional *view shows the speaker and listener exchanging turns at speaking and listening; for example, A speaks while B listens; then B speaks while A listens. The* transactional *view shows that each person serves simultaneously as speaker and listener; at the same time that you send messages, you are also receiving messages from your own communications and also from the reactions of the other person(s).*

Also, in a transactional view the elements of communication are seen as interdependent (never independent). Each exists in relation to the others. A change in any one element of the process produces changes in the other elements. For example, you are talking with a group of your friends and your mother enters the group. This change in "audience" will lead to other changes. Perhaps you or your friends will change what you are saying or how you are saying it. Regardless of what change is introduced, other changes will be produced as a result.

People in communication act and react on the basis of the present situation plus their history, past experiences, attitudes, cultural beliefs, and a host of related issues. One implication of this is that actions and reactions in communication are determined not only by what is said, but also by the way the person interprets what is said. Your responses to a movie, for example, do not depend solely on the words and pictures in the film but also on your previous experiences, present emotions, knowledge, physical well-being, and lots more. Another implication is that two people listening to the same message will often derive two very different meanings. Although the words and symbols are the same, each person interprets them differently.

Can you give an example of a communication which clearly illustrates the transactional nature of communication?

This principle of inevitability has
created lots of controversy (Motley,
1990a, b; Bavelas, 1990; Beach,
1990). Some assumed that this
principle meant that all behavior
communicates—that communication
and behavior were identical.
Therefore, the reasoning went, you
cannot *not* communicate because
you cannot *not* behave. Others
argue that the original intention was
to emphasize that behavior *in an
interactional situation* communicates;
therefore, if you are interacting with
another person and if your behavior
is perceived, it will communicate
something. What arguments could
you advance to support or refute
any of these notions?

Communication Is Inevitable

Communication often takes place even though a person does not intend
or want to communicate. Take, for example, a student sitting in the back
of the room with an expressionless face, perhaps staring out the window.
Although the student might claim not to be communicating with the instructor, the instructor may derive any of a variety of messages from this
behavior. Perhaps the instructor assumes that the student lacks interest,
is bored, or is worried about something. In any event, the teacher is receiving messages even though the student might not intentionally be
sending any (Watzlawick, Beavin, & Jackson, 1967; Motley, 1990a, b; Bavelas, 1990). This does not mean that all behavior is communication. For instance, if the student looked out the window and the teacher did not notice, no communication would take place. The two people must be in an
interactional situation and the behavior must be perceived by some other
person for the principle of inevitability to operate.

Notice too that when you are in an interactional situation, you cannot
not respond to the messages of others. For example, if you notice someone winking at you, you must respond in some way. Even if you do not
respond actively or openly, that lack of response is itself a response, and it
communicates. You cannot *not* respond. Again, if you don't notice the
winking, then obviously there was no communication.

**Figure 1.3 Some Occupations that
Rely on Communication.**
*(This flyer was prepared by Harper-
Collins College Publishers and was
originally titled "What Can You Do
With a Communication Degree?")*

Communication researcher Alan Rubin (1979) found that the reasons children watch television is (1) to learn, (2) to pass the time, (3) for companionship, (4) to forget, (5) for stimulation or arousal, and (6) for relaxation. How does this list compare with the general list of purposes discussed in this chapter? What essential purpose(s) of communication is (are) discussed in this chapter but not included in Rubin's list? Which did Rubin include that are not covered here? What reason might you offer for these differences?

Never say anything on the phone that you wouldn't want your mother to hear at your trial.

—*Sydney Biddle Barrows*

Communication Is Purposeful

You communicate for a purpose; there is some motivation that leads you to communicate. When you speak or write, you are trying to send some message to another and trying to accomplish some goal. Although different cultures will emphasize different purposes and motives (Rubin & Fernandez-Collado, 1992), five general purposes seem relatively common to most if not all forms of communication: to learn, to relate, to help, to influence, and to play.

- to learn   to acquire knowledge of others, the world, and yourself
- to relate   to form relationships with others, to interact with others as individuals
- to help   to assist others by listening, offering solutions
- to influence   to strengthen or change the attitudes or behaviors of others
- to play   to enjoy the experience of the moment

Figure 1.3 (page 19) identifies just some of today's occupations that rely heavily on communication and where these purposes are served throughout the performance of these jobs. In Chapter 4, these purposes are examined from the perspective of listening.

Communication Is Irreversible and Unrepeatable

Communication is an irreversible process. Once you communicate something, you cannot uncommunicate it. You can, of course, try to reduce the effects of your message. You can say, for example, "I really didn't mean what I said." Regardless of how hard you try to negate or reduce the effects of your message, the message itself, once it has been received, cannot be taken back. In a public speaking situation in which the speech is recorded or broadcast, inappropriate messages may have national or even international effects. Here, attempts to reverse what one has said (in, say, trying to offer clarification) often have the effect of further publicizing the original statement.

Because of irreversibility, be careful not to say things you may be sorry for later. Especially in conflict situations, when tempers run high, you need to avoid saying things you may wish to withdraw. Commitment messages—the "I love you" messages and their variants—need also to be monitored. Otherwise, you might commit yourself to a position you may not be happy with later. In group and public communication situations, when the messages are heard by many people, it is especially crucial to recognize the irreversibility.

Communication is also unrepeatable. A communication act can never be duplicated. The reason is simple: everyone and everything is constantly changing. As a result, you can never recapture the exact same situation, frame of mind, or relationship dynamics that defined a previous communication act. For example, you can never repeat meeting someone for the first time, comforting a grieving friend, leading a small group for the first time, or giving a public speech.

You can, of course, try again as when you say, "I'm sorry I came off so forward, can we try again?" But, notice that even when you say this, you have not erased the initial impression. Instead, you try to counteract this initial (and perhaps negative) impression by going through the motions again.

THINKING CRITICALLY ABOUT HUMAN COMMUNICATION

I am convinced that it is of primordial importance to learn more every year than the year before. After all, what is education but a process by which a person begins to learn how to learn?

—PETER USTINOV

The last section of each chapter focuses on critical thinking and reviews and invites reflection on the material in the chapter from a critical thinking perspective.

Thinking About Communication

In approaching the study of human communication, keep the following in mind:

- The study of human communication involves theory and research *as well as* practical skills for increasing communication effectiveness. Seek to understand the theories *and* to improve your communication skills. Each will assist in understanding the other: A knowledge of theory will help you better understand the skills, and a knowledge of skills will help you better understand theory.
- The concepts and principles discussed throughout this book and this course directly relate to your everyday communications. Try, for example, to recall examples from your own communications that illustrate the ideas considered here. This will help to make the material more personal and easier to assimilate.
- Analyze yourself as a critical thinker and a communicator. Self-analysis is essential if you are to use this material in any meaningful sense, say, to change some of your own behaviors. Be open to new ideas, even those that may contradict your existing beliefs.
- Become willing to change your ways of communicating and even your ways of thinking. Carefully assess what you should and should not change, what you should strengthen or revise, and what you should leave as is.

All truly wise thoughts have been thought already thousands of times; but to make them truly ours, we must think them over again honestly, till they take root in our personal experience.

—GOETHE

Thinking About Skills

Throughout this text, you will encounter a wide variety of skills in interpersonal, small group, and public speaking. Try not to limit these skills to the situations described here. Instead, apply these to a wide variety of situations. You will find that skills learned here will transfer to other areas of your life if you do three things (Sternberg, 1987):

- Think about the principles flexibly and recognize exceptions to the rule. Consider where the principles seem useful and where they need to be adjusted. Recognize especially that the principles discussed here are largely the result of research conducted on college students in the United States. Ask yourself if they apply to other groups and other cultures.

- Seek analogies between current situations and those you experienced earlier. What are the similarities? What are the differences? For example, most people repeat relationship problems because they fail to see the similarities (and sometimes the differences) between the old and destructive relationship and the new and soon-to-be equally destructive relationship.
- Look for situations at home, work, and school where you could transfer the skills discussed here. For instance, how can active listening skills improve your family communication? How can brainstorming and problem-solving skills help you deal with work-related difficulties?

Feedback on Concepts and Skills

In this chapter the nature of communication, its major components, and some major communication principles were considered.

1. Communication is the act, by one or more persons, of sending and receiving messages that are distorted by noise, occur within a context, have some effect (and some ethical dimension), and provide some opportunity for feedback.
2. The essentials of communication—the elements present in every communication act—are context (physical, cultural, social-psychological, and temporal); source-receiver; competence; message; channel; noise (physical, psychological, and semantic); sending or encoding processes; receiving or decoding processes; feedback and feedforward; effect; and ethics.
3. Communication messages may be of varied forms and may be sent and received through any combination of sensory organs. Communication messages may also metacommunicate—communicate about other messages. The communication channel is the medium through which the messages are sent.
4. Feedback refers to messages or information that is sent back to the source. It may come from the source itself or from the receiver. Feedforward refers to messages that preface other messages.
5. Noise is anything that distorts the message; it is present to some degree in every communication.
6. Communication always has an effect. Effects may be cognitive, affective, or psychomotor.
7. Communication ethics refers to the moral rightness or wrongness of a message and is an integral part of every effort to communicate.
8. Normally, communication is a package of signals, each reinforcing the other. When these signals oppose each other, the result is contradictory messages.
9. Communication involves both content dimensions and relationship dimensions.

10. Communication sequences are punctuated for processing. Individuals divide the communication sequence into stimuli and responses in different ways.
11. Communication is transactional. Communication is a process of interrelated parts.
12. In any interactional situation, communication is inevitable; you cannot not communicate nor can you not respond to communication.
13. Communication is purposeful. Through communication, you learn, relate, help, influence, and play.
14. Communication is irreversible and unrepeatable. You cannot take back or exactly repeat any message.

Several important communication skills emphasized in this chapter are presented here in summary form (as they are in every chapter). These skill checklists do not include all the skills covered in the chapter but rather are representative of the most important skills. Check your ability to apply these skills. You will gain most from this brief experience if you think carefully about each skill and try to identify instances from your recent communications in which you did or did not act on the basis of the specific skill. Use a rating scale such as the following: (1) = almost always, (2) = often, (3) = sometimes, (4) = rarely, (5) = almost never.

_____ 1. I'm sensitive to contexts of communication. I recognize that changes in the physical, cultural, social-psychological, and temporal contexts will alter meaning.
_____ 2. I look for meaning not only in words but in nonverbal behaviors as well.
_____ 3. I am sensitive to the feedback that I give to others and that others give to me.
_____ 4. I combat the effects of physical, psychological, and semantic noise that distorts messages.
_____ 5. Because communication is a package of signals, I use my verbal and nonverbal messages to reinforce rather than contradict each other and I respond to contradictory messages by identifying and openly discussing the dual meanings communicated.
_____ 6. I listen to the relational messages that other people and I send, and I respond to the relational messages of others to increase meaningful interaction.
_____ 7. I actively look for the punctuation pattern that other people and I use in order to better understand the meanings communicated.
_____ 8. Because communication is transactional, I recognize the mutual influence of all elements and that messages are sent and received simultaneously by each speaker/listener.
_____ 9. Because communication is inevitable, I look carefully for hidden meanings.
_____ 10. Because communication is purposeful, I look carefully at both the speaker's and the listener's purposes.
_____ 11. Because communication is irreversible and unrepeatable, I am especially cautious in communicating messages that I may later wish to withdraw, and I am also aware that any communication act occurs but once.

Skill Development Experiences

1.1 What's Happening?

How would you use the principles of human communication to *describe* what is happening in each of the following situations? Do note that these scenarios are extremely brief and are written only as aids to stimulate you to think more concretely about the axioms. The objective is not to select the one correct principle (each scenario can probably be described by reference to several), but to provide an opportunity to think about the principles as applied to specific situations.

1. A couple, together for 20 years, argue constantly about the seemingly most insignificant things—who takes the dog out, who does the shopping, who decides where to go to dinner, and so on. It has gotten to the point where they rarely have a day without argument and both are seriously considering separating.
2. Tanya and her grandmother can't seem to agree on what Tanya should do or not do. Tanya, for example, wants to go away for the weekend with her friends from college. But her grandmother fears she will come back pregnant and refuses to allow her to go.
3. In the heat of a big argument, Harry said he didn't ever want to see Peggy's family again—"They don't like me and I don't like them." Peggy said she felt the same way about his family. Now, weeks later, there remains a great deal of tension between them, especially when they find themselves with one or both families.
4. Grace and Mark are engaged to be married and are currently senior executives at a large advertising agency. Recently, Grace made a presentation that was not received positively by the other members of the team. Grace feels that Mark, in not defending her proposal, created a negative attitude and actually encouraged others to reject her ideas. Mark says that he felt he could not defend her proposal because others in the room would have felt his defense was motivated by their relationship and not by his positive evaluation of her proposal. So he felt it was best to say nothing.
5. Margo has just taken over as vice president in charge of sales for a manufacturing company. Margo is extremely organized and refuses to waste time on nonessentials. In her staff meetings, she is all business. Several top sales representatives have requested to be assigned to other VPs. They feel Margo works them too hard and doesn't care about them as people.
6. Junko supervises 12 designers who complain that they never know what she really wants. She always seems to like what they have done, but the designs never get final approval. They have asked Junko for feedback, but all she says is that everything is good.

1.2 Analyzing Family Talk

The principles of human communication discussed in this chapter should prove useful in analyzing any communication interaction. To help understand these principles and to gain some practice, apply them to this representation of a family dinner. Carefully study the interaction of the family members and identify each of the principles of communication discussed in the chapter.

Dinner with Margaret and Fred

Cast of Characters:

Margaret:	mother, housewife, junior high school history teacher; 41 years old
Fred:	father, gas station attendant; 46 years old
Diane:	daughter, receptionist at an art gallery; 22 years old
Stephen:	son, college freshman; 18 years old

Margaret is in the kitchen finishing the preparation of dinner—lamb chops, Fred's favorite, though she does not care much for them. Diane is going through some CDs. Stephen is reading one of his textbooks. Fred comes in from work and throws his jacket over the couch; it falls to the floor.

Fred: [*bored but angry, looking at Stephen*] What did you do with the car last night? It stunk like rotten eggs. And you left your school papers all over the backseat.

Stephen: [*as if expecting the angry remarks*] What did I do now?

Fred: You stunk up the car with your pot or whatever you kids smoke, and you left the car a mess. Can't you hear?

[Stephen says nothing; goes back to looking at his book but without really reading]

Margaret: All right, everybody, dinner's ready. Come on. Wash up and sit down.

[At dinner]

Diane: Mom, I'm going to the shore for the weekend with some friends from work.

Margaret: Okay. When will you be leaving?

Diane: Friday afternoon, right after work.

Fred: Like hell you're going. No more going to the shore with that group.

Margaret: Fred, they're nice people. Why shouldn't she go?

Fred: Because I said so, okay? Finished. Closed.

Diane: [*mumbling*] I'm 22 years old and he gives me problems.[*Turning to Fred*] You make me feel like a kid, like some stupid little kid.

Fred: Get married. Then you can tell your husband what to do.

Diane: I wish I could.

Stephen: But nobody'll ask her.

Margaret: Why should she get married? She's got a good life—a good job, nice friends, a good home. Listen, I was talking with Elizabeth and Cara this morning and they both feel they've just wasted their lives. They raised a family and what have they got? They got nothing. [*To Diane*] And don't think sex is so great either; it isn't, believe me.

Fred:	Well, they're idiots.
Margaret:	[*snidely*] They're idiots? Yeah, I guess they are.
Diane:	Joanne's getting married.
Margaret:	Who's Joanne?
Stephen:	That creature who lives with that guy Michael.
Fred:	Watch your mouth, Stephen. Don't be disrespectful to your mother or I'll teach you how to act right.
Margaret:	Well, how do you like the dinner?

[Prolonged silence]

Diane:	Do you think I should be in the wedding party if Joanne asks me? I think she will; we always said we'd be in each other's wedding.
Margaret:	Sure, why not? It'll be nice.
Fred:	I'm not going to no wedding, no matter who's in it.
Stephen:	Me neither.
Diane:	I hope you'll both feel that way when I get married.
Stephen:	By then I'll be too old to remember I got a sister.
Margaret:	How's school?
Stephen:	I hate it. It's so big. Nobody knows anybody. You sit in these big lecture halls and listen to some creep talk. I really feel lonely and isolated, like nobody knows I'm alive.
Fred:	Listen to that college talk. Get yourself a woman and you won't feel lonely, instead of hanging out with those potheads.

[Diane looks at Margaret, giving a sigh as if to say, "Here we go again"]

Margaret:	[*to Diane, in a whisper*] I know.
Diane:	Mom? Do you think I'm getting fat?
Stephen:	Yes.
Fred:	Just don't get fat in the stomach or you'll get thrown out of here.
Margaret:	No, I don't notice it.
Diane:	Well, I just thought I might be.
Stephen:	[*pushing his plate away*] I'm finished; I'm going out.
Fred:	Sit down and finish your supper. You think I work all day for you to throw the food away? You wanna go smoke your dope?
Stephen:	No. I just want to get away from you—forever.
Margaret:	You mean we both work all day; it's just that I earn a lot more.
Fred:	No, I mean I work and you baby-sit.
Margaret:	Teaching junior high school history isn't baby-sitting.
Fred:	Well, what is it, then? You don't teach them anything.
Margaret:	[*to Diane*] You see? You're better off single. I should've stayed single. Instead . . . Oh, well. I was young and stupid. It was my own fault for getting involved with a loser. Just don't you make the same mistake.
Fred:	[*to Stephen*] Go ahead. Leave the table. Leave the house. Who cares what you do?

1. Communication is a package of signals.
   - What instances show communication as a package of signals? Are there any examples of mixed or contradictory messages?
   - What effects do you suppose these messages will have on subsequent interactions?
2. Communication involves both content and relationship dimensions.
   - How do each of the characters deal with the self-definitions of the other characters? For example, how does Fred deal with the self-definition of Margaret? How does Margaret deal with the self-definition of Fred?
   - Are any problems caused by the failure to recognize the distinction between the content and the relationship levels of communication?
3. Communication sequences are punctuated for processing.
   - Select any two characters and indicate how they differ in their punctuation of any specific sequence of events. Do the characters realize that they are each arbitrarily dividing the sequence of events differently?
   - What problems might a failure to recognize the arbitrary nature of punctuation create?
4. Communication is transactional.
   - How is the process nature of communication illustrated in this interaction? For example, why is it impossible to identify specific beginnings and endings for any of the varied interactions? Are there instances in which individual characters attempt to deny the process nature of interactions?
   - In what ways are the messages of the different characters interdependent?
5. Communication is inevitable.
   - Do the characters communicate significant messages, even though they may attempt not to?
   - In what ways do the characters communicate simply by their physical presence or by the role they occupy in the family?
6. Communication is purposeful.
   - Do the characters seem to realize the number of different purposes their messages are communicating?
   - How many different purposes of communication can you identify from the dialogue?
7. Communication is irreversible and unrepeatable.
   - Do you think the characters would have (at a later date) wished they had not communicated any of these messages? Why?
   - Can you identify any message in this dialogue that would have different meaning if said at another time and in another context?

CHAPTER TWO

The Self in Communication

Chapter Concepts	Chapter Goals	Chapter Skills
	After completing this chapter, you should be able to	**After completing this chapter, you should be able to**
Self-Concept	1. define *self-concept* and explain how it develops	communicate with an understanding of your self-concept, your strengths, and your weaknesses
Self-Awareness	2. explain *self-awareness* and the Johari Window	increase your own self-awareness
	3. explain how you can increase self-awareness	
Self-Esteem	4. define *self-esteem* and explain the ways to increase it	increase your self-esteem
Self-Disclosure	5. define *self-disclosure* and explain its major rewards and dangers	evaluate the costs and rewards of self-disclosure and regulate your disclosures accordingly
	6. explain the factors that influence self-disclosure and why people avoid self-disclosing	
Thinking Critically About the Self and Communication	7. explain the role of the self in influencing communications	understand how your self-concept, awareness, and esteem influence your own communications
		regulate your self-disclosures on the basis of the potential rewards and dangers

In all communications, the most important part is yourself. Who you are and how you see yourself influence the way you communicate and how you respond to others. In this chapter, we explore the self: the self-concept and how it develops, self-awareness and ways to increase it, self-esteem, and self-disclosure, that form of communication in which you reveal something of who you are.

What person has had the greatest influence on your self-concept? On whom have you had a great influence?

SELF-CONCEPT

Your image of who you are is your **self-concept** and is made up of your feelings and thoughts about your strengths and weaknesses, your abilities and limitations. Your self-concept develops from the image of you that others have, the comparisons you make between yourself and others, and the way you evaluate your own thoughts and behaviors (Figure 2.1).

Others' Images of You

If you wished to see the way your hair looked, you would probably look in a mirror. But what would you do if you wanted to see how friendly or how assertive you are? According to the concept of the **looking-glass self** (Cooley, 1922), you would look at the image of yourself that others reveal to you through their behaviors and especially through the way they treat you and react to you.

Of course, you would not look to just anyone. Rather, you would look to those who are most significant in your life—your *significant others.* As a child you would look to your parents and then to your elementary schoolteachers, for example. As an adult you might look to your friends and romantic partners. If these significant others think highly of you, you will see a positive self-image reflected in their behaviors; if they think little of you, you will see a more negative image.

Social Comparisons

Another way you develop your self-concept is to compare yourself with others (Festinger, 1954). Again, you do not choose just anyone. Rather, when you want to gain insight into who you are and how effective or competent you are, you look to your peers. For example, after an exami-

Even when we are quite alone, how often do we think with pleasure or pain of what others think of us—of their imagined approbation or disapprobation.
—*CHARLES DARWIN*

Others' Images
How do significant others see me?

Self-Concept

Social Comparisons
How do I compare to my peers?

Your Interpretations and Evaluations
How do I evaluate my own feelings and behaviors?

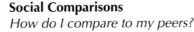

Figure 2.1 The Sources of Self-Concept

Drawing by Levin, © 1993
The New Yorker Magazine, Inc.

"*Please, Lord, enough already.*"

Some research evidence (e.g., Swann, 1987) shows that people adapt strategies and enter relationships that will confirm their self-concepts, even when these self-concepts are negative. People, Swann (1987) notes, "gravitate toward social relationships in which they are apt to receive self-confirmatory feedback." Do you do this? Do those you know also do this?

nation you probably want to know how you performed relative to the other students in your class. This gives you a clearer idea as to how effectively you performed. If you play on a baseball team, it's important to know your batting average in comparison with the batting average of others on the team. Absolute scores on the exam or of your batting average may be helpful in telling you something about your performance, but you gain a different perspective when you see your score in comparison with those of your peers. Notice that in the cartoon the man's unstated assumption is that—in comparison with others—he has had more than "his share" of problems and so he asks, "Please, Lord, enough already."

Your Own Interpretations and Evaluations

You also react to your own behavior; you interpret it and evaluate it. These interpretations and evaluations help form your self-concept. For example, let's say you believe that lying is wrong. If you lie, you will probably evaluate this behavior in terms of your internalized beliefs about lying and will react negatively to your own behavior. You might, for example, experience guilt as a result of your behavior contradicting your beliefs. On the other hand, let's say that you pulled someone out of a burning building at great personal risk. You would probably evaluate this behavior positively; you would feel good about this behavior and, as a result, about yourself.

The more you understand about the reasons you view yourself as you do, the better you will understand who you are. You can gain additional insight into yourself by looking more directly at self-awareness and especially at the Johari model of the self.

I believe that when all the dreams are dead, you're left only with yourself. You'd better like yourself a lot.

—RITA MAE BROWN

	Known to self	Not known to self
Known to others	Open self	Blind self
Not known to others	Hidden self	Unknown self

Figure 2.2 The Johari Window
From Group Process: An Introduction to Group Dynamics *by Joseph Luft.*
Reprinted by permission of Mayfield Publishing Company.

SELF-AWARENESS

Self-awareness is basic to all communication. Self-awareness can be explained by examining the several aspects of yourself as they might appear to others as well as to yourself. A commonly used tool for this examination is a metaphoric division of the self into four areas, collectively called the Johari Window (Figure 2.2, Luft, 1969, 1984). The window gets its name from its inventors, *Jo*seph Luft and *Har*ry Ingham.

The Johari Window

> *Each has his past shut in him like the leaves of a book known to him by heart and his friends can only read the title.*
>
> —*Virginia Woolf*

Divided into four areas or "panes," the window pictures different aspects or versions of the self. The four versions are the open self, the blind self, the hidden self, and the unknown self. These areas are not separate from one another but rather are interdependent. As one dominates, the others recede to a greater or lesser degree; or, to stay with our metaphor, as one window pane becomes larger, one or another becomes smaller. The four window panes can be defined in the following way.

CULTURAL VIEWPOINT

Openness to Intercultural Communication

Knowing the importance of intercultural communication is only part of the issue. Having a willingness to communicate interculturally is the other half. Take the following self-test to help you explore your willingness to communicate interculturally.

TEST YOURSELF

How Open Are You Interculturally?

Instructions: Select a specific culture (national, racial, or religious) different from your own, and substitute this culture for the phrase *culturally different person* in each of the questions below. Indicate how open you would be to communicate in each of these situations, using the following scale:

5 = very open and willing
4 = open and willing
3 = neutral
2 = closed and unwilling
1 = very closed and unwilling

_____ 1. Talk with a culturally different person in the presence of those who are culturally similar to you.
_____ 2. Have a "best friendship" with a culturally different person.
_____ 3. Have a long-term romantic relationship with a culturally different person.
_____ 4. Adopt a culturally different child.
_____ 5. Participate in a problem-solving or consciousness-raising group that is composed predominantly of people who are culturally different from you.
_____ 6. Listen openly and fairly to a speech by a culturally different person.
_____ 7. Listen fairly to a public speaker describing this different cultural group.
_____ 8. Ascribe a level of credibility to a culturally different person identical to that ascribed to a culturally similar person—all other things being equal.

Thinking Critically About Your Openness to Intercultural Communication This test was designed to raise questions rather than to provide answers. The questions refer to various aspects of interpersonal, small group, and public communication. High scores for any question or group of questions indicate considerable openness; low scores indicate a lack of openness. Use these numbers for purposes of thinking critically about the following questions rather than to indicate any absolute level of openness or closedness.

- Did you select the group on the basis of how positive or negative your attitudes were? What group would you be most open to interacting with? Least open?
- In which form of communication are you most open? Least open?
- How open are you to learning about the importance of greater intercultural understanding and communication?
- How open are you to learning what members of other groups think of your cultural groups?

[Next Cultural Viewpoint, page 43]

The Open Self

This self represents all the information, behaviors, attitudes, and feelings
about yourself that you and others know. This could include your name,
skin color, sex, age, religion, and political beliefs among other matters.
The "size" of the open self varies according to your personality and according to whom you are relating. With some people you may be open
and with others not. Probably you are selectively open—open about some
things and not about others.

The Blind Self

The blind self represents knowledge about you that others have but
you do not. This might include your habit of finishing other people's
sentences or rubbing your nose when you become anxious. It may
include your tendency to overreact to imagined insults or to compete
for attention. Blind areas—like famous blind spots—interfere with
communication, so it is important to reduce your blind self as much
as possible.

The Unknown Self

The unknown self represents those parts of yourself that neither you nor
others know. This is information that is buried in your subconscious or
that has somehow escaped awareness. You gain insight into the unknown
self in several ways. Sometimes this area is revealed through hypnosis,
dreams, or psychological tests, like the inkblot test devised by the Swiss
psychiatrist Hermann Rorschach. Another way is to explore yourself in
an open, honest, and understanding way with those whom you trust—
parents, lovers, and friends.

The Hidden Self

The hidden self represents all the knowledge you have of yourself but
keep from others. This window pane includes all your successfully kept
secrets. It may include your dreams and fantasies, experiences about
which you are embarrassed, and attitudes, beliefs, and values of which
you may be ashamed. You probably keep secrets from some people and
not from others. For example, you might not tell your parents you are dating someone of another race or religion, but you might tell a close friend.
So too, you might not let your friends know you have difficulty asking for
a date, but you might discuss this problem with a brother or sister.

Increasing Self-Awareness

Because self-awareness is so important in communication you should
make every effort to increase your awareness of your needs, desires,
habits, beliefs, and attitudes. One way to do this is to make a list of those
things important to you. Also make a list of qualities that you think are
characteristic of you. Then observe your own behavior with both lists in
mind. Think of this as a sort of internal dialogue.

　　Another way is to thoughtfully listen to and observe the responses of
those with whom you are interacting. Both verbal and nonverbal forms of
communication can provide clues into yourself. Also, asking direct questions about your behavior can help reduce your blind self. And looking at

*If you wish in this world to advance
Your merits you're bound to enhance;
You must stir it and stump it.
You blow your own trumpet,
Or, trust me, you haven't a chance.*
—W. S. GILBERT

What kinds of communication situations enhance your self-esteem? What kinds decrease your self-esteem? If you wished to enhance a friend's self-esteem, what kinds of messages would you use? What kinds of messages would you avoid?

POWER PERSPECTIVE

Referent Power

You have *referent power* over another person when that person wishes to be like you or identified with you. For example, an older brother may have power over a younger brother because the younger wants to be like his brother. The assumption made by the younger brother is that he will be more like his brother if he behaves and believes as his brother does. Referent power depends greatly on your attractiveness and prestige (as seen by this other person); as these increase, so does identification and, consequently, power. When you are well liked and well respected, of the same sex, and have similar attitudes and experience as this other person, your referent power becomes even greater. And this is why role models are so important; role models, by definition, possess referent power and exert great influence on those looking up to them.

[Next Power Perspective, page 61]

yourself through the eyes of your friends and acquaintances may provide new and valuable perspectives. Most of all, open yourself to others. It is through such openness that you best get to know yourself.

SELF-ESTEEM

Self-esteem refers to the way you feel about yourself. How much do you like yourself? How valuable a person do you think you are? How competent? The answers to these questions reflect your self-esteem—the value that you place on yourself.

The major reason that self-esteem is so important is simply that success breeds success. When you feel good about yourself—about who you are and what you are capable of doing—you will perform more effectively. When you think like a success, you are more likely to act like a success. When you think you're a failure, you're more likely to act like a failure. Increasing self-esteem will, therefore, help you to function more effectively in school, in your interpersonal relationships, and in your career. Here are a few ways to increase your self-esteem.

Attack Your Self-Destructive Beliefs. Self-destructive beliefs are those things that you believe that damage your self-esteem and prevent you from building meaningful and productive relationships. They may be about yourself ("I'm not creative," "I'm boring"), your world ("The world is an unhappy place," "People are out to get me"), and your relationships ("All the good people are already in relationships," "If I ever fall in love, I know I'll be hurt"). Identifying these beliefs will help you examine them critically and see that they are both illogical and self-defeating.

Some theorists (e.g., Albert Ellis, 1988) claim that the way to increase self-esteem would be to discover which faulty beliefs you have concerning who you are and how valuable you are and substitute logical and healthy ones in their place. For example, you would substitute the belief "I must be loved by everyone" with "it would be nice to have people love me, but it isn't necessary or realistic to believe that this will or should ever happen." What do you think of this approach?

If I can talk, I can sing.
If I can walk, I can dance.
—*AFRICAN PROVERB*

What happens to a dream deferred?
Does it dry up
Like a raisin in the sun?
Or does it explode?
—*LANGSTON HUGHES*

Another way of looking at self-destructive beliefs is to identify what Pamela Butler (1981) calls "drivers"—unrealistic beliefs that may motivate you to act in ways that are self-defeating. Butler identifies five such drivers: be perfect, hurry up, be strong, please others, and try hard. If you can hear yourself giving these injunctions, you may have internalized the unproductive and self-defeating drivers:

- The drive to **be perfect** impels you to try to perform at unrealistically high levels. Whether it is work, school, athletics, or appearance, this drive tells you that anything short of perfection is unacceptable and that you are to blame for any imperfections.
- The drive to **hurry up** compels you to do things quickly, to do more than can be reasonably expected in any given amount of time. This drive leads you to become impatient and to always rush.
- The drive to **be strong** tells you that weakness and any of the more vulnerable emotions like sadness, compassion, or loneliness are wrong.
- The drive to **please others** leads you to seek approval from others. Pleasing yourself is secondary and in fact self-pleasure comes from pleasing others. The logic is that if you gain the approval of others then you are a worthy and deserving person; if others disapprove of you, then surely you must be worthless and undeserving.
- The drive to **try hard** makes you take on more responsibilities than anyone can be expected to handle. This driver leads you to take on tasks that would be impossible for any normal person to handle.

Recognizing that you may have internalized such drivers is a first step to eliminating them. A second step involves recognizing that these drivers are in fact unrealistic and self-defeating. Psychotherapist Albert Ellis (1988; Ellis & Harper, 1975) and other cognitive therapists (e.g., Beck, 1988) would argue that you can accomplish this by understanding why these drivers are unrealistic and substituting more realistic ones. For example, following Ellis, you might try substituting the unrealistic belief to please others (always and in everything you do) with a more realistic belief that it would be nice if others were pleased with you, but it certainly isn't essential. A third step consists of giving yourself permission to fail, to be less than perfect, to be normal.

Do recognize that it is the *unrealistic* nature of these drivers that creates problems. Certainly trying hard or being strong are not unhealthy beliefs when these beliefs are realistic. It is only when they become absolute—when you try to be everything to everyone—that they become impossible to attain and create problems.

Engage in Self-Affirmation. Remind yourself of your successes from time to time. Focus on your good deeds, positive qualities, strengths, and virtues. Also, look carefully at the good relationships you have with friends and relatives. Concentrate on your potential, not your limitations (Brody, 1991).

Seek Out Nourishing People. Seek out positive people who are optimistic and make you feel good about yourself. Avoid those who find fault with just about everything. Seek to build a network of supportive others (Brody, 1991).

Research (Brody, 1991) shows that girls and boys as young as 2 years old respond differently to success and failure. For example, boys show more pride in their successes than do girls. Girls, on the other hand, react to failure with greater shame. Girls also allow a single failure to affect the way they feel about themselves more than do boys.

Work on Projects That Will Result in Success. Success builds self-esteem. Each success will make achieving the next success a little easier. When a project does fail, remember it does not mean that you are a failure. Everyone fails sometime. Successful people know how to deal with failure—they know failure is something that happens, not something inside you. Further, your failing once does not mean that you will fail the next time. Put failure in perspective; do not make it an excuse for not trying again.

Realize That You Do Not Have to Be Loved by Everyone. No one is. Many, however, believe that everyone should love them. The problem with this is that it leads you to believe that you must always please others.

What kinds of communication situations seem to enhance your self-esteem? What kinds seem to decrease your self-esteem? What kinds of messages would you use to enhance a child's self-esteem? What kinds would you avoid?

ETHICAL ISSUE

Introducing Lying and Emotional Appeals

The following dialogue raises questions about two ethical issues discussed in future Ethical Issue boxes: lying and using fear and emotional appeals. What do you feel would be ethical or unethical in each case?

FRANK: father
LAURA: mother
BARBARA: daughter
JEFF: son
ALEX: son

Frank, Barbara, Jeff, and Alex are sitting in the living room.

FRANK: Look. I don't want anything said to your mother about this. Do you hear me? Not one word.
ALEX: Pop, I really think she should know.
BARBARA: She has a right to know. She has more of a right to know than anyone else.
JEFF: Yeah. I agree. You can't keep this from her. You have no right.
FRANK: I don't give a damn what you kids think. I want her to continue thinking that everything is the way it was. The first one to open their trap is going to have my foot in it.
ALEX: OK, but I don't like it.
JEFF: Okay.
BARBARA: I think it stinks but okay.

Assuming that all remain true to their promise, are all four guilty of lying by omission? Are all four equally guilty? Would your answer be different if:

When an individual is kept in a situation of inferiority, the fact is that he does become inferior.
—SIMONE DE BEAUVOIR

Research has shown that when people are made self-aware (for example, sitting them in a room facing a large mirror while listening to their own voices), they are more likely to resist the temptation to engage in unethical behavior (for example, cheat on a test) (Diener & Walbom, 1976). Although 7 percent of the self-aware group cheated, 71 percent of the not self-aware group cheated. Also, self-aware people make more accurate assessments of their own feelings and thoughts and their own personalities than not self-aware people (Pryor, 1980; Aronson, Wilson, & Akert, 1994). Are you less likely to engage in unethical behavior when you are especially aware of yourself? Do you make more accurate judgments when self-aware?

- Frank just learned he was going to die in the next six months, Laura was in poor health, and Frank feared that the shock might kill her?
- Frank was found by one of his children with a girlfriend whom he has been seeing romantically for years?
- Frank got a large pay raise or pay cut?

Are Barbara, Alex, and Jeff unethical because they agree to act against their conscience? Would your answer to this question depend on the age of the children?

[Exit Jeff; Enter Laura]

LAURA: Barbara, I can't believe what you're telling me. Of the three of you kids, you were the last one I would think would want to marry someone of another race and religion. After all I did for you? I can't believe you're going to do this to me. I'll never be able to face the rest of the family. You're destroying everything. You're throwing away everything we tried to do for you. I just want to die. Your father is going to have a heart attack.

FRANK: Listen. You marry that creep and we're through. You'll never be allowed in this house again. Don't ever call; don't ever write. You marry this guy and you have no family. And your kids will have no grandparents. We will never ever ever see you again. To us, you'll be dead.

ALEX: And I'm going to get the guys together and knock that guy's teeth out if I ever see him around here.

FRANK: Now, Alex, I don't think that's going to be necessary.

Are these parents and brother ethical in their use of emotional and fear appeals? Is Frank's threat ethical? Is Alex's physical threat (and Frank's implicit agreement with it) any different ethically from the emotional or interpersonal threats? What (if anything) would you have to know to answer this question? For example, would your answer be different if:

- Laura were honestly expressing her feelings or if she were using this appeal merely as a persuasive strategy to keep Barbara from marrying outside her race and religion?
- Frank thought that this type of appeal was the only one that would keep Barbara from marrying this man and that she would—later in life—be grateful to him?
- The issue centered on Barbara's intention to change her own religion and join a religious cult?
- Barbara were 18 years old, or if she were 55?

[Next Ethical Issue, page 79]

How does self-disclosure with a close friend differ from self-disclosure on, say, a television talk show? How do the rewards and problems involved in these situations differ?

SELF-DISCLOSURE

Self-disclosure is a type of communication in which you reveal information about yourself (Jourard, 1968, 1971a, 1971b). Because self-disclosure is communication, overt statements about the self as well as slips of the tongue, unconscious nonverbal movements, and public confessions would all be considered forms of self-disclosure. Usually, however, the term *self-disclosure* is used to refer to the conscious revealing of information, such as the statements, "I'm afraid to compete; I guess I'm afraid I'll lose" or "I love you" or "I finally saved enough and I'm buying a car this week."

Self-disclosure is "information"—something previously unknown by the receiver. This may vary from the relatively commonplace ("I'm really afraid of that French exam") to the extremely significant ("I'm so depressed, I feel like committing suicide"). Often, when we think of self-disclosure, we think of information that is in our hidden self that we actively keep others from learning.

In addition to disclosing information about yourself, you might also disclose information about those close to you, if it has a significant bearing on your life, social status, or professional capabilities. Thus, self-disclosure could refer to your own actions or the actions of, say, your parents or children, since these have a direct relationship to who you are.

Self-expression must pass into communication for its fulfillment.
—PEARL S. BUCK

Michael Korda (1975), in *Power! How to Get It. How to Use It,* advises: "Never reveal all of yourself to other people; hold back something in reserve so that people are never quite sure if they really know you." What do you think of this advice? Is it applicable to all relationships?

Self-disclosure involves at least one other individual. For self-disclosure to occur, the communication must involve at least two persons. It cannot be an intrapersonal act; the information must be received and understood by another individual.

TEST YOURSELF
How Willing to Self-Disclose Are You?

Instructions: Respond to each of the following statements by indicating the likelihood that you would disclose such items of information to, say, other members of this class in an *interpersonal* situation, one on one; in a *small group* situation with say five or six others; and in a *public communication* setting where you speak to all members of the class. Use the following scale, filling in all three columns:

1 = would definitely self-disclose
2 = would probably self-disclose
3 = don't know
4 = would probably not self-disclose
5 = would definitely not self-disclose

Information	Interpersonal Communication	Small Group Communication	Public Communication
1. My attitudes toward other religions, nationalities, and races			
2. My economic status			
3. My feelings about my parents			
4. My sexual fantasies			
5. My physical and mental health			
6. My ideal mate			
7. My drinking and/or drug behavior			
8. My most embarrassing moment			
9. My unfulfilled desires			
10. My general self-concept			

Novelist and philosopher Albert Camus in *The Fall* says: "We rarely confide in those who are better than we are." Do you find this a generally accurate observation?

. . . know your own value, whatever it may be, and act upon that principle; but take great care to let nobody discover that you do know your own value. Whatever real merit you have, other people will discover; and people always magnify their own discoveries, as they lessen those of others.
—LORD CHESTERFIELD

The dyadic effect may not be universal. For example, some research (Won-Doornink, 1985) finds that although Americans are likely to follow the dyadic effect, Koreans do not. Does this dyadic effect operate in cultures with which you are familiar? What problems might be created by the failure to recognize that the dyadic effect does not hold in all cultures?

Thinking Critically About Self-Disclosure This test, and ideally its discussion with others who also complete it, should get you started thinking about your own self-disclosing behavior. Consider, for example, are there certain topics you are less willing to disclose than others? Are you more likely to disclose positive secrets than negative ones? Are you more likely to communicate interpersonally than in small group or public situations? Are there topics about which you wish you had the opportunity to self-disclose but somehow can't find the right situation to do so? As a listener are there topics you would rather not hear about from certain people?

Factors Influencing Self-Disclosure

Self-disclosure occurs more readily in small groups than in large groups. Dyads (groups of two people) are the most hospitable setting for self-disclosure. With one listener, you can attend to the responses carefully. You can monitor the disclosures, continuing if there is support and stopping if there is not. With more than one listener, such monitoring becomes difficult since the responses are sure to vary among the listeners.

Sometimes self-disclosure takes place in group and public speaking situations. In consciousness-raising groups and in meetings like those of Alcoholics Anonymous, members may disclose their most intimate problems to 10 or perhaps hundreds of people at the same time. In these situations, group members are pledged to be totally supportive. These and similar groups are devoted specifically to encouraging self-disclosure and to giving each other support for the disclosures.

Because you disclose on the basis of support you receive, you probably disclose to people you like (Derlega, Winstead, Wong, & Greenspan, 1987) and to people you trust (Wheeless & Grotz, 1977). In turn, you probably also come to like those to whom you disclose (Berg & Archer, 1983).

You are more likely to disclose when the person you are with discloses. This dyadic effect probably leads you to feel more secure and, in fact, reinforces your own self-disclosing behavior. Disclosures are also more intimate when they are made in response to the disclosures of others (Berg & Archer, 1983).

Competent people engage in self-disclosure more than less competent people. Perhaps competent people have greater self-confidence and more positive things to reveal. Similarly, their self-confidence may make them more willing to risk possible negative reactions (McCroskey & Wheeless, 1976).

Not surprisingly, personality influences self-disclosure. Highly sociable and extroverted people self-disclose more than those who are less sociable and more introverted. People who are apprehensive about talking in general also self-disclose less than do those who are more comfortable in communicating.

You are also more likely to disclose about some topics than others. For example, you are probably more likely to self-disclose information about your job or hobbies than about your sex life or financial situation (Jourard, 1968, 1971a). You are also more likely to disclose favorable information than unfavorable information. Generally, the more personal and negative the topic, the less likely you will be to self-disclose.

The popular stereotype of gender differences in self-disclosure—aptly illustrated in the accompanying cartoon—emphasizes men's reluctance to

Judy Pearson (1980) has argued that it is sex role, not biological gender, that accounts for the differences in self-disclosure. "Masculine" women, for example, self-disclosed to a lesser extent than did women who scored low on masculinity scales. Further, "feminine" men self-disclosed to a greater extent than those who scored low on femininity scales. Do your own observations and experiences support this idea?

Copyright 1990, Distributed by Los Angeles Times syndicate. Reprinted with permission.

speak about themselves, especially their feelings. For the most part, research supports this generally accepted view. One notable exception occurs in initial encounters. Here men will disclose more intimately than women, perhaps "in order to control the relationship's development" (Derlega, Winstead, Wong, & Hunter, 1985). Women also self-disclose more to members of the extended family than do men (Komarovsky, 1964; Argyle & Henderson, 1985; Moghaddam, Taylor, & Wright, 1993).

CULTURAL VIEWPOINT

Culture and Self-Disclosure

Culture exerts powerful influence on self-disclosures. For example, people in the United States disclose more than those in Great Britain, Germany, Japan, or Puerto Rico (Gudykunst and Kim, 1992;

What do you think of "outing"—
the process of making public that a
noted personality is gay or lesbian?
Under what conditions do you
think outing is acceptable?
Unacceptable? An excellent
communication perspective is
provided by Gross (1991).

Gudykunst, 1994). American students also disclose more than students from nine different Middle East countries (Jourard, 1971).

There are also important similarities across cultures. For example, people from Great Britain, Germany, the United States, and Puerto Rico are alike in that they are all more apt to disclose personal information such as hobbies, interests, and attitudes and opinions on politics and religion and are less apt to disclose information on finances, sex, personality, and interpersonal relationships (Jourard, 1971a).

Some cultures view the disclosing of one's inner feelings as a weakness. Among some groups, for example, it would be considered "out of place" for a man to cry at a happy occasion like a wedding, while that same crying would go unnoticed in some Latin cultures. Similarly, in Japan it is considered undesirable to reveal personal information, whereas in much of the United States it is considered desirable and is even expected (Barnlund, 1989; Hall & Hall, 1987).

The potential rewards and dangers of self-disclosure, then, must be examined in terms of the particular cultural rules. As with all cultural rules, following them brings approval and violating them brings disapproval.

[Next Cultural Viewpoint, page 66]

The Rewards and Dangers of Self-Disclosure

Whether or not you self-disclose will depend on your assessment of the possible rewards and dangers. Here are some of the most important.

The Rewards of Self-Disclosure

In order to have a conversation with someone you must reveal yourself.

—JAMES BALDWIN

Self-disclosure contributes to self-knowledge; it helps you gain a new perspective on yourself and a deeper understanding of your own behavior. In therapy, for example, insight often comes while you are disclosing. Through self-disclosure, then, you may come to understand yourself more thoroughly.

Self-disclosure improves your coping abilities; it helps you to deal with problems, especially guilt. You may fear that you will not be accepted because of something you have done or because of some feeling or attitude you have. Because you feel these things are a basis for rejection, you may develop guilt. By self-disclosing such a feeling and receiving support rather than rejection, you may be better able to deal with guilt, perhaps reducing or even eliminating it.

Self-disclosure often improves communication. You understand the messages of others largely to the extent that you understand the individuals. You can tell what certain nuances mean, when the person is serious or joking, and when the person is being sarcastic out of fear or out of resentment. You might study a person's behavior or even live together for years, but if that person rarely self-discloses, you are far from understanding that individual as a complete person.

At times self-disclosure occurs more in temporary than permanent relationships—for example, between strangers on a train or plane, a kind of "in-flight intimacy" (McGill, 1985). In this situation, two people set up an intimate self-disclosing relationship during a brief travel period, but they do not pursue it beyond that point. When, if ever, are you more likely to engage in this type of in-flight intimacy?

Self-disclosure helps you establish meaningful relationships. Without self-disclosure, relationships of any meaningful depth seem impossible. By self-disclosing, you tell others that you trust, respect, and care enough about them and your relationship to reveal yourself. This in turn leads the other individual to self-disclose and forms at least the start of a meaningful relationship, one that is honest and open and goes beyond trivialities.

The Dangers of Self-Disclosure

The many advantages of self-disclosure should not blind you to its very real risks (Bochner, 1984). When you self-disclose you risk personal and social rejection. You usually self-disclose to a person you expect will be supportive. Of course, the person you think will be supportive may turn out to reject you. Parents, normally the most supportive of all interpersonal relations, frequently reject children who self-disclose their homosexuality, their plans to marry someone of a different race, or their belief in another faith. Your best friends, your closest intimates, may reject you for similar self-disclosures.

Sometimes self-disclosure results in material losses. Politicians who disclose that they have been in therapy may lose the support of their own political party and find that voters are unwilling to vote for them. Teachers who disclose disagreement with the school administrators may find themselves denied tenure, teaching undesirable schedules, and victims of "budget cuts." In the business world, self-disclosures of alcoholism or drug addiction are often met with dismissal, demotion, or transfer.

Remember that self-disclosure, like any communication, is irreversible (see Chapter 1). You cannot self-disclose and then take it back. Nor can you erase the conclusions and inferences listeners have made on the basis of your disclosures.

THINKING CRITICALLY ABOUT THE SELF AND COMMUNICATION

Because the self is so crucial in every communication act, it is essential that you carefully weigh the role of the self in your communication decisions. Your self-concept, self-awareness, and self-esteem will influence how positively or negatively you communicate and how defensive or supportive you will be. They will also influence how others communicate with you. Thus, when you want to figure out ways of improving your own communications, consider the self-image that you are projecting. Attacking your self-destructive beliefs, engaging in self-affirmation—seeking out nourishing people, for example—will not only help you to increase self-esteem but will also make you a more effective communicator.

Similarly, think critically about the consequences of self-disclosing. As we noted earlier, attitudes toward self-disclosure vary from culture to culture and these must be considered in deciding whether to and how to self-disclose. Moreover, decisions to self-disclose will be based on several other factors. Among these is your concern for your rela-

I never intended to become a run-of-the-mill person.
—BARBARA JORDAN

tionship with the person or persons to whom you are self-disclosing (Will this add tension to the relationship? Might it place an unfair burden on the friendship?). You would also probably consider the appropriateness of the context in which you are self-disclosing (Is this the right time, place, and circumstance? Should you disclose interpersonally, in a small group, or more publicly?) and the way in which the person to whom you are self-disclosing responds (sympathetically and supportively or indifferently, perhaps even hostilely?). And, of course, you would weigh the consequences of your self-disclosure (Can you afford to lose your job? Might it cause your friend some pain?).

Then there are times when you may be on the receiving end of self-disclosure. Here, too, you need to consider the cultural rules and customs. In addition, remember that when someone is disclosing to you, he or she is simultaneously seeking your support and placing enormous trust in you. Listen attentively, not only to what is said, but also to the feelings that underlie the words. Paraphrase the speaker so that you show both sympathy and understanding. Openly express your support during and after the disclosures with both words and gestures. Refrain from criticizing or passing judgments on the speaker. Do not betray the trust of the person making the disclosures by telling others or using the information against that person. This last might, depending on the disclosure, create a moral dilemma for you. If your friend reveals that he or she intends to commit suicide, you would probably want to reveal this to appropriate professionals who can provide help to your friend. Table 2.1 summarizes some of these guidelines.

Add a third to your two ears even if it be an imaginary one, for the news is so enchanting that two ears is not enough.
—HAUSA PROVERB

Have you ever been involved in a self-disclosure experience where these general principles were violated? What happened?

TABLE 2.1 A SUMMARY OF SELF-DISCLOSURE GUIDELINES

In Self-Disclosing:	In Responding to the Self-Disclosing of Others:
1. Is the motivation to improve the relationship?	1. Are you trying to feel what the other person is feeling?
2. Does the self-disclosure impose burdens on your listener?	2. Are you using effective and active listening skills?
3. Is the self-disclosure appropriate to the context and the relationship between yourself and your listener?	3. Are you communicating supportiveness (verbally and nonverbally) to the discloser?
4. Is the other person disclosing also? If not, might this be a sign of disinterest?	4. Are you refraining from criticism and evaluation?
5. Might the self-disclosure place too heavy a burden on you?	5. Will you maintain confidentiality?

Feedback on Concepts and Skills

In this chapter we looked at the most important part of the communication process: the self. We discussed (1) self-concept and how it develops, (2) self-awareness and how to increase it, (3) self-esteem and how to increase it, and (4) self-disclosure and how we might be more effective disclosers.

1. Self-concept refers to the image that you have of yourself and is composed of feelings and thoughts about both your abilities and your limitations.
2. Self-concept develops from the image that others have of you, the comparisons you make between yourself and others, and your own interpretations and evaluations of your thoughts and behaviors.
3. In the Johari Window model of the self, there are four major areas: the open self, the blind self, the hidden self, and the unknown self.
4. To increase self-awareness, analyze yourself, listen to others to see yourself as they do, actively seek information from others about yourself, see yourself from different perspectives, and increase your open self.
5. Self-esteem refers to the value a person puts on himself or herself.
6. Among the ways to increase self-esteem are to attack your self-destructive beliefs, engage in self-affirmation, seek out nourishing people, work on projects that result in success, and recognize that you do not have to be loved by everyone.
7. Self-disclosure refers to a form of communication in which information about the self that is normally kept hidden is communicated to another person.
8. Self-disclosure is more likely to occur when the potential discloser is with one other person, when the discloser likes or loves the listener, when the listener also discloses, when the discloser feels competent, when the discloser is highly sociable and extroverted, and when the topic of disclosure is fairly impersonal and is also positive.
9. The rewards of self-disclosure include increases in self-knowledge, in the ability to cope with difficult situations and guilt, in communication efficiency, and in the chances for a meaningful relationship.
10. The dangers of self-disclosure include personal and social rejection, material loss, and intrapersonal difficulties.
11. Before self-disclosing, consider the cultural rules operating, the motivation for the self-disclosure, the possible burdens you might impose on your listener, the appropriateness of the self-disclosure, the disclosures of the other person, and the possible burdens that your self-disclosure might impose on you.
12. When listening to disclosures, take into consideration the cultural rules governing the communication situation, try to feel what the discloser is feeling, practice the skills of effective and active listening, support the discloser, refrain from criticism and evaluation, and keep the disclosures confidential.

The skills for increasing self-awareness and self-esteem and for effective self-disclosure are critical to effective communication in all its forms.

Check your ability to apply these skills. If you wish, use the following rating scale: (1) = almost always, (2) = often, (3) = sometimes, (4) = rarely, (5) = almost never.

_____ 1. I seek to understand my self-concept and be realistic about my strengths and my weaknesses.

_____ 2. I actively seek to increase self-awareness by talking with myself, listening to others, reducing my blind self, seeing myself from different perspectives, and increasing my open self.

_____ 3. I seek to increase my self-esteem by engaging in self-affirmation, seeking out nourishing people, working on projects that will likely succeed, and recognizing that I do not have to be loved by everyone.

_____ 4. I regulate my disclosures on the basis of the unique communication situation.

_____ 5. In deciding whether or not to self-disclose I take into consideration (1) the cultural rules, (2) my motivation, (3) the possible burdens on my listener, (4) the appropriateness to the other person and the context, (5) the other person's disclosures, and (6) the possible burdens the disclosures may impose on me.

_____ 6. I respond to the disclosures of others by trying to feel what the other person is feeling, using effective and active listening skills, expressing supportiveness, refraining from criticism and evaluation, and keeping the disclosures confidential.

Skill Development Experiences

2.1 I'd Prefer to Be

This exercise should enable members of the class to get to know one another better and at the same time get to know themselves better. The questions should encourage each individual to increase awareness of some facet(s) of his or her thoughts or behaviors. The "I'd Prefer to Be" game is played in a group of four to six people.

1. Each person individually rank-orders each of the clusters of preferences presented below using 1 for the most preferred and 3 for the least preferred choice.
2. The players then consider each of the categories in turn, each member giving his or her rank order.
3. Members may refuse to reveal their rankings for any category by saying, "I pass." The group is not permitted to question the reasons for any member's passing.
4. When a member has revealed his or her rankings for a category, group members may ask questions relevant to that category. These questions may be asked after any individual member's account or may be reserved until all members have given their rankings for a particular category.

1. _____ intelligent
   _____ wealthy
   _____ physically attractive
2. _____ movie star
   _____ senator
   _____ successful businessperson
3. _____ blind
   _____ deaf
   _____ mute
4. _____ on a date
   _____ reading a book
   _____ watching television
5. _____ loved
   _____ feared
   _____ respected
6. _____ alone
   _____ with a group of people
   _____ with one person
7. _____ brave
   _____ reliable
   _____ insightful
8. _____ bisexual
   _____ heterosexual
   _____ homosexual
9. _____ the loved
   _____ the lover
   _____ the good friend
10. _____ introvert
    _____ extrovert
    _____ ambivert
11. _____ a tree
    _____ a rock
    _____ a flower
12. _____ a leader
    _____ a follower
    _____ a loner

Thinking Critically About Preferences

1. What do the choices reveal about the individual? Why would it be dangerous to categorize people or draw conclusions about people on the basis of these choices?
2. What is the degree of similarity of the group as a whole? Were cultural differences evident? Do the members show relatively similar choices or wide differences? What does this mean in terms of the members' ability to communicate with one another?
3. Do the members accept/reject the choices of other members? Are some members disturbed by the choices other members make? If so, why? Are some apathetic? Why? Did hearing the choices of one or more members make you want to get to know them better?

2.2 Deciding About Self-Disclosure

Should you self-disclose or not? Here are several instances of impending self-disclosure. For each, indicate whether or not you think the self-disclosure would be appropriate. Specify your reasons for each of your judgments. In making your decision, consider each of the guidelines identified in this chapter.

1. A student plagiarized a term paper in anthropology. He is sorry, especially since the plagiarized paper only earned a grade of C+. He wants to disclose to his instructor and redo the paper.
2. Robert, a college sophomore, has just discovered he is HIV-positive. He wants to tell his parents and his best friends but fears their rejection. His major advisor at school seems sensitive and empathic and he wonders if he should tell this instructor. He wants the support of his friends and family and yet doesn't want them to reject him or treat him differently.
3. Tom has fallen in love with another woman and wants to end his relationship with Cathy. He wants to call Cathy on the phone, break his engagement, and disclose his new relationship.
4. Sam is 27 years old and has been living in a romantic relationship with another man for the past several years. Sam wants to tell his parents, with whom he has been very close throughout his life, but can't seem to get up the courage. He decides to tell them in a long letter.
5. Mary and Jim have been married for 12 years. Mary has disclosed a great deal to Jim about her past romantic encounters, fears, insecurities, ambitions, and so on. Yet Jim doesn't reciprocate. He almost never shares his feelings and has told Mary almost nothing about his life before they met. Mary wonders if she should begin to limit her disclosures.

2.3 Experiencing Self-Disclosure

This experience is an extremely powerful one for demonstrating the topics normally kept secret, the reasons for secrecy, and the willingness to be supportive; it derives from Egan (1970). The procedure is simple: On an index card write a statement of information that is currently in your hidden self. Do not put your names on these cards; the statements are to be dealt with anonymously. These cards will be collected and read aloud to the entire group. The exercise will work best if members make no negative comments (verbal or nonverbal) as the cards are read aloud. After hearing the statements from the cards, consider:

1. Can you classify the statements into categories—for example, sexual problems, attitudes toward family, self-doubts, and so forth?
2. Why do you suppose this type of information is kept hidden? What advantages might hiding this information have? What disadvantages?

3. How would you react to people who disclosed such statements to you? For example, what difference, if any, would it make in your relationship?
4. What type of person is likely to have a large hidden self and a small open self? A large open self and a small hidden self?
5. Would your open self be larger than that of other group members? Smaller? The same size? Would your hidden self be larger? Smaller? The same size?

CHAPTER THREE

Perception

Chapter Concepts	Chapter Goals After completing this chapter, you should be able to	Chapter Skills After completing this chapter, you should be able to
The Perception Process	1. define perception and describe its stages of sensation, organization, and evaluation	perceive others with a knowledge that perceptions are influenced by who you are and by the external stimulus
Processes Influencing Perception	2. explain the processes that influence interpersonal perception	perceive others while avoiding the common perceptual barriers
Critical Perception: Making Perceptions More Accurate	3. explain the suggestions for increasing accuracy in perception	perceive others with a variety of strategies and while following perceptual guidelines
Thinking Critically About Perception	4. explain the techniques for perception checking	use perception checking as appropriate

What you perceive and what you think about it; who you judge positively and who negatively; and how others perceive and judge you will be influenced by a wide range of factors. **Perception**—the process of becoming aware of the many stimuli impinging on your senses—influences what messages you take in and what meaning you give them. Perception is therefore central to the study of communication in all its forms. Here we look at how perception works, the processes that influence it, and how you can make your perceptions more accurate.

Perception is complex. There is no one-to-one relationship between the messages that occur—in the sounds of the voice, the writings on paper—and the messages that eventually reach your brain. What occurs may differ greatly from what reaches your brain. Further, although two people may be exposed to the same stimulus, each will interpret it differently—not unlike our heroes in the accompanying cartoon. The three steps involved in the process explain how perception works. These stages are not separate; they are continuous and blend into and overlap one another (see Figure 3.1).

THE PERCEPTION PROCESS

At the *sensation* stage, one or another of your five senses responds to a stimulus: you hear, see, smell, taste, feel, or use all of these at the same time. For example, when you hold a slice of pizza, you feel it, see it, taste and smell it, and at the same time hear the sounds around you.

At the *organization* stage, you organize the sensory stimulations according to various principles. One principle is that of proximity: You perceive people or messages that are physically close to one another as a unit. For example, you perceive people you often see together as a unit (such as a couple). You also assume that verbal and nonverbal signals sent at about the same time are related and constitute a unified whole. Another principle is closure: you perceive as closed, or complete, a figure or message that is actually unclosed or incomplete. For example, you perceive a broken circle as complete even though part of it is missing; you fill in messages you hear only partially with parts that seem logically to complete the messages.

At the *interpretation-evaluation* stage you give the stimulation meaning and evaluate or judge it. This step is highly subjective; your interpretations-and-evaluations are not based solely on the outside stimulus, but are also greatly influenced by your experiences, needs, wants, value systems, beliefs about the way things are or should be, current physical or emotional states, expectations, and so on. Similarly, they are influenced by cultural factors—your cultural training and values. Two men walking arm in arm, young children competing in school and on the sports field, and a woman or man in a leopard-skin coat will all be evaluated differently depending on your cultural values.

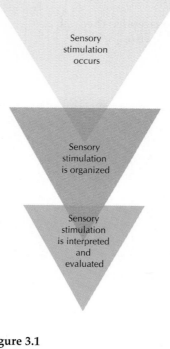

Figure 3.1
The Perception Process

Horley Schwadron

....

TEST YOURSELF

How Accurate Are You at People Perception?

Instructions: Respond to each of the following statements with T (true) if the statement is usually accurate in describing your behavior and F (false) if the statement is usually inaccurate.

_____ 1. I base most of my impressions of people on the first few minutes of our meeting.

_____ 2. When I know some things about another person, I fill in what I don't know.

_____ 3. I make predictions about people's behaviors that generally prove to be true.

_____ 4. I have clear ideas of what people of different national, racial, and religious groups are really like.

_____ 5. I reserve making judgments about people until I learn a great deal about them and see them in a variety of situations.

_____ 6. On the basis of my observations of people, I formulate guesses (that I am willing to revise), rather than firmly held conclusions.

_____ 7. I pay special attention to people's behaviors that might contradict my initial impressions.

_____ 8. I delay formulating conclusions about people until I have lots of evidence.

_____ 9. I avoid making assumptions about what is going on in someone else's head on the basis of their behaviors.

_____ 10. I recognize that people are different and don't assume that everyone is like me.

Everyone complains of the badness of his memory, but nobody of his judgment.
—LaRochefoucauld

Thinking Critically About Your Perceptions This brief perception test was designed to raise questions considered in this chapter and not to provide you with a specific perception score. The first four questions refer to tendencies to judge others on the basis of first impressions (question 1), implicit personality theories (2), prophecies (3), and stereotypes (4). Ideally you would have answered "false" to these four questions because they represent sources of distortion. Questions 5 through 10 refer to specific guidelines for increasing accuracy in people perception: looking for a variety of cues (5), formulating hypotheses rather than conclusions (6), being especially alert to contradictory cues (7), delaying conclusions until more evidence is in (8), avoiding the tendency to mind read (9), and recognizing the diversity in people (10). Ideally you would have answered "true" to these six questions because they represent suggestions for increased accuracy in perception. Do recognize, however, that situations vary widely and these suggestions will prove useful only most of the time, not all the time. You may want to identify situations in which these suggestions should not be taken.

PROCESSES INFLUENCING PERCEPTION

Seeing is deceiving. It's eating that's believing.

—JAMES THURBER

Between the occurrence of the stimulation (the uttering of the message, presence of the person, smile, or wink of the eye) and its interpretation-evaluation, perception is influenced by several psychological processes. Here we identify five major ones (Cook, 1971; Rubin & McNeil, 1985): implicit personality theory, the self-fulfilling prophecy, primacy-recency, stereotyping, and attribution (Figure 3.2).

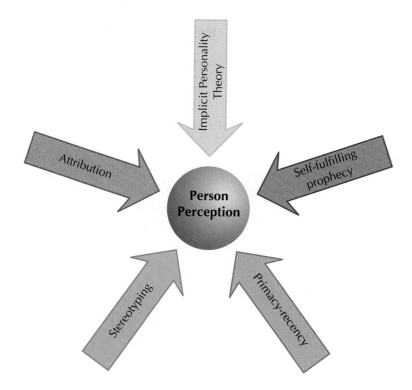

Figure 3.2 Processes Influencing Perception

These processes influence what you see and fail to see; what you assume to be true or false about another person. These processes help to explain why you make some predictions and decline to make others about people. Note, however, that each process also contains potential barriers to accurate perception. These barriers can exert significant influence on both your perceptions and your interpersonal interactions. We discuss these potential barriers along with the psychological processes.

Personality Theory

Consider the following brief statements. Note the characteristic in parentheses that best seems to complete the sentence:

John is energetic, eager, and (intelligent, unintelligent).
Mary is bold, defiant, and (extroverted, introverted).
Joe is bright, lively, and (thin, fat).
Jane is attractive, intelligent, and (likable, unlikable).
Susan is cheerful, positive, and (attractive, unattractive).
Jim is handsome, tall, and (interesting, boring).

Certain choices seem right and others, wrong. What makes some seem right is the implicit personality theory, a system of rules that tells you which characteristics go with each other. Most people's rules tell them that a person who is energetic and eager is also intelligent. Of course, there is no logical reason why an unintelligent person could not be energetic and eager.

The culture in which you were raised greatly influenced the specific theories you now hold. So remember that your theories may not be held by others. The widely documented "halo effect" is a function of this implicit personality theory. If you believe an individual has several positive qualities, you may conclude that she or he has other positive qualities. The "reverse halo effect" operates similarly. If you know a person has several negative qualities, you might conclude the person also has other negative qualities.

Beware: Potential Barriers

The tendency to develop a personality theory and then to perceive an individual as conforming to the theory can lead you to:

- perceive qualities in an individual that your "theory" tells you should be present when they actually are not. For example, you see "goodwill" in the "charitable" acts of a friend when tax reduction may be the real motive.
- ignore or distort qualities or characteristics that do not conform to your theory. For example, you may ignore negative qualities in your friends that you would easily perceive in your enemies.

Self-fulfilling Prophecy

A **self-fulfilling prophecy** occurs when you make a prediction or formulate a belief that comes true because you made the prediction and acted as if it were true (Merton, 1957; Insel & Jacobson, 1975). There are four basic steps in the self-fulfilling prophecy:

It is with our judgments as with our watches; no two go just alike, yet each believes his own.
—ALEXANDER POPE

What implicit personality theory do others have of you? How do the theories held by your close friends differ from those held by your casual acquaintances? Who has the more accurate theory? Why?

A widely known example of the self-fulfilling prophecy is the Pygmalion effect. In one study, for example, teachers were told that certain pupils, whose names were actually selected at random, were expected to do exceptionally well, that they were late bloomers. At the end of the term, these students actually performed at a higher level than the others (Rosenthal & Jacobson, 1968; Insel & Jacobson, 1975). How do you account for this? Has someone's predictions about you ever influenced you?

1. You make a prediction or formulate a belief about someone (often yourself) or a situation. For example, you predict that Pat is awkward in interpersonal situations.
2. You act toward that person or situation as if the prediction or belief is true. For example, you act toward Pat as if she were in fact awkward.
3. Because you act as if the belief were true, it becomes true. Because of the way you act toward Pat, she becomes tense and manifests awkwardness.
4. Your effect on the person or the resulting situation strengthens your beliefs. Seeing Pat's awkwardness reinforces your belief that Pat is in fact awkward.

If you expect people to act in a certain way, your predictions will frequently come true because of the self-fulfilling prophecy. Consider, for instance, people who enter a group situation convinced that other members will dislike them. Almost invariably they are proved right, perhaps because they act in a way that encourages people to respond negatively. Such people fulfill their own prophecies.

A widely known example of the self-fulfilling prophecy is the **Pygmalion effect** (Rosenthal & Jacobson, 1968). In one study, teachers were told that certain pupils were expected to do exceptionally well, that they were late bloomers. The experimenters actually selected the names at random. The students did perform at a higher level than the other students. The teacher's expectations probably generated extra attention to the students, thereby positively affecting their performance.

Have you ever made a prophecy about someone? Did the prophecy have any effect on your attitudes and behaviors toward this other person? Was it a self-fulfilling prophecy?

Beware: Potential Barriers

The tendency to fulfill your own prophecies can lead you to:

- influence another's behavior to conform to your prophecy.
- see what you predicted rather than what really is. For example, it can lead you to perceive yourself as a failure because you made this prediction rather than because of any actual failures.

What can you do to combat the stereotypes you hear in the messages of your friends, family members, or people with whom you work?

Primacy-Recency

If what comes first exerts the most influence, we have a **primacy effect.** If what comes last (or is the most recent) exerts the most influence, we have a **recency effect.** In an early study on primacy-recency effects in interpersonal perception, Solomon Asch (1946) read a list of adjectives describing a person to a group and found that the effects of order were significant. Students more positively evaluated a person described as "intelligent, industrious, impulsive, critical, stubborn, and envious" than a person described as "envious, stubborn, critical, impulsive, industrious, and intelligent." The implication is that we use early information to provide a general idea of what a person is like, then later information to make the general idea more specific. The obvious practical implication of primacy-recency is that the first impression you make is likely to be the most important. Through this first impression, others filter additional information to formulate a picture of who they perceive you to be.

Primacy-recency provides the public speaker with guidance as to how to arrange the arguments in a speech. If you have three arguments, for example, put the weakest one in the middle—the position least likely to be remembered. If your listeners have no real conviction about your position, lead off with your strongest argument to get the listeners on your side. Public speaking audiences—like interpersonal ones—also form a general impression of the speaker and then filter everything else through this initial impression.

Beware: Potential Barriers

Your tendency to give greater weight to early information and to interpret later information in light of these early impressions can lead you to:

- formulate a "total" picture of an individual on the basis of initial impressions that may not be typical or accurate. For example, you might form an image of someone as socially ill at ease. If you based this impression on watching the person at a stressful job interview or during the first few minutes of a long political campaign, it is likely to be wrong.
- discount or distort later perceptions to avoid disrupting your initial impression. For instance, you may fail to see signs of deceit in someone who made a good first impression.

Stereotypes

A frequently used shortcut in perception is stereotyping. The term stereotype originated in printing; it referred to the plate that printed the same image over and over. A sociological or psychological stereotype is a fixed impression of a group of people. We all have attitudinal stereotypes—of national, religious, and racial groups, and of criminals, prostitutes, teachers, or plumbers.

If you have these fixed impressions, you might, on meeting a member of a particular group, see that person primarily as a member of that group. When you apply all the characteristics you assign to members of

Manage every second of a first meeting. Do not delude yourself that a bad impression can be easily corrected. Putting things right is a lot harder than getting them right first time.

—DAVID LEWIS

What is the first impression that people—say, your classmates—form of you? On what do they base these first impressions? Do men and women develop essentially the same first impressions of you?

I make up my mind about people in the first ten seconds, and I very rarely change it.

—MARGARET THATCHER

What stereotypes do you maintain? Were you taught them as a child? Did you formulate them on the basis of your personal interactions with this group of people? How accurate do you think they are?

POWER PERSPECTIVE

Strategic Self-Presentation

How do you get others to like you and to see you as a competent and capable person? Here are a few strategies (Jones & Pittman, 1982; Jones, 1990):

When you use **ingratiation** you may express lots of agreement with the opinions of the other person, compliment the other, or do favors for this person. Or you might emphasize your positive qualities. In using these strategies, however, you run the risk of being seen as a sycophant, as one who is willing to do anything to be liked. When you use **self-promotion** you try to present yourself as exceptionally competent so that the other person will respect you. The obvious problem with this tactic is that you may be perceived as incompetent on the theory that really competent people demonstrate competence; they don't talk about it.

When you use **exemplification** you present yourself as worthy, moral, and virtuous. The downside to this is that you may appear as sanctimonious, as "holier than thou," a quality that most people dislike. When you use **supplication** you present yourself as helpless and in need of assistance: "Can you type my paper? I'm such a bad typist." The supplicant runs the risk, however, of being seen as demanding, incompetent, or perhaps lazy.

[Next Power Perspective, page 81]

that group, you run the risk of missing a great deal that is unique to the individual. If you meet someone who is homeless, for example, you might have a host of characteristics for "homeless" that you are ready to apply. Also, you may see various characteristics in this person's behavior that you would not see if you did not know this person was homeless. Stereotypes prevent you from seeing an individual.

Beware: Potential Barriers

Grouping people into classes and then responding to individuals primarily as members of that class can lead you to:

- perceive someone as having those qualities (usually negative) that you believe characterize the particular group (for example, all Venusians are lazy); therefore, you fail to appreciate the multifaceted nature of all people and all groups.
- ignore the unique characteristics of an individual and therefore fail to benefit from the special contributions each can bring to an encounter.

Attribution

Attribution is a process by which we try to explain the motivation for a person's behavior. One way to do this is to ask if the person was in control of the behavior. For example, say you invited your friend Desmond to dinner for seven o'clock and he arrives at nine. Consider how you would respond to each of these reasons:

1. Reason 1: I just couldn't tear myself away from the beach. I really wanted to get a great tan.
2. Reason 2: I was driving here when I saw some young kids mugging an old couple. I broke it up and took the couple home. They were so frightened that I had to stay with them until their children arrived. Their phone was out of order, so I had no way of calling to tell you I'd be late.
3. Reason 3: I got in a car accident and was taken to the hospital.

Assuming you believe all three explanations, you would attribute very different motives to Desmond's behavior. With reasons 1 and 2, you would conclude that Desmond was in control of his behavior; with reason 3, that he was not. Further, you would probably respond negatively to reason 1 (Desmond was selfish and inconsiderate) and positively to reason 2 (Desmond was a good Samaritan). Because Desmond was not in control of his behavior in reason 3, you would probably not attribute either positive or negative motivation to his behavior. Instead you would probably feel sorry that he got into an accident.

You probably make similar judgments based on controllability in numerous situations. Consider, for example, how you would respond to the following situations:

- Doris fails her history midterm exam.
- Sidney got fired.

Notice how this theory has recently been used as a defense strategy in some of the recent widely publicized trials of the Menendez brothers or Lorena Bobbit, for example. If you were a member of the jury, would this type of defense influence you?

- Margie is 150 pounds overweight and is complaining that she feels awful.
- Thomas's wife has just filed for divorce and he is feeling depressed.

You would most likely be sympathetic to each of these people if you feel that they were not in control of what happened. For example, if the examination was unfair, if Sidney lost his job because of employee discrimination, if Margie has a glandular problem, and if Thomas's wife wants to leave him for a wealthy drug dealer. On the other hand, you probably would not be sympathetic toward these people if you felt they were in control of what happened. For example, if Doris partied instead of studied, if Sidney didn't do his job, if Margie ate nothing but junk food and refused to exercise, and if Thomas has been repeatedly unfaithful and his wife finally gave up trying to reform him.

In perceiving, and especially in evaluating, other people's behavior, we frequently ask if they were in control of the behavior. Generally, research shows that if we feel a person was in control of negative behaviors, we will come to dislike him or her. If we believe the person was not in control of negative behaviors, we will come to feel sorry for and not blame the person.

Beware: Potential Barriers

Can you explain with the concept of controllability the attitudes that many people have about the homeless? About drug addicts or alcoholics? About successful politicians, scientists, or millionaires?

Of course, the obvious problem is that we can only make guesses about another person's behaviors. Can we really know if Doris deserved to pass or fail the history exam? Can we really know if Sidney deserved to have his car repossessed? Our inability to discover the absolute truth, however, does not discourage us from making such judgments, from trying to mind read the motives of another person. But, if we realize that our judgments are based on guesses, we might be more apt to seek further information before acting as if they were facts.

You see this tendency to mind read in a wide variety of situations: You forgot my birthday; *you don't love me.* You don't want to go to my parents' for dinner; *you've never liked my parents.* You don't want to go for that interview; *you lack self-confidence.* The italicized words represent attempts to get inside a person's head, to mind read.

Another potential problem is the self-serving bias that operates when you evaluate your own behaviors. It leads you to take credit for the positive and to deny responsibility for the negative. Thus, you are more likely to attribute your own negative behaviors to uncontrollable factors. For example, after getting a D on an exam, you are more likely to attribute it to the difficulty or unfairness of the test.

Roman historian Seneca once observed: "Other men's sins are before our eyes; our own are behind our backs." How would you rephrase Seneca's observation in the terms of attribution theory?

However, you are likely to attribute your positive behaviors to controllable factors—your own strength, intelligence, or personality. After getting an A on an exam, you are more likely to attribute it to your ability or hard work (Bernstein, Stephan, & Davis 1979). So this self-serving bias may distort your attributions.

The self-serving bias, however, has at least one benefit—it helps protect our self-esteem. Our self-esteem is enhanced by attributing negative behaviors to outside, uncontrollable forces and positive behaviors to internal, controllable forces.

Another problem is the tendency of overattribution—attributing everything a person does to one or two obvious characteristics. For example,

To see ourselves as others see us is a most salutary gift. Hardly less important is the capacity to see others as they see themselves.
—ALDOUS HUXLEY

attributing a person's behavior to alcoholic parents or to being born blind or into great wealth. And so we say Sally has difficulty forming meaningful relationships because she grew up in a home of alcoholics, Alex overeats because he's blind, and Lillian is irresponsible because she never had to work for her money. Most behaviors and personality characteristics are the product of a wide variety of factors; it is almost always a mistake to select one factor and attribute everything to it.

CRITICAL PERCEPTION: MAKING PERCEPTIONS MORE ACCURATE

Successful communication depends in part on your accuracy in perception. You can increase this accuracy by (1) employing strategies for reducing uncertainty, and (2) following some suggested guidelines.

Critical Perception Strategies

Communication involves a gradual process of reducing uncertainty about each other. With each interaction you learn more about each other and gradually come to know each other on a more meaningful level. The three main strategies for achieving this reduction in uncertainty are passive, active, and interactive (Berger & Bradac, 1982).

Passive Strategies

When you observe another person without his or her knowledge, you are using **passive strategies.** Usually, you can learn more about someone while observing him or her engaged in an active task, preferably interacting with other people in social (and informal) situations. In such informal situations people are less apt to monitor their behaviors and are more likely to reveal their true selves.

Active Strategies

When you actively seek out information about someone in any way other than direct interaction with the person, you are using **active strategies.** For example, you can ask others about the person: "What is she like?" "Does he work out?" "Does she date guys younger than she is?" You can also manipulate the situation in such a way that you observe the person in more specific and more revealing contexts. Employment interviews, theatrical auditions, and student teaching are some of the ways in which the situation can be manipulated to observe how the person might act and react and hence to reduce uncertainty about the person.

Interactive Strategies

When you interact with the individual, you are using **interactive strategies.** For example, you can ask questions: "Do you enjoy sports?" "What did you think of that computer science course?" "What would you do if you got fired?" You also gain knowledge of another by disclosing information about yourself. Your self-disclosure creates a relaxed environment that encourages subsequent disclosures from the person about whom you wish to learn more.

Here are three theorems paraphrased from the theory of uncertainty reduction, a theory concerned with how communication reduces the uncertainty you have about another person (Berger & Calabrese, 1975): (1) the more people communicate, the more they like each other; (2) the more people communicate, the more intimate their communications will be; and (3) the more nonverbally expressive people are, the more they like each other. How would you go about testing the accuracy of any one of these theorems?

Drawing by Leo Cullum; © 1981
The New Yorker Magazine, Inc.

"Let's take the next one, Stoddard. These people aren't going anywhere."

You probably use these strategies all the time to learn about each other. Unfortunately, many people feel that they know a person well enough after only employing passive strategies. But all three types of strategy are useful; employing all three will strengthen the accuracy of your perceptions.

Critical Perception Guidelines

In addition to perception checking, to thinking critically about the perceptual processes discussed earlier, and to employing all three uncertainty reduction strategies, consider the following suggestions.

Recognize Your Role in Perception
Your emotional and physiological state will influence the meaning you give to your perceptions. The sight of raw clams may be physically upsetting when you have a stomachache but mouthwatering when you are hungry.

Formulate Hypotheses

On the basis of your observations of behaviors, formulate hypotheses to test against additional information and evidence rather than drawing conclusions you then look to confirm. **Delay formulating conclusions** until you have had a chance to process a wide variety of cues, a simple skill that our elevator passengers in the accompanying cartoon have not learned.

Look for a Variety of Cues

The more cues pointing to the same conclusion, the more likely it is that your conclusion will be correct. **Be especially alert to contradictory cues,** cues that refute your initial hypotheses. It is relatively easy to perceive cues that confirm your hypotheses but more difficult to acknowledge contradictory evidence.

Avoid Mind Reading

Regardless of how many behaviors you observe and how carefully you examine them, you can only *guess* what is going on in someone's mind. A person's motives are not open to outside inspection; you can only make assumptions based on overt behaviors. Substitute perception checking ("Did you realize that my birthday was Thursday?") for **mind reading** ("You forgot my birthday because you don't really love me").

How might the processes influencing perception (implicit personality theory, self-fulfilling prophecy, primacy-recency, stereotyping, and attribution) influence your perception of people who are homeless? What guidelines for increasing the accuracy of your perceptions are particularly relevant to this specific situation?

Beware of Your Own Biases

Know when your perceptual evaluations are unduly influenced by your own biases, for example, perceiving only the positive in people you like and only the negative in people you do not like.

Seek Validation

Compare your perceptions with those of others. Do others see things in the same way you do? If not, ask yourself if your perceptions may be in some way distorted.

CULTURAL VIEWPOINT

Being Sensitive to Cultural Differences

Perhaps the most prevalent intercultural barrier occurs when you fail to recognize or respond sensitively to cultural differences, especially those concerning values, attitudes, and beliefs. You can easily see and accept different hairstyles, clothing, and foods; in basic values and beliefs, however, you may assume that down deep we are really all alike. We aren't. When you assume similarities and ignore differences, you implicitly communicate that your ways are the right ways and that the ways of others are not important to you. Take a simple example. An American invites a Filipino co-worker to dinner. The Filipino politely refuses. The American is hurt and feels that the Filipino does not want to be friendly. The Filipino is hurt and concludes that the invitation was not extended sincerely. Here, it seems, both the American and the Filipino assume that their customs for inviting people to dinner are the same when, in fact, they are not. A Filipino expects to be invited several times before accepting a dinner invitation. When an invitation is given only once it is viewed as insincere.

Within every cultural group there are wide and important differences. As all Americans are not alike, neither are all Indonesians, Greeks, Mexicans, and so on. When we ignore these differences we are guilty of stereotyping. A good case in point was seen during the furor over the film *The Last Temptation of Christ*. While Cardinal O'Connor, Archbishop of New York, condemned the film, professor of sociology Father Andrew Greeley praised it and labeled it "a profound religious challenge" (*The New York Times*, August 14, 1988, p. 21). Both are Catholic priests, but each sees the same message quite differently.

Recognizing differences between another culture and your own and recognizing differences among members of a particular culture—and communicating this recognition and understanding—are sure to aid intercultural communication.

[Next Cultural Viewpoint, page 83]

THINKING CRITICALLY ABOUT PERCEPTION

In addition to your perception of another's behaviors (verbal or nonverbal), you can also perceive what you think another person is feeling or thinking (Laing, Phillipson, & Lee, 1966; Littlejohn, 1992). You can, for example, perceive Pat kissing Chris. This is a simple, relatively direct perception of some behavior. But you can also sense (or perceive)—on the basis of the kiss—that Pat loves Chris. Notice the difference: You have observed the kiss but have not observed the love. (Of course, you could continue in this vein and from your conclusion that Pat loves Chris, conclude that Pat no longer loves Terry. That is, you can always formulate a conclusion on the basis of a previous conclusion. The process is unending.)

The important point to see here is that when your perceptions are based on something observable (the kiss), you have a greater chance of being accurate when you describe this kiss or even when you interpret and evaluate it. But as you move further away from your actual observation, your chances of being accurate decrease—when you try to describe or evaluate the love. Generally, when you draw conclusions on the basis of what you think someone is thinking as a result of the behavior, you have a greater chance of making errors than when you stick to conclusions about what you observe yourself.

The ability to accurately read another person's perceptions is a skill not easily mastered. There are so many factors that can get in the way of an accurate interpretation that it is almost always best to engage in **perception checking.** In its most basic form, perception checking consists of two steps.

1. Describe (in tentative terms) what you think is happening. Try to do this as descriptively (not evaluatively) as you can. Some examples:

   You seem depressed. You say you feel fine about the breakup, but you don't seem happy.
   You don't seem to want to go out this evening.
   You seemed disturbed when he said . . .
   You sound upset with my plans.

2. Ask the other person for confirmation. Be careful that your request for confirmation does not sound like you already know the answer.
   Avoid phrasing your questions defensively, for example, "You really don't want to go out, do you? I knew you didn't when you turned on that lousy television." Instead, ask for confirmation in as supportive a way as possible: "Would you rather watch TV?" Some examples:

   Are you really okay about the breakup?
   Do you feel like going out or would you rather stay home?
   Are you disturbed?
   Did my plans upset you?

As these examples illustrate, the goal of perception checking is not to prove that your initial perception is correct but to explore further the thoughts and feelings of the other person. With this simple technique, you lessen your chances for misinterpreting another's feelings. At the same time, you give the other person an opportunity to elaborate on his or her thoughts and feelings.

Feedback on Concepts and Skills

In this chapter we discussed the way we receive messages through perception and explained how perception works, the processes that influence it, and how to make our perceptions more accurate.

1. Perception refers to the process by which we become aware of the many stimuli impinging on our senses.
2. Perception occurs in three stages: sensory stimulation occurs, sensory stimulation is organized, and sensory stimulation is interpreted-evaluated.
3. The following processes influence perception: (1) implicit personality theory, (2) self-fulfilling prophecy, (3) primacy-recency, (4) stereotyping, and (5) attribution.
4. Implicit personality theory refers to the private personality theory that individuals hold and that influence how they perceive other people.
5. The self-fulfilling prophecy occurs when you make a prediction or formulate a belief that comes true because you have made the prediction and acted as if it were true.
6. Primacy-recency refers to the relative influence of stimuli as a result of their order. If what occurs first exerts greater influence, we have a primacy effect. If what occurs last exerts greater influence, we have a recency effect.
7. Stereotyping refers to the tendency to develop and maintain fixed, unchanging perceptions of groups of people and to use these perceptions to evaluate individual members, ignoring their individual, unique characteristics.
8. Attribution refers to the process by which we try to explain the motivation for a person's behavior. Whether or not the person was in control of the behavior will influence how we evaluate the behavior or explain the motivation for a person's behavior.

Throughout this discussion of perception, a variety of skills were identified and are presented here in summary. Check your ability to apply these skills: (1) = almost always, (2) = often, (3) = sometimes, (4) = rarely, (5) = almost never.

_____ 1. Recognizing how primacy-recency works, I actively guard against first impressions that might prevent accurate perceptions of future events; I formulate hypotheses rather than conclusions.
_____ 2. To guard against the self-fulfilling prophecy, I take a second look at my perceptions when they conform too closely to my expectations.
_____ 3. I bring to consciousness my implicit personality theories.
_____ 4. I recognize stereotyping in the messages of others and avoid it in my own communications.
_____ 5. I am aware of and am careful to avoid mind reading, the self-serving bias, and overattribution in trying to account for another person's behavior.
_____ 6. I use perception checking when in doubt or when further information is needed.

Skill Development Experiences

3.1 Understanding the Barriers to Perception

This exercise is designed to reinforce an understanding of the processes of perception. Read the following dialogue and identify the processes of perception that may be at work here.

PAT: All I had to do was to spend two seconds with him to know he's an idiot. I said I went to Graceland and he asked what that was. Can you believe it? Graceland! The more I got to know him, the more I realized how stupid he was. A real loser; I mean, really.

CHRIS: Yeah, I know what you mean. Well, he is a jock, you know.

PAT: Jocks! The worst. And I bet I can guess who he goes out with. I'll bet it's Lucy.

CHRIS: Why do you say that?

PAT: Well, I figure that the two people I dislike would like each other. And I figure you must dislike them too.

CHRIS: For sure.

PAT: By the way, have you ever met Marie? She's a computer science major so you know she's bright. And attractive—really attractive.

CHRIS: Yes, I went out of my way to meet her, because she sounded like she'd be a nice person to know.

PAT: You're right. I knew she'd be nice as soon as I saw her.

CHRIS: We talked at yesterday's meeting. She's really complex, you know. I mean really complex. Really.

PAT: Whenever I think of Marie, I think of the time she helped that homeless man. There was this homeless guy—real dirty—and he fell, running across the street. Well, Marie ran right into the street and picked this guy up and practically carried him to the other side.

CHRIS: And you know what I think of when I think of Lucy? The time she refused to visit her grandmother in the hospital. Remember? She said she had too many other things to do.

PAT: I remember that—a real selfish egomaniac. I mean really.

Identifying these barriers in this dialogue should have been relatively easy. Seeing the barriers to perception operate in ourselves and in others with whom we interact is a lot more difficult. For the next several days, record all personal examples of the four barriers to accurate perception. Record also the specific context in which they occurred.

After you have identified the various barriers, share your findings in groups of five or six or with the entire class. As always, disclose only what you wish to disclose. You may find it worthwhile to discuss some or all of these questions:

1. What barrier seems most frequent?
2. What problems did the barrier cause?
3. What advantages do we gain when we avoid making first impressions? When we avoid using implicit theories? When we avoid making prophecies? When we avoid stereotyping?
4. What disadvantages are there in avoiding these shortcuts to people perception?

3.2 Who?

The purpose of this exercise is to explore some of the cues that people give and that others perceive and use in formulating inferences about the knowledge, abilities, and personality of these others. The exercise should serve as a useful summary of the concepts and principles of perception.

The entire class should form a circle so that each member may see each other member without straining. If members do not know all the names of their classmates, name tags should be used.

Each student should examine the following list of phrases and should write the name of one student to whom he or she feels each statement applies in the column marked "Who." Be certain to respond to all statements. Although one name may be used more than once, the experience will prove more effective if a wide variety of names are chosen. Unless the class is very small, no name should be used more than two times. Write in the names before reading any further.

Who?

_____ 1. Goes to the professional theater or opera a few times a year
_____ 2. Has been to at least three different countries
_____ 3. Watches soap operas on a regular basis
_____ 4. Has recently seen a pornographic (XXX-rated) movie
_____ 5. Is a member of an organized sports team
_____ 6. Watches television for three or more hours a day
_____ 7. Has cried over a movie in the last few months
_____ 8. Fluently speaks a foreign language
_____ 9. Has many close friends
_____ 10. Knows how potatoes should be planted
_____ 11. Knows the difference between a hacksaw and a jigsaw
_____ 12. Knows the ingredients of a bloody Mary
_____ 13. Knows how to make a hollandaise sauce
_____ 14. Can name all 12 signs of the zodiac
_____ 15. Has a car in the immediate family costing more than $35,000
_____ 16. Would aid a friend even at great personal sacrifice
_____ 17. Would like, perhaps secretly, to be a movie star
_____ 18. Writes poetry
_____ 19. Knows where Rwanda is
_____ 20. Knows the political status of Puerto Rico
_____ 21. Keeps a diary or a journal
_____ 22. Knows what _prime rate_ means
_____ 23. Is an extremely logical (critical) thinker
_____ 24. Is very religious

_____ 25. Wants to go to graduate, law, or medical school
_____ 26. Would vote in favor of gay rights legislation
_____ 27. Is going to make a significant contribution to society
_____ 28. Is going to be a millionaire
_____ 29. Is a real romantic
_____ 30. Would emerge as a leader in a small group situation

Thinking Critically About Person Perception

After the names have been written for each statement by each student, the following procedure might prove useful. The instructor selects a statement (there is no need to tackle the statements in the order they are given here), and asks someone specifically, or the class generally, what names were put down. Before the person whose name was put down is asked if the phrase is correctly or incorrectly attributed to him or her, some or all of the following questions may be considered.

- What was there about this person that led you to think that this phrase applied to him or her? What specific verbal or nonverbal cues led you to your conclusion?
- What additional cues would you need to raise your degree of certainty?
- Is your response at all a function of a stereotype you might have of this individual's ethnic, religious, racial, or sexual identification?
- Did anyone give contradictory cues? Explain the nature of these contradictory cues.
- How do you communicate your "self" to others? How do you communicate what you know, think, feel, and do to your peers?

CHAPTER FOUR

Listening

Chapter Concepts	Chapter Goals After completing this chapter, you should be able to	Chapter Skills After completing this chapter, you should be able to
The Listening Process	1. define *listening*	use listening to learn, relate, influence, play, and help as appropriate
	2. explain the five steps in the listening process	listen more effectively during each of the five listening stages
Effective Listening	3. explain the four dimensions of listening and the guidelines for regulating these characteristics	adjust your listening on the basis of the four dimensions of listening: participatory and passive, empathic and objective, nonjudgmental and critical, and surface and depth listening
Active Listening	4. define *active listening* and explain its functions and techniques	use active listening when appropriate
Thinking Critically About Listening	5. explain the guidelines for listening for truth and accuracy	listen critically for truth and accuracy

There can be little doubt that you listen a great deal. Upon awakening you listen to the radio. On the way to school you listen to friends, people around you, screeching cars, singing birds, or falling rain. In school you listen to the instructor, to other students, and of course to yourself. You listen to friends at lunch and return to class to listen to more instructors; you go to work and listen to co-workers, supervisors, or customers; you arrive home and again listen to family and friends. You listen to CDs, radio, or television. All in all, you probably listen for a good part of your waking day.

In this chapter we continue our discussion of the way we receive messages, this time focusing on listening: the importance of listening, how listening works, the ways in which listening may and should vary depending on the situation, and a special type of listening called *active listening*.

If you measured importance by the time you spend on an activity, then listening would be your most important communication activity. According to one study, conducted in 1929 (Rankin), listening occupies 45 percent of a person's communication time; speaking is second with 30 percent; reading (10 percent) and writing (9 percent) follow. According to another study of college students, conducted in 1980 (Barker, Edwards, Gaines, Gladney, & Holley), listening also occupies the most time: 53 percent compared to reading (17 percent), speaking (16 percent), and writing (14 percent).

Another way to appreciate the importance of listening is to look at the benefits you derive from effective listening. Five of these benefits, organized around the five purposes of communication considered in Chapter 1, are summarized in Table 4.1.

They [higher management] believe more and more that listening skills are crucial to job performance and are demanding that managers do something about it. Listening can no longer be sloughed off as just one more item in the vocabulary of communication.

—WARREN REED

THE LISTENING PROCESS

You listen in five stages: receiving, understanding, remembering, evaluating, and responding (Figure 4.1). Note that listening is circular: The responses of Person A serve as the stimuli for Person B, whose responses, in turn, serve as the stimuli for Person A, and so on.

Receiving

Hearing (as opposed to listening) begins and ends with this first stage of receiving. Hearing just happens when you open your ears or get within range of some auditory stimuli. Listening, on the other hand, is quite different. **Listening** begins (but does not end) with receiving messages the speaker sends. Messages are both verbal and nonverbal; they consist of words as well as gestures, facial expressions, variations in volume and rate, and more as we will see when we discuss them in chapters 5 and 6.

TABLE 4.1 THE BENEFITS OF EFFECTIVE LISTENING

Effective Listening Will Result in Increasing Your Ability to	Because You Will	For Example
learn: to acquire knowledge of others, the world, and yourself	profit from the insights of others who have learned or seen what you have not	listening to Peter about his travels to Cuba will help you learn more about Peter and about life in Cuba
to avoid problems and difficulties	hear and be able to respond to warnings of impending problems before they develop or escalate and become impossible to control	listening to student reactions (instead of saying "Students just don't want to work hard") will help the teacher plan more relevant classes
to make more reasoned and reasonable decisions	acquire more information relevant to decisions you'll be called on to make in business or in personal life	listening to the difficulties your sales staff has (instead of saying "You're not trying hard enough") may help you offer more pertinent sales training
relate, to gain social acceptance and popularity	find that people come to like those who are attentive and supportive	others will increase their liking for you once they see your genuine concern for them, communicated through attentive and supportive listening
influence the attitudes and behaviors of others	find that people are more likely to respect and follow those they feel have listened to and understood them	workers are more likely to follow your advice once they feel you have really listened to their insights and concerns
play	know when to suspend critical and evaluative thinking and when to simply engage in passive and accepting listening	listening to the anecdotes of co-workers will allow you to gain a more comfortable balance between the world of work and the world of play
help others	hear more, empathize more, and come to understand others more deeply	listening to your child's complaints about her teacher (instead of saying "Now what did you do wrong?") will increase your ability to help your child cope with school and her teacher

In what other ways might you visualize the listening process?

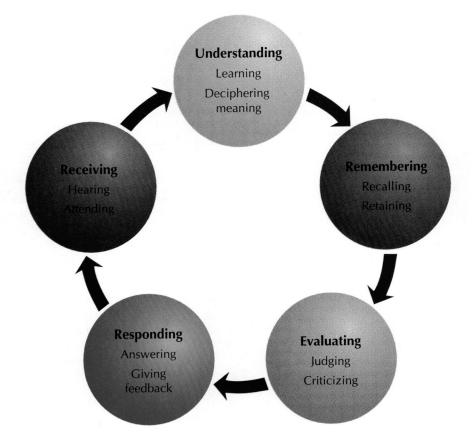

Figure 4.1 A Five-Step Model of the Listening Process
This model draws on a variety of previous models that listening researchers have developed (e.g., Alessandra, 1986; Barker, 1990; Brownell, 1987; Steil, Barker, & Watson, 1983).

At this stage you note not only what is said (verbally and nonverbally) but also what is omitted. You not only receive the politician's summary of accomplishments in education but also the omission of failures in improved health care programs or education, for example.

In this receiving stage, the following suggestions should prove useful:

There is no such thing as a worthless conversation, provided you know what to listen for.
—JAMES NATHAN MILLER

- focus your attention on the speaker's verbal and nonverbal messages, on what is said and what is not said;
- avoid distractions in the environment;
- focus your attention on the speaker's messages, not on what you will say next;
- maintain your role as listener; avoid interrupting the speaker until he or she is finished;
- confront mixed messages (messages that communicate different and contradictory meanings)—something the *Born Loser* cartoon characters might profit from.

BORN LOSER reprinted by permission of NEA, Inc.

Understanding

Understanding occurs when you learn what the speaker means. Understanding includes both the thoughts that are expressed as well as the emotional tone that accompanies them, for example, the urgency or the joy or sorrow expressed in the message.

In achieving understanding:

- relate the speaker's new information to what you already know (e.g., In what way will this new proposal change our present health care?);
- see the speaker's messages from the speaker's point of view; avoid judging the message until it is fully understood as the speaker intended it;
- ask questions for clarification, if necessary; ask for additional details or examples if needed; and
- rephrase (paraphrase) the speaker's ideas.

Remembering

Messages that you receive and understand need to be retained at least for some period of time. In some small group and public speaking situations you can augment your memory by taking notes or by taping the messages. In most interpersonal communication situations, however, such note taking would be considered inappropriate, although you often do write down a phone number, an appointment, or directions.

What you remember is not what was actually said, but what you think (or remember) was said. Memory for speech is not reproductive; it is reconstructive. You don't simply reproduce in your memory what the speaker said; rather, you reconstruct the messages you hear into a system that makes sense to you—a concept noted in the discussion of perception

Have you ever stopped someone in midsentence to say, "I know just what you are going to say." Well, guess what? you don't know.
—MARY LYNNE HELDMANN

From listening comes wisdom, and from speaking repentance.
—ITALIAN PROVERB

In what ways are listening in public speaking and listening interpersonally the same? In what ways are they different? Does the five-stage model adequately describe both types of listening? If not, how might you revise the model to better describe all kinds of listening?

in Chapter 3. To illustrate this important concept, try to memorize the list of 12 words presented below (Glucksberg & Danks, 1975). Don't worry about the order; only the number remembered counts. Take about 20 seconds to memorize as many words as possible. Don't read any further until you have tried to memorize the list.

Word List

bed	awake
dream	night
comfort	slumber
rest	tired
wake	eat
sound	snore

Now close the book and write down as many words from the list as you can remember. Don't read any further until you have tested your own memory. If you are like my students, you not only remembered most of the words, but also added at least one word: *sleep*. Most people recall *sleep* being on the list, but, as you can see, it wasn't. What happened was that you didn't just reproduce the list; you reconstructed it. In this case you gave the list meaning by including the word *sleep*. This happens with all types of messages; they are reconstructed into a meaningful whole and in the process a distorted version is often remembered.

To ensure more accurate remembering:

Have you ever "remembered" what was not said in an interpersonal, group, or public communication situation?

- identify the central ideas and the major support advanced;
- summarize the message in an easier to retain form, but do not ignore crucial details or qualifications;
- repeat names and key concepts to yourself or, if appropriate, aloud; and

- if this is a formal talk with a recognizable organizational structure, identify this pattern and use it (see it in your mind) to organize what the speaker is saying.

Evaluating

Evaluating consists of judging the messages. At times you may try to evaluate the speaker's underlying intent, often without much conscious awareness. For example, Elaine tells you she is up for a promotion and is really excited about it. You may then try to judge her intention. Does she want you to use your influence with the company president? Is she preoccupied with the possible promotion, thus telling everyone? Is she looking for a pat on the back? Generally, if you know the person well, you will be able to identify the intention and respond appropriately.

In other situations, the evaluation is more in the nature of a critical analysis. For example, you would evaluate proposals in a business meeting while listening to them. Are they practical? Will they increase productivity? What is the evidence? Are there more practical alternative proposals?

At this stage of listening try to:

- resist evaluation until you fully understand the speaker's point of view;
- assume that the speaker is a person of goodwill and give the speaker the benefit of any doubt by asking for clarification on issues you object to (e.g., Are there any other reasons for accepting this new proposal?);
- distinguish facts from inferences (see Chapter 5), opinions, and personal interpretations by the speaker; and
- identify any biases, self-interests, or prejudices that may lead the speaker to unfairly slant information presented.

ETHICAL ISSUE

Introducing Censorship and Secrets

This dialogue is a continuation of the one in Chapter 2 and identifies two more ethical issues: censoring interactions and revealing secrets. What do you feel would be ethical or unethical in each case?

Frank: father
Laura: mother
Barbara: daughter
Jeff: son
Alex: son

FRANK: Listen, Alex. I hear you've been hanging out with the Franklin brothers. I want that stopped. I don't want you hanging around with—hell, I don't want you even *seeing*—the Franklins. Even from a distance. They're bad news.

LAURA: He's right, Alex. Stay away from them from now on.

FRANK: Don't act like a know-it-all. You listen to your mother.

LAURA: You hear us, Alex? Do you?

FRANK: We mean it, Alex. We want you to stay far away from those guys.

Are these parents justified in trying to censor interactions between their son and others they consider undesirable? Would you have to have additional information about the Franklins to make your decision? How would you answer if:

- the Franklin brothers were drug dealers and were trying to persuade Alex to run drugs for them?
- the Franklin brothers had AIDS?
- the Franklin brothers were of a different race or religion?
- Alex was mentally retarded or 11 years old or on parole?

[Exit Alex; Enter Jeff]

JEFF: Listen, everyone. Kim told me something today that I want to tell you. I promised her I wouldn't tell anyone but I just have to tell you.

LAURA: Well, maybe you shouldn't. I mean, if you promised Kim maybe you shouldn't tell us.

JEFF: No, no, I really want to—I have to.

FRANK: Your mother's right. If you promised to keep a secret, then keep it. You'll be the better person for it.

JEFF: Well, if you all promise to keep it a secret, it'll be OK.

Would it be wrong for Jeff to reveal the secret? Would your answer depend on the kind of secret? If so, what would you have to know about the secret to answer this question? What would you answer if:

- Kim broke up with her boyfriend yesterday for the third time this month (and they are both 14 years old)?
- Kim, 17 years old, plans to commit suicide?
- Kim is heavily into drugs?
- Kim was 4 and Jeff was 5? Kim was 4 and Jeff was 32? Kim and Jeff were both 19?
- if the family members kept the secret confidential?

[Next Ethical Issue, page 108]

Responding

The opposite of talking isn't listening. The opposite of talking is waiting.

—Fran Lebowitz

Responding occurs in two phases: (1) responses you make while the speaker is talking and (2) responses you make after the speaker has stopped talking. Responses made while the speaker is talking should be supportive and should acknowledge that you are listening. These include what nonverbal researchers call backchanneling cues, such as "I see," "yes," "uh-huh," that let the speaker know you are paying attention.

Responses after the speaker has stopped talking are generally more elaborate and might include empathy ("I know how you must feel"); asking for clarification ("Do you mean this new health plan will replace the old one or will it be just a supplement?"); challenging ("I think your evidence is weak"); and agreeing ("You're absolutely right and I'll support your proposal when it comes up for a vote").

In responding:

- be supportive of the speaker throughout the talk by using varied backchanneling cues; using only one (for example, saying "uh-huh" throughout) will make it appear that you are not listening but are merely on automatic pilot;
- express support for the speaker in your final responses; and
- own your own responses; state your thoughts and feelings as your own, using "I" messages. (Say "I think the new proposal will entail greater expense than you outlined" rather than "Everyone will object to the plan's cost.")

EFFECTIVE LISTENING

Before reading about the principles of effective listening, examine your own listening habits and tendencies by taking the accompanying self-test.

TEST YOURSELF
How Good a Listener Are You?

Respond to each question with the following scale:

1 = always
2 = frequently
3 = sometimes
4 = seldom
5 = never

_____ 1. I listen by participating; I interject comments throughout the conversation.
_____ 2. I listen to what the speaker is saying and feeling; I try to feel what the speaker feels.
_____ 3. I listen without judging the speaker.
_____ 4. I listen to the literal meanings that a speaker communicates; I don't look too deeply into hidden meanings.
_____ 5. I listen passively; I generally remain silent and take in what the other person is saying.
_____ 6. I listen objectively; I focus on the logic of the ideas rather than on the emotional meaning of the message.
_____ 7. I listen critically, evaluating the speaker and what the speaker is saying.
_____ 8. I look for the hidden meanings; the meanings that are revealed by subtle verbal or nonverbal cues.

POWER PERSPECTIVE

Power Through Listening

While many books and articles have been devoted to achieving power through speaking, few have asked about achieving power through listening. And yet, a glance at the benefits of listening (Table 4.1) offers convincing proof that listening effectively is a means to your own empowerment. The learning that results gives you obvious power (especially expert, page 288, and information or persuasion power, page 349) and increases the perception of competence, one of the essential components of credibility (Chapter 15). Listening effectiveness in relating and in helping (and perhaps even in playing) make you more likable and contribute greatly to the character and charisma you are seen to possess. The most obvious dimension relating to power is that with effectiveness in listening comes greater ability to influence the attitudes and behaviors of others.

[Next Power Perspective, page 97]

Thinking Critically About Listening These statements focus on the ways of listening discussed in this chapter. All ways are appropriate at times and all ways are inappropriate at times—it depends. So the only responses that are really inappropriate are "always" and "never." Effective listening is listening that is appropriate to the specific communication situation. Review these statements and try to identify situations in which each statement would be appropriate and situations in which each statement would be inappropriate.

Participatory and Passive Listening

The key to effective listening in most situations is to participate. Perhaps the best preparation for participatory listening is to *act* like one who is participating (physically and mentally) in the communication exchange. For many people, this may be the most abused rule of effective listening. Recall, for example, how your body almost automatically reacts to important news: Almost immediately you assume an upright posture, cock your head to the speaker, and remain relatively still and quiet. You do this almost reflexively because this is how you listen most effectively. Even more important than this physical alertness is mental alertness. As a listener, participate in the communication interaction as an equal partner with the speaker, as one who is emotionally and intellectually ready to engage in the sharing of meaning.

Effective participatory listening is expressive. Let the listener know that you are participating in the communication interaction. Nonverbally, maintain eye contact, focus your concentration on the speaker rather than on others present, and express your feelings facially. Verbally, ask appropriate questions, signal understanding with "I see" or "yes," and express agreement or disagreement as appropriate.

A special type of participatory listening is active listening (Gordon, 1975). **Active listening** involves facilitating the speaker to express what he or she wants to express. It's a way of listening that helps the speaker to further explore thoughts and feelings and to feel safe in expressing these.

Passive listening, however, is not without merit, and some recognition of its values is warranted. **Passive listening** —listening without talking or directing the speaker in any nonverbal way—is a powerful means of communicating acceptance. Passive listening allows the speaker to develop his or her thoughts and ideas in the presence of another person who accepts but does not evaluate, who supports but does not intrude. By listening passively, you provide a supportive and receptive environment. Once that has been established, you may wish to participate in a more active way, verbally and nonverbally.

How would you describe your last few communication experiences in terms of participatory and passive listening?

Another form of passive listening is just to sit back, relax, and let the auditory stimulation wash over you without exerting any significant energy and especially without your directing the stimuli in any way, as in listening to music for pure enjoyment rather than to make critical evaluations.

In regulating participatory and passive listening, keep the following guidelines in mind:

- Avoid preoccupation with yourself or with external issues. Avoid focusing on your own performance in the interaction or on rehearsing your responses. Also avoid focusing on matters that are irrelevant to the interaction—what you did Saturday night or your plans for this evening.

NANCY reprinted by permission of UFS, Inc.

- Because you can process information faster than the average rate of speech, there is often a time lag. Use this time to summarize the speaker's thoughts, formulate questions, and draw connections between what the speaker says and what you already know. Avoid daydreaming, the natural tendency to let your mind wander to perhaps more pleasant thoughts.
- Be careful that you listen to what the speaker is really saying and instead hear what you expect to hear. You know that Lin frequently complains about grades, so when Lin tells you about problems with an instructor, you automatically "hear" Lin complaining (again) about grades.

Is it not also arrogant to assume that we can fully understand what the other person intends without giving full attention to that person?
—CARLEY H. DODD

CULTURAL VIEWPOINT

Men and Women as Listeners

Deborah Tannen opens her chapter on listening in her best-selling *You Just Don't Understand: Women and Men in Conversation* with several anecdotes illustrating that when men and women talk, men lecture and women listen (also see Tanner, 1994a, b). The lecturer is positioned as the superior, as the teacher, the expert. The listener is positioned as the inferior, as the student, the nonexpert.

Women, according to Tannen, seek to build rapport and establish a closer relationship and so use listening to achieve these ends. For example, women use more listening cues that let the other person know they are paying attention and are interested. Men not only use fewer listening cues but interrupt more and will often change the topic to one they know more about, is less relational or people oriented, or is more factual—for example, sports statistics, economic developments, or political problems. Men, research shows, play up their expertise, emphasize it, and use it in dominating the conversation. Women play down their expertise.

Now you might be tempted to conclude from this that women play fair in conversation and that men don't; for example, men consistently seek to put themselves in a position superior to women. But, that may be too simple an explanation. Research shows, however, that men communicate this way not only with women but with other men as well. Men are not showing disrespect for their female conversational partners but are simply communicating as they normally do. Women too communicate as they do not only with men but also with other women.

Tannen argues that the goal of a man in conversation is to be accorded respect and so he seeks to display his knowledge and expertise even if he has to change the topic to one he knows a great deal about. A woman, on the other hand, seeks to be liked and so she expresses agreement, rarely interrupts a man to take her turn as speaker, and gives lots of cues (verbally and nonverbally) to indicate that she is listening.

Men and women also show that they are listening in different ways. A woman is more apt to give lots of listening cues such as interjecting "yeah," "uh-uh," nodding in agreement, and smiling. A man is more likely to listen quietly, without giving lots of listening cues as feedback. Tannen also argues, however, that men do listen less to women than women listen to men. The reason, says Tannen, is that listening places the person in an inferior position, whereas speaking places the person in a superior position.

There is no evidence to show that these differences represent any negative motives on the part of men to prove themselves superior or of women to ingratiate themselves. Rather, these differences in listening, according to Tannen, are largely the result of the way in which men and women have been socialized.

[Next Cultural Viewpoint, page 99]

Empathic and Objective Listening

If you want to understand what a person means and what a person is feeling, you need to listen with **empathy.** When you empathize with others you feel with them, you see the world as they see it, you feel what they feel. Only when you achieve this can you understand another's meaning fully.

There is no easy method of achieving empathy. But it is something you should work toward. It is important, for example, that a student see the teacher's point of view. And it is equally important for the teacher to see the student's point of view. Popular students might intellectually understand why an unpopular student feels depressed, but that will not enable them to understand emotionally the feelings of depression. To accomplish that, they must put themselves in the position of the unpopular student, role play a bit, and begin to feel that student's feelings and think his or her thoughts. Then the popular students will be in a better position to understand and genuinely empathize. (See Chapter 7 for specific suggestions for developing and communicating empathy.)

Although empathic listening is preferred for most communication situations, there are times when you need to go beyond empathy and measure the meanings and feelings against some objective reality. It is important to listen to a friend tell you how the entire world hates him or her and to understand how your friend feels and why. But then you need

to look a bit more objectively at your friend and at the world and perhaps see the paranoia or self-hatred at work. Sometimes you have to put your empathic responses aside and listen with objectivity and detachment.

In adjusting your empathic and objective listening focus, keep the following recommendations in mind:

- Seek to understand both thoughts and feelings. Do not consider your listening task finished until you have understood what the speaker is feeling as well as thinking.
- Avoid "offensive listening," the tendency to listen to bits and pieces of information that will enable you to attack the speaker or find fault with something the speaker has said.
- Beware of the "friend or foe" factor that may lead you to distort messages because of your attitudes toward another person. For example, if you think Freddy is stupid, then it will take added effort to listen objectively to Freddy's messages and to hear anything that is clear or insightful.

Nonjudgmental and Critical Listening

Effective listening is both nonjudgmental and critical. It involves listening with an open mind with a view toward understanding. But it also involves listening critically with a view toward making some kind of evaluation or judgment. Clearly, listening for understanding (nonjudgmentally) should come first. Only after you have fully understood the message should you evaluate or judge. Listening with an open mind is often difficult. It is not easy, for example, to listen to arguments against some cherished belief or to criticisms of something you value highly. Listening often stops when a hostile or critical remark is made. Admittedly, to continue listening with an open mind is difficult, yet it is in precisely these situations that it is especially important to listen fairly.

Supplement open-minded listening with critical listening. Listening with an open mind will help you understand the messages; listening with a critical mind will help you analyze and evaluate the messages. This is especially true in the college environment. It is easy simply to listen to an instructor and take down what is said. Yet it is important that you also evaluate and critically analyze what is said. Instructors have biases too; at times consciously and at times unconsciously, these biases creep into scholarly discussions. Identify and bring these to the surface. The vast

Do you find yourself falling into the friend-or-foe fallacy, where you listen with positive expectations to a friend and negative expectations to an enemy? How might this tendency get you into trouble?

A good memory and a tongue tied in the middle is a combination which gives immortality to conversation.
—MARK TWAIN

majority of teachers will appreciate critical responses. These responses demonstrate that someone is listening and will help to stimulate further examination of ideas.

In adjusting your nonjudgmental and critical listening, focus on the following guidelines:

- Keep an open mind. Avoid prejudging. Delay evaluation until you have fully understood the intent and the content of the message being communicated.
- Avoid filtering out difficult messages. Avoid distorting messages through oversimplification or leveling—the tendency to eliminate details and to simplify complex messages so that they are easier to remember. Also avoid filtering out unpleasant or undesirable messages; you may miss the very information you need to change your assumptions or your behaviors.
- Recognize your own biases; we all have them. These may interfere with accurate listening and cause you to distort message reception through the process of **assimilation**—the tendency to interpret what you hear or think you hear according to your own biases, prejudices, and expectations. For example, are your ethnic, national, or religious biases preventing you from appreciating the speaker's point of view? Biases may also lead to **sharpening**—the tendency for a particular item of information to take on increased importance because it seems to confirm the listener's stereotypes or prejudices.
- Use critical listening when evaluations and judgments are called for. Use nonjudgmental listening when you want to express support.

Can you recall a specific example of assimilation where you were the speaker or the listener?

Surface and Depth Listening

In Shakespeare's *Julius Caesar,* Marc Antony, delivering Caesar's funeral oration, says: "I come to bury Caesar, not to praise him. . . . The evil that men do lives after them. . . . The good is oft interred with their bones." And later: "For Brutus is an honourable man. . . . So are they all, all honourable men." But Antony, as we know, did come to praise Caesar and to convince the crowd that Brutus was not an honorable man. He came to incite the crowd to avenge the death of Caesar, his friend.

In most messages there is an obvious meaning that a literal reading of the words and sentences reveals. But there is often another level of meaning. Sometimes, as in *Julius Caesar,* it is the opposite of the expressed literal meaning; sometimes it seems totally unrelated. In reality, few messages have only one level of meaning. Most function on two or three levels at the same time. Consider the parent who seems on the surface to be complaining about working too hard may, on a deeper level, be asking for some expression of appreciation. The child who talks about the unfairness of the other children in the playground may be asking for affection and love, for some expression of caring, for some indication that you understand. To appreciate these other meanings you need to engage in depth listening.

Become sensitive to different levels of meaning. If you respond only to the surface-level communication (the literal meaning), we will miss the opportunity to make meaningful contact with the other person's feelings

There is only one cardinal rule: one must always listen to the patient.

—OLIVER SACKS

and real needs. If you say to your parent, "You're always complaining. I bet you really love working so hard," you may be failing to answer this very real call for understanding and appreciation.

In regulating your surface and depth listening, consider the following guidelines:

- Focus on both verbal and nonverbal messages. Recognize both consistent and inconsistent "packages" of messages and take these cues as guides for inferring the meaning the speaker is trying to communicate. Ask questions when in doubt. Listen also to what is omitted. Remember that we communicate by what we leave out as well as by what we include.
- Listen for both content and relational messages (Chapter 1). The student who constantly challenges the teacher is on one level communicating disagreement over content; the student is debating the issues. However, on another level—the relationship level—the student may well be voicing objections to the instructor's authority or authoritarianism. If the instructor is to deal effectively with the student, he or she must listen and respond to both types of messages.
- Do not disregard the literal (surface) meaning of interpersonal messages in your attempt to uncover the more hidden (deep) meanings. If you do, you will quickly find that your listening problems disappear—because no one will talk to you anymore. Balance your attention between the surface and the underlying meanings. Respond to the various levels of meaning in the messages of others as you would like others to respond to yours—sensitively but not obsessively, readily but not overambitiously.

ACTIVE LISTENING

Active listening owes its development to Thomas Gordon (1975) who made it a cornerstone of his P-E-T (Parent-Effectiveness-Training) technique. Consider the following exchange:

Speaker:	I have to do this entire budget report over again. I really worked on that project and now I have to do it over again.
Listener 1:	That's not too bad; most people have to do their first reports over again. That's the norm of the office.
Listener 2:	So what? You don't intend to stay at this job. Anyway, you're getting paid by the hour, what do you care what you do?
Listener 3:	You should be pleased with a simple rewrite. Peggy and Michael both had to redo their entire projects.
Listener 4:	You have to rewrite that report you were working on for the last three weeks? You sound really angry and hurt.

All four listeners are probably anxious to make the speaker feel better. But they go about it in very different ways and, we can be sure, with very different results. Listeners 1 and 2 try to lessen the significance of the

In what situations would you consider active listening inappropriate and ineffective?

rewrite. This response is extremely common and may be well intended but it does little to promote meaningful communication and understanding. Listener 3 tries to give the rewrite a positive spin. By their responses, however, these listeners are also saying that the speaker should not be feeling as he or she does. They are also saying the speaker's feelings are not legitimate and should be replaced with more logical feelings.

Listener 4, however, is different. Listener 4 uses active listening, a process of sending back to the speaker what you as a listener think the speaker meant—both in content and in feelings. Active listening is not merely repeating the speaker's exact words, but rather putting together into some meaningful whole your understanding of the speaker's total message.

The Functions of Active Listening

Active listening serves several important functions. First, it helps you as a listener check your understanding of what the speaker said and, more important, what he or she meant. Reflecting back perceived meanings to the speaker gives the speaker an opportunity to offer clarification. In this way, future messages will have a better chance of being relevant.

Second, through active listening you express acceptance of the speaker's feelings. Note that in the sample responses given, the first three listeners challenged the speaker's feelings. The active listener (listener 4), who reflected back to the speaker what he or she thought was said, gave the speaker acceptance. Rather than challenging the speaker's feelings, listener 4 echoed them in a caring manner. In addition to accepting the speaker's feelings, listener 4 also identified them explicitly ("You sound angry and hurt"), again allowing an opportunity for correction.

Third, active listening stimulates the speaker to explore feelings and thoughts. The response of listener 4 encourages the speaker to elaborate on his or her feelings. This further exploration also encourages the speaker to solve his or her own problems by providing the opportunity to talk them through.

The Techniques of Active Listening

Three simple techniques may prove useful in learning the process of active listening.

Paraphrase the Speaker's Thoughts

State in your own words what you think the speaker meant. This helps ensure understanding and also shows the speaker you are interested. The paraphrase also gives the speaker a chance to elaborate on or extend what was originally said. Thus, when listener 4 echoes the speaker's thought, the speaker may next elaborate on why rewriting the budget report meant so much. Perhaps the speaker fears that his or her other reports will be challenged or that this now means the hoped-for promotion will not be forthcoming. Finally, in your paraphrase, be especially careful not to lead the speaker in the direction you think he or she should go. Paraphrases should be objective descriptions.

Express Understanding of the Speaker's Feelings

In addition to paraphrasing the content, echo the feelings the speaker expressed or implied ("I can imagine how you must have felt. You must have felt horrible."). Just as the paraphrase helps you check your perception of the content, the expression of feelings will help you check your perception of the speaker's feelings. This will also allow the speaker to see his or her feelings more objectively. This is especially helpful when the speaker feels angry, hurt, or depressed.

You've no doubt used those techniques on many occasions. What effects did they have?

When you echo the speaker's feelings, you also stimulate the speaker to elaborate. Most of us hold back our feelings until we are certain they (and we) will be accepted. When we feel acceptance, we then feel free to go into more detail. Active listening gives the speaker this important opportunity. In echoing feelings, be careful not to over- or understate the speaker's feelings. Try to echo these feelings as accurately as you can.

Ask Questions

Asking questions ensures your own understanding of the speaker's thoughts and feelings and secures additional information ("How did you feel when you read your job appraisal report?"). The questions should provide just enough stimulation and support for the speaker to express his or her thoughts and feelings. These questions will further confirm your interest and concern for the speaker. Be careful not to pry into unrelated areas or challenge the speaker in any way.

THINKING CRITICALLY ABOUT LISTENING

It takes two to speak the truth—one to speak, and another to listen.
—HENRY DAVID THOREAU

Earlier we noted the importance of regulating your listening between nonjudgmental and critical listening. In addition, however, listening critically depends also on assessing the truth and accuracy of the information and the honesty and motivation of the speaker (also see Chapter 15). Thus, in addition to keeping an open mind and delaying judgments, it is necessary to focus on other issues as well. Here are a few examples:

- Is what the speaker says the truth as far as you understand it? For example, is this car really that great? Are there any disadvantages to this particular car?
- Has the speaker presented the information in enough detail? Have crucial parts been left out? For example, has the speaker identified all the costs?
- Is the speaker being honest? Is the speaker's motivation merely self-gain? For example, might this speaker be distorting the facts merely to make a sale and earn a commission?
- Does the speaker use fallacious reasoning such as stating that X causes Y when the evidence merely confirms that X and Y occur together? Are conclusions about "all" or "most people" based on a sample that is both large and representative of the population?
- Does the speaker rely too heavily on emotional appeals? Are these appeals legitimate?
- Has the speaker the credibility you want and expect? For example, is the speaker competent and knowledgeable about the topic?

Feedback on Concepts and Skills

In this chapter we discussed the way we listen and how listening may be made more effective.

1. Listening serves a variety of purposes; we listen to learn, to relate to others, to influence the attitudes, beliefs, and behaviors of others, to play, and to help.
2. Listening is a five-step process consisting of receiving, understanding, remembering, evaluating, and responding.
3. Receiving is essentially the hearing process; the messages from another person are received at this stage.
4. Understanding is the stage of comprehension; you make sense out of the messages.
5. The remembering stage refers to the fact that messages and your understanding of them are retained in your memory for at least some time.
6. In evaluating you judge the messages and apply your critical thinking skills to them.
7. The final stage, responding, includes both the responses you make while the speaker is speaking and the responses you may make after the speaker has stopped talking.
8. Effective listening involves a process of making adjustments—depending on the situation—along such dimensions as participatory and passive listening, empathic and objective listening, nonjudgmental and critical listening, and surface and depth listening.

9. Active listening is a special type of listening that enables you to check your understanding of what the speaker means, express your acceptance of the speaker's feelings, and stimulate the speaker to further explore his or her thoughts and feelings.

10. The techniques of active listening include paraphrasing, expressing understanding of the speaker's feelings, and asking questions.

Throughout this discussion of listening, a variety of skills were identified and are presented here in summary. Check your ability to apply these skills: (1) = almost always, (2) = often, (3) = sometimes, (4) = rarely, (5) = almost never.

_____ 1. I recognize that listening serves a variety of purposes and I adjust my listening on the basis of my purposes, for example, to learn, relate, influence, play, and help.

_____ 2. I realize that listening is a multistage process and I regulate my listening behavior as appropriate in receiving, understanding, remembering, evaluating, and responding.

_____ 3. In receiving messages, I seek to increase my chances of effective listening by, for example, focusing attention on the speaker's verbal and nonverbal messages, avoiding distractions, and focusing attention on what the speaker is saying and not on what I'm going to say next.

_____ 4. I facilitate understanding in listening by relating new information to what I already know and trying to see the messages from the speaker's point of view.

_____ 5. In remembering the speaker's messages I try to identify the central ideas and the major supporting materials, summarize the main ideas, and repeat important concepts to etch them more firmly in my mind.

_____ 6. In evaluating messages I first make sure I understand what the speaker means from his or her point of view and seek to identify any sources of bias or self-interest.

_____ 7. In responding I am supportive of the speaker and I own my own thoughts and feelings.

_____ 8. I am especially careful to adjust my listening on the basis of the immediate situation between participatory and passive, empathic and objective, nonjudgmental and critical, and surface and depth listening.

_____ 9. I practice active listening when appropriate by paraphrasing the speaker's meaning, by expressing my understanding of the speaker's feelings, and by asking questions.

_____ 10. I listen for truth and accuracy.

Skill Development Experiences

4.1 Paraphrasing to Ensure Understanding

For each of the messages presented below, write an acceptable paraphrase. After you complete the paraphrases, ask another person if he or she would accept them as objective restatements of thoughts and feelings.

Rework the paraphrases until the other person agrees that they are accurate. A sample paraphrase is provided in number 1.

1. I can't deal with my parents' constant fighting. I've seen it for the last ten years and I really can't stand it anymore.

   Paraphrase: You have trouble dealing with their fighting. You seem really upset by this last fight.

2. Did you hear I got engaged to Jerry? I'm the happiest person in the world.

3. I got a C on that paper. That's the worst grade I've ever received. I just can't believe that I got a C. This is my major. What am I going to do?

4. I really had a scare with the kids the other night. They went out to the night game at the high school. They didn't walk in till two A.M. I thought I'd die.

5. That rotten, inconsiderate pig just up and left. He never even said good-bye. We were together for six months and after one small argument he leaves without a word. And he even took my bathrobe—that expensive one he bought for my last birthday.

6. I'm just not sure what to do. I really love Chris. She's the sweetest kid I've ever known. I mean, she'd do anything for me. But she really wants to get married. I do too and yet I don't want to make such a commitment. I mean that's a long-term thing. And, much as I hate to admit it, I don't want the responsibility of a wife, a family, a house. I really don't need that kind of pressure.

4.2 Experiencing Active Listening

For each of the situations described below, supply at least one appropriate active listening response.

1. Your friend Phil has just broken up a love affair and is telling you about it. "I can't seem to get Chris out of my mind," he says. "All I do is daydream about what we used to do and all the fun we used to have."

2. You and your friend are discussing the recent chemistry examination. Your friend says: "I didn't get an A. I got a B+. What am I going to do now? I feel like a failure."

3. A young nephew tells you that he cannot talk with his parents. No matter how hard he tries, they just don't listen. "I tried to tell them that I can't play baseball and I don't want to play baseball," he confides. "But they ignore me and tell me that all I need is practice."

4. A friend just won $20,000 on a quiz show but is depressed because she lost the championship and the chance to compete for the grand prize of $150,000. She says: "I knew the answer, but I just couldn't think fast enough. That money could have solved all my problems."

5. Your mother has been having a difficult time at work. She was recently passed up for a promotion and received one of the lowest merit raises given in the company. "I'm not sure what I did wrong," she

tells you. "I do my work, mind my own business, don't take my sick days like everyone else. How could they give that promotion to Helen who's only been with the company for two years? Maybe I should just quit."

6. Your friend, looking real depressed, meets you on the street and says: "I can't believe it, I just got a phone call from the clinic. I'm HIV positive and I don't know what to do."

CHAPTER FIVE

Verbal Messages

Chapter Concepts	Chapter Goals After completing this chapter, you should be able to	Chapter Skills After completing this chapter, you should be able to
Language and Meaning	1. identify the characteristics of meaning and their implications for human communication	communicate with a recognition of denotation and connotation look for meanings in people look for meanings in the context
Barriers in Thinking and Communicating	2. define the barriers to thinking and communicating and ways to avoid them	identify the barriers in the thinking and communicating of others and avoid them in your own thinking and communicating
Disconfirmation	3. explain disconfirmation and distinguish it from confirmation and rejection	regulate your confirmations as appropriate
	4. explain the nature of racism, sexism, and heterosexism and how these may be viewed as forms of disconfirmation	avoid racist, sexist, and heterosexist language and, in general, language that puts down other groups
Thinking Critically About Verbal Messages	5. explain the suggestions for thinking critically about verbal messages	identify conceptual distortions in your own and in the language of others and avoid them in your own messages

I n communication you use two major signal systems—the verbal and the nonverbal. This chapter focuses on the verbal system: language as a system for communicating meaning; the verbal barriers that prevent clear thinking and clear communication; and disconfirmation, a particularly insightful way of looking at racist, sexist, and heterosexist speech.

LANGUAGE AND MEANING

Of all the functions of language, the communication of meaning from one person to another is surely the most significant. The following principles identify the characteristics of meaning and should help to erase some common misconceptions.

Meanings: Denotative and Connotative

Two general types of meaning are essential to identify: denotation and connotation. **Denotation** refers to the meaning you would find in a dictionary; it is the meaning that members of the culture assign to a word. **Connotation** refers to the emotional meaning that specific speakers-listeners give to a word. Take as an example the word *death*. To a doctor this word might mean (or *denote*) the time when the heart stops. This is an ob-

Why is it relatively easy for two people to agree on a word's denotative meaning and so difficult for the same two people to agree on its connotative meaning? For example, consider securing agreement on the connotative meaning of *religion, democracy, wealth,* and *freedom.*

P. Steiner

"When I use a word," Humpty Dumpty said in rather a scornful tone, "it means just what I choose it to mean; neither more nor less."
—LEWIS CARROLL,
THROUGH THE LOOKING-GLASS

How would a dictionary entry for the connotative meaning of a word look? Can you construct a connotative dictionary entry for a word such as *gold* or *school* or *professor*? What factors or characteristics does your connotative meaning entry include?

jective description of a particular event. On the other hand, to the dead person's mother (upon being informed of her son's death), the word means (or *connotes*) much more. It recalls her son's youth, ambition, family, illness, and so on. To her it is a highly emotional, subjective, and personal word. These emotional, subjective, or personal reactions are the word's connotative meaning. The denotation of a word is its objective definition. The connotation of a word is its subjective or emotional meaning.

Semanticist S. I. Hayakawa (Hayakawa & Hayakawa, 1990) coined the terms *snarl words* and *purr words* to further clarify the distinction between denotation and connotation. **Snarl words** are highly negative ("She's an idiot"; "He's a pig"; "They're a bunch of losers"). **Purr words** are highly positive ("She's a real sweetheart"; "He's a dream"; "They're the greatest").

Snarl and purr words, although they may sometimes seem to have denotative meaning and to refer to the "real world," are actually connotative in meaning. These terms do not describe people or events in the real world but rather the speaker's feelings about these people or events.

Meanings Are in People

If you wanted to know the meaning of the word *love,* you would probably turn to a dictionary. There you would find, according to Webster's: "The attraction, desire, or affection felt for a person who arouses delight or admiration or elicits tenderness, sympathetic interest, or benevolence." This is the denotative meaning.

But where would you turn if you wanted to know what Pedro means when he says "I'm in love"? Of course, you'd turn to Pedro to discover his meaning. It is in this sense that meanings are not in words but in people. Consequently, to uncover meaning, you need to look into people and not merely into words.

An example of the confusion that can result when this relatively simple fact is not taken into consideration is provided by Ronald D. Laing, H. Phillipson, and A. Russell Lee (1966) and analyzed with insight by Paul Watzlawick (1977). A couple on the second night of their honeymoon are sitting at a hotel bar. The woman strikes up a conversation with the couple next to her. The husband refuses to communicate with the couple and becomes antagonistic toward his wife and the couple. The wife then grows angry because he has created such an awkward and unpleasant situation. Each becomes increasingly disturbed, and the evening ends in a bitter conflict with each convinced of the other's lack of consideration. Eight years later, they analyze this argument. Apparently *honeymoon* had meant different things to each. To the husband it was a "golden opportunity to ignore the rest of the world and simply explore each other." He felt his wife's interaction with the other couple implied there was something lacking in him. To the wife *honeymoon* meant an opportunity to try out her new role as wife. "I had never had a conversation with another couple as a wife before," she said. "Previous to this I had always been a 'girlfriend' or 'fiancée' or 'daughter' or 'sister.'"

Also recognize that as you change, you also change the meanings you created out of past messages. Thus, although the message sent may not have changed, the meanings you created from it yesterday and the meanings you create today may be quite different. Yesterday, when a special someone said, "I love you," you created certain meanings. But today,

POWER PERSPECTIVE

Powerful Speech

One of the ways you communicate power is by using powerful language. Here are some suggestions for communicating power, based largely on research in the United States (Johnson, 1987; Kleinke, 1986; Molloy, 1981; Ng & Bradac, 1993).

1. Avoid hesitations; they make you sound unprepared and uncertain.
2. Avoid uncertainty expressions; these communicate a lack of commitment, direction, and conviction.
3. Avoid overpoliteness; such forms signal your subordinate status.
4. Avoid disqualifiers (*I didn't read the entire article, but . . .*); they may call into question the validity of your statements.
5. Avoid tag questions (questions that ask for agreement: *That was great, wasn't it?*); these may signal your own uncertainty.
6. Avoid slang and vulgar expressions; these usually signal low social class and little power.

[Next Power Perspective, page 125]

"What good does it do to send signals to someone who just scrambles them?"

Drawing by Wm. Hamilton; © 1990 The New Yorker Magazine, Inc.

Consider the implication of this principle for intercultural communication. Consider, for example, the differences in meaning for such words as *woman* to an American and an Iranian, *religion* to a born-again Christian and an atheist, and *lunch* to a Chinese rice farmer and a Wall Street executive. What communication principles might help you communicate effectively your meaning in these situations?

when you learn that the same "I love you" was said to three other people or when you fall in love with someone else, you drastically change the meanings you perceive from those three words.

Meanings Are Context Based

Verbal and nonverbal communications exist in a **context,** and that context to a large extent determines the meaning of any verbal or nonverbal behavior. The same words or behaviors may have totally different meanings when they occur in different contexts. For example, the greeting, "How are you?" means "Hello" to someone you pass regularly on the street but means "Is your health improving?" when said to a friend in the hospital. A wink to an attractive person on a bus means something completely different from a wink that signifies a put-on or a lie. Similarly, the meaning of a given signal depends on the other behavior it accompanies or is close to in time. Pounding a fist on the table during a speech in support of a politician means something quite different from that same gesture in response to news of a friend's death. Divorced from the context, it is impossible to tell what meaning was intended from just examining the signals. Of course, even if we know the context in detail, we still might not be able to decipher the meaning of the verbal or nonverbal message.

Especially important is the cultural context, a context emphasized throughout this text. The cultural context will influence not only the meaning assigned to speech and gesture but whether your meaning is friendly, offensive, lacking in respect, condescending, sensitive, and so on.

Can you identify conversational maxims taught by your own culture? What happens when you violate such maxims?

Cultural Maxims

Each culture has its own style of communication, its own principles governing communication. For example, in much of the United States we operate with the maxim that communication be truthful; that is, we expect that what the other person says will be the truth and you no doubt follow that maxim by telling the truth yourself. Similarly, we operate with the maxim that what we talk about will be relevant to the conversation. Thus, if you are talking about A, B, and C and someone brings up D, you would assume that there is a connection between A, B, and C on the one hand and D on the other. It is interesting to examine the maxims that are unlike those that are followed throughout most of the United States. Here are just three.

The Maxim of Peaceful Relations In research on Japanese conversations and group discussions a maxim of keeping peaceful relationships with others may be noted (Midooka, 1990). The ways in which such peaceful relationships may be maintained will vary with the person with whom you are interacting. For example, in Japan, your status or position in the hierarchy will influence the amount of self-expression you are expected to engage in. Similarly, there is a great distinction made between public and private conversations. In public, this maxim is much more important than it is in private conversations where they may be violated.

The Maxim of Politeness In some cultures, especially Asian, it is especially important to "save face," to avoid being embarrassed or embarrassing others. When this maxim operates, it may actually violate other maxims. For example, the maxim of politeness may require that you not tell the truth, a situation that would violate the maxim of quality (Fraser, 1990).

The Maxim of Self-Denigration This maxim, observed in the conversations of Chinese speakers, may require that a speaker avoid taking credit for some accomplishment or make less of some ability or talent (Gu, 1990). To put oneself down here is a form of politeness that seeks to elevate the person to whom you are speaking.

[Next Cultural Viewpoint, page 111]

Never give advice in a crowd.
—ARAB PROVERB

BARRIERS IN THINKING AND COMMUNICATING

There is a close connection between thinking and communicating—a theme we have emphasized throughout this book. Consequently, the barriers we identify here relate to both problems in thinking and in communication. The connection is simple: Distortions in thought lead to distortions in language; distortions in language (because we think in and with our language) further distort our thinking.

It is not only true that the language we use puts words in our mouths; it also puts notions in our heads.
—WENDELL JOHNSON

Here is a photo of an Alanon meeting. In keeping with the group's anonymity policy, no faces are revealed. From what you know of Alanon and similar groups, what maxims do they follow that might not be followed in, say, communication in class or at work?

Let's look at six possible barriers to thinking and communicating (Haney, 1973; DeVito, 1974; Rothwell, 1982). These barriers may appear in interpersonal, small group, and public speaking.

Polarization

*Con was a thorn to brother Pro—
On Pro we often sicked him:
Whatever Pro would claim to know
Old Con would contradict him!*
—CHRISTOPHER MORLEY

Polarization is the tendency to look at the world in terms of opposites and to describe it in extremes—good or bad, positive or negative, healthy or sick, intelligent or stupid. It is often referred to as the fallacy of "either-or" or "black and white." Most people exist somewhere between the extremes. Yet we have a strong tendency to view only the extremes and to categorize people, objects, and events in terms of these polar opposites.

We create problems when we use the absolute form in inappropriate situations. For example, "The politician is either for us or against us." These options do not include all possibilities. The politician may be for us in some things and against us in other things, or may be neutral. During the Vietnam War, people were categorized as either hawks or doves. But clearly many people were neither and many were hawks on certain issues and doves on others.

Correcting Polarization

In correcting this tendency to polarize, beware of implying (and believing) that two extreme classes include all possible classes—that an individual must be one or the other, with no alternatives. Most people, most events, most qualities exist between polar extremes. When others imply that there are only two sides or alternatives, look for the middle ground.

Intensional Orientation

Have you ever reacted to the way something was labeled or described rather than to the actual item? Have you ever bought something because of its name rather than because of the actual object? If so, you were probably responding intensionally.

Intensional orientation (the *s* in *intensional* is intentional) refers to the tendency to view people, objects, and events in the way they are talked about—the way they are labeled. For example, if Sally is labeled "uninteresting" you would, responding intensionally, evaluate her as uninteresting before listening to what she had to say. The tendency would be to see Sally through a filter imposed by the label "uninteresting." **Extensional orientation,** on the other hand, is the tendency to look first at the actual people, objects, and events and only afterwards at their labels. In this case, it would mean looking at Sally without any preconceived labels, guided by what she says and does, not by the words used to label her.

Correcting Intensional Orientation

The way to avoid intensional orientation is to extensionalize. Give your main attention to the people, things, and events in the world as you see them and not as they are presented in words. For example, when you meet Jack and Jill, observe and interact with them. Then form your impressions. Don't respond to them as "greedy, money-grubbing landlords" because Harry labeled them this way. Don't respond to Carmen as "lazy and inconsiderate" because Elaine told you she was.

Fact-Inference Confusion

Often, when you listen or speak, you don't distinguish between statements of fact and those of inference. Yet, there are great differences between the two. Barriers to clear thinking can be created with inferences are treated as facts.

For example, you can say, "She is wearing a blue jacket," as well as "He is harboring an illogical hatred." Although the sentences have similar structures, they are different. You can observe the jacket and the blue color, but how do you observe "illogical hatred"? Obviously, this is not a descriptive but an inferential statement. It is one you make on the basis not only of what you observe, but on what you infer. For a statement to be considered factual it must be made by the observer after observation and must be limited to what is observed (Weinberg, 1959).

Reprinted by permission: Tribune Media Services.

There is nothing wrong with making inferential statements. You must make them to talk about much that is meaningful to you. The problem arises when you act as if those inferential statements are factual. Consider the following anecdote (Maynard, 1963): A woman went for a walk one day and met a friend whom she had not seen, heard from, or heard of in ten years. After an exchange of greetings, the woman said: "Is this your little boy?" and her friend replied, "Yes, I got married about six years ago." The woman then asked the child, "What is your name?" and the little boy replied, "Same as my father's." "Oh," said the woman, "then it must be Peter."

How did the woman know the boy's father's name when she had no contact with her friend in the last ten years? The answer is obvious, but only after we recognize that in reading this short passage we have made an unconscious inference. Specifically, we have inferred that the woman's friend is a woman. Actually, the friend is a man named Peter.

You may test your ability to distinguish facts from inferences by taking the accompanying fact-inference test (based on the tests constructed by Haney, 1973).

TEST YOURSELF
Can You Distinguish Facts from Inferences?

Instructions: Carefully read the following report and the observations based on it. Indicate whether you think the observations are true, false, or doubtful on the basis of the information presented in the report. Write T if the observation is definitely true, F if the observation is definitely false, and ? if the observation may be either true or false. Judge each observation in order. Do not reread the observations after you have indicated your judgment, and do not change any of your answers.

A well-liked college teacher had just completed making up the final examinations and had turned off the lights in the office. Just then a tall, broad figure with dark glasses appeared and demanded the examination. The professor opened the drawer. Everything in the drawer was picked up and the individual ran down the corridor. The dean was notified immediately.

_____ 1. The thief was tall, broad, and wore dark glasses.

_____ 2. The professor turned off the lights.

_____ 3. A tall figure demanded the examination.

_____ 4. The examination was picked up by someone.

_____ 5. The examination was picked up by the professor.

_____ 6. A tall, broad figure appeared after the professor turned off the lights in the office.

_____ 7. The man who opened the drawer was the professor.

_____ 8. The professor ran down the corridor.

_____ 9. The drawer was never actually opened.

_____ 10. Three persons are referred to in this report.

Thinking Critically About Facts and Inferences After you answer all ten questions, form small groups of five or six and discuss the answers. Look at each statement from each member's point of view. For each statement, ask yourself, "How can I be absolutely certain that the statement is true or false?" You should find that only one statement can be clearly identified as True and only one as False; eight should be marked "?"

Correcting Fact-Inference Confusion

Any inferential statements should be made tentatively. Recognize that they may prove to be wrong. Inferential statements should leave open the possibility of alternatives. If, for example, you treat the statement "Our biology teacher was fired for poor teaching" as factual, you eliminate any alternatives. When making inferential statements, be psychologically prepared to be proved wrong. If you are prepared to be wrong, you will be less hurt if you are shown to be wrong.

Be especially sensitive to this distinction when you are listening. Most talk is inferential. Beware of the speaker (whether in interpersonal, group, or public speaking) who presents everything as fact. Analyze closely and you'll uncover a world of inferences.

Static Evaluation

People change and forget to tell each other.
—LILLIAN HELLMAN

Static evaluation is the tendency to retain evaluations without change despite the fact that the reality to which they refer is constantly changing. Often a verbal statement we make about an event or person remains static, but the event or person may change enormously. Alfred Korzybski (1933) used an interesting illustration. In a tank we have a large fish and many small fish, the natural food for the large fish. Given freedom in the tank, the large fish will eat the small fish. If we partition the tank, separating the large fish from the small fish by a clear piece of glass, the large fish will continue to attempt to eat the small fish but will fail, knocking instead into the glass partition.

Eventually, the large fish will "learn" the futility of attempting to eat the small fish. If we now remove the partition, the small fish will swim all around the big fish, but the big fish will not eat them. In fact, the large fish will die of starvation while its natural food swims all around. The large fish has learned a pattern of behavior, and even though the actual territory has changed, the map remains static.

While we would probably all agree that everything is in a constant state of flux, do we act as if we know this? Do we act in accordance with the notion of change or just accept it intellectually? Do we realize, for example, that because we have failed at something once, we need not fail again? Our evaluations of ourselves and of others must keep pace with the rapidly changing real world; otherwise our attitudes and beliefs will be about a world that no longer exists.

Correcting Static Evaluation

The basic fact of today is the tremendous pace of change in human life.
—JAWAHARLAL NEHRU

To guard against static evaluation, date your statements and especially your evaluations. Remember that Pat Smith$_{1984}$ is not Pat Smith$_{1995}$; academic abilities$_{1992}$ are not academic abilities$_{1995}$. T. S. Eliot, in "The Cocktail Party," said, "What we know of other people is only our memory of the moments during which we knew them. And they have changed since then . . . at every meeting we are meeting a stranger." In listening, look carefully at messages that claim that what was true still is. It may or may not be. Look for change.

Allness

We can never know all or say all about anything. The parable of the six blind men and the elephant is an excellent example of an **allness** orientation and its problems. You may recall the John Saxe poem that tells of six blind men of Indostan who examine an elephant, an animal they had only heard about. The first blind man touched the elephant's side and concluded the elephant was like a wall. The second felt the tusk and said the elephant must be like a spear. The third held the trunk and concluded the elephant was like a snake. The fourth touched the knee and knew the elephant was like a tree. The fifth felt the ear and said the elephant was like a fan. And the sixth grabbed the tail and said that the elephant was like a rope.

Each reached his own conclusion; each argued that he was correct and that the others were wrong. Each was correct, and at the same time, wrong. We are all in the position of the six blind men. We never see all of anything. We never experience anything fully. We see a part, then conclude what the whole is like. We have to draw conclusions on the basis of insufficient evidence (we always have insufficient evidence). We must recognize that when we make judgments based only on a part, we are making inferences that can later prove wrong.

Correcting Allness

A useful device to help remember the nonallness orientation is to end each statement, verbally or mentally, with "etc."—a reminder that there is more to learn, more to know, and more to say, that every statement is inevitably incomplete. Do be careful, however, that you do not use the etc. as a substitute for being specific.

Indiscrimination

Indiscrimination refers to the failure to distinguish between similar but different people, objects, or events. It occurs when we focus on classes and fail to see that each is unique and needs to be looked at individually. Everything is unique. Everything is unlike everything else.

Our language, however, provides us with common nouns such as *teacher, student, friend, enemy, war, politician, liberal.* These lead us to focus on similarities—to group together all teachers, all students, and all politicians. At the same time, the terms divert attention away from the uniqueness of each person, each object, and each event.

This misevaluation is at the heart of stereotyping on the basis of nationality, race, religion, sex, and affectional orientation. A stereotype, you'll remember from Chapter 3, is a fixed mental picture of a group that is applied to each individual in the group without regard to his or her unique qualities.

Most stereotypes are negative and denigrate the group to which they refer. Some, however, are positive. A particularly clear example is the popular stereotype of Asian American students. The stereotype is that these students are successful, intelligent, and hardworking.

How many examples of the barriers to language and verbal interaction (polarization, intensional orientation, fact-inference confusion, allness, static evaluation, and indiscrimination) can you find in one evening of television?

Whether the stereotypes are positive or negative, they create the same problem. They provide us with shortcuts that are often inappropriate. For instance, when you meet a particular person, your first reaction may be to pigeonhole him or her into some category—perhaps religious, national, or academic. Then you assign to this person all the qualities that are part of your stereotype. Regardless of the category you use or the specific qualities you are ready to assign, you fail to give sufficient attention to the individual's unique characteristics. Two people may both be Christian, Asian, and lesbian, for example, but each will be different from the other. Indiscrimination is a denial of another's uniqueness.

Correcting Indiscrimination

A useful antidote to indiscrimination is the **index.** This verbal or mental subscript identifies each individual as an individual even though both may be covered by the same label. Thus, politician$_1$ is not politician$_2$, teacher$_1$ is not teacher$_2$. The index helps us to discriminate among without discriminating against.

DISCONFIRMATION

Before reading about disconfirmation, take the self-test to examine your own behavior.

TEST YOURSELF
How Confirming Are You?

Instructions: In your typical communications, how likely are you to display the following behaviors? Use the following scale in responding to each statement:

    5 = always
    4 = often
    3 = sometimes
    2 = rarely
    1 = never

_____ 1. I acknowledge the presence of another person both verbally and nonverbally.

_____ 2. I acknowledge the contributions of the other person by, for example, supporting or taking issue with what the person says.

_____ 3. During the conversation, I make nonverbal contact by maintaining direct eye contact, touching, hugging, kissing, and otherwise demonstrating acknowledgment of the other person.

_____ 4. I communicate as both speaker and listener, with involvement, and with a concern and respect for the other person.

_____ 5. I signal my understanding of the other person both verbally and nonverbally.

_____ 6. I reflect back the other person's feelings as a way of showing that I understand these feelings.

_____ 7. I ask questions as appropriate concerning the other person's thoughts and feelings.

_____ 8. I respond to the other person's requests, by, for example, returning phone calls and answering letters within a reasonable time.

_____ 9. I encourage the other person to express his or her thought and feelings.

_____ 10. I respond directly and exclusively to what the other person says.

Thinking Critically About Confirmation and Disconfirmation All ten statements are phrased so that they express confirming behaviors. Therefore, high scores (say, above 35) reflect a strong tendency to engage in confirmation. Low scores (say, below 25) reflect a strong tendency to engage in disconfirmation. Don't assume, however, that all situations call for confirmation and that only insensitive people are disconfirming. You may wish to consider the situations in which disconfirmation would be, if not an effective response, at least a legitimate one.

A useful way to introduce disconfirmation and its alternatives confirmation and rejection is to consider a specific situation: Pat arrives home late one night. Chris is angry and complains about Pat's coming home so late. Consider some responses Pat might make:

1. Stop screaming. I'm not interested in what you're babbling about. I'll do what I want, when I want. I'm going to bed.
2. What are you so angry about? Didn't you get in three hours late last Thursday, when you went to that office party? So knock it off.
3. You have a right to be angry. I should have called when I was going to be late, but I got involved in an argument at work and I couldn't leave until it was resolved.

In (1) Pat dismisses Chris's anger and even indicates a dismissal of Chris as a person. In (2) Pat rejects the validity of Chris's reasons for being angry but does not dismiss Chris's feelings of anger or Chris as a person. In (3) Pat acknowledges Chris's anger and the reasons for being angry. In addition Pat provides some kind of explanation and in doing so shows that Chris's feelings and Chris as a person are important and deserve to know what happened. The first response is an example of disconfirmation, the second of rejection, and the third of confirmation.

The psychologist William James once observed that "No more fiendish punishment could be devised, even were such a thing physically possible, than that one should be turned loose in society and remain absolutely unnoticed by all the members thereof." In this often-quoted observation James identifies the essence of disconfirmation (Watzlawick, Beavin, & Jackson, 1967; Veenendall & Feinstein, 1990).

Disconfirmation is a communication pattern in which we ignore someone's presence as well as that person's communications. We say, in effect, that this person and what this person has to say are not worth serious attention or effort—that this person and this person's contributions are so unimportant or insignificant that there is no reason to concern ourselves with them.

Note that disconfirmation is not the same as _rejection._ **Rejection** is disagreeing with the person; you indicate your unwillingness to accept something the other person says or does. In disconfirming someone, however, you deny that person's significance; you claim that what this person says or does simply does not count.

Confirmation is the opposite communication pattern. We not only acknowledge the presence of the other person but we also indicate our acceptance of this person, of this person's definition of self, and of our relationship as defined or viewed by this other person.

Disconfirmation and confirmation may be communicated in a wide variety of ways. Table 5.1 shows just a few and parallels the self-test presented earlier so that you can see clearly not only the confirming but also the opposite, disconfirming behaviors. As you review this table, try to imagine a specific illustration for each of the ways of communicating disconfirmation and confirmation (Galvin & Brommel, 1991; Pearson, 1993).

TABLE 5.1 CONFIRMATION AND DISCONFIRMATION

Confirmation	Disconfirmation
1. Acknowledge the presence of the other verbally or nonverbally	1. Ignore the presence of the other person
2. Acknowledge the contributions of the other by either supporting or taking issue with what the other says	2. Ignore what the other says; express (nonverbally and verbally) indifference to anything the other says
3. Make nonverbal contact by maintaining direct eye contact, touching, hugging, kissing, and otherwise demonstrating acknowledgment of the other	3. Make no nonverbal contact; avoid direct eye contact; avoid touching other person
4. Engage in dialogue—communication in which both persons are speakers and listeners, both are involved, and both are concerned with and have respect for each other	4. Engage in monologue—communication in which one person speaks and one person listens, there is no real interaction, and there is no real concern or respect for each other
5. Demonstrate understanding of what the other says and means	5. Jump to interpretation or evaluation rather than working at understanding what the other means
6. Reflect back the other's feelings to demonstrate your understanding of these feelings	6. Express your own feelings, ignore feelings of the other, or give abstract intellectualized responses
7. Ask questions of the other concerning both thoughts and feelings	7. Make statements about yourself; ignore any lack of clarity in the other's remarks
8. Acknowledge the other's requests; answer the other's questions, return phone calls, and answer letters	8. Ignore the other's requests; fail to answer questions, return phone calls, and answer letters
9. Encourage the other to express thoughts and feelings	9. Interrupt or otherwise make it difficult for the other to express himself or herself
10. Respond directly and exclusively to what the other says	10. Respond tangentially by acknowledging the other's comment but then shifting the focus of the message in another direction

We can gain insight into a wide variety of offensive language practices by viewing them as types of disconfirmation, as language that alienates and separates. The three obvious practices are racism, sexism, and heterosexism.

Gossiping

According to the *Random House Dictionary*, gossip is "idle talk or rumor, especially about the personal or private affairs of others." Gossip is an inevitable part of our daily interactions; at times it is harmless, even flattering. At other times, however, it may not be so harmless and may in fact be unethical. When is gossip unethical? Why is it immoral to say certain things? Ethical philosopher Sissela Bok (1983) identifies three kinds of gossip that she considers unethical. First, it is unethical to reveal information that you have promised to keep secret. In situations where that is impossible (Bok offers the example of a teenager who confides a suicide plan), the information should be revealed only to those required to know it and not to the world at large.

Second, gossip is unethical when you know it to be false and pass it on nevertheless. When you try to deceive your listeners by spreading gossip you know to be false, your communications are unethical.

Third, gossip is unethical when it invades the privacy to which everyone has a right. Invasive gossip is especially unethical when the gossip can hurt the individual involved.

These conditions are not easy to identify in any given instance, but they do provide us with excellent starting points for asking ourselves whether or not a discussion of another person is ethical. How would you respond to each of these situations?

- Is it ethical to reveal seemingly private information if you were not explicitly told to keep it secret?
- Under what conditions would revealing another person's secrets be ethical? Are there times when the failure to reveal such secrets would be unethical?
- You are in a conversation and observe the following: Ricky and Lyn are discussing Terry. Ricky makes a number of statements about Terry that you know to be false. Is it ethical for you to say nothing? Does it matter whether these statements about Terry are positive or negative?
- Is it ethical to observe someone (without his or her knowledge) and report your observations to others? For example, would it be ethical to observe your communication professor on a date with a student or smoking marijuana and then report these observations back to your communication classmates?
- What ethical guidelines would you propose for revealing secrets?

[Next Ethical Issue, page 127]

There is only one thing in the world worse than being talked about, and that is not being talked about.

—Oscar Wilde

Gossip is the opiate of the oppressed.

—Erica Jong

Research shows (Walker & Blaine, 1991) that negative gossip is passed on more than is positive gossip. Negative gossip seems to arouse a higher level of anxiety and thus encourages greater communication than does positive gossip. Do you find this to be true?

What forms of disconfirmation do you encounter most often in college? At work? What effects do such disconfirming messages have?

Racism

According to Andrea Rich (1974), "any language that, through a conscious or unconscious attempt by the user, places a particular racial or ethnic group in an inferior position is racist." **Racist language** expresses racist attitudes. It also, however, contributes to the development of racist attitudes in those who use or hear the language.

Racist terms are used by members of one culture to disparage members of other cultures—their customs or their accomplishments. Racist language emphasizes differences rather than similarities and separates rather than unites members of different cultures. Generally, racist language is used by the dominant group to establish and maintain power over other groups. The social consequences of racist language in terms of employment, education, housing opportunities, and general community acceptance are well known.

It has often been pointed out (Bosmajian, 1974; Davis, 1973) that there are aspects of language that may be inherently racist. For example, in one examination of English there were found 134 synonyms for *white*. Of these, 44 have positive connotations (for example, "clean," "chaste," and "unblemished") and only 10 have negative connotations (for example, "whitewash" and "pale"). The remaining were relatively neutral. Of the 120 synonyms for *black* 60 had unfavorable connotations ("unclean," "foreboding," and "deadly") and none had positive connotations.

Andrea Rich (1974) observes: "The language of racism is not merely reflective of racist thought and attitude in the culture; its use also produces racist thought in those exposed to it and helps to shape certain forms of racist behavior." Do you agree with this? Do you think this also holds when members of a particular culture refer to themselves with racist terms?

Consider such phrases as the following:

- the Korean doctor
- the Chicano prodigy
- the African-American mathematician
- the white nurse

In some cases, of course, the racial identifier may be relevant as in, say, "The Korean doctor argued for hours with the French [doctors] while the Mexicans tried to secure a compromise." Here the aim might be to identify the nationality of the doctor or the specific doctor (as you would if you forgot her or his name).

One of the interesting things about cultural identifiers is that some people want to know them and others don't seem to care what is a person's race or religion or sexual orientation, for example. In most cases, the degree to which a person wants a cultural identifier will vary with the topic. Consider, for example, how you feel about each of the following sentences. Would you want to know the cultural identifiers? Would you find it helpful to know? Would such identifiers influence the way you thought about or evaluated what a speaker says? Which cultural identifiers concerning the speaker would you consider relevant for each of these theses? Which cultural identifiers would you consider irrelevant? Note that each of the items can be read positively or negatively; respond to both.

1. the affectional orientation of someone who argues that gays and lesbians should (not) be allowed the same adoption rights as heterosexuals
2. the religion of someone arguing that religious schools should (not) be publicly supported
3. the sex of a person arguing that men need to learn to communicate with women/the sex of a person arguing that women need to learn to communicate with men
4. the race of someone arguing that the school should (not) be named in honor of Malcolm X
5. the religion or affectional orientation of someone arguing that the city must (not) recognize domestic partnerships as equal under the law to marriage
6. the religion, sex, or age of someone arguing that condoms must (not) be made available to elementary and junior high school students without any restrictions based on parental objections
7. the race or nationality of someone arguing that affirmative action programs must be retained (abolished)
8. the sex, age, or affectional orientation of someone arguing that sexual harassment is (not) a real problem in the workplace
9. the religion or sexual orientation of someone arguing that AIDS education must stress abstinence, not safe sex/the religion or sexual orientation of someone arguing that AIDS education must stress safe sex, not abstinence
10. the race or sex of someone arguing that interracial marriages and interracial adoptions should be encouraged (discouraged)

Words can destroy. What we call each other ultimately becomes what we think of each other, and it matters.

—JEANNE J. KIRKPATRICK

Gender Differences in Language

The best way to start thinking about gender differences in language is to think about your own beliefs. The following self-test will help.

TEST YOURSELF
Gender Differences

Instructions: Here are ten statements about the "differences" between the speech of women and men. For each of the following statements, indicate whether you think the statement describes women's speech (W), men's speech (M), or women's and men's speech equally (=).

_____ 1. This speech is logical rather than emotional.

_____ 2. This speech is vague.

_____ 3. This speech is endless, not concise, and jumps from one idea to another.

_____ 4. This speech is highly businesslike.

_____ 5. This speech is polite.

_____ 6. This speech uses weak forms (for example, the weak intensifiers like *so* and *such*) and few exclamations.

_____ 7. This speech contains tag questions (for example, questions appended to statements that ask for agreement, such as "Let's meet at ten o'clock, *okay?*").

_____ 8. This speech is euphemistic (contains polite words as substitutes for some taboo or potentially offensive terms) and uses few swear terms.

_____ 9. This speech is generally effective.

_____ 10. This speech is not forceful and not in control.

Thinking Critically About Gender Differences After responding to all ten statements, consider the following: (1) On what evidence did you base your answers? (2) How strongly do you believe that your answers are correct? (3) What do you think might account for sex differences in verbal behavior? That is, how did the language differences that might distinguish the sexes, come into existence? (4) What effect might these language differences (individually or as a group) have on communication (and relationships generally) between the sexes? *Do not read any further* until you have responded to the above statements and questions.

The ten statements were drawn from the research of Cheris Kramarae (1974a, 1974b, 1977, 1981; also see Coates & Cameron, 1989), who argues that these "differences"—with the exception of statements 5 and 8 (women's speech is often more "polite")—are actually stereotypes of women's and men's speech that are not in fact confirmed in analyses of actual speech. According to Kramarae, then, you should have answered "women's and men's speech equally" for statements 1, 2, 3, 4, 6, 7, 9, and 10 and "women's speech" for statements 5 and 8. Perhaps we see these "differences" in cartoons or on television, and this teaches us that they actually characterize real speech.

Reexamine your answers to the above ten statements. Were your answers based on your actual experience with the speech of women and men or might they have been based on popular beliefs about women's and men's speech?

[Next Cultural Viewpoint, page 132]

Sexism

The National Council of Teachers of English has proposed guidelines for nonsexist (gender-free, gender-neutral, or sex-fair) language. These concern the use of generic *man,* the use of generic *he* and *his,* and sex role stereotyping (Penfield, 1987).

Generic Man

The word *man* refers most clearly to an adult male. To use the term to refer to both men and women emphasizes maleness at the expense of femaleness. Similarly the terms *mankind* or *the common man* or even *caveman* imply a primary focus on adult males. Gender-neutral terms can easily be substituted. Instead of *mankind,* you can say *humanity, people,* or *human beings.* Instead of *the common man,* you can say *the average person* or *ordinary people.* Instead of *cavemen,* you can say *prehistoric people* or *cave dwellers.*

Similarly, the use of such terms as *policeman* or *fireman* and other terms that presume maleness as the norm and femaleness as a deviation from this norm are clear and common examples of sexist language. Consider using nonsexist alternatives for these and similar terms; make these alternatives (for example, *police officer* and *firefighter*) a part of your active vocabulary. What alternatives can you offer for each of such terms as these: *man, countryman, manmade, manpower, repairman, doorman, stewardess, waitress, salesman, mailman,* and *actress?*

Generic He and His

The use of the masculine pronoun to refer to any individual regardless of sex is certainly declining. But it was only as far back as 1975 that all college textbooks, for example, used the masculine pronoun as generic. There seems to be no legitimate reason why the feminine pronoun could not alternate with the masculine pronoun in referring to hypothetical individuals, or why such terms as *he and she* or *her and him* could not be used instead of just *he* or *him.* Alternatively, we can restructure our sentences to eliminate any reference to gender. Here are a few examples from the NCTE Guidelines (Penfield, 1987):

Sexist	Gender-Free
The average student is worried about his grades.	The average student is worried about grades.
Ask the student to hand in his work as soon as he is finished.	Ask students to hand in their work as soon as they are finished.

We hold these truths to be self-evident, that all men and women are created equal.
—ELIZABETH CADY STANTON

Some quotations in this text use *man* and *he* generically. How would you reword them in today's language? Look through one of your textbooks. Can you find examples of sexist language? Sexist photos? Can you find examples of sexist language in your own speech?

Julia Stanley, for example, researched terms indicating sexual promiscuity and found 220 terms referring to a sexually promiscuous woman but only 22 terms for a sexually promiscuous man (Thorne, Kramarae, & Henley, 1983). Assuming the widely held assumption that the importance of a concept to a culture is reflected in the number of terms for the concept that the language has, how would you explain this difference in terms for promiscuity?

Sex Role Stereotyping

The words we use often reflect a sex role bias, the assumption that certain roles or professions belong to men and others belong to women. In eliminating sex role stereotyping, avoid, for example, making the hypothetical elementary schoolteacher female and the college professor male. Avoid referring to doctors as male and nurses as female. Avoid noting the sex of a professional with terms such as "female doctor" or "male nurse." When you are referring to a specific doctor or nurse, the person's sex will become clear when you use the appropriate pronoun: *Dr. Smith wrote the prescription for her new patient* or *The nurse recorded the patient's temperature himself.* Here are a few additional examples. How would you rephrase these?

1. You really should get a second doctor's opinion. Just see what he says.
2. Johnny went to school today and met his kindergarten teacher. I wonder who she is?
3. Everyone needs to examine his own conscience.
4. The effective communicator is a selective self-discloser; he discloses to some people about some things some of the time.
5. The effective waitress knows when her customers need her.
6. The history of man is largely one of technology replacing his manual labor.

I don't see the big deal about sexual behavior. Why do we need this excuse to hate? It should be a nonissue.

—CYBILL SHEPHERD

Heterosexism

A close relative of sexism is heterosexism. The term is a relatively new addition to our list of linguistic prejudices. As the term implies, **heterosexist language** refers to language used to disparage gay men and lesbians. As with racist language, we see heterosexism in the derogatory terms used for lesbians and gay men as well as in more subtle forms of language usage. For example, if you qualify a profession—as in "gay athlete" or "lesbian doctor"—the effect is to state that athletes and doctors are not normally gay or lesbian. Further, you would be highlighting the affectional orientation of the athlete and the doctor in a context where it may have no relevance. This practice, of course, is the same as qualifying by race or gender already noted.

Still another instance of heterosexism—and perhaps the most difficult to deal with—is the presumption of heterosexuality. Usually, people assume the person they are talking to or about is heterosexual. Usually they are correct because the majority of the population is heterosexual. At the same time, however, note that it denies the lesbian and gay identity a certain legitimacy. The practice is very similar to the presumption of whiteness and maleness that we have made significant inroads in eliminating. Here are a few additional suggestions for avoiding heterosexist or what some call homophobic language.

- Avoid offensive nonverbal mannerisms that parody stereotypes when talking about gays and lesbians.

It is interesting to note that the terms denoting some of the major movements in art, for example, *impressionism* and *cubism,* were originally applied negatively. The terms were taken on by the artists and eventually became positive. A parallel can be seen in the use of the word *queer* by some of the more militant lesbian and gay organizations. Their purpose in using the term is to make it lose its negative connotation. Do you think this is a generally effective technique? Would it work with racist, sexist, and heterosexist terms equally?

- Avoid "complimenting" gay men and lesbians because "they don't look it." To gays and lesbians, it's not a compliment. Similarly, expressing disappointment that a person is gay—often thought to be a compliment when said in such comments as "What a waste!"—is not really a compliment.
- Avoid the assumption that every gay or lesbian knows what every other gay or lesbian is thinking. It's very similar to asking a Japanese why Sony is investing heavily in the United States or, as one comic put it, asking an African-American "What do you think Jesse Jackson meant by that last speech?"
- Avoid denying individual differences. Saying things like "lesbians are so loyal" or "gay men are so open with their feelings," which ignore the reality of wide differences within any group, are potentially insulting to all groups.
- Avoid **overattribution,** the tendency to attribute just about everything a person does, says, and believes to being gay or lesbian. This tendency helps to recall and perpetuate stereotypes.
- Remember that relationship milestones are important to all people. Ignoring anniversaries or birthdays of, say, a relative's partner is resented by everyone.

THINKING CRITICALLY ABOUT VERBAL MESSAGES

The first need of a free people is to be able to define their own terms and have those terms recognized by their oppressors.
—STOKLEY CARMICHAEL

In thinking critically about verbal messages and the various principles (as well as the principles covered in any section of this text), think about them flexibly and recognize that there are exceptions to each rule. Consider where the principles seem useful and where they need to be adjusted to the unique situation. Recognize especially that the principles discussed here are largely the result of research conducted in the United States. Ask yourself if they apply in other cultures.

Also, be ready to analyze and evaluate ideas instead of just accepting them just because they appear in a textbook or because they are mentioned by a teacher. Ask yourself: Is this principle true generally? For what situations is it especially true? Is it worthwhile? Does it effectively explain communication? Does it offer any practical implications?

Critically decode and encode verbal messages. The verbal messages you send or are about to send as well as those you receive need to be evaluated and critically analyzed. One of the most important types of messages that need careful regulation are those of self-disclosure. Remember the benefits and the dangers and regulate your disclosures after critical analysis.

A chief concern should be to recognize what critical thinking theorists call "conceptual distortions" and what we have called "barriers to verbal interaction." Avoid the barriers and substitute a more critical, more realistic analysis. Be especially careful to avoid dividing an issue into two extremes and then assuming they represent all ways of looking at things (polarization); confusing the label with what it stands for (intensional orientation); confusing inferences with facts (fact-inference confusion); acting as if you know all about anything (allness); treating a person as unchanging (static evaluation); and assuming that all people are the same because they are covered by the same label, for example, teachers, Asians, or homeless people (indiscrimination).

Feedback on Concepts and Skills

In this chapter we considered verbal messages. We looked at meaning and its implications for communication, the barriers in thinking and communicating, and the concept of disconfirmation.

1. Meaning is central to the process of communication. Meanings may be denotative or connotative, are in people (not simply in words), may metacommunicate, and depend on context.
2. Polarization occurs when we divide reality into two unrealistic extremes, such as black and white, good and bad.
3. Intensional orientation occurs when we respond to the way something is talked about or labeled rather than to the reality. Extensional orientation is the tendency to respond to things as they are, not how they are labeled or talked about.
4. Fact-inference confusion occurs when we treat inferences as if they were facts.
5. Static evaluation occurs when we ignore change and assume that reality is static.
6. Allness refers to the tendency to assume that one knows all there is to know, or that what has been said is all there is to say.
7. Indiscrimination occurs when we group unlike things together and assume that because they have the same label, they are all alike.
8. Disconfirmation refers to the process of ignoring the presence and the communications of others. Confirmation refers to accepting, supporting, and acknowledging the importance of the other person.
9. Racist, sexist, and heterosexist language puts down and negatively evaluates various cultural groups.

The study of meaning and the barriers in thinking, communicating, and in talking with others have important implications for developing the skills of effective communication. Check your ability to apply these skills. Use a rating scale such as: (1) = almost always, (2) = often, (3) = sometimes, (4) = rarely, (5) = almost never.

_____ 1. I take special care to make spoken messages clear and unambiguous, especially when using terms for which people will have very different connotative meanings.

_____ 2. I try to understand not only the objective, denotative meanings but also the subjective, connotative meanings.

_____ 3. I recognize snarl and purr words as describing the speaker's feelings and not objective reality.

_____ 4. I focus attention not only on words but on the person communicating, recognizing that meanings are largely in the person.

_____ 5. Words may refer to the real world (objects, people, and events) but also to other words. Language is metacommunication system; it can be used to talk about itself.

_____ 6. I communicate as sender/listener with a recognition that the meaning of a term will depend greatly on the context in which it occurs.

_____ 7. I avoid polarization by using "middle ground" terms and qualifiers in describing the world and especially people.

_____ 8. I avoid responding (intensionally) to labels as if they are objects; instead, I respond extensionally and look first at the reality and only then at the words.

_____ 9. I distinguish facts from inferences and respond to inferences with tentativeness.

_____ 10. I mentally date my statements and thus avoid static evaluation.

_____ 11. I end my statements with an implicit etc. in recognition that there is always more to be known or said.

_____ 12. I avoid indiscrimination by treating each person and situation as unique.

_____ 13. I avoid disconfirmation and instead use responses that confirm the other person.

_____ 14. I avoid racist, sexist, and heterosexist language and, in general, language that puts down other groups.

Skill Development Exercises

5.1 Thinking with E-Prime

The expression _E-prime_ (E') refers here to the mathematical equation $E - e = E'$ where E = the English language and e = the verb _to be._ E', therefore, stands for normal English without the verb _to be._ D. David Bourland, Jr. (1965–1966; Wilson, 1989; Joyner, 1993) argued that if we wrote and spoke without the verb _to be,_ we would describe events more accurately. The verb _to be_ often suggests that qualities are in the person or thing rather than in the observer making the statement. It is easy to forget that these statements are evaluative rather than purely descriptive. For example, when you say, "Johnny is a failure," you imply that failure is somehow within Johnny instead of a part of someone's evaluation of Johnny. This type of thinking is especially important in making statements about yourself. When you say, for example, "I'm not good at mathematics" or "I'm unpopular" or "I'm lazy," you imply that these qualities are _in_ you. But these are simply evaluations that may be incorrect or, if at least partly accurate, may change. The verb _to be_ implies a permanence that is simply not true of the world in which we live.

To appreciate further the difference between statements that use the verb *to be* and those that do not, try to rewrite the following sentences without using the verb *to be* in any of its forms–*is, are, am, was*, etc. Sample E-prime responses are provided in number 1.

1. *I'm a poor student.*
   E-prime responses: *"I received an 'F' in Accounting." "I have to rewrite my last paper." "Professor Windez said I had poor study habits."*
2. They are inconsiderate.
3. What is meaningful communication?
4. Is this valuable?
5. Happiness is a dry nose.
6. Love is a useless abstraction.
7. Is this book meaningful?
8. Was the movie any good?
9. Dick and Jane are no longer children.
10. This class is boring.

5.2 Identifying Barriers in Language in Action

Here is a brief dialogue that was written to illustrate the various barriers to communication discussed in this unit as they might apply as two people talk. Read over the dialogue and identify the barriers illustrated. Also consider why these statements establish barriers and how the people in the dialogue might have avoided the barriers.

PAT: Look, do you care about me or don't you? If you do then you'll go away for the weekend with us like we planned originally.

CHRIS: I know we planned to go but I got this opportunity to put in some overtime and I really need the extra money.

PAT: Look, a deal is a deal. You said you'd go and that's all that really matters.

CHRIS: Pat! You never give me a break, do you? I just can't go; I have to work.

PAT: All right, all right. I'll go alone.

CHRIS: Oh, no you don't. I know what will happen.

PAT: What will happen?

CHRIS: You'll go back to drinking again. I know you will.

PAT: I will not. I don't drink anymore.

CHRIS: Pat, you're an alcoholic and you know it.

PAT: I am not an alcoholic.

CHRIS: You drink, don't you?

PAT: Yes, occasionally.

CHRIS: Occasionally? Yeah, you mean two or three times a week, don't you?

PAT: That's occasionally. That's not being an alcoholic.

CHRIS: Well, I don't care how much you drink or how often you drink. You're still an alcoholic.

PAT: Anyway, what makes you think I'll drink if I go away for the weekend?

CHRIS: All those weekend ski trips are just excuses to drink. I've been on one of them—remember?

PAT: Well, see it your way, my dear. See it your way. I'll be gone right after I shower. *[Thinking]: I can't wait to get away for the weekend.*

CHRIS: *[Thinking] Now, what have I done? Our relationship is finished.*

5.3 Confirming, Rejecting, and Disconfirming

Classify the following responses as confirmation, rejection, or disconfirmation and develop original responses to illustrate all three types of responses.

Enrique receives this semester's grades in the mail; they are a lot better than previous semesters' grades but are still not great. After opening the letter, Enrique says: "I really tried hard to get my grades up this semester." Enrique's parents respond:

_____ Going out every night hardly seems like trying very hard.

_____ What should we have for dinner?

_____ Keep up the good work.

_____ I can't believe you've really tried your best; how can you study with the stereo blasting in your ears?

_____ I'm sure you've tried real hard.

_____ That's great.

_____ What a rotten day I had at the office.

_____ I can remember when I was in school; got all B's without ever opening a book.

Pat, who has been out of work for the past several weeks, says: "I feel like such a failure; I just can't seem to find a job. I've been pounding the pavement for the last five weeks and still nothing." Pat's friend responds:

_____ I know you've been trying real hard.

_____ You really should get more training so you'd be able to sell yourself more effectively.

_____ I've told you a hundred times: you need that college degree.

_____ I've got to go to the dentist on Friday. Boy, do I hate that.

_____ The employment picture is real bleak this time of the year but your qualifications are really impressive. Something will come up soon.

_____ You are not a failure. You just can't find a job.

_____ What do you need a job for? Stay home and keep house. After all, Chris makes more than enough money to live in style.

_____ What's five weeks?

_____ Well, you'll just have to try harder.

CHAPTER SIX

Nonverbal Messages

Chapter Concepts	Chapter Goals	Chapter Skills
	After completing this chapter, you should be able to	After completing this chapter, you should be able to
Body Movements	1. define and provide examples of the five kinds of body movements	regulate your own body movements and gestures to communicate desired meanings
Facial and Eye Movements	2. describe the types of information communicated by the face and the eyes	use facial and eye expressions to communicate meanings
Spatial and Territorial Communication	3. explain the four distances and give examples of the communications occurring at each distance	communicate with an understanding of the messages of space and territory
	4. define *territoriality* and *marker*	
Artifactual Communication	5. explain artifactual communication and how color, clothing, and space decoration communicate	use artifacts to communicate and interpret meanings
Touch Communication	6. explain the major meanings communicated by touch	use appropriate touch to communicate varied meanings
		act sensitively to cultural differences in touching preferences and avoidance tendencies
Paralanguage	7. define *paralanguage* and its role in making judgments	vary rate, pausing, quality, tempo, and volume to communicate intended meanings
Time Communication	8. explain how time communicates and the nature of cultural and psychological time	use and interpret time cues in cultural perspective
Thinking Critically About Nonverbal Communication	9. explain the suggestions for thinking critically about nonverbal communication	recognize that what you perceive is only a part of the total nonverbal expression
		connect and relate the various nonverbal cues into a meaningful whole

What would your life be like if you were able to read a person's nonverbal behavior and tell what the person was thinking and feeling? What would it be like with your friends? Your co-workers? Your family? And what if others could do the same with you? What would your interpersonal and professional lives be like if everyone could read your thoughts and feelings from simply observing your nonverbal messages? This kind of mind reading is obviously impossible. And yet we do know a great deal about nonverbal messages and how they are used in communication. And that is the focus of this chapter—to discuss some of what we know about the nonverbal messages communicated by the body, face, and eyes, by the way space is used, by vocal variation, and by the way in which time is treated.

BODY MOVEMENTS

Table 6.1 summarizes some of the ways in which you can communicate with your body, an area of nonverbal communication often referred to as **kinesics** (Ekman & Friesen, 1969). Examine this table and try to identify other meanings that these types of movements may communicate.

	NAME AND FUNCTION	EXAMPLES
	EMBLEMS directly translate words or phrases; especially culture specific	"Okay" sign, "come here" wave, hitchhiker's sign
	ILLUSTRATORS accompany and literally "illustrate" verbal messages	Circular hand movements when talking of a circle; hands far apart when talking of something large
	AFFECT DISPLAYS communicate emotional meaning	Expressions of happiness, surprise, fear, anger, sadness, disgust/contempt
	REGULATORS monitor, maintain, or control the speaking of another	Facial expressions and hand gestures indicating "keep going," "slow down," or "what else happened?"
	ADAPTORS satisfy some need	Scratching one's head

Table 6.1
Five Body Movements

In reviewing this table also note that the meanings that you might assign to any given hand movement will not be the same as those a member of another culture would assign. Although some meanings seem universal, most vary widely from one culture to another (Axtell, 1993). For example, in America you would wave hello or good-bye with your whole hand moving from side to side. In much of Europe this gesture would mean "no." Instead, you would wave hello or good-bye with the palm of your hand exposed and with your fingers going up and down. In Greece, however, this would be considered insulting to the person to whom you are waving.

FACIAL AND EYE MOVEMENTS

The facial area, including the eyes, is probably the single most important source of nonverbal messages.

Facial Communication

Throughout your interpersonal interactions, your face communicates, especially your emotions. In fact, facial movements alone seem to communicate the degree of pleasantness, agreement, and sympathy felt; the rest of the body doesn't provide any additional information. But for other aspects—for example, the intensity with which an emotion is felt—both facial and bodily cues are used (Graham & Argyle, 1975; Graham, Bitti, & Argyle, 1975).

Some nonverbal researchers claim that facial movements may communicate at least the following eight emotions: happiness, surprise, fear, anger, sadness, disgust, contempt, and interest (Ekman, Friesen, &

What do the facial expressions in this photo communicate? On the basis of the facial expressions and other nonverbal cues, what might you assume is going on among the people in this photo?

Research shows that women smile more than men when making negative comments or expressing negative feelings (Shannon, 1987). What implications does this have for male-female communication? What implications might this have for childrearing? For teaching?

Ellsworth, 1972). Others propose that in addition, facial movements may also communicate bewilderment and determination (Leathers, 1986).

Try to communicate surprise using only facial movements. Do this in front of a mirror and try to describe in as much detail as possible the specific movements of the face that make up surprise. If you signal surprise like most people, you probably use raised and curved eyebrows, long horizontal forehead wrinkles, wide-open eyes, a dropped-open mouth, and lips parted with no tension. Even if there were differences—and clearly there would be from one person to another—you could probably recognize the movements listed here as indicative of surprise. In the FAST (Facial Affect Scoring Technique), the face is divided into three main parts: eyebrows and forehead, eyes and eyelids, and the lower face from the bridge of the nose down (Ekman, Friesen, & Tomkins, 1971). Judges then try to identify various emotions by observing the different parts of the face and writing descriptions for the various emotions similar to the one just given for surprise. In this way we can study more effectively just how the face communicates the various emotions.

Of course, some emotions are easier to communicate and to decode than others. For example, in one study, happiness was judged with an accuracy ranging from 55 to 100 percent, surprise from 38 to 86 percent, and sadness from 19 to 88 percent (Ekman, Friesen, & Ellsworth, 1972). Research finds that women and girls are more accurate judges of facial emotional expression than men and boys (Argyle, 1988; Hall, 1984).

As you learned the nonverbal system of communication, you also learned certain facial management techniques; for example, to hide certain emotions and to emphasize others. Here are four types of facial management techniques that you will quickly recognize as being frequently and widely used:

- intensifying to exaggerate a feeling—for example, exaggerating surprise when friends throw you a party
- deintensifying to underplay a feeling—for example, covering up your own joy in the presence of a friend's bad news
- neutralizing to hide a feeling—for example, covering up your sadness so as not to depress others
- masking to replace or substitute the expression of one emotion for another—for example, expressing happiness to cover up disappointment

You probably learned these facial management techniques along with the display rules that told you what emotions to express when; they are the rules of appropriateness. For example, when someone gets bad news in which you may secretly take pleasure, the display rule dictates that you frown and otherwise nonverbally signal your displeasure. If you violate these display rules, you will be judged insensitive.

The Facial Feedback Hypothesis

According to the facial feedback hypothesis your facial expression influences your level of positive and negative physiological arousal (Capella, 1993; Larsen, Kasimatis, & Frey, 1992). It has been found, for example, that

"I'm going out to log some face time with the dog."

POWER PERSPECTIVE

Persuasive Power Signals

Much research has addressed the issue of the nonverbal factors related to your ability to persuade and influence others (Burgoon, Buller, & Woodall, 1989).

Clothing and other artifactual symbols of authority help you to influence others. Although most people deny that they would be so influenced, research shows that they would in fact be more susceptible to influence attempts to people in, for example, a respected uniform.

Affirmative nodding, facial expressions, and gestures help you express your concern for the other person and for the interaction and help you establish your charisma, an essential component of credibility. Self-manipulations (playing with your hair or touching your face, for example) and backward leaning will damage your persuasiveness.

Public speakers are more persuasive when they maintain physically closer relationships with their listeners and are relatively relaxed.

[Next Power Perspective, page 136]

subjects who exaggerated their facial expressions showed higher physiological arousal than subjects who suppressed these expressions. Those who neither exaggerated nor suppressed their expressions had arousal levels between these two extremes (Lanzetta, Cartwright-Smith, & Kleck, 1976; Zuckerman, Klorman, Larrance, & Spiegel, 1981). So not only does your facial expression influence the judgments and impressions that others have of you; they also influence your own level of emotional arousal (Hess, Kappas, McHugo, Lanzetta, et al., 1992).

The Influence of Context

The same facial expressions are perceived differently if people are supplied with different contexts. For example, when a smiling face is presented looking at a glum face, the smiling face is judged to be vicious and taunting. But when the same smiling face was presented looking at a frowning face, it was judged to be peaceful and friendly (Cline, 1956).

The wide variations in facial communication that we observe in different cultures seem to reflect which reactions are permissible and which are not, rather than a difference in the way in which emotions are facially expressed (Matsumoto, 1991). For example, Japanese and American students watched a film of an operation (Ekman, 1985). The students were videotaped in both an interview situation about the film and alone while watching the film. When alone, the students showed very similar reactions; but in the interview, the American students displayed facial expressions indicating displeasure whereas the Japanese students did not show any great emotion. Thus, the difference may not be in the way different cultures express emotions but rather in the cultural rules for displaying emotions in public.

Eye Movements

An eye can threaten like a loaded and leveled gun, or it can insult like hissing or kicking; or, in its altered mood, by beams of kindness, it can make the heart dance for joy.
—RALPH WALDO EMERSON

From Ben Jonson's poetic observation "Drink to me only with thine eyes, and I will pledge with mine" to the scientific observations of contemporary researchers (Hess, 1975; Marshall, 1983), the eyes are regarded as the most important nonverbal message system.

The messages communicated by the eyes vary depending on the duration, direction, and quality of the eye behavior. For example, in every culture there are rather strict, though unstated, rules for the proper duration for eye contact. In one study conducted in England, the average length of gaze is 2.95 seconds. The average length of mutual gaze (two persons gazing at each other) is 1.18 seconds (Argyle & Ingham, 1972; Argyle, 1988). When eye contact falls short of this amount, members (of some cultures) may think the person is uninterested, shy, or preoccupied. When the appropriate amount of time is exceeded, members might perceive the person as showing unusually high interest.

The direction of the eye also communicates. According to our culture, you glance alternatively at the other person's face, then away, then again at the face, and so on. The rule for the public speaker is to scan the entire audience; not focusing for too long or ignoring any one area of the audience. When you break these directional rules, you communicate different meanings—abnormally high or low interest, self-consciousness, nervousness over the interaction, and so on. The quality—how wide or how narrow your eyes get during interaction—also communicates meaning, especially interest level and such emotions as surprise, fear, and disgust.

The Functions of Eye Movements

With eye movements you communicate a variety of messages. You can seek feedback with your eyes. In talking with someone, you look at her or him intently, as if to say, "Well, what do you think?"

You can also inform the other person that the channel of communication is open and that he or she should now speak. We see this in the college classroom, when the instructor asks a question and then locks eyes with a student. Without saying anything, the instructor expects that student to answer the question.

What messages did you send by eye movements today? What messages did you receive?

Eye movements may also signal the nature of a relationship, whether positive (an attentive glance) or negative (eye avoidance). You can also signal your power through "visual dominance behavior" (Exline, Ellyson, & Long, 1975). The average speaker, for example, maintains a high level of eye contact while listening and a lower level while speaking. When people want to signal dominance, they may reverse this pattern—maintaining a high level of eye contact while talking but a lower level while listening.

Eye contact can also change (psychologically) the physical distance between yourself and another person. When you catch someone's eye at a party, for example, you become psychologically close even though far apart. By avoiding eye contact—even when physically close as in a crowded elevator—you increase the psychological distance between you.

Women make eye contact more and maintain it longer (both in speaking and in listening) than do men. This holds true whether the woman is interacting with other women or with men. This difference in eye behavior may result from women's tendency to display their emotions more than men (Wood, 1994).

Eye Avoidance Functions

The eyes are "great intruders," observed sociologist Erving Goffman (1967). When you avoid eye contact or avert your glance, you help others to maintain their privacy. You might do this when you see a couple arguing in public. You turn your eyes away (though your eyes may be wide open) as if to say, "I don't mean to intrude; I respect your privacy." Goffman refers to this behavior as **civil inattention.**

Eye avoidance can also signal lack of interest—in a person, a conversation, or some visual stimulus. At times, you might hide your eyes to block off unpleasant stimuli or close your eyes to block out visual stimuli and thus heighten other senses. For example, you might listen to music with your eyes closed. Lovers often close their eyes while kissing, and many prefer to make love in a dark or dimly lit room.

Pupil Dilation

Those lovely lamps, these windows of the soul.
—GUILLAME DE SALLUSTE, SEIGNEUR DU BARTAS

In the fifteenth and sixteenth centuries in Italy, women put drops of belladonna (which literally means "beautiful woman") into their eyes to dilate the pupils so they would look more attractive. Contemporary research supports the logic of these women; people judge dilated pupils as more attractive (Hess, 1975). Your pupils enlarge when you are interested in something or emotionally aroused. Perhaps you judge dilated pupils as more attractive because you judge an individual's dilated pupils to indicate interest in you. More generally, Ekhard Hess (1975) has claimed that pupils dilate in response to positively evaluated attitudes and objects, and constrict in response to negatively evaluated attitudes and objects.

ETHICAL ISSUE

Lying

Actions lie louder than words.
—CAROLYN WELLS

According to the *Random House Dictionary,* a *lie* is "a false statement made with deliberate intent to deceive; a falsehood; something intended or serving to convey a false impression." As this definition makes clear, lying may also be committed by omission as well as commission. When you omit something relevant to the issue at hand, and this omission leads others to draw incorrect inferences, you have lied just as surely as if you had made a false statement (Bok, 1978).

Similarly, although many lies are verbal, some are nonverbal and most seem to involve at least some nonverbal elements. The innocent facial expression—despite the commission of some punishable act—and the knowing nod instead of the honest expression of ignorance are common examples of nonverbal lying. Lies may range from the "white lie" that stretches the truth to the "big lie" in which one formulates falsehoods so elaborate that everyone comes to believe they are true.

There are probably as many reasons for lying as there are lies; each situation is different. But if we boiled it down, we would probably find that people lie for two main reasons: (1) to gain some reward or

(2) to avoid some punishment. In one study of white lies in interpersonal communication, four reward categories were identified as motivating lying (Camden, Motley, & Wilson, 1984): to gain basic needs such as money, to increase desired relationships with others, to protect one's self-esteem, and to gain some personal satisfaction.

Each person is likely to feel differently about whether or not an act constitutes lying and if it does, is it wrong or unethical. Consider, for example, would you define the following instances as lying? For those you do consider lying, is it unethical? What other information would you want to know about each of these situations before rendering a judgment?

- telling a best friend that you are feeling fine when you are actually depressed
- lying to your employer about your HIV status since it bears no relationship to your ability to do your job
- lying to co-workers about your romantic relationship status
- allowing an interviewer to believe you have experience when you really do not (though you never actually say you do have experience)
- allowing an audience to believe that you formulated the arguments you're advancing when they come from a secondary source

[Next Ethical Issue, page 160]

SPATIAL AND TERRITORIAL COMMUNICATION

Your use of space speaks as surely and loudly as words and sentences. Speakers who stand close to their listener, with their hands on the listener's shoulders and their eyes focused directly on those of the listener, communicate something very different from speakers who stand in a corner with arms folded and eyes downcast. Similarly, the executive office suite on the top floor with huge windows, private bar, and plush carpeting communicates something totally different from the 6-by-6-foot cubicle occupied by the rest of the workers. Proxemics refers to the messages communicated by the way you treat space and territoriality to the influence that the specific territory has on your communication behavior.

Spatial Distances

Edward Hall (1959, 1966) distinguishes four distances that define the type of relationship between people (see Figure 6.1).

In **intimate distance**, ranging from actual touching to 18 inches, the presence of the other individual is unmistakable. Each person experiences the sound, smell, and feel of the other's breath. You use intimate distance

Some nonverbal researchers (Burgoon & Hale, 1988) argue that when people violate the expected distance in conversation, attention shifts from the topic to the person. Do you notice this? What else happens when expected distances are violated?

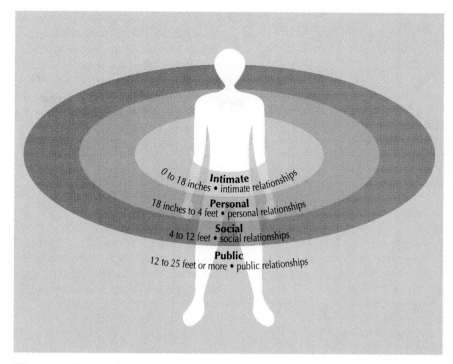

Figure 6.1 Proxemic Distances

for lovemaking and wrestling, for comforting and protecting. This distance is so short that most people do not consider it proper in public.

Personal distance refers to the protective "bubble" that defines your personal distance, ranging from 18 inches to 4 feet. This imaginary bubble keeps you protected and untouched by others. You can still hold or grasp another person at this distance but only by extending your arms, allowing you to take certain individuals such as loved ones into your protective bubble. At the outer limit of personal distance, you can touch another person only if both of you extend your arms.

Social distance, ranging from 4 to 12 feet, you lose the visual detail you have at personal distance. You conduct impersonal business and interact at a social gathering at this social distance. The more distance you maintain in your interactions, the more formal they appear. In offices of high officials, the desks are positioned so the official is assured of at least this distance from clients.

Public distance, from 12 to more than 25 feet, protects you. At this distance you could take defensive action if threatened. On a public bus or train, for example, you might keep at least this distance from a drunkard. Although at this distance you lose fine details of the face and eyes, you are still close enough to see what is happening.

Influences on Space Communication

Several factors influence the way we treat space in communication. Here are a few examples of how status, culture, context, subject matter, sex, and age influence space communication (Burgoon, Buller, & Woodall, 1989):

Why do you suppose people who are angry or tense need greater space around them? Do you find this true from your personal experiences?

- People of equal **status** maintain shorter distances between themselves than do people of unequal status. When status is unequal, the higher-status person may approach the lower-status person more closely than the lower-status person may approach the higher-status person.
- Members of different **cultures** treat space differently; for example, European Americans stand fairly far apart when conversing, compared with those from southern European and Middle Eastern cultures, who stand much closer.
- The larger the physical **context** you are in, the smaller the interpersonal space.
- When discussing personal **subjects** you maintain shorter distances than with impersonal subjects. Also, you stand closer to someone praising you than to someone criticizing you.
- Your **sex** influences your spatial relationships. Women generally stand closer than men.
- As people **age** there is a tendency for the spaces to become larger. Children stand much closer than do adults. This is some evidence that these distances are learned behaviors.

"It's quite natural, you know, he's just marking territory."

Courtesy Andre Noel.

Territoriality

Territoriality, a term that comes to us from ethology (the study of animals in their natural habitat), refers to the ownership-like reaction toward a particular space or object. The size and location of human territory also say something about status (Sommer, 1969; Mehrabian, 1976). An apartment or office in midtown Manhattan or downtown Tokyo is extremely high-status territory since the cost restricts it to the wealthy.

Status is also indicated by the unwritten law granting the right of invasion. In some cultures and in some organizations, for example, higher-status individuals have more of a right to invade the territory of others than vice versa. The president of a large company can invade the territory of a junior executive by barging into her or his office, but the reverse would be unthinkable.

Like animals, humans also mark their territory. We make use of three types of markers: central, boundary, and ear markers (Hickson & Stacks, 1989). Table 6.2 identifies the function of these markers and gives some examples.

In one of O. Henry's stories, the narrator says: "She plucked from my lapel the invisible strand of lint (the universal act of woman to proclaim ownership)." What do you think of this observation? Is this an act proclaiming "ownership"? Is it limited to women? Do men use similar gestures to proclaim "ownership"?

Have you seen any examples of marking behavior today? Look around your home and at your belongings. Can you identify examples of *central, boundary,* and *ear* markers?

TABLE 6.2 THREE TYPES OF MARKERS

Marker	Function	Examples
Central	To reserve a territory	A drink at the bar, books on your desk, and a sweater over the chair let others know that this territory belongs to you
Boundary	To set boundaries between your territory and that of others	The bar in the supermarket checkout line, the armrests separating your chair from those on either side
Ear	To identify your possessions	Trademarks, initials, nameplates, and initials on a shirt or attaché case

ARTIFACTUAL COMMUNICATION

Artifactual messages are those made by human hands. Thus, color, clothing, jewelry, and the decoration of space would be considered artifactual. Let's look at each of these briefly.

Color Communication

There is some evidence that colors affect us physiologically. For example, respiratory movements increase with red light and decrease with blue light. Similarly, eye blinks increase in frequency when eyes are exposed to red light and decrease when exposed to blue. This seems consistent with our intuitive feelings about blue being more soothing and red more arousing. After changing a school's walls from orange and white to blue, the blood pressure of the students decreased while their academic performance increased.

Colors surely influence perceptions and behaviors (Kanner, 1989). People's acceptance of a product, for example, is largely determined by its package. The very same coffee taken from a yellow can was described as weak, from a dark brown can too strong, from a red can rich, and from a blue can mild. Even our acceptance of a person may depend on the colors worn. Consider, for example, the comments of one color expert (Kanner, 1989): "If you have to pick the wardrobe for your defense lawyer heading into court and choose anything but blue, you deserve to lose the case." Black is so powerful it could work against the lawyer with the jury. Brown lacks sufficient authority. Green would probably elicit a negative response.

Clothing and Body Adornment

People make inferences about who you are, in part, by the way you dress. Whether these inferences are accurate or not, they will influence what people think of you and how they react to you. Your social class, your seriousness, your attitudes (for example, whether you are conservative or liberal), your concern for convention, your sense of style and perhaps even your creativity will all be judged, at least in part, by the way you dress.

Similarly, college students will perceive an instructor dressed informally as friendly, fair, enthusiastic, and flexible and the same instructor dressed formally as prepared, knowledgeable, and organized (Malandro, Barker, & Barker, 1989). Your jewelry also communicates messages about you. Wedding and engagement rings are obvious examples that communicate specific messages. College rings and political buttons likewise communicate specific messages. If you wear a Rolex watch or large precious stones, for example, others are likely to infer that you are rich. Men who wear earrings will be judged differently from men who don't.

The way you wear your hair communicates about who you are—from caring about being up-to-date to a desire to shock, to perhaps a lack of concern for appearances. Men with long hair, to take just one example, will generally be judged as less conservative than those with shorter hair.

CULTURAL VIEWPOINT

Gift Giving as Communication

One aspect of nonverbal communication that is frequently overlooked is the giving of gifts, a practice in which rules and customs vary according to each culture. Here are a few situations where gift giving backfired and created barriers rather than bonds. These examples are designed to heighten your awareness of both the importance of gift giving and of recognizing intercultural differences. What might have gone wrong in each of these situations (Axtell, 1993)?

1. An American brings chrysanthemums to a Belgian colleague and a clock to a Chinese colleague. Both react negatively.
2. Upon meeting an Arab businessman for the first time—someone with whom you wish to do considerable business—you present him with a gift. He becomes disturbed.
3. When visiting an Arab family in Oman, you bring a bottle of your favorite brandy for after dinner. Your host seems annoyed.
4. Arriving for dinner at the home of a Kenyan colleague, you present flowers as a dinner gift. Your host accepts them politely but looks puzzled.
5. In arriving for dinner at the home of a Swiss colleague, you bring 14 red roses. Your host accepts them politely but looks strangely at you.

Possible reasons:

1. Chrysanthemums in Belgium and clocks in China are both reminders of death.
2. Gifts given at the first meeting may be interpreted as a bribe; thus should be avoided.
3. Alcohol is prohibited by Islamic law, so should be avoided when selecting gifts for most Arabs.
4. In Kenya, flowers are brought only to express condolence.
5. In Switzerland red roses are a sign of romantic interest. Also, an even number of (or 13) flowers is generally considered bad luck, so should be avoided.

[Next Cultural Viewpoint, page 140]

Space Decoration

The way you decorate your private spaces also tells about you. The office with mahogany desk and bookcases and oriental rugs communicates your importance and status within the organization, just as the metal desk and bare floors indicate a worker much further down in the hierarchy.

Similarly, people will make inferences about you based on the way you decorate your home. The expense of the furnishings may communicate your status and wealth; their coordination, your sense of style. The magazines may reflect your interests while the arrangement of chairs around a television set may reveal how important watching television is to you. Bookcases lining the walls reveal the importance of reading. In fact, there is probably little in your home that would not send messages that others would use in making inferences about you. Computers, widescreen televisions, well-equipped kitchens, and oil paintings of greatgrandparents, for example, all say something about the people who live in the home.

Similarly, the lack of certain items will communicate something about you. Consider what messages you would get from a home where there is no television, phone, or books.

Who would touch whom—say, by putting an arm on the other person's shoulder or by putting a hand on the other person's back—in the following pairs: teacher and student, doctor and patient, manager and worker, minister and parishioner, police officer and accused, business executive and secretary? What reasons might you offer to explain these differences?

Touch communication (**haptics**) is perhaps the most primitive form of communication (Montagu, 1971). Touch develops before the other senses; even in the womb the child is stimulated by touch. Soon after birth the child is fondled, caressed, patted, and stroked. In turn, the child explores its world through touch and quickly learns to communicate a variety of meanings through touch.

Touching varies greatly from one culture to another. For example, African Americans touch each other more than do European Americans. Similarly, touching declines from kindergarten to the sixth grade for European Americans but not for African American children (Burgoon, Buller, & Woodall, 1989). Similarly, Japanese touch each other much less than do Anglo-Saxons, who in turn touch much less than do southern Europeans (Morris, 1977; Burgoon, Buller, & Woodall, 1989).

The Meanings of Touch

Nancy Henley (1977) argues that touching demonstrates the assertion of male power over women. Men may, says Henley, touch women during their daily routine. In the restaurant, office, and school, for example, men touch women and thus indicate "superior status." When women touch men, on the other hand, the interpretation that it designates a female-dominant relationship is not acceptable (to men). So men may explain and interpret this touching as a sexual invitation. What do you think of Henley's observations?

Nonverbal researchers have identified the major meanings of touch (Jones & Yarbrough, 1985). Here are five of the most important.

- Touch may communicate such **positive emotions** as support, appreciation, inclusion, sexual interest or intent, and affection.
- Touch often communicates **playfulness,** affectionately or aggressively.
- Touch may also **control** or direct the behaviors, attitudes, or feelings of the other person. In attention getting, for example, you touch the person to gain his or her attention, as if to say "look at me" or "look over here."
- **Ritual** touching centers on greetings and departures, for example, shaking hands to say hello or good-bye, or hugging, kissing, or putting your arm around another's shoulder when greeting or saying farewell.
- **Task-relatedness** touching occurs while you are performing some function, for example, removing a speck of dust from another person's face or helping someone out of a car.

Touch Avoidance

"There is a very simple rule about touching," the manager continued. "When you touch, don't take. Touch the people you manage only when you are giving them something— reassurance, support, encouragement, whatever."

—KENNETH BLANCHARD AND
SPENCER JOHNSON

Much as you have a tendency to touch and be touched, you also have a tendency to avoid touch from certain people or in certain circumstances. Researchers in nonverbal communication have found some interesting relationships between touch avoidance and other significant communication variables (Andersen & Leibowitz, 1978). For example, touch avoidance is positively related to communication apprehension; those who fear oral communication also score high on touch avoidance. Touch avoidance is also high with those who self-disclose little. Both touch and self-disclosure are intimate forms of communication; thus people who are reluctant to get close to another person by self-disclosing also seem reluctant to get close by touching.

Older people have higher touch-avoidance scores for opposite-sex persons than do younger people. As we get older we are touched less by

Why do you suppose the rules for touching and touch avoidance operate differently on the ball field than they do, say, in a cafeteria or in a classroom?

members of the opposite sex. This decreased frequency may lead us to avoid touching.

Males score higher on same-sex touch avoidance than do females, which matches our stereotypes. Men avoid touching other men, but women may and do touch other women. On the other hand, women have higher touch-avoidance scores for opposite-sex touching than do men.

PARALANGUAGE

Paralanguage refers to the vocal (but nonverbal) dimension of speech. It refers to how you say something not what you say. An old exercise to increase a student's ability to express different emotions, feelings, and attitudes was to have the student say a sentence while accenting or stressing different words. One popular sentence was, "Is this the face that launched a thousand ships?" Significant differences in meaning are easily communicated depending on where the stress is placed. Consider the following variations:

1. **Is** this the face that launched a thousand ships?
2. Is **this** the face that launched a thousand ships?
3. Is this **the face** that launched a thousand ships?
4. Is this the face that **launched** a thousand ships?
5. Is this the face that launched **a thousand ships**?

Each sentence communicates something different; in fact, each asks a different question even though the words are the same. All that distinguishes the sentences is stress, one aspect of paralanguage.

In addition to stress or pitch, paralanguage includes such vocal characteristics as rate, volume, and rhythm. It also includes vocalizations you make in crying, whispering, moaning, belching, yawning, and yelling (Trager, 1958, 1961; Argyle, 1988). A variation in any of these features communicates. When you speak quickly, for example, you communicate something different from when you speak slowly. Even though the words might be the same, if the speed (or volume, rhythm, or pitch) differs, the meanings people receive will also differ.

Judgments About People

Do you make judgments about another's personality on the basis of the person's paralinguistic cues? For example, do you conclude that those who speak softly feel inferior, believing that no one wants to listen and nothing they say is significant? Do you assume that people who speak loudly have overinflated egos? Do those who speak with no variation, in a complete monotone, seem uninterested in what they are saying? Might you generalize to their having a lack of interest in life in general? All these conclusions are based on little evidence; yet they seem to persist in much popular talk.

People can accurately judge the status (whether high, middle, or low) of speakers from 60-second voice samples (Davitz, 1964). In one study, many listeners made their judgments in fewer than 15 seconds. Speakers judged to be of high status were also given higher credibility than speakers rated middle and low.

Listeners can also accurately judge the emotional states of speakers from vocal expression alone. In these studies, speakers recite the alphabet or numbers while expressing emotions. Some emotions are easier to identify than others; it is easy to distinguish between hate and sympathy but more difficult to distinguish between fear and anxiety. And, of course, listeners vary in their ability to decode, and speakers in their ability to encode emotions (Scherer, 1986).

Judgments About Communication Effectiveness

In one-way communication (when one person is doing all or most of the speaking and the other person is doing all or most of the listening), those who talk fast (about 50 percent faster than normal) are more persuasive.

People agree more with a fast speaker than with a slow speaker and find the fast speaker more intelligent and objective (MacLachlan, 1979).

When we look at comprehension, rapid speech shows an interesting effect. When the speaking rate is increased by 50 percent, the comprehension level only drops by 5 percent. When the rate is doubled, the comprehension level drops only 10 percent. These 5 percent and 10 percent losses are more than offset by the increased speed; thus the faster rates are much more efficient in communicating information. If the speeds are more than twice normal speech, however, comprehension begins to fall dramatically.

Do exercise caution in applying this research to all forms of communication (MacLachlan, 1979). While the speaker is speaking, the listener is generating or framing a reply. If the speaker talks too rapidly, there may not be enough time to compose this reply and the listener may become resentful. Furthermore, the increased rate may seem so unnatural that the listener may focus on the speed rather than the thought.

TIME COMMUNICATION

Temporal communication (**chronemics**) concerns the use of time—how you organize it, react to it, and the messages it communicates (Bruneau, 1985, 1990). Cultural and psychological time are two aspects of particular interest in human communication.

Cultural Time

Two types of cultural time are especially important: formal and informal time. In the United States and in most of the world, **formal time** is divided into seconds, minutes, hours, days, weeks, months, and years. Some cultures, however, may use phases of the moon or the seasons to delineate time periods. In the United States, if your college is on the semester system, your courses are divided into 50- or 75-minute periods that meet two or three times a week for 14-week periods. Eight semesters of 15 or 16 50-minute periods per week equal a college education. As these examples illustrate, formal time units are arbitrary. The culture establishes them for convenience.

Informal time refers to the use of general time terms—for example, "forever," "immediately," "soon," "right away," "as soon as possible." This area of time creates the most communication problems because the terms have different meanings for different people.

Attitudes toward time vary from one culture to another. In one study, for example, the accuracy of clocks was measured in six cultures—Japan, Indonesia, Italy, England, Taiwan, and the United States. Japan had the most accurate and Indonesia had the least accurate clocks. A measure of the speed at which people in these six cultures walked, found that the Japanese walked the fastest, the Indonesians the slowest (LeVine & Bartlett, 1984).

Another interesting aspect of cultural time is your "social clock" (Neugarten, 1979). Your culture and your more specific society maintains a time schedule for the right time to do a variety of important things, for example, the right time to start dating, to finish college, to buy your own

I believe one thing: that today is yesterday and tomorrow is today and you can't stop.
—MARTHA GRAHAM

home, to have a child. And you no doubt learned about this clock as you were growing up. On this basis of this social clock you then evaluate your own social and professional development. If you are on time with the rest of your peers—for example, you all started dating at around the same age or you're all finishing college at around the same age—then you will feel well adjusted, competent, and a part of the group. If you are late, you will probably experience feelings of dissatisfaction.

Psychological Time

Psychological time refers to the importance we place on the past, present, and future. In a past orientation, we have particular reverence for the past. We relive old times and regard the old methods as the best. We see events as circular and recurring, so the wisdom of yesterday is applicable also to today and tomorrow. In a present orientation, we live in the present; for now, not tomorrow. In a future orientation, we look toward and live for the future. We save today, work hard in college, and deny ourselves luxuries because we are preparing for the future.

Alexander Gonzalez and Philip Zimbardo (1985) have provided some interesting conclusions about ourselves based on the way we view time. Before reading these conclusions take the time to test yourself.

....

TEST YOURSELF
What Time Do You Have?

Instructions: For each statement, indicate whether the statement is true (T) or untrue (F) of your general attitude and behavior. (A few statements are purposely repeated to facilitate scoring and analyzing your responses.)

_____ 1. Meeting tomorrow's deadlines and doing other necessary work comes before tonight's partying.

_____ 2. I meet my obligations to friends and authorities on time.

_____ 3. I complete projects on time by making steady progress.

_____ 4. I am able to resist temptations when I know there is work to be done.

_____ 5. I keep working at a difficult, uninteresting task if it will help me get ahead.

_____ 6. If things don't get done on time, I don't worry about it.

_____ 7. I think that it's useless to plan too far ahead because things hardly ever come out the way you planned anyway.

_____ 8. I try to live one day at a time.

_____ 9. I live to make better what is rather than to be concerned about what will be.

_____ 10. It seems to me that it doesn't make sense to worry about the future, since fate determines that whatever will be, will be.

_____ 11. I believe that getting together with friends to party is one of life's important pleasures.

_____ 12. I do things impulsively, making decisions on the spur of the moment.

_____ 13. I take risks to put excitement in my life.

_____ 14. I get drunk at parties.

_____ 15. It's fun to gamble.

_____ 16. Thinking about the future is pleasant to me.

_____ 17. When I want to achieve something, I set subgoals and consider specific means for reaching those goals.

_____ 18. It seems to me that my career path is pretty well laid out.

_____ 19. It upsets me to be late for appointments.

_____ 20. I meet my obligations to friends and authorities on time.

_____ 21. I get irritated at people who keep me waiting when we've agreed to meet at a given time.

_____ 22. It makes sense to invest a substantial part of my income in insurance premiums.

_____ 23. I believe that "A stitch in time saves nine."

_____ 24. I believe that "A bird in the hand is worth two in the bush."

_____ 25. I believe it is important to save for a rainy day.

_____ 26. I believe a person's day should be planned each morning.

_____ 27. I make lists of things I must do.

_____ 28. When I want to achieve something, I set subgoals and consider specific means for reaching those goals.

_____ 29. I believe that "A stitch in time saves nine."

Thinking Critically About Your Time Orientation This time test measures seven different factors. If you selected true (T) for all or most of the questions within any given factor, you are probably high on that factor. If you selected untrue (F) for all or most of the questions within any given factor, you are probably low on that factor.

The first factor, measured by questions 1–5, is a future, work motivation, perseverance orientation. These people have a strong work ethic and are committed to completing a task despite difficulties and temptations. The second factor (questions 6–10) is a present, fatalistic, worry-free orientation. High scorers on this factor live one day at a time, not necessarily to enjoy the day but to avoid planning for the next day or anxiety about the future.

The third factor (questions 11–15) is a present, pleasure-seeking, partying orientation. These people enjoy the present, take risks and engage in a variety of impulsive actions. The fourth factor (questions 16–18) is a future, goal-seeking and planning orientation. These people derive special pleasure from planning and achieving a variety of goals.

The fifth factor (questions 19–21) is a time-sensitivity orientation. People who score high are especially sensitive to time and its role in social obligations. The sixth factor (questions 22–25) is a future, practical action orientation. These people do what they have to do—take practical actions—to achieve the future they want.

The seventh factor (questions 26–29) is a future, somewhat obsessive daily planning orientation. High scorers on this factor make daily "to do" lists and devote great attention to specific details.

Source: From "Time in Perspective" by Alexander Gonzalez and Philip G. Zimbardo. Reprinted with permission from *Psychology Today* magazine. Copyright © 1985 Sussex Publishers, Inc.

Know the true value of time; snatch, seize, and enjoy every moment of it. No idleness, no laziness, no procrastination; never put off till tomorrow what you can do today.

—LORD CHESTERFIELD

Consider some of the findings on psychological time. Future income is positively related to future orientation; the more future oriented you are, the greater your income is likely to be. Present orientation is strongest among lowest-income males.

The time orientation you develop depends on your socioeconomic class and your personal experiences. The researchers who developed this scale and upon whose research these findings are based, observe: "A child with parents in unskilled and semiskilled occupations is usually socialized in a way that promotes a present-oriented fatalism and hedonism. A child of parents who are managers, teachers, or other professionals learns future-oriented values and strategies designed to promote achievement" (Gonzalez & Zimbardo, 1985). Similarly, the future-oriented person who works for tomorrow's goals will frequently look down on the present-oriented person as lazy and poorly motivated for enjoying today and not planning for tomorrow. In turn, the present-oriented person may see those with strong future orientations as obsessed with amassing wealth or rising in status.

Different time perspectives also account for much intercultural misunderstanding because different cultures often teach their members drastically different time orientations. For example, members from some Latin cultures would rather be late for an appointment than end a conversation abruptly or before it has come to a natural end. The Latin sees this behavior as politeness. But others may see this as impolite to the person with whom he or she had the appointment (Hall & Hall, 1987).

> When I look at the future, it's so bright it burns my eyes.
> —OPRAH WINFREY

Culture and Nonverbal Communication

Culture influences the way you communicate nonverbally, both as a sender of messages and as a receiver-interpreter of messages. Here are just a few examples.

Americans consider direct eye contact an expression of honesty and forthrightness, but the Japanese often view this as a lack of respect. The Japanese will glance at the other person's face rarely and then only for very short periods (Axtell, 1993).

In the United States if you live next door to someone, you are almost automatically expected to be friendly and to interact with that person. It seems so natural that we probably don't even consider that this is a cultural expectation not shared by all cultures. In Japan, the fact that your house is next to another's does not imply that you should become close or visit each other. Consider, therefore, the situation in which a Japanese buys a house next to an American. The Japanese may well see the American as overly familiar and as taking friendship for granted. The American may see the Japanese as distant, unfriendly, and unneighborly. Yet, each person is merely fulfilling the expectations of his or her own culture (Hall & Hall, 1987).

Even the meanings you assign to different colors will depend on your culture (Dreyfuss, 1971). In China, for example, red is used for joyous and festive occasions, whereas in Japan it signifies anger and danger. Blue signifies defeat for the Cherokee Indian, but virtue and truth for the Egyptian. In the Japanese theater, blue is the color for villains. Yellow signifies happiness and prosperity in

Egypt, but in tenth-century France yellow colored the doors of criminals. Green communicates femininity to certain American Indians, fertility and strength to Egyptians, and youth and energy to the Japanese. Purple signifies virtue and faith in Egypt, grace and nobility in Japan.

[Next Cultural Viewpoint, page 159]

THINKING CRITICALLY ABOUT NONVERBAL COMMUNICATION

In thinking critically about nonverbal communication try following these suggestions.

- Analyze your own nonverbal communication patterns. If you are to use this material in any meaningful way, for example, to change some of your behaviors, then self-analysis is essential.
- Observe. Observe. Observe. Observe the behaviors of those around you as well as your own. See in everyday behavior what you read about here and discuss in class.
- Resist the temptation to draw conclusions from nonverbal behaviors. Instead, develop hypotheses (educated guesses) about what is going on and test the likelihood of their being correct on the basis of other evidence.
- Connect and relate. Although the areas of nonverbal communication are presented separately in textbooks and in many class lectures, in actual communication situations, they all work together. See the forest as well as the trees.

Feedback on Concepts and Skills

In this chapter we explored nonverbal communication—communication without words—and looked at the ways in which messages are communicated by body movements, facial and eye movements, space and territoriality, artifacts, touch, paralanguage, and time.

1. Five types of body movements are especially important: emblems (nonverbal behaviors that rather directly translate words or phrases), illustrators (nonverbal behaviors that accompany and literally "illustrate" the verbal messages), affect displays (nonverbal movements that communicate emotional meaning), regulators (nonverbal movements that coordinate, monitor, maintain, or control the speaking of another individual), and adaptors (nonverbal behaviors that are emitted without conscious awareness and that usually serve some kind of need, as in scratching an itch).

2. Facial movements may communicate a wide variety of emotions. The most frequently studied are happiness, surprise, fear, anger, sadness, and disgust/contempt. Facial Management Techniques enable you to control revealing the emotions you feel.
3. The Facial Feedback Hypothesis claims that facial display of an emotion can lead to physiological and psychological changes.
4. Eye movements may seek feedback, inform others to speak, signal the nature of a relationship, and compensate for increased physical distance.
5. Pupil size shows one's interest and level of emotional arousal. Pupils enlarge when one is interested in something or is emotionally aroused in a positive way.
6. Proxemics refers to the communicative function of space and spatial relationships. Four major proxemic distances are: (1) intimate distance ranging from actual touching to 18 inches; (2) personal distance, ranging from 18 inches to 4 feet; (3) social distance, ranging from 4 to 12 feet; and (4) public distance, ranging from 12 to more than 25 feet.
7. Your treatment of space is influenced by such factors as status, culture, context, subject matter, sex, age, and positive or negative evaluation of the other person.
8. Territoriality refers to one's possessive reaction to an area of space or to particular objects. Markers are devices that identify a territory as ours; these include central, boundary, and ear markers.
9. Artifactual communication refers to messages that are human-made, for example, the use of color, clothing and body adornment, and space decoration.
10. Touch communication (or haptics) may communicate a variety of meanings, the most important being positive affect, playfulness, control, ritual, and task-relatedness. Touch avoidance refers to our desire to avoid touching and being touched by others.
11. Paralanguage refers to the vocal but nonverbal dimension of speech. It includes rate, pitch, volume, resonance, and vocal quality as well as pauses and hesitations. On the basis of paralanguage we make judgments about people, conversational turns, and believability.
12. Time communication (chronemics) refers to the messages communicated by our treatment of time. Cultural time focuses on how our culture defines and teaches time, and with the difficulties created by the different meanings people have for informal time terms. Psychological time focuses on time orientations, whether past, present, or future.

Throughout our discussion we covered a wide variety of communication skills. Check your ability to apply these skills. Use the following rating scale: (1) = almost always, (2) = often, (3) = sometimes, (4) = rarely, (5) = almost never.

_____ 1. I recognize messages communicated by body gestures and facial and eye movements.

_____ 2. I take into consideration the interaction of emotional feelings and nonverbal expressions of the emotion; each influences the other.

_____ 3. I recognize that what I perceive is only a part of the total non-verbal expression.

_____ 4. I use my eyes to seek feedback, to inform others to speak, to signal the nature of my relationship with others, and to compensate for increased physical distance.

_____ 5. I give others the space they need, for example, giving more space to those who are angry or disturbed.

_____ 6. I am sensitive to the markers (central, boundary, and ear) of others and use these markers to define my own territories.

_____ 7. I use artifacts to communicate the desired messages.

_____ 8. I am sensitive to the touching behaviors of others and distinguish among those touches that communicate positive emotion, playfulness, control, ritual, and task-relatedness.

_____ 9. I recognize and respect each person's touch-avoidance tendency. I am especially sensitive to cultural and gender differences in touching preferences and in touch-avoidance tendencies.

_____ 10. I vary paralinguistic features (rate, pausing, quality, tempo, and volume) to communicate my intended meanings.

_____ 11. I specify what I mean when I use informal time terms.

_____ 12. I interpret time cues from the cultural perspective of the person with whom I am interacting.

Skill Development Experience

6.1 Recognizing Verbal and Nonverbal Message Functions

Although verbal and nonverbal communication are presented in separate chapters, in normal communication they work together. You speak with facial expression, you express sorrow with your entire body and with your words. Six ways in which verbal and nonverbal messages interact are usually identified (Ekman, 1965; Knapp & Hall, 1993). For each function identify a specific and original example to illustrate how verbal and nonverbal messages occur together.

To accent	Nonverbal signals may highlight or emphasize some part of the verbal message, for example, smiling to emphasize your pleasure.
To complement	Nonverbal signals may reinforce or complete your verbal message as when you laugh when telling a funny story.
To contradict	You may contradict your verbal messages by, for example, winking to show you should not be taken seriously.
To regulate	Nonverbal signals may communicate your desire to control the flow of verbal messages, for example, leaning forward to indicate your desire to speak.

To repeat	Using your fingers to echo your verbal "okay" or motioning with your hand as you say "Let's go" are examples of nonverbal signals repeating the verbal.
To substitute	Nonverbal signals may also take the place of verbal messages as when, for example, you simply nod your head to indicate agreement.

6.2 Interacting in Space

Presented here are diagrams of tables and chairs. Imagine that the situation is in the school cafeteria and that this is the only table not occupied. In the space marked X is seated the person described above the

1. A young man or woman to whom you are physically attracted and whom you would like to date but to whom you have never spoken

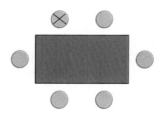

2. A person whom you find physically unattractive and to whom you have never spoken

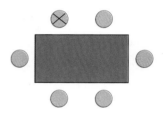

3. A person you dated once and had a miserable time with and whom you would never date again

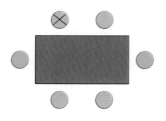

4. A person you have dated a few times and would like to date again

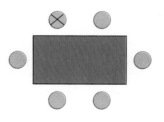

5. An instructor who gave you an undeserved F in a course last semester and whom you dislike intensely

6. Your favorite instructor, whom you would like to get to know better

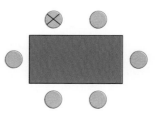

diagram. Indicate by placing an *X* in the appropriate circle where you would sit.

Thinking Critically About Space

1. Why did you select the positions you did? How does the position you selected better enable you to achieve your purpose?
2. Assume that you were already seated in the position marked *X*. Do you think that the person described would sit where you indicated you would (assuming that the feelings and motives are generally the same)? Are there significant sex differences? Significant status differences?
3. What does the position you selected communicate to the person already seated? In what ways might this nonverbal message be misinterpreted? How would your subsequent nonverbal (and perhaps verbal) behavior reinforce your intended message? That is, what would you do to ensure that the message you intended to communicate is in fact the message communicated and received?
4. What is the relationship between distance and liking? What is the relationship between distance and status?

6.3 Coloring Meanings

This exercise is designed to raise questions about the meanings that colors communicate and focuses on the ways in which advertisers and marketers use colors to influence our perceptions of a particular product. The color spectrum is presented below with numbers from 1 to 25 to facilitate identifying the colors that you select for the objects noted below.

Assume that you are working for an advertising agency and that your task is to select colors for the various objects listed below. For each object select the major color as well as the secondary colors you would use in its

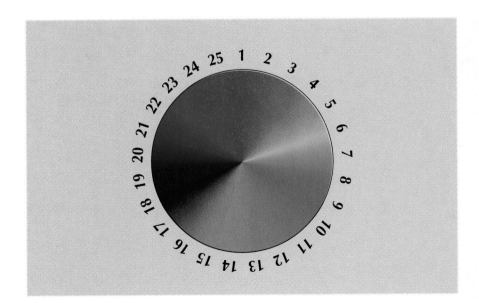

packaging. Record these in the spaces provided by selecting the numbers corresponding to the colors of the spectrum.

Objects	Major Color	Secondary Colors
Toothpaste	_____	_____
An especially rich ice cream	_____	_____
A low-calorie, low-cholesterol ice cream	_____	_____
Puppy food	_____	_____
Packaging for up-scale jewelry store	_____	_____
Diet soda	_____	_____
Rich, creamy chocolate	_____	_____
Children's shampoo	_____	_____
Glass wax	_____	_____
A textbook in human communication	_____	_____

Thinking Critically About Color Communication

After each person has recorded his or her decisions, discuss these in small groups of five or six or with the class as a whole. You may find it helpful to consider the following:

1. What meanings did you wish to communicate for each of the objects for which you chose colors?
2. How much agreement is there among the group members that these meanings are the appropriate ones for these products?
3. How much agreement is there among group members on the colors selected?
4. How effectively do the various colors communicate the desired meanings?
5. Pool the insights of all group members and recolor the products. Are these group designs superior to those developed individually? If a number of groups are working on this project at the same time, it may be interesting to compare the final group colors for each of the products.

6.4 Praising and Criticizing

This exercise aims to show that the same verbal statement can communicate praise and criticism depending on the paralinguistic cues that accompany it. Read each of the ten statements, first to communicate praise and second, criticism. One procedure is to seat the class in a circle and begin with one student reading statement No. 1 with a praising meaning, and the next student reading the same statement with a criticizing meaning. Continue around the circle until all ten statements are read.

1. Now that looks good on you.
2. You lost weight.
3. You look younger than that.

4. You're gonna make it.
5. That was some meal.
6. You really know yourself.
7. You're an expert.
8. You're so sensitive. I'm amazed.
9. Your parents are really something.
10. Are you ready? Already?

Thinking Critically About Paralanguage

After all the statements are read from both a praising and a criticizing perspective, consider these questions:

1. What specific paralinguistic cues communicate praise? Criticism?
2. What paralinguistic cue was most helpful in enabling the speaker to communicate praise or criticism?
3. Most people would claim it is easier to decode than to encode the praise or criticism. Was this true in this experience? Why or why not?
4. Although this exercise focused on paralanguage, the statements were probably read with different facial expressions, eye movements, and body postures. How would you describe these other nonverbals when communicating praise and criticism?

PART TWO

The Contexts of Human Communication

CHAPTER SEVEN

Interpersonal Communication: Conversation and Conflict

Chapter Concepts	Chapter Goals	Chapter Skills
	After completing this chapter, you should be able to	After completing this chapter, you should be able to
The Conversation Process	1. explain the 5-stage model of conversation and define each of its stages 2. explain the suggestions for opening, maintaining, and closing a conversation	open, maintain, and close conversations effectively
Conversational Effectiveness	3. explain the seven qualities of conversational effectiveness	use the qualities of conversational effectiveness as appropriate to the specific situation
Interpersonal Conflict	4. define interpersonal conflict, the major myths, and its positive and negative effects	engage in interpersonal conflict with a realistic understanding of the myths and potential effects
Conflict Management	5. explain the suggestions for dealing with conflict productively	engage in conflict management using fair fight strategies
Before and After the Conflict	6. explain the suggestions for preparing for and for concluding conflict encounters	prepare for and follow up the conflict productively
Thinking Critically About Interpersonal Conversation and Conflict	7. explain mindfulness, flexibility, and metacommunication as skills to regulate more specific skills	communicate with an appropriate degree of mindfulness flexibility, and metacommunication

Your work relationships, friendships, and romantic relationships depend on your ability to communicate interpersonally. Interpersonal communication is simply communication between two persons who have a clearly established relationship. Thus interpersonal communication would include what takes place between a waiter and a customer, a son and his father, two people in an interview, and so on. This definition makes it almost impossible to have a two-person communication that is not interpersonal. Almost inevitably, there is some relationship between two persons. Even the stranger in the city who asks directions from a resident has a clearly defined relationship as soon as the first message is sent. Sometimes this "relational" or "dyadic" definition is extended to include small groups of persons, such as families or groups of three or four friends.

Interpersonal communication, like any behavior, varies from extremely effective to extremely ineffective; no interpersonal encounter is a total failure or a total success. Some, however, are more effective than others. In the first part of this unit we consider conversation, its stages and its qualities of effectiveness, those qualities that foster meaningful, honest, and mutually satisfying interactions and relationships (Bochner & Kelly, 1974). They are also the qualities that make you effective in presenting yourself and in achieving your goals (Wiemann, 1977; Wiemann & Backlund, 1980; Spitzberg & Hecht, 1984; Spitzberg & Cupach, 1984, 1989; Rubin and Nevins, 1988). In the second part, we examine the qualities of effectiveness given their severest test: in interpersonal conflict.

THE CONVERSATION PROCESS

The process of conversation takes place in five steps: opening, feedforward, business, feedback, and closing (Figure 7.1).

Opening

Your first step is to open the conversation, usually with some kind of greeting: "Hi," "How are you?" "Hello, this is Joe." Greetings can be verbal or nonverbal and are usually both (Krivonos & Knapp, 1975;

Conversation is the socializing instrument par excellence, and in its style one can see reflected the capacities of a race.
—JOSÉ ORTEGA Y GASSET

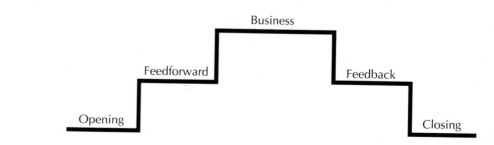

Figure 7.1
The Conversation Process

Knapp, 1984). Verbal greetings include, for example, verbal salutes ("Hi," "Hello"), initiation of the topic ("The reason I called . . ."), making reference to the other ("Hey, Joe, what's up?"), and personal inquiries ("What's new?" How are you doing?"). Nonverbal greetings include waving, smiling, shaking hands, and winking. Usually, you greet another person both verbally and nonverbally—you smile when you say hello.

Greetings serve several purposes (Krivonos & Knapp, 1975; Knapp & Vangelista, 1992). They can **signal a stage of access;** they open up the channels of communication for more meaningful interaction and are good examples of **phatic communion,** the "small talk" that paves the way for the "big talk." Greetings can **reveal important information about the relationship between the two persons.** For example, a big smile and a warm "Hi, it's been a long time" signals that the relationship is still a friendly one. Greetings can also **help maintain the relationship.** You see this function served between workers who pass each other frequently. This greeting-in-passing assures you that even though you do not stop and talk for an extended period that you still have access to each other.

The opening of the conversation is the part that seems to cause the most anxiety or apprehension; you may wish to pause at this point and take the self-test on your own apprehension in conversations.

....

TEST YOURSELF
How Apprehensive Are You in Interpersonal Conversations?

Instructions: Although we often think of apprehension or fear of speaking in connection with public speaking, each of us has a certain degree of apprehension in all forms of communication. The following brief test is designed to measure your apprehension in interpersonal conversations.

This questionnaire consists of six statements concerning your feelings about interpersonal conversations. Indicate in the space provided the degree to which each statement applies to you by marking whether you (1) strongly agree, (2) agree, (3) are undecided, (4) disagree, or (5) strongly disagree with each statement. There are no right or wrong answers. Do not be concerned that some of the statements are similar to others. Work quickly; just record your first impression.

_____ 1. While participating in a conversation with a new acquaintance, I feel very nervous.

_____ 2. I have no fear of speaking up in conversations.

_____ 3. Ordinarily I am very tense and nervous in conversations.

_____ 4. Ordinarily I am very calm and relaxed in conversations.

_____ 5. While conversing with a new acquaintance, I feel very relaxed.

_____ 6. I'm afraid to speak up in conversations.

Thinking Critically About Conversation Apprehension To obtain your apprehension score, use the following formula:

18 plus scores for items 2, 4, and 5;
minus scores for items 1, 3, and 6.

A score above 18 shows some degree of apprehension. Of course, conversations vary widely in the degree to which they may lead to apprehension. For which types do you experience the greatest anxiety? The least? Do others experience apprehension when talking with you?

Source: From *An Introduction to Rhetorical Communication*, 6th ed., by James C. McCroskey. Englewood Cliffs, NJ: Prentice-Hall, 1993. Reprinted by permission of the author.

Feedforward

At the second step, you usually give some kind of **feedforward** in which you might seek to:

- open the channels of communication, usually with some **phatic** message—a message that opens the channels of communication rather than communicates any significant denotative information, for example, "Haven't we met before?" or "Nice day, isn't it?"
- preview future messages, for example, "I'm afraid I have bad news for you" or "Listen to this before you make a move" or "I'll tell you all the gory details."
- **altercast,** to place the receiver in a specific role and request that the receiver respond to you in terms of this assumed role (Weinstein & Deutschberger, 1963; McLaughlin, 1984); for example, "But you're my best friend, you have to help me" or "As an advertising executive, what do you think of corrective advertising?"
- disclaim, to persuade the listener to hear your message as you wish it to be heard (Hewitt & Stokes, 1975); for example, "Don't get me wrong, I'm not sexist" or "I didn't read the entire report, but . . ." or "Don't say anything until you hear my side."

Business

A good conversationalist is not one who remembers what was said, but says what someone wants to remember.
—JOHN MASON BROWN

The third step is the "business," the substance or focus of the conversation. *Business* is a good term to use for this stage because it emphasizes that most conversations are goal-directed. You converse to fulfill one or several of the general purposes of communication: to learn, relate, influence, play, or help (Chapter 1). The business is conducted through an exchange of speaker and listener roles. Here you talk about Jack, what happened in class, or your vacation plans. This is obviously the longest part of the conversation and the reason for both the opening and the feedforward.

The defining feature of conversation is that the roles of speaker and listener are exchanged throughout the interaction. Usually, brief (rather than long) speaking turns characterize mutually satisfying conversations. Here are just a few suggestions for achieving this back-and-forth motion and mutual satisfaction.

- Ask questions of clarification and extension to show that you are listening and that you are interested.
- Ask for opinions and ideas to draw the person into the conversation and to initiate an exchange of thoughts.

- Paraphrase important ideas to make sure you understand what the speaker is thinking and feeling and give the speaker an opportunity to correct or modify your paraphrase ("Do you mean you're going to quit your job?").
- Strive for a balance between speaking and listening, at least in most conversations. Ask yourself for good reasons if your speaking time is greatly different from your listening time.
- Beware of detouring, when you take a word or idea from something said and then go off on a tangent. Too many of these tangents loses you the opportunity to achieve any depth in conversation.
- Avoid interruptions. Generally, interruptions that take the speaking turn away from the speaker damage a conversation by preventing each person from saying what he or she wants to say. When interruptions are excessive they may result in monologues rather than dialogues.
- Use backchanneling cues, cues that you send back to the speaker about your reactions but that do not take away the speaker's turn at speaking (Burgoon, Buller, & Woodall, 1989; Kennedy & Camden, 1988; Pearson & Spitzberg, 1990)—for example, indicating **agreement** or disagreement through smiles or frowns, gestures of approval or disapproval, or brief comments such as "right" or "never" or **involvement** or boredom with the speaker through attentive posture, forward leaning, and focused eye contact. You can also give the speaker **pacing** cues, for example, to slow down by raising your hand near your ear and leaning forward or to speed up by continued nodding of your head. Also, you can ask for **clarification** with, for example, a puzzled facial expression, perhaps coupled with a forward lean.
- Pay attention to turn-taking cues. Look for verbal and nonverbal cues that tell you that the speaker wants to maintain or give up the turn as speaker and when a listener wants to say something (or simply remain a listener).
- Pay attention to leave taking cues, signals that the other person wants to end the conversation. See the discussion of ways of closing a conversation below.

Feedback

Conversation is a game of circles.
—RALPH WALDO EMERSON

The fourth step is the reverse of the second. Here you reflect back on the conversation to signal that as far as you're concerned the business is completed: "So, you may want to send Jack a get well card," "Wasn't that the craziest class you ever heard of?" or "I'll call for reservations while you shop for what we need." Of course, the other person may not agree that the business is completed and may therefore counter with, for example, "But what hospital is he in?" When this happens, you normally would go back a step and continue the business.

Feedback can be looked upon in terms of five important dimensions: positive-negative, person focused–message focused, immediate-delayed, low monitoring–high monitoring, and critical-supportive. To use feedback effectively, then, you need to make educated choices along these dimensions (Figure 7.2).

Figure 7.2

Five Dimensions of Feedback

It may be argued that, generally at least, your interpersonal relationships would be characterized as existing toward the left side of the figure. This "feedback model of relationships" would characterize close or intimate personal relationships as involving feedback that is strongly positive, person-focused, immediate, low in monitoring, and supportive. Acquaintance relationships might involve feedback somewhere in the middle of these scales. Relationships with relative strangers or with those you dislike would involve feedback closer to the right side of the scales, for example, negative, message-focused, delayed, highly monitored, and critical. What arguments for or against this feedback model can you advance?

Positive	__:__:__:__:__:__:__	Negative
Person–focused	__:__:__:__:__:__:__	Message–focused
Immediate	__:__:__:__:__:__:__	Delayed
Low monitoring	__:__:__:__:__:__:__	High monitoring
Supportive	__:__:__:__:__:__:__	Critical

Positive-Negative. Positive feedback (applause, smiles, head nods signifying approval) tells the speaker that the message is being well received and that he or she should continue speaking in the same general mode. Negative feedback (boos, frowns and puzzled looks, and gestures signifying disapproval) tells the speaker that something is wrong and that adjustments need to be made.

Person Focused–Message Focused. Feedback may center on the person ("You're sweet," "You have a great smile") or on the message ("Can you repeat that phone number?" "Your argument is a good one"). Especially in giving criticism (as in public speaking) is it important to make clear that your feedback relates to, say, the organization of the speech and not to the speaker personally.

Immediate-Delayed. In interpersonal situations, feedback is most often sent immediately after the message is received. In other communication situations, however, the feedback may be delayed. When you applaud to ask questions of the public speaker, the feedback is more delayed. Instructor evaluation questionnaires completed at the end of the course provide feedback long after the class began. In interview situations, the feedback may come weeks afterward. In media situations, some feedback comes immediately—through Nielsen ratings, for example—while other feedback comes much later through viewing and buying patterns.

Low Monitoring–High Monitoring. Feedback varies from the spontaneous and totally honest reaction (low-monitored feedback) to the carefully constructed response designed to serve a specific purpose (high-monitored feedback). In most interpersonal situations you probably give feedback spontaneously; you allow your responses to show with little monitoring. At other times, however, you may be more guarded as when your boss asks you how you like your job or when your grandfather asks what you think of his new motorcycle outfit.

Supportive-Critical. Feedback is supportive when it confirms the speaker's definition of self, when it encourages the speaker, or when it defends the speaker in some way. When you console or compliment someone or when you try to make the person feel better about himself or herself, you are giving supportive feedback. Critical feedback, on the other hand, is evaluative. When you give critical feedback you judge another's performance, as in, for example, evaluating a speech, coaching someone learning a new skill, or reprimanding a subordinate on the job.

The Closing

The fifth and last step, the opposite of the first step, is the closing, the good-bye (Knapp, Hart, Friedrich, & Shulman, 1973; Knapp & Vangelista, 1992). Like the opening, the closing may be verbal or nonverbal but is usually a combination of both verbal and nonverbal. Most obviously, the closing signals the end of accessibility. Just as the opening signaled access, the closing signals the end of access. The closing usually also signals some degree of supportiveness; for example, you express your pleasure in interacting: "Well, it was good talking with you." The closing may also summarize the interaction.

Using the Model

Not all conversations will be easily divided into these five steps. Often the opening and the feedforward are combined as when you see someone on campus, for example, and say "Hey, listen to this" or when, in a work situation, someone might say, "Well, folks, let's get the meeting going." In a similar way, the feedback and the closing might be combined: "Look, I've got to think more about this commitment, okay?"

As already noted, the business is the longest part of the conversation. The opening and the closing are usually about the same length and the feedforward and feedback are usually about equal in length. When these relative lengths are severely distorted, you may feel that something is wrong. For example, when someone uses a long feedforward or too short an opening, you might suspect that what is to follow is extremely serious. Of course, what is defined as too long or too short, for example, will be influenced by the culture.

This model may also help identify skill weaknesses and help distinguish effective and satisfying from ineffective and unsatisfying conversations. Consider, for example, the following violations and how they can damage an entire conversation.

- using openings that are insensitive, for example, "Wow, you've gained a few pounds."
- using overly long feedforwards that make you wonder if the other person will ever get to the business
- omitting feedforward before a truly shocking message (for example, the death or illness of a friend or relative) that leads you to see the other person as insensitive or uncaring
- doing business without the normally expected greeting, as when, for example, you go to a doctor who begins the conversation by saying, "Well, what's wrong?"
- omitting feedback, which leads you to wonder if the other person heard what you said or cared about it
- omitting an appropriate closing that makes you wonder if the other person is disturbed or angry with you

Talking is like playing on the harp; there is as much in laying the hands on the strings to stop their vibration as in twanging them to bring out their music.

—Oliver Wendell Holmes, Sr.

POWER PERSPECTIVE

Understanding Power Plays

No interpersonal relationship exists without a power dimension; all interactions invariably involve power maneuvers and consequences. Here are three discussed by Claude Steiner in *The Other Side of Power* (1981).

In **Nobody Upstairs** the individual refuses to acknowledge your request. The maneuver takes the form of not listening to what you are saying, regardless of how many times you say it. Sometimes "nobody upstairs" takes the form of ignoring commonly accepted (but unspoken) rules such as not opening another person's mail or not going through another person's wallet. The power play takes the form of expressing ignorance of the rules: "I didn't know you didn't want me to look in your wallet."

In **You Owe Me** an individual does something for you and then demands something in return. As humorist Erma Bombeck put it, "Guilt is the

continued

gift that keeps on giving." This maneuver is played frequently by friends and co-workers who want you to do something for them. They then bring up all they have done for you and use that to get you to do something for them.

In **Thought Stoppers** someone literally stops your thinking and especially stops you from expressing your thoughts. Thought stoppers may take a number of different forms. Perhaps the most common is the interruption. Before you can finish your thought, the other person interrupts you and either completes it or goes off on another topic. Other thought stoppers include the use of profanity and raising one's voice to drown you out. Regardless of the specific form, it shifts the speaker role from you to the other person.

[Next Power Perspective, page 170]

Do you come to like people who demonstrate the qualities of interpersonal communication effectiveness discussed here? What do you think is the most important quality for increasing liking?

CONVERSATIONAL EFFECTIVENESS

Skill in conversation depends on your ability to make adjustments along a number of dimensions. Recall that your listening effectiveness depends on your ability to make adjustments among participatory and passive or empathic and objective listening and that feedback effectiveness depends on adjustments between positive and negative and immediate and delayed feedback, for example. In a similar way your effectiveness in conversations depends on your ability to make adjustments along dimensions such as (1) openness, (2) empathy, (3) positiveness, (4) immediacy, (5) interaction management, (6) expressiveness, and (7) other-orientation (Figure 7.3). Your decisions would be based on all the factors discussed throughout this book—for example, the context, your relationship with the other person, the topic of conversation, the cultural influences, and so on.

As you read the discussions of these concepts, keep in mind that the most effective communicator (1) is flexible and adapts to the individual situation; (2) is mindful and aware of the situation and the available com-

Figure 7.3
The Dimensions of Interpersonal Effectiveness

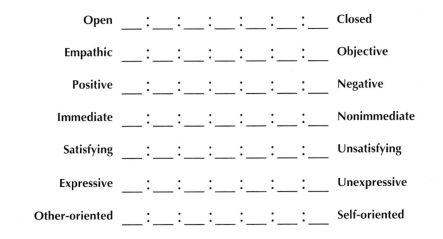

Open	__:__:__:__:__:__:__	Closed
Empathic	__:__:__:__:__:__:__	Objective
Positive	__:__:__:__:__:__:__	Negative
Immediate	__:__:__:__:__:__:__	Nonimmediate
Satisfying	__:__:__:__:__:__:__	Unsatisfying
Expressive	__:__:__:__:__:__:__	Unexpressive
Other-oriented	__:__:__:__:__:__:__	Self-oriented

William Shakespeare noted that "conversation should be pleasant without scurrility, witty without affectation, free without indecency, learned without conceitedness, novel without falsehood." How would you define effective conversation?

munication choices; and (3) uses metacommunication to avoid any real or potential ambiguity. These concepts are discussed in greater detail in the section "Thinking Critically About Interpersonal Conversation and Conflict" at the end of the chapter.

CULTURAL VIEWPOINT

Intercultural Communication Effectiveness

In applying the skills for interpersonal effectiveness, be sensitive to the cultural differences among people. What may prove effective for upper-income people working in the IBM subculture of Boston or New York may prove ineffective for lower-income people working as fruit pickers in Florida or California. What works in Japan may not work in Mexico. The direct eye contact that signals immediacy in much of the United States may be considered rude or too intrusive in Hispanic and other cultures. The empathy that most Americans will welcome may be uncomfortable for the average Korean (Yun, 1976). The specific skills discussed in this chapter are considered generally effective in much of the United States and among most people living in the United States. But note that these skills and the ways in which we communicate them are not universal throughout the world or even throughout the entire United States.

Effectiveness in intercultural communication requires that you be (Kim, 1991):

- **open** to new ideas and to differences among people
- **flexible** in ways of communicating and in adapting to the communications of the culturally different
- **tolerant** of other attitudes, values, and ways of doing things
- **creative** in seeking varied ways to communicate

These qualities—along with some knowledge of the other culture and the general skills of effectiveness—"should enable a person to approach each intercultural encounter with the psychological posture of an interested learner . . . and to strive for the communication outcomes that are as effective as possible under a given set of relational and situational constraints" (Kim, 1991).

[Next Cultural Viewpoint, page 175]

If we understand others' languages, but not their culture, we can make fluent fools of ourselves.

—WILLIAM B. GUDYKUNST

Openness

Openness refers to your willingness to self-disclose, to reveal information about yourself and also to your openness in listening to the other person. Openness also involves the degree to which you "own" your own feelings and thoughts, the degree to which you acknowledge responsibility for your thoughts and feelings. Consider the difference among these sentences:

Why do statements such as "You make me so angry," "You make me feel stupid," and "You never want to have any fun" cause interpersonal difficulties?

1. Your behavior was grossly inconsiderate.
2. Everyone thought your behavior was grossly inconsiderate.
3. I was really disturbed when you told my father he was an old man.

Comments 1 and 2 do not evidence ownership of feelings. In 1, the speaker accuses the listener of being inconsiderate without assuming any of the responsibility for the judgment. In 2, the speaker assigns responsibility to the convenient but elusive "everyone" and again assumes none of the responsibility. In comment 3, however, we see a drastic difference. Note that here the speaker takes responsibility for his or her own feelings ("*I* was really disturbed").

When you own your own messages (a way of communication which most theorists would recommend) you use **I-messages** instead of **you-messages**. Instead of saying, "You make me feel so stupid when you ask what everyone else thinks but don't ask my opinion," the person who owns his or her feelings says "I feel stupid when you ask everyone else what they think but don't ask me." When you own your feelings and thoughts, when you use I-messages, you say in effect, "This is how *I* feel," "This is how *I* see the situation," "This is what *I* think," with the *I* always paramount. Instead of saying, "This discussion is useless," one would say, "*I'm* bored by this discussion," or "*I* want to talk more about myself," or any other such statement that includes a reference to the fact that *I* am making an evaluation and not describing objective reality. By doing so, you make it explicit that your feelings are the result of the interaction between what is going on in the world outside your skin (what others say, for example) and what is going on inside your skin (your perceptions, preconceptions, attitudes, and prejudices, for example).

ETHICAL ISSUE

Questions and Answers

Here are a few communication situations that raise ethical issues. Consider each of these questions that others might ask of you; all are questions asking for information that you are presumed to have. For each question there are extenuating circumstances that may militate against your responding fully or even truthfully (these are noted as the Thought you are thinking as you consider your answer). How do you respond?

Question: *A friend asks your opinion*: How do I look?
Thought: *You look terrible but I don't want to hurt your feelings.*
Question: *An interviewer asks*: You seem a bit old for this type of job. How old are you?
Thought: *I am old for this job but I need it anyway. I don't want to turn the interviewer off because I really need this job. Yet, I don't want to reveal my age either.*
Question: *A 15-year-old asks*: Was I adopted? Who are my real parents?

Empathy

To **empathize** with someone is to feel as that person feels. When you feel empathy for another, you are able to experience what the other is experiencing from that person's point of view. Empathy does **not** mean that you agree with what the other person says or does. You never lose your own identity or your own attitudes and beliefs. To **sympathize,** on the other hand, is to feel **for** the individual—to feel sorry for the person, for example. To empathize is to feel the same feelings in the same way as the other person does. Empathy, then, enables you to understand, emotionally and intellectually, what another person is experiencing. The other half of this aspect of communication is to remain objective and view what the speaker says and feels as a totally disinterested third-party observer would.

Most people find it easier to communicate empathy in response to a person's positive statements (Heiskell & Rychiak, 1986). So perhaps you will have to exert special effort to communicate empathy for negative statements. When you experience empathy and wish to communicate it back to the speaker, try the following:

How can you tell when another person feels empathy toward you?

- Confront mixed messages. Confront messages that seem to be communicating conflicting feelings to show you are trying to understand the other person's feelings. For example, "You say that it doesn't bother you but I seem to hear a lot of anger coming through."
- Avoid judgmental and evaluative (nonempathic) responses. Avoid *should* and *ought* statements that tell the other person how he or she *should* feel. For example, avoid expressions such as "Don't feel so bad," "Don't cry," "Cheer up," "In time you'll forget all about this," and "You should start dating others; by next month you won't even remember her name."
- Use reinforcing comments. Let the speaker know that you understand what the speaker is saying and encourage the speaker to continue talking about this issue. For example, use comments such as *"I see," "I get it," "I understand," "yes,"* and *"right."*

How empathic do you consider yourself to be? Who is the most empathic person you've ever met? How did this person communicate this empathic feeling?

Women are never disarmed by compliments. Men always are.
—OSCAR WILDE

• Demonstrate interest by maintaining eye contact. Avoid scanning the room or focusing on objects or persons other than the person with whom you are interacting. Maintain physical closeness (avoid large spaces between yourself and the other person), lean toward the other person, and show your interest and agreement with your facial expressions, nods, and eye movements.

Positiveness

In most situations you strive to increase **positiveness,** although you should not ignore the importance of communicating negatively. For example, people who smile while giving criticism are believed less than those who use more negative expressions. If you communicated your criticism to one of your work assistants in too positive a tone, you would probably defeat the purpose of your criticism.

Generally, however, you want to communicate positiveness. You can state positive attitudes and you can "stroke" the person with whom you interact. Positiveness in attitudes also refers to a positive feeling for the general communication situation. A negative response to a communication makes you feel almost as if you are intruding, and communication is sure to break down.

Positiveness can be seen most clearly in the way you phrase statements. Consider these two sentences:

1. You look horrible in stripes.
2. You look your best, I think, in solid colors.

The first sentence is critical and will almost surely encourage an argument. The second sentence, on the other hand, expresses the speaker's thought clearly and positively and encourages responses that are cooperative.

In communicating positiveness:

• Don't exaggerate; positive comments and compliments work best when they are realistic and not blown out of proportion
• Be specific; instead of saying, "I liked your speech," say why you liked the speech: "Your introduction really got my attention; I especially liked the anecdote about your first day on campus."

Hager © 1992, Reprinted with special permission of King Features Syndicate.

A plastic compliment is a compliment that starts out feeling good but ends up feeling bad. "You sound good for a kid who can't carry a tune," "That looks good considering you made it," or "I like you no matter what anybody says" are examples.
—JEAN ILLSLEY CLARKE

- Own your own messages; say "I liked your report" instead of "your report was well received."
- Make sure your verbal and nonverbal messages are consistent; if your comments are genuinely felt, then your verbal and nonverbal messages are likely to be consistent; if you are only pretending to be positive, your nonverbals may betray your real feelings.

Immediacy

Immediacy refers to the degree to which the speaker and listener are connected or jointed. High immediacy refers to extreme closeness and connection; low immediacy to distance and a lack of togetherness. The communicator who demonstrates high immediacy conveys a sense of interest and attention, a liking for and an attraction to the other person. People generally respond favorably to high immediacy.

You can communicate immediacy in several ways:

Teacher immediacy behaviors, both verbal and nonverbal, are significantly related to student learning.
—JOAN GORHAM

- Maintain appropriate eye contact and limit looking around at others.
- Maintain a physical closeness, which suggests a psychological closeness.
- Use a direct and open body posture, for example, by arranging your body to keep others out.
- Smile and otherwise express that you are interested in and care about the other person.
- Use the other person's name, for example, say "Joe, what do you think?" instead of "What do you think?" Say, "I like that, Mary" instead of "I like that."
- Focus on the other person's remarks. Make the speaker know that you heard and understood what was said and will base your feedback on it. For example, use questions that ask for clarification or elaboration. Also, refer to the speaker's previous remarks.
- Reinforce, reward, or compliment the other person. Make use of such expressions as "I like your new outfit" or "Your comments were really to the point."

There are times when you may want to communicate a lack of immediacy, for example, in discouraging romantic advances, in criticizing a subordinate, or in registering a complaint. Obviously, in these situations, you would seek to avoid using the suggestions offered above.

Interaction Management (Satisfaction)

The effective communicator *manages the interaction to the satisfaction of both parties.* In most cases you would manage the interaction so that neither person feels ignored or on stage, so that each can contribute to the total communication interchange. Maintaining your role as speaker or listener and passing back and forth the opportunity to speak are interaction management skills. If one person speaks all the time and the other listens all the time, effective conversation becomes difficult if not impossible. Here are two additional suggestions for effective interactive management:

Groucho Marx once observed, "Years ago, I tried to top everybody, but I don't anymore. I realized it was killing conversation. When you're always trying for a topper you aren't really listening. It ruins communication." How would you explain "conversational killers"?

- Avoid interrupting the other person; interruption signals that what you have to say is more important than what the other person is saying and puts the other person in an inferior position. The result is dissatisfaction with the conversation.
- Keep the conversation flowing and fluent without long and awkward pauses that make everyone uncomfortable.

One of the best ways to look at interaction management is to take the self-test "Are You a High Self-Monitor?" This test will help you to identify the qualities that make for the effective management of interpersonal communication situations.

High self-monitors place relatively great emphasis on, and therefore pay considerable attention to, exterior appearances when choosing whether or not to date someone. Low self-monitors place relatively great emphasis on, and are therefore sensitive to, the interior qualities of their prospective dating partners.
—MARK SNYDER

TEST YOURSELF
Are You a High Self-Monitor?

Instructions: These statements concern personal reactions to a number of different situations. No two statements are exactly alike, so consider each statement carefully before answering. If a statement is true, or mostly true, as applied to you, write T. If a statement is false, or not usually true, as applied to you, write F.

_____ 1. I find it hard to imitate the behavior of other people.
_____ 2. I guess I do put on a show to impress or entertain people.
_____ 3. I would probably make a good actor.
_____ 4. I sometimes appear to others to be experiencing deeper emotions than I actually am.
_____ 5. In a group of people, I am rarely the center of attention.
_____ 6. In different situations and with different people, I often act like very different persons.
_____ 7. I can only argue for ideas I already believe.
_____ 8. In order to get along and be liked, I tend to be what people expect me to be rather than who I really am.
_____ 9. I may deceive people by being friendly when I really dislike them.
_____ 10. I am always the person I appear to be.

Thinking Critically About Self-Monitoring Give yourself one point for each of questions 1, 5, and 7 that you answered F. Give yourself one point for each of the remaining questions that you answered T. Add up your points. If you are a good judge of yourself and scored 7 or above, you are probably a high self-monitoring individual; 3 or below, you are probably a low self-monitoring individual.

Self-monitoring, the manipulation of the image that you present to others in your interpersonal interactions, is integrally related to interpersonal interaction management. High self-monitors carefully adjust their behaviors on the basis of feedback from others so that they produce the most desirable effect. Low self-monitors are not concerned with the image they present to others. Rather, they communicate their thoughts and feelings with no attempt to manipulate the impressions they create. Most of us lie somewhere between the two extremes.

High self-monitors are more apt to take charge of a situation, are more sensitive to the deceptive techniques of others, and are better able to detect self-monitoring or impression management techniques when used by others.

High self-monitors prefer to interact with low self-monitors, over whom they are able to assume positions of influence and power (Snyder, 1986). These, of course, are the extremes; most of us engage in selective self-monitoring. For example, if you go for a job interview, you are more likely to monitor your behaviors than if you are talking with a group of friends.

Source: This test appeared in Mark Snyder, "The Many Me's of the Self-Monitor," *Psychology Today* 13 (March 1980): 34.

Expressiveness

Expressiveness refers to the degree to which you display involvement in the interpersonal interaction. The expressive speaker plays the game instead of just watching it as a spectator. Expressiveness is similar to openness in its concern with involvement. It includes taking responsibility for your thoughts and feelings, encouraging expressiveness or openness in others, and providing appropriate feedback.

This quality also includes taking responsibility for both talking and listening and in this way is similar to interaction management. In conflict situations, expressiveness involves fighting actively and stating disagreement directly. Expressiveness means using I-messages in which you accept responsibility for your thoughts and feelings, for example, "I'm bored when I don't get to talk" or "I want to talk more," rather than you-messages ("you ignore me," "you don't ask my opinion"). It is the opposite of fighting passively, withdrawing from the encounter, or attributing responsibility to others.

When you want to communicate expressiveness, consider the following:

- Practice active listening by paraphrasing, expressing understanding of the thoughts and feelings of the other person, and asking relevant questions.
- Avoid clichés and trite expressions that signal a lack of personal involvement and originality.
- Avoid sending mixed messages—messages (verbal or nonverbal) that are communicated simultaneously but that contradict each other— and address those you detect in others.
- Address messages that somehow seem unrealistic to you (for example, statements claiming that the break-up of a long-term relationship is completely forgotten or that failing a course doesn't mean anything).
- Use I-messages to signal personal involvement and a willingness to share your feelings. Instead of saying "You never give me a chance to make any decisions," say "I'd like to contribute to the decisions that affect both of us."
- Use appropriate variations in vocal rate, pitch, volume, and rhythm to convey involvement and interest and by allowing your facial muscles to reflect and echo this inner involvement.
- Use gestures appropriately; too few gestures may signal disinterest, while too many may communicate discomfort, uneasiness, and awkwardness.

How expressive are you? Ask a close friend to comment on your expressiveness. Do your opinions match?

When, for example, you want to discourage a talkative person or when you want to avoid leading the speaker in any way, you may wish to limit your expressiveness. Your own expressiveness reinforces the other person and as a result the more that person will talk. If you want to discourage the other person from talking, you need to limit your expressiveness.

Other-Orientation

Other-orientation is the opposite of self-orientation and is the generally desired mode of communication. It involves the ability to communicate attentiveness and interest in the other person and in what is being said. Without other-orientation each person pursues his or her own goal; cooperation and working together to achieve a common goal are absent.

Other-orientation demonstrates consideration and respect—for example, asking if it's all right to dump your troubles on someone before doing so or asking if your phone call comes at an inopportune time before launching into your conversation. Other-orientation involves acknowledging others' feelings as legitimate: "I can understand why you're so angry; I would be too."

You can communicate other-orientation in a number of ways:

- Use eye contact, smiles, and head nods; lean toward the other person; display feelings and emotions through appropriate facial expression.
- Avoid focusing on yourself (as in primping or preening, for example) or on anyone other than the person to whom you're speaking (through frequent or prolonged eye contact or body orientation).
- Ask the other person for suggestions, opinions, and clarification as appropriate. Statements such as "How do you feel about it?" or "What do you think?" will go a long way toward focusing the communication on the other person.
- Express agreement when appropriate. Comments such as "You're right" or "That's interesting" help to focus the interaction on the other person, which encourages greater openness.
- Use minimal responses to encourage the other person to express himself or herself. Minimal responses are those brief expressions that encourage another to continue talking without intruding on his or her thoughts and feelings or directing him or her to go in any particular direction. For example, "yes," "I see," or even "a-ha" or "hmm" are minimal responses that tell the other person that you are interested in his or her continued comments.
- Use positive affect statements to refer to the other person and to his or her contributions to the interaction; for example, "I really enjoy talking with you" or "That was a clever way of looking at things" are positive affect statements that are often felt but rarely expressed.

There are times when you may want to be more self-oriented and self-focused. For example, in employment interview situations, the interviewee is expected to talk about himself or herself and to do more of the speaking than the listening. On the other hand, if you are being interviewed because of something you accomplished, you obviously don't want to focus the conversation on the interviewer; rather, you're expected

What quality of interpersonal communication effectiveness most closely draws you to others? What quality is the most difficult for you to incorporate into your own interpersonal behaviors? Why?

Which strategies (unproductive as well as productive) do you use in your own interpersonal conflicts? Which strategies do you most resent others using on you? Will this discussion influence you to change the way in which you engage in interpersonal conflict?

to focus the conversation on yourself. In this situation, you would obviously not ask the interviewer for suggestions or opinions or use minimal responses to encourage the interviewer to express himself or herself. But, you would be positive, use focused eye contact, lean toward the other person, and so on.

INTERPERSONAL CONFLICT

Where there is no difference, there is only indifference.
—LOUIS NIZER

Tom wants to go to the movies and Sara wants to stay home. Tom's insisting on going to the movies interferes with Sara's staying home and Sara's determination to stay home interferes with Tom's going to the movies. Randy and Grace have been dating. Randy wants to get married; Grace wants to continue dating. Each has opposing goals and each interferes with the other's attaining these goals.

As experience shows, relational conflicts can be of various types: goals to be pursued ("We want you to go to college and become a teacher or a doctor, not a disco dancer"); allocation of resources such as money or

Never go to bed mad. Stay up
and fight.

—PHYLLIS DILLER

time ("I want to spend the tax refund on a car, not on new furniture");
decisions to be made ("I refuse to have the Jeffersons over for dinner");
or behaviors that are considered appropriate or desirable by one person
and inappropriate or undesirable by the other ("I hate it when you get
drunk, pinch me, ridicule me in front of others, flirt with others, dress
provocatively . . .").

Myths About Conflict

One of the problems in dealing with interpersonal conflict is that we may
be operating with false assumptions about what conflict is and what it
means. For example, do you think the following are true or false?

- If two people in a relationship fight, it means their relationship is a
  bad one.
- Fighting hurts an interpersonal relationship.
- Fighting is bad because it reveals our negative selves—for example,
  our pettiness, our need to be in control, our unreasonable expectations.

What beliefs do you have about
interpersonal conflict? How do
these beliefs influence the way you
engage in interpersonal conflict?

As in most cases, simple answers are usually wrong. The three assumptions above may all be true or may all be false—it depends. In and of
itself, conflict is neither good nor bad. Conflict is a part of every interpersonal relationship, between parents and children, brothers and sisters,
friends, lovers, co-workers. If it isn't, then the relationship is probably
dull, irrelevant, or insignificant. It is not so much the conflict that creates
the problem as the way in which the individuals approach and deal with
the conflict. Because of this, the major portion of this chapter focuses on
ways of managing conflict rather than avoiding it.

Content and Relationship Conflicts

In one sentence, how would you
describe your style of conflict?

Using concepts developed earlier (Chapter 1), you can distinguish between content and relationship conflict. **Content conflict** centers on objects, events, and persons in the world that are usually, but not always, external to the parties involved in the conflict. These include the millions of
issues that we argue and fight about every day—the value of a particular
movie, what to watch on television, the fairness of the last examination or
job promotion, and the way to spend your savings.

Relationship conflicts are equally numerous and include such conflict situations as a younger brother who does not obey his older
brother, two partners who each want an equal say in making vacation
plans, and the mother and daughter who each want to have the final
word concerning the daughter's life-style. Here the conflicts are concerned not so much with some external object as with the relationships
between the individuals, with such issues as who is in charge, the
equality of a primary relationship, and who has the right to set down
rules of behavior.

Content and relationship conflicts are easier to separate in a textbook
than they are in real life, where many conflicts contain elements of both.
But it helps if you can recognize which issues pertain primarily to content
and which pertain primarily to relationship.

The Negatives and Positives of Conflict

Among the potential negative aspects of conflict is that it may lead to increased negative regard for your "opponent" (who may be your best friend or lover). Conflict frequently leads to a depletion of energy better spent on other areas. At times conflict may lead you to close yourself off from the other person. When you hide your true self from an intimate, you prevent meaningful communication.

The major positive value of interpersonal conflict is that it forces you to examine a problem and work toward a potential solution. If productive conflict strategies are used, the relationship may emerge from the encounter stronger, healthier, and more satisfying than before. Also, the fact that you are trying to resolve a conflict usually means that you feel the relationship is worth the effort; otherwise you would walk away from such a conflict.

Conflict enables each participant to state what he or she wants and—if the conflict is resolved effectively—perhaps to get it. For example, let's say that I want to spend our money on a new car (my old one is unreliable) and you want to spend it on a vacation (you feel the need for a change of pace). Through our conflict and its resolution, we hopefully learn what each really wants. We may then be able to figure out a way for both of us to get what we want. I might accept a good used car and you might accept a less expensive vacation. Or we might buy a used car and take an inexpensive motor trip. Either of these solutions would satisfy both of us; they are win-win solutions. But of us win, both of us get what we wanted.

CONFLICT MANAGEMENT

Throughout the process of resolving conflict, avoid the common but damaging strategies that can destroy a relationship. At the same time, consciously apply those strategies that will help resolve the conflict and even improve the relationship. Here we consider five general strategies, each of which has a destructive and a productive dimension.

Avoidance and Fighting Actively

Avoidance may involve actual physical flight. You may leave the scene of the conflict (walk out of the apartment or go to another part of the office or shop), fall asleep, or blast the stereo to drown out all conversation. It may also take the form of emotional or intellectual avoidance. Here you may leave the conflict psychologically by not dealing with any of the arguments or problems raised.

Instead of avoiding the issues, take an active role in your interpersonal conflicts. Don't close your ears (or mind), blast the stereo, or walk out of the house during an argument. This is not to say that a cooling-off period is not at times desirable. It is to say, instead, that if you wish to resolve conflicts, you need to confront them actively.

Another part of active fighting involves taking responsibility for your thoughts and feelings. For example, when you disagree with your partner or find fault with her or his behavior, take responsibility for these feelings. Say, for example, "I disagree with . . ." or "I don't like it when you . . ."

Every difficulty slurred over will be a ghost to disturb your repose later on.

—CHOPIN

Power Plays: Ignoring and Neutralizing

What do you do when confronted by power plays such as Nobody Upstairs, You Owe Me, or Thought Stoppers? One commonly employed response is to ignore the power play and allow the other person to control the conversation and us. Some people ignore power plays because they don't recognize them as consistent patterns of behavior. They don't realize that this other person behaves this way repeatedly in order to maintain power. Others ignore this behavior for fear that any objection might start an argument. They therefore elect the lesser of the two evils and ignore the power play.

Another response is what Steiner calls neutralizing the power play. In this type of response, you treat the power play as an isolated instance (rather than as a pattern of behavior) and object to it. For example, you might say quite simply, "Please don't come into my room without knocking first" or "Please don't look in my wallet without permission."

[Next Power Perspective, page 171]

Avoid statements that deny your responsibility, for example, "Everybody thinks you're wrong about . . ." or "Chris thinks you shouldn't . . ."

Force and Talk

When confronted with conflict, many people prefer not to deal with the issues but rather to physically force their position on the other person. The force may be emotional or physical. In either case, however, the issues are avoided and the person who "wins" is the one who exerts the most force. This is the technique of warring nations, children, and even some normally sensible and mature adults. This is surely one of the most serious problems confronting relationships today, but many approach it as if it were of only minor importance or even something humorous, as in the accompanying cartoon.

More than over 50 percent of both single and married couples report that they have experienced physical violence in their relationship. If we add symbolic violence (for example, threatening to hit the other person or throwing something), the percentages are above 60 percent for singles and above 70 percent for marrieds (Marshall & Rose, 1987). In another study, 47 percent of a sample of 410 college students reported some experience with violence in a dating relationship. In most cases the violence was reciprocal—both people in the relationship used violence. In cases where only one person was violent, the research results are conflicting. For example, Deal and Wampler (1986) found that in cases where one partner was violent, the aggressor was significantly more often the female partner. Earlier research found a similar sex difference (for example, Cate, Henton, Koval, Christopher, & Lloyd, 1982). Other research, however, has found that the popular conception of men being more likely to use force than women is indeed true (Deturck, 1987): Men are more apt than women to use violent methods to achieve compliance.

One of the most puzzling findings is that many victims of violence interpret it as a sign of love. For some reason, they see being beaten, verbally abused, or raped as a sign that their partner is fully in love with

Drawing by Ziegler; © 1993
The New Yorker Magazine, Inc.

"What's amazing to me is that this late in the game we still have to settle our differences with rocks."

Power Plays: Cooperating

In addition to dealing with power plays by ignoring and neutralizing them, you can also respond cooperatively. This generally preferred response consists of the following (Steiner, 1981):

a. Express your feelings. Tell the person that you are angry or annoyed or disturbed by his or her behavior.

b. Describe the behavior to which you object. Tell the person—in language that describes rather than evaluates—the specific behavior that you object to, for example, reading your mail, persisting in trying to hug you.

c. State a cooperative response that you both can live with comfortably. Tell the person in a cooperative tone what you want; for example: "I want you to stop reading my mail." "I want you to stop trying to hug me when I tell you to stop."

A cooperative response to Nobody Upstairs might go something like this: "I'm angry (*statement of feelings*) that you persist in opening my mail. You have opened my mail four times this past week alone (*description of the behavior to which you object*). I want to open my own mail. If there is anything in it that concerns you, I will let you know (*statement of cooperative response*)." How would you respond cooperatively to the power plays You Owe Me and Thought Stoppers, following the three-part strategy suggested here?

[Next Power Perspective, page 194]

them. Many victims, in fact, accept the blame for contributing to the violence instead of blaming their partners (Gelles & Cornell, 1985).

The only real alternative to force is talk. Instead of force, we need to talk and listen. The qualities of openness, empathy, and positiveness, for example, discussed earlier are suitable starting points.

Gunnysacking and Present Focus

A gunnysack is a large bag usually made of burlap. As a conflict strategy, **gunnysacking** refers to the practice of storing up grievances so we may unload them at another time. The immediate occasion may be relatively simple (or so it might seem at first), such as someone's coming home late without calling. Instead of arguing about this, the gunnysacker unloads all past grievances. The birthday you forgot, the time you arrived late for dinner, the hotel reservations you forgot to make are all noted. As you probably know from experience, gunnysacking begets gunnysacking. When one person gunnysacks, the other person gunnysacks. The result is that we have two people dumping their stored-up grievances on one another. Frequently the original problem never gets addressed. Instead, resentment and hostility escalate.

Focus your conflict on the here and now rather than on issues that occurred two months ago. Similarly, focus your conflict on the person with whom you are fighting, and not on the person's mother, child, or friends.

Attack and Acceptance

An attack can come in many forms. In **personal rejection,** for example, one party to a conflict withholds love and affection. He or she seeks to win the argument by getting the other person to break down in the face of this withdrawal. The individual acts cold and uncaring in an effort to demoralize the other person. In withdrawing affection, the individual hopes to make the other person question his or her own self-worth. Once the other is demoralized and feels less than worthy, it is relatively easy for the rejector to get his or her way. The person, in other words, holds out the renewal of love and affection as a reward for resolving the conflict in his or her favor.

Much like fighters in a ring, each of us has a "belt line." When you attack someone by hitting below the belt, a tactic called **beltlining,** you can inflict serious injury. When you hit above the belt, however, the person is able to absorb the blow. With most interpersonal relationships, especially those of long standing, we know where the belt line is. You know, for example, that to hit Pat with the inability to have children is to hit below the belt. You know that to hit Chris with the failure to get a permanent job is to hit below the belt. Hitting below the belt line causes all persons involved added problems. Keep blows to areas your opponent can absorb and handle.

Express positive feelings for the other person and for the relationship between the two of you. In fact, recent research shows that positiveness is a crucial factor in the survival of a relationship (Gottman, 1994). Throughout any conflict, many harsh words will probably be exchanged, later to be regretted. The words cannot be unsaid or uncommunicated, but they can be partially offset by the expression of positive statements. If you are engaged in combat with someone you love, remember that you are fighting with a loved one and express that feeling. "I love you very much, but I still don't want your mother on vacation with us. I want to be alone with you."

Verbal Aggressiveness and Argumentativeness

An especially interesting perspective on conflict is emerging from the work on verbal aggressiveness and argumentativeness (Infante & Rancer, 1982; Infante, 1988; Infante & Wigley, 1986).

Verbal aggressiveness is a method of winning an argument by inflicting psychological pain—by attacking the other person's self-concept. It is a type of disconfirmation in that it seeks to discredit the person's view of himself or herself. This is often the talk that leads to force (Infante & Wigley, 1986; Infante, Sabourin, Rudd, & Shannon, 1990; Infante, Riddle, Horvath, & Tumlin, 1992).

On the other hand, **argumentativeness,** contrary to popular usage, refers to a quality to be cultivated rather than avoided. It refers to your willingness to argue for a point of view, your tendency to speak your mind on significant issues. It is the mode of dealing with disagreements that is the preferred alternative to verbal aggressiveness. Before reading about ways to increase your argumentativeness, take the following heavily researched test of argumentativeness.

....

TEST YOURSELF

How Argumentative Are You?

This questionnaire contains statements about controversial issues. Indicate how often each statement is true for you personally according to the following scale:

1 = *almost never true*
2 = *rarely true*
3 = *occasionally true*
4 = *often true*
5 = *almost always true*

_____ 1. While in an argument, I worry that the person I am arguing with will form a negative impression of me.

_____ 2. Arguing over controversial issues improves my intelligence.

_____ 3. I enjoy avoiding arguments.

_____ 4. I am energetic and enthusiastic when I argue.

_____ 5. Once I finish an argument, I promise myself that I will not get into another.

_____ 6. Arguing with a person creates more problems for me than it solves.

_____ 7. I have a pleasant, good feeling when I win a point in an argument.

_____ 8. When I finish arguing with anyone, I feel nervous and upset.

_____ 9. I enjoy a good argument over a controversial issue.

_____ 10. I get an unpleasant feeling when I realize I am about to get into an argument.

_____ 11. I enjoy defending my point of view on an issue.

_____ 12. I am happy when I keep an argument from happening.

_____ 13. I do not like to miss the opportunity to argue a controversial issue.
_____ 14. I prefer being with people who rarely disagree with me.
_____ 15. I consider an argument an exciting intellectual challenge.
_____ 16. I find myself unable to think of effective points during an argument.
_____ 17. I feel refreshed and satisfied after an argument on a controversial issue.
_____ 18. I have the ability to do well in an argument.
_____ 19. I try to avoid getting into arguments.
_____ 20. I feel excitement when I expect that a conversation I am in is leading to an argument.

Thinking Critically About Argumentativeness To compute your argumentativeness score follow these steps:

1. add your scores on items 2, 4, 7, 9, 11, 13, 15, 17, 18, and 20.
2. add 60 to the sum obtained in Step 1.
3. add your scores on items 1, 3, 5, 6, 8, 10, 12, 14, 16, 19.
4. to compute your argumentativeness score, subtract the total obtained in step 3 from the total obtained in step 2.

The following guidelines will help you interpret your score:

scores between 73 and 100 indicate high argumentativeness
scores between 56 and 72 indicate moderate argumentativeness
scores between 20 and 55 indicate low argumentativeness

Generally, those who score high in argumentativeness have a strong tendency to state their position on controversial issues and argue against the positions of others. A high scorer sees arguing as exciting, intellectually challenging, and as an opportunity to win a kind of contest.

The moderately argumentative person possesses some of the qualities of the highly argumentative and some of the qualities of the low argumentative. The person who scores low in argumentativeness tries to prevent arguments. This person experiences satisfaction not from arguing, but from avoiding arguments. The low argumentative sees arguing as unpleasant and unsatisfying. Not surprisingly this person has little confidence in his or her ability to argue effectively.

The researchers who developed this test note that both high and low argumentatives may experience communication difficulties. The high argumentative, for example, may argue needlessly, too often, and too forcefully. The low argumentative, on the other hand, may avoid taking a stand even when it seems necessary. Persons scoring somewhere in the middle are probably the more interpersonally skilled and adaptable, arguing when it is necessary but avoiding the many arguments that are needless and repetitive. Does your experience support this observation?

Source: This scale was developed by Dominic Infante and Andrew Rancer and appears in Infante and Rancer (1982).

....

Here are some suggestions for cultivating argumentativeness and for preventing it from degenerating into aggressiveness (Infante, 1988):

• Treat disagreements as objectively as possible; avoid assuming that because someone takes issue with your position or your interpretation that they are attacking you as a person.
• Avoid attacking the other person (rather than the person's arguments), even if this would give you a tactical advantage; it will

Which strategies (unproductive as well as productive) do you use in your own interpersonal conflicts? Which do you most resent others using? Why? Will this discussion influence you to change the way you engage in interpersonal conflict?

probably backfire at some later time and make your relationship more difficult. Center your arguments on issues rather than personalities.

- Reaffirm the other person's sense of competence; compliment the other person as appropriate.
- Avoid interrupting; allow the other person to state her or his position fully before you respond.
- Stress equality (see Chapter 1) and stress the similarities that you have with the other person; stress your areas of agreement before attacking the disagreements.
- Express interest in the other person's position, attitude, and point of view.
- Avoid presenting your arguments too emotionally; using an overly loud voice or interjecting vulgar expressions will prove offensive and eventually ineffective.
- Allow the other person to save face; never humiliate the other person.

BEFORE AND AFTER THE CONFLICT

If you are to make conflict truly productive you will need to consider a few suggestions for preparing for the conflict and for using the conflict as a method for relational growth.

Before the Conflict

Try to fight in private. In front of others, you may not be willing to be totally honest; you may feel you have to save face and therefore must win the fight at all costs. You also run the risk of incurring resentment and hostility by embarrassing your partner in front of others.

Although conflicts arise at the most inopportune time, we can choose the time when we will try to resolve them. Confronting your partner when she or he comes home after a hard day of work may not be the right time for resolving a conflict. Make sure you are both relatively free of other problems and ready to deal with the conflict at hand.

Know what you're fighting about. Only when you define your differences in specific terms, can you begin to understand them and, hence, resolve them. Fight about problems that can be solved. Fighting about past behaviors or about family members or situations over which you have no control solves nothing.

After the Conflict

Learn from the conflict and from the process you went through in trying to resolve it. For example, can you identify the fight strategies that aggravated the situation? Does your partner need a cooling-off period? Do you need extra space when upset? Can you tell when minor issues are going to escalate into major arguments? Does avoidance make matters worse? What issues are particularly disturbing and likely to cause difficulties? Can these be avoided?

What one characteristic of interpersonal communication effectiveness do you think is the most important for effective intercultural communication?

Keep the conflict in perspective. Be careful not to blow it out of proportion, when you begin to define your relationship in terms of conflict. Avoid the tendency to see disagreement as inevitably leading to major blow-ups. Conflicts in most relationships actually occupy a very small percentage of the couple's time and yet in the couple's recollection, arguments often loom extremely large.

Attack your negative feelings. Negative feelings frequently arise because unfair fight strategies such as personal rejection, manipulation, or force, were used to undermine the other person. Resolve surely to avoid such unfair tactics in the future, but at the same time let go of guilt and blame, for yourself and your partner. If you think it would help, discuss these feelings with your partner or even a therapist.

Increase the exchange of rewards and cherishing behaviors to demonstrate your positive feelings and that you are over the conflict. It's a good way of saying you want the relationship to survive and to flourish.

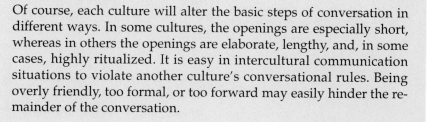

CULTURAL VIEWPOINT

Conversation, Conflict, and Culture

Of course, each culture will alter the basic steps of conversation in different ways. In some cultures, the openings are especially short, whereas in others the openings are elaborate, lengthy, and, in some cases, highly ritualized. It is easy in intercultural communication situations to violate another culture's conversational rules. Being overly friendly, too formal, or too forward may easily hinder the remainder of the conversation.

You cannot shake hands with a clenched fist.

—INDIRA GANDHI

The reasons that such violations may have significant consequences is that you may not be aware of these rules and hence may not see violations as cultural differences but rather as aggressiveness, stuffiness, or pushiness—and almost immediately dislike the person and put a negative cast on the future conversation.

Also, members of different cultures are likely to pursue conflict differently. For example, in a study of Chinese and American students, it was found that Chinese students were more likely to pursue a conflict with a non-Chinese than with a Chinese student. Americans, on the other hand, were more likely to pursue a conflict with another American than with a non-American (Leung, 1988).

Members of different cultures will also view conflict management techniques differently. For example, one study (Collier, 1991) found that African-American men preferred clear argument and a focus on problem-solving while African-American women preferred assertiveness and respect. Mexican-American men emphasized mutual understanding through discussing the reasons for the conflict while women focused on support for the relationship. Anglo-American men preferred direct and rational argument while women preferred flexibility. These examples underlie the important principle that different cultures will view interpersonal conflict techniques differently.

[Next Cultural Viewpoint, page 191]

THINKING CRITICALLY ABOUT INTERPERSONAL CONVERSATION AND CONFLICT

Because each conversation and each conflict is unique, the qualities of interpersonal effectiveness cannot be applied indiscriminately. You need to know how the skills themselves should be applied. We suggest that you be mindful, flexible, and that you use metacommunication skills as appropriate.

Mindfulness

After you have learned a skill or rule you may have a tendency to apply it without thinking or "mindlessly," without, for example, considering the novel aspects of a situation. For instance, after learning the skills of active listening, many will use them in response to all situations. Some of these responses will be appropriate but others will prove inappropriate and ineffective. In interpersonal and even in small group situations (Elmes & Gemmill, 1990), apply the skills mindfully (Langer, 1989).

Langer (1989) offers several suggestions for increasing mindfulness:

• Create and recreate categories. See an object, event, or person as belonging to a wide variety of categories. Avoid storing in memory an image of a person, for example, with only one specific label; it will be difficult to recategorize it later.

- Be open to new information even if it contradicts your most firmly held stereotypes.
- Be open to different points of view. This will help you avoid the tendency to blame outside forces for your negative behaviors ("that test was unfair") and internal forces for the negative behaviors of others ("Pat didn't study," "Pat isn't very bright"). Be willing to see your own and others' behaviors from a variety of perspectives.
- Be careful of relying too heavily on first impressions, what is sometimes called premature cognitive commitment (Chanowitz & Langer, 1981; Langer, 1989). Treat your first impressions as tentative, as hypotheses.

Flexibility

Respond to each of the following statements according to the following scale:

A = almost always true
B = frequently true
C = sometimes true
D = infrequently true
E = almost never true

_____ 1. People should be frank and spontaneous in conversation.

_____ 2. When angry, a person should say nothing rather than say something he or she will be sorry for later.

_____ 3. When talking to your friends, you should adjust your remarks to suit them.

_____ 4. It is better to speak your gut feelings than to beat around the bush.

_____ 5. If people would open up to each other the world would be better off.

The preferred answer to all five of these statements, taken from research on rhetorical sensitivity, is C, and this underscores the importance of flexibility (Hart & Burks, 1972; Hart, Carlson, & Eadie, 1980) in all interpersonal encounters. Here are a few suggestions for cultivating flexibility:

- Recall the principle of indiscrimination (Chapter 5)—no two things or situations are exactly alike. Ask yourself what is different about this situation?
- Recall that communication always takes place in a context (Chapter 1); ask yourself what is unique about this specific context that might alter your communications. Will cultural differences play a role in this communication?
- Recall that everything is in a constant state of change (Chapter 5) and therefore responses that were appropriate yesterday may not be appropriate today. Responding protectively when your child is 5 might be appropriate; at 18 that same response may be inappropriate. Also, recognize that sudden changes may also exert great influence on communication: the death of a lover, the knowledge of a fatal illness, the birth of a child, a promotion are just a few examples.

- Recall that everyone is different. Thus, you may need to be frank and spontaneous when talking with a close friend about your feelings, but you may not want to be so open when talking with your grandmother about the dinner she prepared that you disliked.

Metacommunicational Ability

Much talk concerns people, objects, and events in the world. But you can also talk about your talk—you can metacommunicate (Chapter 1). Your interpersonal effectiveness will often hinge on this ability to metacommunicate. Let's say that someone says something positive but in a negative way; for example, "Yes, I think you did . . . a good job," but with no enthusiasm and an avoidance of eye contact. You are faced with several alternatives. You may respond to the message as positive or as negative.

A third alternative, however, is to talk about the message and say something like, "I'm not sure I understand if you're pleased or displeased with what I did. You said you were pleased but I detect dissatisfaction in your voice. Am I wrong?" In this way, you may avoid lots of misunderstandings.

Here are a few suggestions for increasing your metacommunicational effectiveness:

- Give clear feedforward. This will help the other person get a general picture of the message that will follow; it will provide a kind of schema which makes information processing and learning easier.
- Confront contradictory or inconsistent messages. At the same time, explain your own messages, which may appear inconsistent to your listener.
- Explain the feelings that go with the thoughts. Often people communicate only the thinking part of their message with the result that listeners are not able to appreciate the other parts of your meaning.
- Paraphrase your own complex messages. Similarly, to check on your own understanding of another's message, paraphrase what you think the other person means and ask if you are accurate.
- Ask questions. If you have doubts about another's meaning, don't assume; instead, ask.
- When you do talk about your talk, do so only to gain an understanding of the other person's thoughts and feelings. Avoid substituting talk about talk for talk about a specific problem.

Feedback on Concepts and Skills

In this chapter we looked at the nature of interpersonal communication, especially the qualities that make for effectiveness in interpersonal communication (in general) and in interpersonal conflict.

1. The conversation process consists of at least five steps: opening, feedforward, business, feedback, and closing.

2. The qualities of interpersonal communication effectiveness are openness, empathy, positiveness, immediacy, interaction management, expressiveness, and other-orientation.

3. Useful guides to fair fighting are: fight actively; use talk instead of force; focus on the present rather than gunnysacking; express acceptance instead of attacking the other person; and use your skills in argumentation, not in verbal aggressiveness.

4. In thinking critically about both interpersonal effectiveness and interpersonal conflict, do so mindfully, flexibly, and with metacommunication as appropriate.

The skills covered in this chapter are vital to effective interpersonal interactions and relationships. Check your ability to use these skills. Use the following rating scale: (1) = almost always, (2) = often, (3) = sometimes, (4) = rarely, (5) = almost never.

_____ 1. I open conversations with comfort and confidence.

_____ 2. I use feedforward that is appropriate to my message and purpose.

_____ 3. I exchange roles as speaker and listener to maintain mutual conversational satisfaction.

_____ 4. I vary my feedback as appropriate on the basis of positiveness, focus (person or message), immediacy, degree of monitoring, and supportiveness.

_____ 5. I close conversations at the appropriate time and with the appropriate parting signals.

_____ 6. I practice an appropriate degree of openness.

_____ 7. I communicate empathy to others.

_____ 8. I express supportiveness.

_____ 9. I communicate positiveness in attitudes and through stroking others.

_____ 10. I express equality in my interpersonal interactions.

_____ 11. I communicate confidence in voice and bodily actions.

_____ 12. I express immediacy both verbally and nonverbally.

_____ 13. I manage interpersonal interactions to the satisfaction of both parties.

_____ 14. I self-monitor my verbal and nonverbal behaviors in order to communicate the desired impression.

_____ 15. I communicate expressiveness verbally and nonverbally.

_____ 16. I communicate other-orientation in my interactions.

_____ 17. I avoid using unproductive methods of conflict resolution.

_____ 18. I make active use of fair-fighting guides.

_____ 19. I approach communication situations with an appropriate degree of mindfulness.

_____ 20. I engage in communication with cultural awareness.

_____ 21. I am flexible in the way I communicate and adjust my communications on the basis of the unique situation.

_____ 22. I use metacommunication to clarify ambiguous meanings.

Skill Development Experiences

7.1 Giving and Receiving Compliments

One of the most difficult forms of interpersonal communication is giving compliments gracefully and comfortably. This exercise is designed to help you gain some experience in phrasing these seemingly simple sentences. Presented below are several situations that might normally call for giving the other person a compliment. For each situation, write at least two compliments that are appropriate to the situation.

1. Your friend has just received an A on the history final. Sample Response: *That's just great. You're going to have a great GPA this semester.*
2. Your mother has just prepared an exceptional dinner.
3. Your kid brother tells you he hit a home run in the little league game.
4. Your teacher gave an exceptionally interesting lecture.
5. Your classmate has just received a scholarship to graduate school.
6. Your friend comes to class in a new outfit that looks particularly good.
7. A stranger on a train moves over so that you can sit down.
8. A friend offers to lend you the money you need to buy that new pair of jeans.
9. A waiter has given your table particularly good service.
10. A colleague from work not only remembers your birthday but gives you a really great gift.

Perhaps even more difficult than giving compliments is receiving them without awkwardness and uneasiness. Too often people respond to compliments in inappropriate ways that make it even more difficult for the person offering the compliment. Respond to the following compliments by (a) acknowledging the compliment and your pleasure in receiving it, and (b) thanking the person for the compliment.

1. That was a persuasive argument you made. You're articulate. Sample Response: *Thanks. I appreciate that. I worked all last night on that seemingly off-the-cuff speech.*
2. Wow! You look terrific.
3. You should have no trouble getting that job. You have everything they're asking for—intelligence, communication ability, and dedication.
4. Your hair looks great. How did you do it?
5. You really are an expert at the computer.
6. I appreciate your helping me with this term paper. You're a good friend.
7. That dinner was the best I've had all year.
8. Your latest book was the best I've read all year. You have a great writing style—so smooth and easy.
9. You deserved that scholarship.
10. I truly enjoyed this class. It was the best class I had all semester.

7.2 Speaking Positively

This exercise is performed by the entire class. One person is "it" and takes a seat in the front of the room or in the center of the circle. (It is possible, though not desirable, for the person to stay where she or he normally sits.) Going around the circle or from left to right, each person says something positive about the person who is "it." For this exercise, only volunteers should be chosen. Students should be encouraged but not forced to participate. It is best done when the students know each other fairly well.

Persons must tell the truth; that is, they are not allowed to say anything about a person that they do not believe. At the same time, however, all statements must be positive. Persons may, however, "pass" and say nothing. No one may ask why something was said or not said. The positive words may refer to the person's looks, behavior, intelligence, clothes, mannerisms, and so on. One may also say, "I don't know you very well, but you seem friendly," or "You seem honest," or whatever. These statements, too, must be believed to be true.

After everyone has said something, another person becomes "it." After all volunteers have been "it," consider the following questions individually.

1. Describe your feelings when thinking about becoming "it."
2. If you were "it" are you pleased that you volunteered? If you were not "it" are you now displeased?
3. How do you feel now that the exercise is over? Did it make you feel better? Why do you suppose it had the effect it did?
4. What implications may be drawn from this exercise for application to everyday living?

7.3 Dealing with Conflict Starters

For each situation write: (a) an unproductive response, a response that will aggravate the potential conflict and (b) a productive response, a response that will lessen the potential conflict. Why do you assume these responses will do as you predict? What principles of conflict management can you derive from this?

Conflict Starters

1. You're late again. You're always late. Your lateness is so inconsiderate of my time and my interests.
2. I just can't bear another weekend of sitting home watching television. I'm just not going to do that again.
3. Who forgot to phone for reservations?
4. Well, there goes another anniversary and another anniversary that you forgot.
5. You think I'm fat, don't you?
6. Just leave me alone.
7. Did I hear you say your mother knows how to dress?
8. We should have been more available when he needed us. I was always at work.
9. Where's the pepper? Is there no pepper in this house?
10. The Romeros think we should spend our money and start enjoying life.

CHAPTER EIGHT

Interpersonal Relationships

Chapter Concepts	Chapter Goals	Chapter Skills
	After completing this chapter, you should be able to	After completing this chapter, you should be able to
Relationship Stages	1. explain the six-stage model of interpersonal relationships	adjust your communication patterns on the basis of the desired relationship goal
Relationship Theories	2. identify the factors that lead to interpersonal attraction	effectively manage the factors of interpersonal attractiveness, the rewards and costs in relationships, and the breadth and depth of a relationship
	3. explain the theory of costs and rewards	
	4. explain social penetration theory and define *breadth* and *depth*	
Thinking Critically About Interpersonal Relationships	5. identify the popular beliefs about relationships	challenge illogical beliefs about relationships

Think about your important relationships. How did they develop? For example, can you identify the stages your relationships passed through? Why did you develop these friendships and romantic relationships? Are your relationships developing? Deteriorating? What makes some relationships grow and prosper and others decay and die? These are some of the questions we explore in this chapter. More specifically, we look at communication in relationships, the stages of relationships (from contact to dissolution), and the theories that try to explain why we develop the relationships we do, and why some relationships last and some don't.

RELATIONSHIP STAGES

Most relationships, possibly all, pass through stages (Knapp, 1984; Wood, 1982). We do not become intimate friends or lifetime lovers immediately. Rather, we grow into an intimate relationship gradually, through a series of steps or stages. The six-stage model presented in Figure 8.1 describes the significant stages in developing relationships. For each specific relationship, you might wish to modify and revise the basic model. As a general description of relationship development, however, the stages are fairly standard. The five stages are contact, involvement, intimacy, deterioration, and dissolution. These stages describe relationships as they are, not as they should be.

Contact

At this stage, you first make **perceptual contact:** you see, hear, and smell the person. According to some researchers (Zunin, 1972), it is during this stage—within the first four minutes of interaction—that you decide whether or not to pursue the relationship. Also at this stage physical appearance is important because physical dimensions are open to easy inspection. Yet, qualities such as friendliness, warmth, openness, and dynamism are also revealed at this stage. If you like the individual and want to pursue the relationship, you proceed to **interactional contact,** when you begin to communicate.

Another way of looking at the process of initiating conversations is to examine the infamous "opening line," which can be of three basic types (Kleinke, 1986). *Cute-flippant* openers are humorous, indirect, and ambiguous as to whether or not the one opening the conversation really wants an extended encounter. Examples Kleinke recalls include: "Is that really your hair?" "I bet the cherry jubilee isn't as sweet as you are."

Innocuous openers are highly ambiguous as to whether these are simple comments that might be made to just anyone or whether they are in fact openers designed to initiate an extended encounter. Examples include:

How long does it take you to decide whether to pursue a relationship with someone you have just met? Is four minutes too short a time? Too long?

Figure 8.1
A Six-Stage Relationship Model
Note that there are three types of ar-
rows. The Exit arrows show that each
stage offers the opportunity to exit the
relationship. After saying "hello," you
can say "good-bye" and exit. The ver-
tical or "movement" arrows between
the stages represent your ability to
move to another stage. You can move
to a stage that is more intense (say
from involvement to intimacy) or less
intense (from intimacy to deteriora-
tion). You can also go back to a former
stage. For example, you may have es-
tablished an intimate relationship but
no longer want to maintain it at that
level. At the same time, you are rela-
tively pleased with the relationship, so
it is not really deteriorating. You just
want it to be less intense. So, you
might go back to the involvement stage
and reestablish the relationship at that
more comfortable level.

The "self-reflexive" arrows return
to the beginning of the same level or
stage. These signify that any relation-
ship may become stabilized at any
point. You may, for example, maintain
a relationship at the intimate level
without the relationship deteriorating
or reverting to the less intense stage of
involvement. Or you might remain at
the "Hello, how are you?" stage—
the contact stage—without further
involvement.

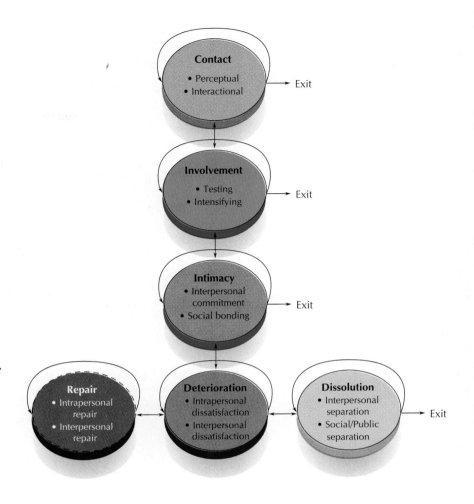

What is the best opening line you have ever heard? What is the worst? What makes one great and another terrible?

"What do you think of the band?" "I haven't been here before. What's good on the menu?" "Could you show me how to work this machine?"

Direct openers clearly demonstrate the speaker's interest in meeting the other person. Examples include: "I feel a little embarrassed about this, but I'd like to meet you." "Would you like to have a drink after dinner?" "Since we're both eating alone, would you like to join me?"

According to Kleinke (1986), the most preferred opening lines by both men and women are generally those that are direct or innocuous. The least preferred lines by both men and women are those that are cute-flippant; women, however, dislike these openers more than men.

Involvement

At this stage a sense of mutuality, of being connected develops. Here you experiment and try to learn more about each other. At the initial phase of involvement a kind of **testing** goes on. You want to see if your initial judg-ment—made perhaps at the contact stage—proves reasonable. And so you try to get to know the other person better and ask, perhaps, "Where do you work?" or "What are you majoring in?" Assuming you are com-mitted to getting to know the other person further, you might continue

How important to you is a person's cultural background at the involvement stage for friendship? For romantic relationships? Can certain cultural characteristics prevent one of your friendship or romantic relationships from progressing from involvement to intimacy?

your interaction by **intensifying** your involvement. If this is to be a romantic relationship, then you might date at this stage. You begin to see each other as unique individuals.

In many Western cultures, such as the United States, it is at this stage (and into the intimacy stage) that the group memberships of your partner become less important. In many other cultures, one's group memberships are always important and never diminish in their impact on the relationship (Moghaddam, Taylor, & Wright, 1993). If it is to be a friendship, you might share your mutual interests, for example, go to the movies or to a sporting event.

Throughout the relationship process, but especially during the involvement and early stages of intimacy, you test your partner; you try to find out how your partner feels about the relationship—somewhat like the characters in the accompanying cartoon. Among the often-used strategies are these (Bell & Buerkel-Rothfuss, 1990; Baxter & Wilmot, 1984):

Drawing by Cline; © 1994
The New Yorker Magazine, Inc.

"You say you love me, but I'm not on your speed dial."

What dating strategies have you used? What dating strategies have been used on you? Were they effective?

- Directness: you ask your partner directly how he or she feels, or you self-disclose, assuming that your partner will also self-disclose

- Endurance: you subject your partner to various negative behaviors (for example, behaving badly or making inconvenient requests), assuming that if your partner endures them, he or she is really serious about the relationship.

- Public presentation: for example, you might introduce your partner as your "boyfriend" or "girlfriend" and see how your partner responds.

- Separation: separating yourself physically to see how the other person responds; if your partner calls, then you know that he or she is interested in the relationship.

- Third party: you might question mutual friends as to your partner's feelings and intentions.

Intimacy

At the intimacy stage, you further commit yourself to the other person. You may establish a primary relationship in which this individual becomes your best or closest friend or lover. The intimacy stage usually divides itself quite neatly into two phases: an **interpersonal commitment** phase, in which you commit yourselves to each other in a private way, and a **social bonding** phase, in which the commitment is made public—perhaps to family and friends, perhaps to the public at large through formal announcements. Here you become a unit, an identifiable pair.

Notice that this discussion is based on the assumption that you decide which relationships to pursue and which not to pursue. And this is certainly true in most of the United States where, for example, you are expected to form romantic relationships with people of your own choosing. In other parts of the world, however, relationships such as marriages are still arranged, as, for example, in some parts of India. In fact, children are frequently wed as early as age 6 or 7. It's interesting to note that when people in arranged marriages were compared with people in self-chosen marriages after five years, those in arranged marriages indicated a greater intensity of love (Gupta & Singh, 1982; Moghaddam, Taylor, & Wright, 1993).

Of course, not everyone strives for intimacy (Bartholomew, 1990). Some may consciously desire intimacy but so fear its consequences that they avoid it. Others dismiss intimacy, defensively denying their need for more and deeper interpersonal contact. To some people relational intimacy is extremely risky. To others, it involves only low risk. For example, how true of your attitudes are the following statements?

- It is dangerous to get really close to people.
- I'm afraid to get really close to someone because I might get hurt.
- I find it difficult to trust other people.
- The most important thing to consider in a relationship is whether I might get hurt.

People who agree with these statements (and other similar statements), which come from recent research on risk in intimacy (Pilkington & Richardson, 1988), perceive intimacy to involve great risk. Such people, it has been found, have fewer close friends, are less likely to be involved in a romantic relationship, have less trust in others, have a low level of dating assertiveness, and are generally less sociable than those who see intimacy as involving little risk.

Intimacy and Love

In the popular mind the intimacy stage is the stage of falling in love. This is the time you "become lovers" and commit yourselves to being romantic partners. It is interesting and important to note, however, that *love* means very different things to different people. To illustrate this important concept, take the following love test, "What Kind of Lover Are You?"

What Kind of Lover Are You?

Do you agree with Russian novelist Leo Tolstoy who said: "To say that you can love one person all your life is like saying you can keep one candle burning as long as you live"?

Instructions: Respond to each of the following statements with T (if you believe the statement to be a generally accurate representation of your attitudes about love) or F (if you believe the statement does not adequately represent your attitudes about love).

_____ 1. My lover and I have the right physical "chemistry" between us.

_____ 2. I feel that my lover and I were meant for each other.

_____ 3. My lover and I really understand each other.

_____ 4. My lover fits my ideal standards of physical beauty/handsomeness.

_____ 5. I try to keep my lover a little uncertain about my commitment to him/her.

_____ 6. I believe that what my lover doesn't know about me won't hurt him/her.

_____ 7. My lover would get upset if he/she knew of some of the things I've done with other people.

_____ 8. When my lover gets too dependent on me, I want to back off a little.

_____ 9. To be genuine, our love first required _caring_ for a while.

_____ 10. I expect to always be friends with my lover.

_____ 11. Our love is really a deep friendship, not a mysterious, mystical emotion.

_____ 12. Our love relationship is the most satisfying because it developed from a good friendship.

_____ 13. In choosing my lover, I believed it was best to love someone with a similar background.

_____ 14. A main consideration in choosing my lover was how he/she would reflect on my family.

_____ 15. An important factor in choosing a partner is whether or not he/she would be a good parent.

_____ 16. One consideration in choosing my lover was how he/she would reflect on my career.

_____ 17. When things aren't right with my lover and me, my stomach gets upset.

_____ 18. Sometimes I get so excited about being in love with my lover that I can't sleep.

_____ 19. When my lover doesn't pay attention to me, I feel sick all over.

_____ 20. I cannot relax if I suspect that my lover is with someone else.

_____ 21. I try to always help my lover through difficult times.

_____ 22. I would rather suffer myself than let my lover suffer.

_____ 23. When my lover gets angry with me, I still love him/her fully and unconditionally.

_____ 24. I would endure all things for the sake of my lover.

Remember only this of our hopeless love
That never til Time is done
Will the fire of the heart and the fire of the mind be one.
—EDITH SHWELL

Thinking Critically About Love This scale is designed to enable you to identify those styles that best reflect your own beliefs about love. The statements refer to the six types of love that we discuss below: eros, ludus, storge, pragma, mania, and agape. "True" answers represent your agreement and "false" answers represent your disagreement with the type of love to which the statements refer. Statements 1–4 are characteristic of the eros lover. If you answered "true" to these statements, you have a strong eros component to your love style. If you answered "false," you have a weak eros component. Statements 5–8 refer to ludus love;,9–12 to storge love, 13–16 to pragma love, 17–20 to manic love, and 21–24 to agapic love.

Source: This scale comes from Hendrick and Hendrick (1990) and is reprinted by permission. It is based on the work of Lee (1976), as is our discussion of the six types of love.

Eros: Beauty and Sensuality. The **erotic** lover focuses on beauty and physical attractiveness, sometimes to the exclusion of qualities we might consider more important and more lasting. The erotic lover has an idealized image of beauty that is unattainable in reality. Consequently, the erotic lover often feels unfulfilled.

Ludus: Entertainment and Excitement. **Ludus** love is seen as fun, a game to be played. To the ludic lover, love is not to be taken too seriously; emotions are to be held in check lest they get out of hand and make trouble. Passions never rise to the point at which they get out of control. The ludic lover retains a partner only so long as the partner is interesting and amusing. When the partner is no longer interesting enough, it is time to change.

Storge: Peaceful and Slow. Like ludus, **storge** lacks passion and intensity. Storgic lovers do not set out to find lovers but to establish a companion-like relationship with someone they know and can share interests and activities. Storgic love develops over a period of time rather than in one mad burst of passion. Storgic love is often characterized by the same qualities that characterize friendship: mutual caring, compassion, respect, and concern for the other person.

Pragma: Practical and Traditional. The **pragma** lover is practical and wants compatibility and a relationship in which important needs and desires will be satisfied. The pragma lover views love as a useful relationship, one that makes life easier. So the pragma lover asks such questions of a potential mate as "Will this person earn a good living?" "Can this person cook?" and "Will this person help me advance in my career?"

Mania: Elation and Depression. The **manic** lover loves intensely and at the same time fears the loss of the love. With little provocation, for example, the manic lover may experience extreme jealousy. The manic lover needs to give and receive constant attention and affection. When this doesn't happen, depression, jealousy, and self-doubt may be experienced and may lead to the extreme lows characteristic of this type of lover.

Agape: Compassionate and Selfless. **Agape** (ah-gah-pay) is compassionate, egoless, self-giving love. The agapic lover loves even people with whom he or she has no close ties. This lover loves the stranger on

Research (Lee, 1976; Hendrick & Hendrick, 1990) shows that men generally score higher on erotic, mania, and ludus love and women score higher on storge and pragma. Does your experience support these findings?

. . . since love and fear can hardly exist together, if we must choose between them, it is far safer to be feared than loved.
—Niccolò Machiavelli, The Prince

What cultural attitudes was satirist Ambrose Bierce referring to when he defined love as "a temporary insanity curable by marriage or by removal of the patient from the influences under which he incurred the disorder"?

the road, and the fact that they will probably never meet again has nothing to do with it. Agape is a spiritual love, offered without concern for personal reward or gain. The agapic lover loves without expecting that the love will be returned or reciprocated.

CULTURAL VIEWPOINT

Attitudes About Relationships

The attitudes you have about relationships are largely determined by your culture. This important fact can be best appreciated by reading the following brief excerpt from Wade and Tavris (1994):

A young wife leaves her house one morning to draw water from the local well, as her husband watches from the porch. On her way back from the well, a stranger stops her and asks for some water. She gives him a cupful, and then invites him home to dinner. He accepts. The husband, wife, and guest have a pleasant meal together. The husband, in a gesture of hospitality, invites the guest to spend the night—with his wife. He accepts. In the morning, the husband leaves early to bring home breakfast. When he returns, he finds his wife again in bed with the visitor.

The question is: At what point in this story does the husband feel angry?

The answer is: It depends on the culture to which you belong (Hupka, 1981). An American husband would feel rather angry at a wife who had an extramarital affair; and a wife would feel rather angry at being offered to a guest as if she were a lamb chop. But these reactions are not universal.

- *A Pawnee Indian husband of the nineteenth century would be enraged at any man who dared ask his wife for water.*
- *An Ammassalik Eskimo husband finds it perfectly honorable to offer his wife to a stranger, but only once. He would be angry to find his wife and the guest having a second encounter.*
- *A Toda husband at the turn of the century in India would not be angry at all. The Todas allowed both husband and wife to take lovers, and women were even allowed to have several husbands. Both spouses might feel angry, though, if one of them had a sneaky affair; without announcing it publicly.*

How are your beliefs about your relationships influenced by the culture in which you were raised? A good start exploring that relationship is provided in the self-test in "Thinking Critically About Interpersonal Relationships" at the end of the chapter.

[Next Cultural Viewpoint, page 199]

Deterioration

Relational deterioration refers to the weakening of bonds that hold people together. The process may be sudden or gradual. Sometimes a relationship rule (say, the rule of fidelity) is broken and the relationship ends almost immediately. At other times, displeasures grow over time and the relationship dies gradually.

The first phase of relationship deterioration is usually **intrapersonal dissatisfaction:** You begin to feel that this relationship may not be as important as you had previously thought. If this intrapersonal dissatisfaction continues, you may pass into the second phase, **interpersonal deterioration.** Here you would withdraw and grow further and further apart. You would share less of your free time and conflicts may become more and more common and their resolution increasingly difficult.

The causes of relationship deterioration are many. Here are just a few:

- Reasons for establishing the relationship have diminished. When the reasons you developed the relationship change drastically, the relationship may deteriorate. For instance, when loneliness is no longer lessened, the relationship may suffer. When stimulation is weak, one or both may begin to look elsewhere. When attractiveness fades, an important reason for establishing the relationship in the first place is lost. We know, for example, that when relationships break up, it is usually the more attractive partner who leaves (Blumstein & Schwartz, 1983).

- Changes in one or both parties may encourage relational deterioration. Psychological changes such as the development of different intellectual interests or incompatible attitudes may create problems, as may behavioral changes such as preoccupation with business or schooling.

- Sexual problems rank among the top three problems in most studies of newlyweds (Blumstein & Schwartz, 1983). Research clearly shows that it is the quality, not the quantity of a sexual relationship that is crucial. When the quality is poor, partners may seek sexual affairs outside the primary relationship. And research on the effects of this is again clear: Extrarelational affairs contribute significantly to breakups for all couples, whether married or cohabiting, heterosexual or homosexual. Even "open relationships"—ones based on sexual freedom outside the primary relationship—experience these problems and are more likely to break up than the traditional "closed" relationship (Blumstein & Schwartz, 1983).

- Unhappiness with work often leads to difficulties with relationships and is often associated with relationship breakup. Most people cannot separate work problems from their relationships (Blumstein & Schwartz, 1983). This is true for heterosexual and homosexual couples.

- In surveys of problems among couples, financial difficulties loom large. Money is important in relationships largely because of its close connection with power; the one who earns more money has more power to control the relationship. Money also creates problems because men and women view it differently. To many men, money is power. To many women, it is security and independence (Blumstein & Schwartz, 1984). Conflicts over how to spend the money can easily result from such different perceptions.

Never get involved with someone who wants to change you.
—QUENTIN CRISP

What other reasons for relationship deterioration can you identify?

Why do you think self-disclosure declines during relationship deterioration?

Do you find differences in the way men and women talk about relationships in their development, maintenance, or deteriorating stages?

Communication is to a relationship what breathing is to maintaining life.
—VIRGINIA SATIR

Allen Fay (1988) argues: "Lying in an intimate relationship undermines the relationship. Even if your partner doesn't know about the lie and never finds out, the relationship will probably still be damaged. You have devalued your partner and will therefore have less respect for her/him and for yourself." Do you agree with Fay? What arguments might you advance for or against Fay's assertion?

Communication in Relationship Deterioration

Relational deterioration involves unique, specialized communication. The way you communicate during deterioration is in part a response to the deterioration, but the way you communicate may also contribute further to the deterioration.

Withdrawal is probably the easiest pattern to observe. When people are close emotionally, they can occupy close physical quarters, but when they are growing apart, they need wider spaces. They literally move away from each other. Other nonverbal signs include the failure to engage in eye contact, to look at each other generally, and to touch each other (Miller & Parks, 1982). Verbally, withdrawal involves less talking and especially less listening. It is also seen in the decline of self-disclosing communications.

Deception increases as relationships break down. Sometimes this involves direct and clear-cut lies; at other times the lies are more like exaggerations or omissions.

Relational deterioration often brings an increase in negative evaluations and a decrease in positive evaluations. Where once you praised the other's behaviors, talents, or ideas, you now criticize them. Often the behaviors have not changed significantly. What has changed is your way of looking at them.

Compliments, once given frequently and sincerely, are now rare. Positive stroking is minimal. Nonverbally, we avoid looking directly at the other and seldom smile. We touch, caress, and hold each other infrequently, if at all.

"Sometimes I'm sorry I ever ran away with you."

Drawing by Leo Cullum; © 1992 The New Yorker Magazine, Inc.

Repair

The repair stage is optional and so is indicated by a broken circle. Some relational partners may pause during deterioration and try to repair their relationship. Others, however, may progress—without stopping—to dissolution. The first phase of repair is **intrapersonal repair,** where you analyze what went wrong and consider ways of solving your difficulties. You might at this stage consider changing your behaviors or perhaps changing your expectations. Should you decide that you want to repair the relationship, you might discuss this with your partner at the **interpersonal repair** level. Here you might discuss the problems in the relationship, the corrections you want to see made, and perhaps what you would be willing to do and what you want the other person to do.

You have a wide variety of strategies that may prove useful should you wish to improve your relationship. Here are six:

• Recognize the problem. Your first step is to identify the problem; specify what is wrong with your present relationship (in concrete, specific terms) and what changes are needed to make it better (again, in concrete, specific terms). Try to see the problem from your partner's point of view and to have your partner see the problem from yours. Exchange these perspectives, empathically and with open minds. Try too to be descriptive when discussing grievances, being especially careful to avoid such troublesome terms as *always* and *never*. Also, own your own feelings and thoughts; use I-messages and take responsibility for your feelings instead of blaming your partner.

- Engage in productive conflict resolution. Some of the appropriate tools have already been identified (Chapter 7).
- Pose possible solutions. After the problem is identified, discuss possible solutions, the ways to lessen or eliminate the difficulty. Look for solutions that will enable both of you to win. Try to avoid "solutions" where one person wins and the other person loses. With such win-lose solutions, resentment and hostility are likely to fester.
- Affirm each other. Any strategy of relationship repair should incorporate increasing supportiveness and positive evaluations. For example, it has been found that happily married couples engage in greater positive behavior exchange; they communicate more agreement, approval, and positive affect than do unhappily married couples (Dindia & Fitzpatrick, 1985). Clearly, these behaviors result from the positive feelings these spouses have for each other. But it can also be argued that these expressions help to increase the positive regard that each person has for his or her partner.
- Integrate solutions into normal behavior. Often solutions that are reached after an argument are followed for only a very short time; then the couple goes back to their previous and unproductive behavior patterns. Instead, solutions need to be integrated into your normal behavior; they need to become integral to your everyday relationship behavior.
- Take risks; risk being supportive without any certainty of reciprocity. Risk rejection; make the first move to make up or say you are sorry. Be willing to change, to adapt, to take on new tasks and responsibilities.

Do you agree with William M. Thackery, who said: "To love and win is the best thing, to love and lose the next best"? Can you think of a reason why someone who has loved and lost might disagree with this?

Dissolution

The dissolution stage is cutting the bonds that tie you together. In the beginning it usually takes the form of **interpersonal separation,** where you might move into separate apartments and begin to lead lives apart from each other. If this separation proves acceptable and if the original relationship is not repaired, you enter the phase of **social** or **public separation.** If this is a marriage, this phase corresponds to divorce. Avoidance of each other and a return to being "single" are among the primary characteristics of dissolution.

In cultures that emphasize continuity from one generation to the next and where being "old-fashioned" is evaluated positively—as in, say, China—interpersonal relationships are likely to be long-lasting and permanent. But in cultures where change is seen as positive and being old-fashioned as negative—as in, say, the United States—interpersonal relationships are likely to be more temporary (Moghaddam, Taylor, & Wright, 1993).

Note too that even the consideration of dissolution as an important phase of interpersonal relationships implies that this is a possible option. But in other cultures, relationships such as marriage are forever and cannot be dissolved if things begin to go wrong or even if things go very wrong. More important in such cultures are such issues as how do you maintain a relationship that has problems, what can you do to exist within an unpleasant relationship, and how can you repair a relationship that is troubled (Moghaddam, Taylor, & Wright, 1993).

Censoring Messages and Interactions

Throughout your life, the messages you receive are censored. When you were very young, your parents may have censored certain television programs, magazines, and movies—perhaps even tapes and CDs—that they thought inappropriate, usually because they were either too sexually explicit or too violent.

Similarly, when you were young, your parents may have encouraged you to play with certain children and not to play with others. Sometimes these decisions were based on the character of the other children. Sometimes they may have been based on the racial, religious, or national background of the would-be friends. Today, the most obvious instances where interactions are prevented are those concerning romantic relationships between interracial couples and homosexual relationships. These prohibitions prevent certain people from interacting in the manner in which they choose. Interracial couples run into difficulty finding housing, employment, and, most significantly, acceptance into a community. Gay men and lesbians encounter the same difficulties, and consequently many are forced to live "straight" lives—at least on the surface. The military policy of "don't ask, don't tell, don't pursue" is a perfect example of how the society as a whole forces certain groups to hide their true selves.

Consider the following situations.

- Is it ethical to try to persuade your friends to avoid interacting with Tom and Lisa because you think they are immoral? Because you are jealous of them? Because you know that they are plotting to commit a series of robberies and you don't want your friends implicated? Because you feel they will have a bad influence on your friends?
- Is it ethical for a group to ostracize a person on the basis of sex? Race? Religion? Affectional orientation? Physical condition? Financial condition? Drug behavior? Criminal connections?
- Is it ethical for a someone to turn in his or her parents to the police for alcohol abuse? For smoking marijuana? For using cocaine? For child abuse?
- What ethical guidelines would you propose for the censorship of interactions?

[Next Ethical Issue, page 292]

No person is your friend who demands your silence, or denies your right to grow.

—ALICE WALKER

RELATIONSHIP THEORIES

Why do you develop the relationships you do? Why do you dissolve the relationships you end? Why do you maintain the friendships and romantic relationships you do? Here are a few theories that try to answer these questions.

Interpersonal Attraction

A theory of interpersonal attraction holds that you are attracted to others because you find them attractive (physically and in personality), close or nearby, reinforcing, and similar to you.

If you are like most people, you are attracted to people you find physically attractive and who have a pleasing personality. Further, you probably attribute positive qualities to those you find attractive and negative qualities to those you find unattractive.

People are attracted to those who are physically close to them. For example, you become friends with and form romantic relationships with those you come into contact most often. Physical closeness (proximity) is most important in the early stages of interaction. But if your initial interaction with a person is unpleasant, repeated exposure will not increase attraction. Proximity works when the initial interaction is favorable or neutral.

People are also attracted to those who reward or reinforce them (socially, as with compliments or praise, or materially, as with gifts or a promotion). You also become attracted to those you reward; you come to like people for whom you do favors. Perhaps there is a need to justify going out of your way and so you need to convince yourself that the person is likable and worth the effort.

People are also attracted to people who are similar to them, to people who look, act, think, and have attitudes and preferences much like they do. Attitudinal similarity, in fact, is even more important than cultural

Of all the girls that are so smart
There's none like pretty Sally:
She is the darling of my heart,
And lives in our alley.

—HENRY CAREY

The matching hypothesis predicts that we date and mate those who are similar to us in physical attractiveness. There are some instances in which opposites attract; for example, the introvert who is displeased with being shy might be attracted to an extrovert. But usually we are attracted to those who are similar to us. Do you find this generally true? What comes to your mind when you see couples who differ greatly in physical attractiveness? Do you think that there must be "compensating factors"—for example, that the less attractive person is rich or has prestige or power?

Drawing by Koren; © 1992
The New Yorker Magazine, Inc.

"It's very sensitive of you to realize that men <u>like</u> *to get flowers!"*

Love is a great beautifier.
—LOUISA MAY ALCOTT

similarity (Kim, 1991). People also like those who are similar in nationality, race, ability, physical characteristics, and intelligence.

As long as these attractiveness factors remain, the interpersonal attraction and the relationship built on it is likely to be maintained. When attractiveness fades relative to other potential partners the relationship may deteriorate. Thus, for example, when away from each other for long periods of time (and the factor of proximity is no longer present), the relationship will deteriorate. Absence, research tells us, does not make the heart grow fonder; it makes the heart forget (eventually). Similarly, as physical attractiveness fades (in the eyes of the lover), the relationship may be in trouble.

Rewards and Costs

According to **social exchange theory,** you develop relationships that you think will provide more rewards than costs (Thibaut & Kelley, 1986; Kelley & Thibaut, 1978). The general assumption is that you develop (and will maintain) relationships in which your rewards are greater than your costs. Rewards are those things that fulfill your needs for security: sex, social approval, financial gain, status, and so on. But rewards also involve some cost or "payback." In order to acquire the reward of financial gain, for example, you must take a job and thus give up some freedom (a cost). Using this basic model, the theory puts into perspective our tendency to seek gain or reward while incurring the least cost (punishment or loss).

Equity theory builds on social exchange theory. It claims that not only do we seek to establish relationships in which rewards exceed costs, but

Take a close look at your past and current relationships and analyze their rewards and costs. Does the theory of rewards and costs accurately predict their development, maintenance, or deterioration?

that we experience relationship satisfaction when there is equity in the distribution of rewards and costs between the two persons in the relationship (Berscheid & Walster, 1978; Hatfield & Traupman, 1981). That is, not only do we want our rewards to be greater than our costs; we also want our rewards and our partner's rewards to be proportional to the costs we each pay. Thus, if you pay the larger share of the costs, you expect to receive the larger share of the rewards. In this situation you would be relatively happy. On the other hand, you would be unhappy if you paid the larger share of the costs and your partner derived the larger share of the rewards.

Most people, like the dish and the spoon in the cartoon, will at times regret their relationships when the costs jump or the rewards fall significantly. As long as rewards exceed costs (according to social exchange theory) and as long as costs and rewards are distributed in proportion to the costs paid into the relationship (according to equity theory), your relationship is likely to be maintained. If the costs begin to exceed the rewards and there is an alternative relationship that offers a better ratio of rewards to costs, the original relationship is likely to deteriorate and dissolve and this alternative relationship is likely to be entered into. According to equity theory, the relationship is likely to be maintained if the costs and rewards are distributed in proportion to the costs paid into the relationship and is likely to deteriorate if the person paying the greater share of the costs does not get the greater share of the rewards.

Beauty can't amuse you, but brainwork—reading, writing, thinking—can.
—HELEN GURLEY BROWN

CULTURAL VIEWPOINT

Equity and Culture

Equity is consistent with the capitalistic orientation of Western culture, where each person is paid, for example, according to his or her contributions. The more you contribute to the organization or the relationship, the more rewards you should get out of it. In other cultures, a principle of equality or need might operate. Under equality, each person would get equal rewards, regardless of their own individual contribution. Under need, each person would get rewards according to his or her individual need (Moghaddam, Taylor, & Wright, 1993). Thus, in the United States equity is found to be highly correlated with relationship satisfaction and with relationship endurance (Schafer & Keith, 1980), but in Europe equity seems to be unrelated to satisfaction or endurance (Lujansky & Mikula, 1983).

In one study, for example, subjects in the United States and India were asked to read situations in which a bonus was to be distributed between a worker who contributed a great deal but who was economically well off and a worker who contributed much less but who was economically needy. Their choices were to distribute the bonus equitably (on the basis of contribution), equally, or in terms of need (Berman, Murphy-Erman, & Singh, 1985; (Moghaddam, Taylor, & Wright, 1993). The results are given in the following table.

How equitable are your relationships? Do you give more than you get? Do you get more than you give? If there is inequity, how does it affect the relationship?

True intimacy is a positive force only if it is a combining of strengths and energies with other mature persons for the continued growth of each.

—LEO BUSCAGLIA

How would you describe the relationship between yourself and your best friend, using the concepts of breadth and depth?

Social Penetration

Social penetration theory focuses not on why relationships develop or deteriorate but rather describes relationships in varying degrees of involvement; it focuses on the number of topics that people talk about and their degree of "personalness" (Altman & Taylor, 1973). The *breadth* of a relationship refers to the number of topics you and your partner talk about. The *depth* of a relationship refers to the degree to which you penetrate the inner personality—the core of the individual.

We can represent an individual as a circle and divide that circle into various parts. These parts represent the topics or areas of interpersonal communication, or breadth. Visualize the circle and its parts as consisting of concentric inner circles, rather like an onion. These represent the different levels of communication, or the depth (see Figure 8.2). The circles contain eight topic areas (A through H) and five levels of intimacy (represented by the concentric circles).

In its initial stage a relationship is usually narrow (you discuss few topics) and shallow (you discuss the topics only superficially). As a relationship becomes more intense, you increase both breadth and depth.

When a relationship begins to deteriorate, the breadth and depth will, in many ways, reverse themselves, a process called *depenetration*. For example, while ending a relationship, you might cut out certain topics from your interpersonal communications. At the same time you might discuss the remaining topics in less depth. You would, for example, reduce the level of your self-disclosures and reveal less of your innermost feelings. This reversal does not always work, of course. In some instances of relational deterioration, both the breadth and the depth of interaction increase. For example, when a couple split up and each is finally free from an oppressive relationship, they may—though usually only after a period of time—begin to discuss problems and feelings they would never have discussed when they were together. In fact, they may become extremely close friends and come to like each other

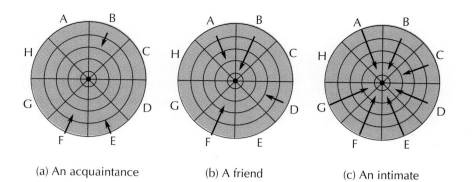

(a) An acquaintance   (b) A friend   (c) An intimate

Figure 8.2
Social Penetration With (a) an Acquaintance, (b) a friend, and (c) an Intimate
Note that in circle (a) only three topics are discussed. Two are penetrated only to the first level and one to the second level. In this type of interaction, the individuals talk about three topic areas and discuss these at rather superficial levels. This is the type of relationship you might have with an acquaintance. Circle (b) represents a more intense relationship. It is both broader and deeper. This is the type of relationship you might have with a friend. Circle (c) represents a still more intense relationship. Here there is considerable breadth and depth. This is the type of relationship you might have with a lover, a parent, or a sibling.

more than when they were together. In these cases the breadth and depth of their relationship may well increase rather than decrease (Baxter, 1983).

THINKING CRITICALLY ABOUT INTERPERSONAL RELATIONSHIPS

One of the best ways to exercise your critical thinking faculties is to examine the beliefs about relationships that you hold.

TEST YOURSELF
Beliefs About Your Relationships

Instructions
For each of the following statements, select the number (1 to 7) of the category that best fits how much you agree or disagree. Enter that number on the line next to each statement.

    agree completely = 7
    agree a good deal = 6
    agree somewhat = 5
    neither agree nor disagree = 4
    disagree somewhat = 3
    disagree a good deal = 2
    disagree completely = 1

Since there is rarely any lasting advantage of ignorance about compatibility, open communication is essential to developing healthy relationships.
—MICHAEL J. BEATTY

Using any of the insights presented in this section, how would you describe the interpersonal communication and the interpersonal relationships of one couple in a television situation comedy or drama?

_____ 1. If a person has any questions about the relationship, then it means there is something wrong with it.

_____ 2. If my partner truly loved me, we would not have any quarrels.

_____ 3. If my partner really cared, he or she would always feel affection for me.

_____ 4. If my partner gets angry at me or is critical in public, this indicates he or she doesn't really love me.

_____ 5. My partner should know what is important to me without my having to tell him or her.

_____ 6. If I have to ask for something that I really want, it spoils it.

_____ 7. If my partner really cared, he or she would do what I ask.

_____ 8. A good relationship should not have any problems.

_____ 9. If people really love each other, they should not have to work on their relationship.

_____ 10. If my partner does something that upsets me, I think it is because he or she deliberately wants to hurt me.

_____ 11. When my partner disagrees with me in public, I think it is a sign that he or she doesn't care for me very much.

_____ 12. If my partner contradicts me, I think that he or she doesn't have much respect for me.

_____ 13. If my partner hurts my feelings, that it is because he or she is mean.

_____ 14. My partner always tries to get his or her own way.

_____ 15. My partner doesn't listen to what I have to say.

Thinking Critically About Relationship Beliefs Aaron Beck, one of the leading theorists in cognitive therapy and the author of the popular _Love Is Never Enough_, claims that all of these beliefs are unrealistic and may well create problems in your interpersonal relationships. The test was developed to help people identify potential sources of difficulty for relationship development and maintenance. The more statements that you indicated you believe in, the more unrealistic your expectations are.

Do you agree with Beck that these beliefs are unrealistic and that they will cause problems? Which belief is the most dangerous to the development and maintenance of an interpersonal relationship?

Review the list—individually or in small groups—and identify with hypothetical or real examples why each belief is unrealistic (or realistic).

Source: This test was taken from Aaron Beck, _Love Is Never Enough_ (New York: Harper & Row, 1988), pp. 67–68. Beck notes that this test was adapted in part from the Relationship Belief Inventory of N. Epstein, J. L. Pretzer, and B. Fleming, "The Role of Cognitive Appraisal in Self-Reports of Marital Communication," _Behavior Therapy_ 18 (1987): 51–69.

Occasionally, thinking is an end in itself, but usually the purpose of thinking is to choose or design a course of action. Sometimes there is a distinct thinking phase and then an action phase. At other times thinking and action are intertwined so that thinking takes place in the course of the action.

—EDWARD DEBONO

Feedback on Concepts and Skills

In this chapter we explored interpersonal relationships—their nature, development, maintenance, deterioration, and repair. We also examined several theories that explain what happens in interpersonal relationships.

1. Relationships are established in stages. At least the following six stages should be recognized: contact, involvement, intimacy, deterioration, repair, and dissolution. Each of these stages can be further broken down into an early and a later phase.

2. Love is perhaps the most important form of intimacy; several types of love were identified: eros, ludus, storge, pragma, mania, and agape.
3. Among the major causes of relationship deterioration are a lessening of the reasons for establishing the relationship; changes in the parties; sexual difficulties; work; and financial problems.
4. Interpersonal attraction depends on attractiveness (physical and personality), proximity, reinforcement, and similarity.
5. Relationships may be considered in terms of exchanging rewards and costs. Rewards are things we enjoy and want. Costs are unpleasant things we try to avoid.
6. Relationships vary in breadth (the number of topics talked about) and depth (the degree of "personalness" or intimacy to which the topics are pursued). Social penetration theory holds that as relationships develop, the breadth and depth increase. When a relationship deteriorates, the breadth and depth will often (but not always) decrease, a process referred to as depenetration.

Check your competence in using these skills for effective relationship development. Use the following rating scale: (1) = almost always, (2) = often, (3) = sometimes, (4) = rarely, (5) = almost never.

_____ 1. I adjust my communication patterns on the basis of the relationship's intimacy.

_____ 2. I can identify changes in communication patterns that may signal relationship deterioration.

_____ 3. I can use the accepted repair strategies to heal an ailing relationship, for example, reversing negative communication patterns, using cherishing behaviors, and adopting a positive action program.

_____ 4. I can apply to my own relationships such communication skills as identifying relational messages; exchanging perspectives due to differences in punctuation; empathic and supportive understanding; and eliminating unfair fight strategies.

_____ 5. I can effectively manage physical proximity, reinforcement, and emphasizing similarities as ways to increase interpersonal attractiveness.

_____ 6. I can identify and to some extent control the rewards and costs of my relationships.

_____ 7. I gradually increase the breadth and depth of a relationship.

Skill Development Experiences

8.1 Exchanging Cherishing Behaviors

William Lederer (1984) suggests that partners make lists of cherishing behaviors they each wish to receive and then exchange the lists. Cherishing behaviors are the small gestures or comments that we enjoy receiving from our relational partner (a smile, a wink, a kiss, a compliment). Cherishing behaviors are specific and positive, are focused on the present and the future (rather than on issues about which you may have argued), are capable of being performed daily, and are easily executed. Each person then practices performing the cherishing behaviors desired by the partner. At first these behaviors may seem self-conscious and awkward. In time, however, they will become a normal part of interaction and will help offset the inevitable costs in any relationship. Compile a list of cherishing behaviors you would like to receive. Have your friend or partner do likewise. Exchange the lists. Agree to exchange a fixed number of cherishing behaviors per day. Continue the exchange for at least five days. Report on your experiences.

8.2 Seeking Affinity

Here are ten affinity-seeking strategies—the techniques we use to get others to like us (Bell & Daly, 1984). Select one of the following situations and indicate—with reference to specific communication behaviors—how you might use any three of the strategies to achieve your goal. In the definitions, the term *Other* is used as shorthand for *other person or persons*.

Situations

1. You're at an employment interview and want the interviewer to like you.
2. You are introduced to Chris and would like to get to know Chris better and perhaps go on a date.
3. You are on a new job and want your co-workers to like you.
4. You just opened a small business in a new neighborhood. You want the people in the area to like you and patronize your store.

Affinity-Seeking Strategies

1. Stimulate and encourage Other to talk about himself or herself; reinforce disclosures and contributions of Other.
2. Ensure that activities with Other are enjoyable and positive.
3. Include Other in your social activities and groupings.
4. Communicate interest in Other.
5. Engage in self-disclosure with Other.
6. Appear to Other as an interesting person to get to know.
7. Appear as one who is able to administer rewards to Other for associating with you.
8. Show respect for Other and help Other to feel positively about himself or herself.
9. Show that you share significant attitudes and values with Other.
10. Communicate supportiveness for Other's thoughts and feelings.

8.3 Communicating with Cards and Songs

This exercise aims (1) to familiarize you with some of the popular conceptions and sentiments concerning interpersonal relationships, and (2) to introduce a wide variety of concepts important in the study of interpersonal relationships.

Bring to class a greeting card or song and show how it expresses a sentiment that is significant for any of the following reasons. (Sentiments in greeting cards and songs are communicated through a number of different channels. Therefore, consider the sentiments communicated through the verbal message but also through the illustrations, the colors, the card's physical form, the type of print, the song's tempo, the music's volume, and so on.) This list, of course, is not exhaustive.

- It uses a concept or theory that can assist us in understanding interpersonal relationships.
- It illustrates a popular problem in interpersonal relationships.
- It illustrates a useful strategy for relationship development, maintenance, repair, or dissolution.
- It suggests a useful question (or hypothesis for scientific study) that should be asked in the study of interpersonal relationships.
- It supports or contradicts some currently accepted theory in interpersonal relationships.

8.4 Understanding Men and Women

This exercise is designed to increase your awareness of matters that may prevent meaningful interpersonal communication between the sexes. It is also designed to encourage meaningful dialogue among class members.

The women and men are separated, one group goes into another classroom. Each group's task is to write on the blackboard all the things that they dislike having the other sex think, believe, do, or say about them in general—and that prevent meaningful interpersonal communication from taking place. After this is done, the groups should change rooms so the men can discuss what the women have written and the women discuss what the men have written. After satisfactory discussion, the groups should get together in the original room. Discussion might center on the following questions.

1. Were there any surprises?
2. Were there any disagreements? That is, did members of one sex write anything that members of the other sex argued they do not believe, think, do, or say?
3. How do you suppose the ideas about the other sex got started?
4. Is there any reliable evidence in support of the beliefs of the men about the women or the women about the men?
5. What is the basis for the dislikes? Or, why was each statement written on the blackboard?
6. What kind of education or training program (if any) do you feel is needed to eliminate these problems?
7. In what specific ways do these beliefs, thoughts, actions, and statements prevent meaningful interpersonal communication?
8. How do you feel now that these matters have been discussed?

CHAPTER NINE

Interviewing

Chapter Concepts	Chapter Goals	Chapter Skills
	After completing this chapter, you should be able to	After completing this chapter, you should be able to
Interviewing Defined	1. define interviewing and its several types	use effectively a variety of interview structures
The Information Interview	2. describe the principles of conducting an information interview	follow the basic guidelines in conducting informative interviews
The Employment Interview	3. explain the principles for effective employment interviewing	follow the basic suggestions in real employment interviews
Questions and Answers	4. explain how questions differ in terms of openness and neutrality	frame questions varying in terms of openness/closedness and neutral/biased depending on the desired purpose
Thinking Critically About the Legality of Interview Questions	5. explain the types of questions that are unlawful	recognize and effectively respond to unlawful questions

I nterviewing includes a range of communication situations—situations much like those you find yourself in as the one doing the interview or the one being interviewed:

- A salesperson tries to sell a client a new car.
- A teacher talks with a student about the reasons the student failed the course.
- A counselor talks with a family about their communication problems.
- A recent graduate applies to IBM for a job in the product development division.
- A building owner talks with a potential apartment renter.
- A minister talks with a parishioner about marital problems.
- A lawyer examines a witness during a trial.
- A theatrical agent talks with a potential client.
- A client discusses with a dating service employee some of the qualities desired in a potential mate.
- A boss talks with an employee about some of the reasons for terminating a contract.

How will interviewing play a part in your professional life? How well prepared do you feel you are in the skills of interviewing? What are your strengths? Your weaknesses?

INTERVIEWING DEFINED

Interviewing is a particular form of interpersonal communication in which two persons interact, largely through a question-and-answer format, to achieve specific goals. Although interviews usually involve two people, some involve more. At job fairs, for example, where many people apply for the few available jobs, interviewers may talk with several persons at once. Similarly, therapy frequently involves entire families, groups of co-workers, or other related individuals. Nevertheless, the two-person interview is certainly the most common and the one we will be referring to throughout this unit.

The interview is different from other forms of communication because it proceeds through questions and answers. Both parties in the interview can ask and answer questions, but most often the interviewer asks and the interviewee answers. The interview has specific goals that guide and structure its content and format. In an employment interview, for example, the interviewer's goal is to find an applicant who can fulfill the tasks of the position. The interviewee's goal is to get the job, if it seems desirable. These goals guide the behaviors of both parties, are relatively specific, and are usually clear to both parties.

We can gain added insight into the nature of interviews by looking at their general structures. Interviews vary from relatively informal talks that resemble everyday conversations to those with rigidly prescribed

What role does interviewing play in interpersonal relationships, say, as you move from contact through involvement to intimacy?

In the hands of a skilled
practitioner [the interview] is like
a sharp knife that can cut away
all the fat of irrelevant detail to get
to the meat of the subject.
—JACK GRATUS

questions in a set order. You would select the interview structure that best fits your specific purpose, or combine the various types and create an interview structure that will best suit your needs (Patton, 1980; Hambrick, 1991):

- **Informal Interview**
  Resembles conversation; general theme is chosen in advance but specific questions arise from the context; useful for obtaining information informally

- **Guided Interview**
  Topics are chosen in advance, but specific question and wordings are guided by the ongoing interaction; useful in assuring maximum flexibility and responsiveness to the dynamics of the situation

- **Standard Open Interview**
  Open-ended questions and their order are selected in advance; useful when standardization is needed, for example, when interviewing several candidates for the same job

- **Quantitative**
  Questions are selected in advance as are the possible response categories, for example, A, B, C, D; agree/disagree; check from 1 to 10; useful when large amounts of information (which can be categorized) are to be collected and statistically analyzed

We can also distinguish among the different types of interviews by the goals of interviewer and interviewee. Some of the most important interviews are persuasion, appraisal, exit, counseling, information, and employment (Stewart & Cash, 1988; Zima, 1983). The information and employment interviews are probably the most important for most college students, so these are covered in considerable length in this chapter. In the information interview we concentrate on the role of the interviewer and in the employment interview, on the role of the interviewee. Of course, the principles for effective information and employment interviews will also prove useful for other types.

The Persuasion Interview

In the **persuasion interview,** the goal is to change an individual's attitudes, beliefs, or behaviors. The interviewer may either ask questions that will lead the interviewee to the desired conclusion or answer questions in a persuasive way. For example, if you go into a showroom to buy a new car, you interview the salesperson. The salesperson's goal is to get you to buy a particular car. He or she attempts to accomplish this by answering your questions persuasively. You ask about mileage, safety features, and finance terms. The salesperson discourses eloquently on the superiority of this car above all others.

All interviews contain elements of both information and persuasion. When, for example, a guest appears on *The Tonight Show* and talks about a new movie, information is communicated. But the performer is also trying to persuade the audience to see the movie.

Do you agree with interviewing researchers Stewart and Cash (1988) when they write: "The persuasive interview has a unique advantage over the public speaker and the mass persuader (radio, television, newspaper). The interviewer can tailor a persuasive effort to fit a particular person, at a particular time, in a particular place"?

The Appraisal Interview

In the **appraisal** or **evaluation interview,** the interviewee's performance is assessed by management, or more experienced colleagues. The general aim is to discover what the interviewee is doing well (and to praise this), and not doing well and why (to correct this). These interviews are important because they help new members of an organization see how their performances match the expectations of those making promotion and firing decisions.

The Exit Interview

The **exit interview** is used widely by organizations in the United States and throughout the world. When an employee leaves a company voluntarily, it is important to know why. All organizations compete for superior workers; if an organization is losing its workers, it must discover why, to prevent others from leaving. This type of interview also provides a method for making the departure as pleasant and efficient as possible for both employee and employer.

The Counseling Interview

Counseling interviews provide guidance. The goal is to help the person more effectively deal with problems with work, friends or lovers, or day-to-day living. For the interview to be of any value, the interviewer must learn a considerable amount about the person's habits, problems, self-perceptions, goals, and so on. With this information, the counselor tries to persuade the person to alter certain aspects of his or her thinking or behaving. The counselor may try to persuade you, for example, to listen more attentively when your spouse argues or to devote more time to your classwork.

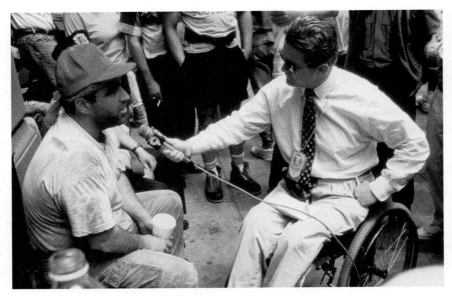

What one person—living or dead, real or fictional—would you most like to interview? What questions would you ask?

THE INFORMATION INTERVIEW

In the **information interview,** the interviewer tries to learn something about the interviewee, usually a person of some reputation and accomplishment. The interviewer asks the interviewee a series of questions designed to elicit his or her views, beliefs, insights, perspectives, predictions, life history, and so on. Examples of the information interview are those published in popular magazines. The television interviews conducted by Jay Leno, Ted Koppel, and Diane Sawyer as well as those conducted by a lawyer during a trial are all information interviews. Each aims to elicit specific information from someone who supposedly knows something others do not.

Let's say that your interview is designed to get information about a particular field—say, the available job opportunities and the preparation you would need to get into desktop publishing. Here are a few guidelines for conducting such an information-gathering interview.

Secure an Appointment

In selecting a person to interview, you might, for example, look through your college catalog for a desktop publishing course and interview the instructor. Or you might call a local publishing company and ask for the person in charge of desktop publishing. Try to learn something about the person before the interview. For example, has the instructor written a book or articles about the field? Look at the book catalog and at indexes to periodicals.

Call or send a letter to request an interview and to identify the purpose of your request. For example, you might say: "I'm preparing for a career in desktop publishing and I would appreciate an interview with you to learn more about the subject. The interview would take about 15 minutes." (This helps because the person now knows it will not take overly long and is more likely to agree to being interviewed.) Generally, it is best to be available at the interviewee's convenience. So indicate flexibility on your part, for example, "I can interview you any day after 12 P.M."

If you find it necessary to conduct the interview by phone, call to set up a time for a future call. For example, you might say: "I'm interested in a career in desktop publishing and I would like to interview you about job opportunities. If you agree, I can call you back at a time that's convenient for you." In this way, you don't run the risk of asking the person to hold still for an interview while he or she is busy.

Prepare Your Questions

This will ensure using the time available to your best advantage. Of course, as the interview progresses, other questions will come to mind and should be asked. But, a prepared list of questions (to be altered or even eliminated as the interview progresses) will help you obtain the information you need most easily.

Use questions that give the interviewee room to discuss the issues you want to raise. Instead of asking "Do you have formal training in desktop publishing?" (a question that asks for only a simple yes or no), you might ask, "Can you tell me about your background in this field?" (a question that is open-ended and allows the person greater freedom).

Establish Rapport with the Interviewer

Open the interview by thanking the person for making the time available and again state your purpose. Many people receive numerous requests and it helps to remind the person of your specific purpose. You might say something like: "I really appreciate your making time for this interview. As I mentioned, I'm interesting in learning about job opportunities in desktop publishing and your expertise and experience in this area will help a great deal."

Ask Permission to Tape the Interview

Generally, it is a good idea to tape the interview. It will ensure accuracy and will also allow you to concentrate on the interviewee rather than on notetaking. But ask permission first. Some people prefer not to have informal interviews taped. Even if the interview is being conducted by phone, ask permission if you intend to tape the conversation.

Close and Follow up the Interview with an Expression of Appreciation

At the end of the interview, thank the person for making the time available, for being informative, cooperative, helpful, or whatever. On the more practical side, this could make it easier to secure a second interview.

Follow up the interview with a brief note of thanks. You might express your appreciation for the person's time, your enjoyment in speaking with the person, and your accomplishing your goal of getting the information you needed. A sample letter might look like this:

---

555 Anystreet
Anytown, Anystate 10000–5555
December 14, 1996

Ms. Anita Brice
Brice Publishers, Inc.
17 Michigan Avenue
Chicago, Illinois 60600–2345

Dear Ms. Brice:

It was a pleasure meeting you on Tuesday. I greatly appreciate your giving me so much of your time and for sharing your insights into desktop publishing.

I now understand the field a lot better and have a clear idea of the kinds of skills I'll need to succeed.

Again, thank you for your time and your willingness to share your expertise.

Sincerely,

Carlos Villas

Carlos Villas

Power, Confidence, and Verbal Messages

The appearance of confidence gives the appearance of power. Here are some suggestions for communicating confidence with particular reference to the interview situation. The general principles, however, apply to all forms of human communication.

- Control your emotions. Once your emotions get the best of you, you will have lost your power and influence, and you will appear to lack confidence.

- Admit your mistakes. Only a confident person can openly admit mistakes and not worry about what others will think.

- Take the initiative in introducing yourself to others and in initiating specific topics of conversation. These behaviors communicate an ability to control the social situation.

- Generally, don't ask for agreement by using tag questions, for example, "That was appropriate, don't you think?" Asking for agreement communicates a lack of confidence.

- Use open-ended questions to involve the other person in the interaction and follow these up with appropriate comments and/or questions.

- Use "you" statements ("What do you think? How do you feel about this?") to signal your personal attention to the other person.

[Next Power Perspective, page 220]

THE EMPLOYMENT INTERVIEW

Perhaps of most concern to college students is the **employment** or **selection interview**. In such an interview, a great deal of information and persuasion will be exchanged. The interviewer will learn about you, your interests, your talents—and, if he or she is clever enough, some of your weaknesses and liabilities. You will be informed about the nature of the company, its benefits, its advantages—and, if you are clever enough, some of its disadvantages and problems. Before reading about the employment interview, you may wish to take the accompanying test on your own apprehension in this situation.

TEST YOURSELF

How Apprehensive Are You in Employment Interviews?

Instructions This questionnaire is composed of five questions concerning your feelings about communicating in the job interview setting. Indicate in the spaces provided, the degree to which each statement adequately describes your feelings about the employment interview. Use the following scale: (1) = strongly agree, (2) = agree, (3) = are undecided, (4) = disagree, or (5) = strongly disagree.

_____ 1. While participating in a job interview with a potential employer, I am not nervous.

_____ 2. Ordinarily, I am very tense and nervous in job interviews.

_____ 3. I have no fear of speaking up in job interviews.

_____ 4. I'm afraid to speak up in job interviews.

_____ 5. Ordinarily, I am very calm and relaxed in job interviews.

Scoring: In computing your score, follow these steps:
1. Reverse your scores for items 2 and 4 as follows:

if you said	reverse it to
1	5
2	4
3	3
4	2
5	1

2. Add the scores from all five items; be sure to use the reverse scores for items 2 and 4 and the original scores for 1, 3, and 5.

Thinking Critically About Apprehension in the Job Interview

1. The higher your score, the greater your apprehension. Since this test is still under development, specific meanings for specific scores are not possible. A score of 25 (the highest possible score) would indicate a strongly apprehensive individual while a score of 5 (the lowest possible score) would indicate a strongly unapprehensive individual. How does your score compare with those of your peers? What score do you think would ensure optimum performance at the job interview?

2. Your apprehension will probably differ somewhat depending on the type of job interview, your responsibilities, the need and desire you have for the job, and so on. What factors would make you especially apprehensive? Do these answers give you clues as to how to lessen your apprehension?
3. It seems clear that persons demonstrating apprehension during a job interview will be perceived less positively than would someone demonstrating confidence and composure. How might you learn to better display confidence?

Source: This test was developed by Joe Ayres, Debbie M. Ayres, and Diane Sharp (1993).

Why is your attitude going into a job interview so important to your eventual success or failure?

The interview sequence might, for convenience, be divided into three main periods: a preparatory period, in which you prepare for the interview; the interview proper; and the postinterview period, in which you reflect on and follow up the interview. The major goal of this discussion is to provide specific suggestions to make the interview work more effectively for you. Although these principles will prove useful for all interviews, we use the employment interview with you as the interviewee for illustration.

Prepare Yourself

This is perhaps the most difficult aspect of the entire interview process. It is also the step that is most often overlooked. Prepare yourself intellectually. Educate yourself as much as possible about relevant topics. Learn something about the company and its specific product or products. Call and ask the company to send you any company brochures, newsletters,

"This is fine, general, but how are your typing skills?"

Joseph Farris

What is your greatest strength as a job applicant going through an employment interview? How might you demonstrate this strength during an actual interview?

or perhaps a quarterly report. If it's a publishing company, familiarize yourself with their books. If it's an advertising agency, familiarize yourself with their major clients and major advertising campaigns.

If you are applying for a job, both you and the company want something. You want a job that will meet your needs. The company wants an employee who will meet its needs. In short, you each want something that the other has. View the interview as an opportunity to engage in a joint effort to each gain something beneficial. If you approach the interview in this cooperative frame of mind, you are much less likely to become defensive, which in turn will make you a more appealing potential colleague.

A great number of jobs are won or lost solely on physical appearance, so also give attention to physical preparation. Dress in a manner that shows you care enough about the interview to make a good impression. At the same time, dress comfortably. Perhaps the most specific advice we can give is to avoid extremes. If in doubt, it is probably best to err on the side of formality: Wear the tie, high heels, or dress.

Bring with you the appropriate materials, whatever they may be. At the very least, bring a pen and paper, an extra copy or two of your résumé and, if appropriate, a business card. If you are applying for a job in which you have experience, you might bring samples of your previous work.

The importance of your résumé cannot be stressed too much. The résumé is a summary of essential information about your experience, goals, and abilities. Often, a job applicant first submits a résumé. If the employer

What are your most important assets as a job candidate? How might you bring these out in an interview?

thinks it is interesting, the candidate is asked in for an interview. Because of the importance of the résumé and its close association with the interview, a sample one-page résumé and some guidelines to assist you in preparing your own are provided below.

---

(1)
Chris Williams
166 Josen Road
Accord, New York 12404–1678
(914) 555–1221

(2) Objective

To secure a position with a college textbook publisher as a sales representative

(3) Education

A.A., Bronx Community College, 1984
B.A., Queens College, 1996 [expected]
Major: Communication, with emphasis in interpersonal and public communication
Minor: Psychology
Courses included: Interpersonal Communication, Public Speaking, Small Group Communication, Interviewing, Organizational Communication, Public Relations, Persuasion: Theory and Practice, Psychology of Attitude Change
Extracurricular activities: Debate team (2 years), reporter on student newspaper (1 year)

(4) Work Experience

Two years, sales clerk in college bookstore (part-time)
Six years in retail sales at Macy's; managed luggage department for last three years

(5) Special Competencies

Working knowledge of major word processing, spreadsheet, and desktop programs
Basic knowledge of college bookstore operation
Speaking and writing knowledge of Spanish

(6) Personal

Enjoy working with computers and people; willing to relocate and travel

(7) References

References from the following people are on file in the office of Student Personnel, Queens College (Flushing, New York 11367–0151):
Dr. Martha Hubbard (Queens College), major advisor and instructor for three courses
Mr. Jack Sprat (Queens College, Bookstore), manager
Professor Mary Contrari (Queens College), debate coach
Dr. Robert Hood (Bronx Community College), communication instructor

(8)

---

1. Your name, address, and phone number are generally centered at the top of the résumé.

2. For some people, employment objectives may be more general than indicated here, for example, "to secure a management trainee position with a transportation company." If you do have more specific goals, put them down. Do not imply that you will take just anything but also do not appear too specific or demanding.

3. Provide more information than simply your educational degree. Even the major department in which you earned your degree might be too vague, so clarify when necessary. If relevant (as it is in this example), specify some of the most relevant courses you have taken. List honors or awards if they are relevant to your educational or job experience. If the awards are primarily educational (for example, Dean's List), list them under the Education heading; if job related, list them under the Work Experience heading.

4. List work experience in chronological order, beginning with your latest position and working back. Depending on your work experience, you may have to pare down what you write; or, you may have little or nothing to write, so will have to search through your history for some relevant experience. Often the dates of the various positions are included.

5. Highlight your special skills. Do you have some foreign language ability? Do you know how to perform statistical analyses? Do you know how to write a computer program? Do you know how to run popular computer software programs? If you do, put it down. Such competencies are relevant to many jobs.

6. You may also include relevant personal information. Since a sales position often involves travel and even relocation, it is especially important to indicate this willingness here.

7. Here, the specific names of people the potential employer may write to are listed. Sometimes phone numbers are included. If your school maintains personnel files for its students, you may simply note that references may be obtained by writing to the relevant office or department (as is done here). Otherwise, include addresses so that the employer may write to these people. Be sure you keep your file up to date. Three or four references are generally enough.

8. Make sure your résumé creates the impression you want to make. Typographical errors, incorrect spelling, poorly spaced headings and entries, and generally sloppy work will not produce the effect you want.

Establish Goals

All interviews have specific objectives. As part of your preparation, fix these goals firmly in mind. Use them to guide the remainder of your preparation and your behavior during and even after the interview.

After establishing your objectives clearly in your own mind, relate your preparation to these goals. For example, ask yourself how your goals might help you answer questions such as how to dress, what to learn about the specific company, and what questions to ask during the interview.

Reprinted courtesy of Bunny Hoest.

"Very impressive...a Hunting major with a Gathering minor."

CULTURAL VIEWPOINT

Acknowledging Cultural Rules and Customs

All cultures—and organizations are much like cultures—have their own rules for communicating (Barna, 1991; Ruben, 1985; Spitzberg, 1991). These rules identify what is appropriate and what is inappropriate, what will bring rewards and what will bring punishments. For example, in many parts of the United States you would call a person you wish to date three or four days in advance. In certain Asian cultures, you might call the person's parents weeks or even months in advance. In American culture, as a kind of general friendly gesture, you might say, "Come over and pay us a visit." To members of some cultures, this comment is sufficient to prompt them to actually visit at their own convenience.

If a young American girl is talking with an older Indonesian man, for example, she is expected to avoid direct eye contact. To an Indonesian, direct eye contact in this situation would be considered disrespectful. In some Southern European cultures men walk arm in arm. Other cultures (in most of the United States, for example) consider this inappropriate.

Acknowledging the rules of another culture is also helpful when first entering a new organizational culture. First learn their rules and customs. Then you'll be able to choose your actions with a knowledge of what is expected and what is viewed as appropriate.

[Next Cultural Viewpoint, page 233]

Prepare Answers and Questions

If the interview is at all important to you, you will probably think about it for some time. Use this time productively by rehearsing the interview's predicted course. Try also to predict the questions that you will be asked.

Think about the questions that are likely to be asked and how you will answer them. Table 9.1 presents a list of questions commonly asked in employment interviews organized around the major topics on the résumé and draws from a variety of interviewing experts (Stewart & Cash, 1984;

TABLE 9.1 COMMON INTERVIEW QUESTIONS

Question Areas	Examples	Suggestions
Objectives and Career Goals	What made you apply to Datacomm? Do you know much about Datacomm? What do you like most about Datacomm? If you took a job with us, where would you like to be in five years? What benefits do you want to get out of this job?	Be positive (and as specific as you can be) about the company. Demonstrate your knowledge of the company. Take a long-range view; no firm wants to hire someone who will be looking for another job in six months.
Education	What do you think of the education you got at Queens College? Why did you major in communication? What was majoring in communication at Queens like? What kinds of courses did you take? Did you do an internship? What were your responsibilities?	Be positive about your educational experience. Try to relate your educational experience to the specific job. Demonstrate competence but at the same time the willingness to continue your education (either formally or informally).
Previous Work Experience	Tell me about your previous work experience. What did you do exactly? Did you enjoy working at Happy Publications? Why did you leave? How does this previous experience relate to the work you'd be doing here at Datacomm? What kinds of problems did you encounter at your last position?	Again, be positive; never knock a previous job. If you do the interviewer will think you may be criticizing them in the near future. Especially avoid criticizing specific people with whom you worked.
Special Competencies	I see here you have a speaking and writing knowledge of Spanish. Could you talk with someone on the phone in Spanish or write letters in Spanish to our customers? Do you know any other languages? How much do you know about computers? Accessing databases?	Before going into the interview, review your competencies. Explain your skills in as much detail as needed to establish their relevance to the job and your own specific competencies.
Personal	Tell me. Who is Chris Williams? What do you like? What do you dislike? Are you willing to relocate? Are there places you would not consider relocating to? Do you think you'd have any trouble giving orders to others? Do you have difficulty working under deadlines?	Place yourself in the position of the interviewer and ask yourself what kind of person you would hire. Stress your ability to work independently but also as a member of a team. Stress your flexibility in adapting to new work situations.
References	Do the people you listed here know you personally or academically? Which of these people know you the best? Who would give you the best reference? Who else might know about your abilities that we might contact?	Be sure the people you list know you well and especially that they have special knowledge about you that is relevant to the job at hand.

Power, Confidence, and Nonverbal Messages

You can also communicate your confidence and its power nonverbally. Here are a few suggestions:

- Avoid excessive movements, especially self-touching. Tapping a pencil, crossing and uncrossing your legs in rapid succession, or touching your face or hair all communicate uneasiness, a lack of social confidence.
- Maintain eye contact. People who maintain eye contact are judged to be more at ease and unafraid to engage in meaningful interaction.
- Allow your facial expressions to reflect your feelings. Smile, for example, to signal positive reactions.
- Avoid vocalized pauses—the "ers" and "ahs"—that frequently punctuate conversations when you are not quite sure of what to say next.
- Maintain reasonably close distances between yourself and those with whom you interact.

[Next Power Perspective, page 238]

Skopec, 1986; Sincoff & Goyer, 1984; Zima, 1983; Seidman, 1991). You may find it helpful to rehearse with this list before going into the interview. Although not all of these questions would be asked in any one interview, be prepared to answer all of them.

Even though the interviewer will ask most of the questions, you also will want to ask questions. In addition to rehearsing some answers to predicted questions, fix firmly in mind the questions you want to ask.

Make an Effective Presentation of Self

This is probably the most important part of the entire procedure. If you make a bad initial impression, it will be difficult to salvage the rest of the interview. Devote special care to the way you present yourself. Arrive on time—in interview situations, this means five to ten minutes early. This will allow you time to relax, get accustomed to the general surroundings, and perhaps fill out any required forms. And it gives you a cushion should something delay you on the way.

Be sure you know the name of the company, the job title, and the interviewer's name. Although you will have much on your mind, the interviewer's name is not one of the things you can afford to forget or mispronounce.

In presenting yourself, try not to be too casual or too formal. When there is doubt, choose increased formality. Slouching back in the chair, smoking, and chewing gum or candy are obvious behaviors to avoid when you are trying to impress an interviewer.

Demonstrate Effective Interpersonal Communication

Throughout the interview, be certain you demonstrate the interpersonal communication skills spelled out in this book. The interview is the ideal place to put into practice all the skills you have learned. Table 9.2 shows seven characteristics of interpersonal effectiveness (from Chapter 7) with special reference to the interview situation.

In addition to demonstrating these qualities of effectiveness, avoid those behaviors that create negative impressions during employment interviews (Table 9.3).

Follow Up

In most cases, follow up an interview with a thank-you note to the interviewer. In this brief, professional letter, thank the interviewer for his or her time and consideration. Reiterate your interest in the company and perhaps add that you hope to hear from him or her soon. Even if you did not get the job, you might ask to be kept in mind for future openings.

This letter gives you an opportunity to resell yourself—to mention qualities you possess and wish to emphasize, but may have been too modest to discuss at the time. It will help you stand out in the mind of the interviewer, since not many interviewees write letters of thanks. It will also remind the interviewer of your interview and tell her or him you are interested in the position. It's a kind of pat on the back to the interviewer and says, in effect, that the interview was an effective one.

TABLE 9.2
EFFECTIVE INTERPERSONAL COMMUNICATION IN AN INTERVIEW SITUATION

Characteristic	Communications
Openness	Answer questions fully. Avoid one-word answers that may signal a lack of interest or knowledge.
Empathy	See the questions from the asker's point of view. Focus your eye contact and orient your body toward the interviewer. Lean forward as appropriate.
Positiveness	Emphasize your positive qualities. Express positive interest in the position. Avoid statements critical of yourself and others. Do note that in some cultures (China is a good example), interviewees are expected to show modesty (Copeland & Griggs, 1985).
Immediacy	Connect yourself with the interviewer throughout the interview by using the interviewer's name, focusing clearly on the interviewer's remarks, and expressing responsibility for your thoughts and feelings.
Interaction management	Ensure the interviewer's satisfaction by being positive, complimentary, and generally cooperative.
Expressiveness	Let your nonverbal behaviors (especially facial expression and vocal variety) reflect your verbal messages and your general enthusiasm. Avoid fidgeting and excessive moving about.
Other-orientation	Focus on the interviewer and on the company. Express agreement and ask for clarification as appropriate.

What would you identify as your weakest qualities when being interviewed for a job? How might you correct this weakness?

TABLE 9.3 WHY PEOPLE FAIL AT INTERVIEWS

Trait	Examples
Unprepared	Forget to bring their résumé, don't show that they know anything about the company
Poor communication skills	Avoid looking at the interviewer, slouch, slur their words, speak in an overly low or rapid voice; give one-word answers, fidget, dress inappropriately
Unpleasant personality	Appear defensive, cocky, lacking in assertiveness, extremely introverted, overly aggressive
Lack of initiative	Fail to pick up on ramifications of interviewer's questions, give one-word answers, don't ask questions as would be appropriate
Poor listening skills	Easily distracted, need to have questions repeated, fail to maintain appropriate eye contact

QUESTIONS AND ANSWERS

The interviewer's principal tool is the question. Understanding the different types of questions may help you to respond to questions more effectively, as in an employment interview, and to ask questions more effectively, as in an information-gathering interview. Questions may be approached in at least the following two dimensions: open/closed and neutral/biased.

Openness

Openness refers to the degree of freedom the interviewee has to respond, both in content and format. At times there is almost unlimited latitude in what may constitute an answer. At the opposite extreme are questions that require only a yes or no. Between these extremes are short-answer questions; those that are relatively closed and to which the responder has only limited freedom in responding. Representative questions varying in terms of openness/closedness arranged on a scale are provided in Figure 9.1. Note that the first of the five questions allows the interviewee the greatest freedom and the last allows the least. The questions in between allow more freedom than a simple yes or no, but less freedom than the most open question.

Part of the art of successful interviewing is to respond with answers that are appropriate to the question's level of openness. Thus, if you are asked a question like number 1 in Figure 9.1, you are expected to speak at some length. If you are asked a question like number 5, then a simple sentence or two should suffice.

Neutrality

Neutrality and its opposite, **bias,** refer to the extent to which the question provides the answer the interviewer wants from the interviewee. Some questions are neutral and do not specify any answer as more appropriate than any other. At the other extreme are questions that are biased, or

OPEN

1. What are some of the problems you see in your family?

2. What are some of the communication problems you see in your family?

3. What communication problems do you see between your children?

4. What do you think can be done to make Pat more communicative?

5. Do you enjoy spending the weekend with the family?

CLOSED

Figure 9.1 Examples of Questions Varying in Openness

loaded. These indicate quite clearly the particular answer the interviewer expects or wants. Compare the following questions:

- How did you feel about managing your own desktop publishing company?
- You must really enjoy managing your own desktop publishing company, don't you?

The first question is neutral and allows the listener to respond in any way; it asks for no particular answer. The second question is biased; it specifies that the interviewer expects a yes. Between the neutrality of "How did you feel about your previous job?" and the bias of "You must have loved your previous job, didn't you?" there are questions that specify with varying degrees of strength the answer the interviewer expects or prefers. For example:

- Did you like your previous job?
- Did you dislike your previous job very much?
- It seems like it would be an interesting job, no?

An interviewer who asks too many biased questions will not learn about the interviewee's talents or experiences but only about the interviewee's ability to give the desired answer. As an interviewee, pay special attention to the biased type of question. Do not give the responses your interviewer expects if they are not what you believe to be correct or know to be the truth. This would be unethical. However, when your responses are not what the interviewer expects, consider explaining why you are responding as you are. For example, to the biased question, "It seems like it would be an interesting job, no?" you might respond: "It was interesting most of the time, but it didn't allow for enough creativity."

THINKING CRITICALLY ABOUT THE LEGALITY OF INTERVIEW QUESTIONS

Can you develop examples of increasingly open questions beginning with "Do you dislike your current job?" Can you develop increasingly closed questions beginning with "What can you do for our company?"

Can any question be totally neutral?

'Tis not every question that deserves an answer.
—THOMAS FULLER

Through the Equal Employment Opportunity Commission, the federal government has classified some questions as unlawful. These are federal guidelines and therefore apply in all 50 states; individual states, however, may have added further restrictions. You may find it interesting to take the self-test (constructed with the good help of Stewart & Cash, 1984, and Zincoff & Goyer, 1984) to see if you can identify which questions are lawful and which are unlawful.

TEST YOURSELF
Can You Identify Unlawful Questions?

Instructions For each question write L (Lawful) if you think the question is legal for an interviewer to ask in an employment interview and U (Unlawful) if you think the question is illegal. For each question you consider unlawful, indicate why you think it is so classified.

_____ 1. Are you married, Tom?

_____ 2. When did you graduate from high school, Mary?

_____ 3. Do you have a picture so I can attach it to your résumé?

_____ 4. Will you need to be near a mosque (church, synagogue)?

_____ 5. I see you taught courses in gay and lesbian studies. Are you gay?

_____ 6. Is Chinese your native language?

_____ 7. Will you have difficulty getting a baby-sitter?

_____ 8. I notice that you walk with a limp. Is this a permanent injury?

_____ 9. Where were you born?

_____ 10. Have you ever been arrested for a crime?

Thinking Critically About the Legality of Employment Interview Questions

All ten questions are unlawful. Review the questions and try to develop the general principles governing the illegality of employment interview questions. Also consider how you would respond to each question if you were asked this in an actual job interview.

Can you identify possible legitimate reasons for asking each of these questions?

The things most people want to know are usually none of their business.

—GEORGE BERNARD SHAW

Do you agree that certain questions should be considered illegal in a job interview? What types of questions do you think should be considered illegal?

Some of the more important areas in which unlawful questions are frequently asked concern age, marital status, race, religion, nationality, citizenship, physical condition, and arrest and criminal records. For example, it is legal to ask applicants whether they meet the legal age requirements for the job and could provide proof of that. But it is unlawful to ask their exact age, even in indirect ways as illustrated in question 2 in the self-test. It is unlawful to ask about a person's marital status (question 1) or about family matters that are unrelated to the job (question 7). An interviewer may ask you, however, to identify a close relative or guardian if you are a minor, or any relative who currently works for the company.

Questions concerning your race (questions 3 and 6), religion (question 4), national origin (question 9), affectional orientation (question 5), age (question 2), handicaps unrelated to job performance (question 8), or even arrest record (question 10) are unlawful, as are questions that get at this same information in oblique ways. (Note, for example, that requiring a picture may be a way of discriminating against an applicant on the basis of sex, race, and age.)

The interviewer may ask you what languages you are fluent in but may not ask what your native language is (question 6), what language you speak at home, or what language your parents speak. The interviewer may ask you if you if are in this country legally but may not ask if you were born in this country or naturalized (question 9).

The interviewer may inquire into your physical condition only insofar as the job is concerned. For example, the interviewer may ask, "Do you have any physical problems that might prevent you from fulfilling your responsibilities at this job?" But the interviewer may not ask about any physical disabilities (question 8). The interviewer may ask you if you have been convicted of a felony but not if you've been arrested (question 10).

These are merely examples of some of the lawful and unlawful questions that may be asked during an interview. Note that even the questions used as examples here might be lawful in specific situations. The test to apply Is simple: Is the information related to your ability to perform the job? Such questions are referred to as BFOQ (bona fide occupational qualification) questions.

Once you have discovered what questions are unlawful, consider how to deal with them if they come up during an interview.

Dealing with Unlawful Questions

Your first strategy should be to deal with such questions by answering the part you do not object to and omitting any information you do not want to give. For example, if you are asked the unlawful question concerning what language is spoken at home, you may respond with a statement such as "I have some language facility in German and Italian," without specifying a direct answer to the question. If you are asked to list all the organizations of which you are a member (an unlawful question in many states, since it is often a way of getting at political affiliation, religion, nationality, and various other areas), you might respond by saying something like: "The only organizations I belong to that are relevant to this job are the International Communication Association and the Speech Communication Association."

Generally, this type of response is preferable to the one that immediately tells the interviewer he or she is asking an unlawful question. In many cases, the interviewer may not even be aware of the legality of various questions and may have no intention of trying to get at information you are not obliged to give. It is easy to conceive of situations in which the interviewer, for example, recognizes the nationality of your last name and wants to mention that he or she is also of the same nationality. If you immediately take issue with the question, you will be creating problems where none really exist.

On the other hand, do recognize that in many employment interviews, the unwritten intention is to keep certain people out, whether it is people who are older or those of a particular marital status, sexual orientation, nationality, religion, and so on. If you are confronted by questions that are unlawful and that you do not want to answer, and if the gentle method described above does not work and your interviewer persists—saying, for example, "Is German the language spoken at home?" or "What other organizations have you belonged to?"—you might counter by saying that such information is irrelevant to the interview and to the position you are seeking. Again, be courteous but firm. Say something like, "This position does not call for any particular language skill and so it does not matter what language is spoken in my home." Or you might say, "The organizations I mentioned are the only relevant ones; whatever other organizations I belong to will certainly not interfere with my ability to perform at this job."

If the interviewer still persists—and it is doubtful that many would after these rather clear and direct responses—you might note that these questions are unlawful and that you are not going to answer them.

Feedback on Concepts and Skills

In this chapter we looked at that unique form of interpersonal communication that relies essentially on a question-and-answer format, the interview. We considered the types of interviews and focused on the principles for the information gathering and the employment interviews. The types of questions used in interviews (and their potential illegality) were identified.

1. Interviewing is a form of interpersonal communication in which two persons interact largely through a question-and-answer format to achieve specific goals.
2. Six types of interviewing are the persuasive interview, the appraisal interview, the exit interview, the counseling interview, the information interview, and the employment interview.
3. In the information interview the following guides should prove useful: Select the person you wish to interview, secure an appointment, prepare your questions, establish rapport with the interviewer, ask permission to tape the interview, ask open-ended questions, and follow up the interview.
4. Before the employment interview, prepare yourself intellectually and physically for the interview; establish your objectives; and prepare answers to predicted questions.
5. During the interview, make an effective presentation of yourself and demonstrate effective interpersonal communication skills.
6. After the interview, mentally review the interview and follow it up with a brief letter.
7. Questions may be indexed in terms of open/closed and neutral/biased. The type of question asked will influence the usefulness of the information obtained.
8. Interviewees should familiarize themselves with possible unlawful questions and develop strategies to deal with them.

Throughout this chapter, we stressed the skills of interviewing. Check your ability to apply these skills. Use the following scale: (1) = almost always, (2) = often, (3) = sometimes, (4) = rarely, (5) = almost never.

_____ 1. I follow the basic guidelines in conducting informative interviews.

_____ 2. Before the interview, I prepare myself intellectually and physically; establish my objectives as clearly as I can; and prepare answers to predicted questions.

_____ 3. During the interview, I make an effective presentation of myself and demonstrate effective interpersonal communication skills.

_____ 4. After the interview, I mentally review the interview and follow it up with a letter.

_____ 5. I can frame questions varying in terms of openness/closedness and neutral/biased depending on my purpose.

_____ 6. I can recognize and respond appropriately to unlawful questions.

Skill Development Experiences

9.1 Expressing Confidence

The following brief dialogue might take place during an initial job interview. Read through the transcript and identify the elements that demonstrate a lack of confidence. Indicate how the applicant might have better represented himself as a more confident, more in-control type of individual.

Mr. Ross:	And you are?
Phil Snap:	Me? Oh, I'm Phil. Mr. Snap. Phil Snap.
Mr. Ross:	So, Mr. Snap, what can I do for you?
Phil Snap:	I'm here for, I mean I'm applying for that job.
Mr. Ross:	So, you'd like a job with Datacomm. Is that right?
Phil Snap:	Well, er, yes. Don't you think that's a good idea? I mean, it's a good company, no?
Mr. Ross:	Tell me about your college career, your courses, your major.
Phil Snap:	Well, I guess, I mean, I took lots of courses in college. Here's my transcript.
Mr. Ross:	I can read your transcript. But I want to hear from you exactly what you did in college.
Phil Snap:	Well, I took courses in, like, liberal arts—history, political science, English, communication, psychology.
Mr. Ross:	Can you be a little more specific?
Phil Snap:	Excuse me. I guess I'm a little nervous. This is my first interview and I really don't know what to say.
Mr. Ross:	[*Smiling*] Are you sure you graduated?
Phil Snap:	Oh, yes, I did. See, it's on the transcript.
Mr. Ross:	Yes, I know. Let me put it this way: Do you think you can do anything for Datacomm?
Phil Snap:	Oh. Yes. Yes.
Mr. Ross:	Okay, Mr. Snap, now exactly what can you do for Datacomm that the next applicant can't do better?
Phil Snap:	Oh, well, I really don't know much about Datacomm. I mean, I may be wrong about this, but I thought I would assist someone and learn the job that way.
Mr. Ross:	Right. What skills can you bring to Datacomm? Why would you make such a good learner?
Phil Snap:	Damn, this isn't as easy as I thought it would be. Well, I'm not very good at giving speeches. But I guess that's not too important anyway, right?
Mr. Ross:	Everything is important, Mr. Snap. But tell me what you are especially good at.
Phil Snap:	Well, I guess I'm kind of good at group stuff—you know, working with people in groups.
Mr. Ross:	No, I'm not sure I know what that means. Tell me.
Phil Snap:	Like, I mean I'm pretty good at just working with people. People think I'm kind of a neat guy.
Mr. Ross:	I don't doubt that, Mr. Snap, but do you have any other talents—other than being a neat guy?
Phil Snap:	I can operate a Showpro system. Is that important?

Mr. Ross:	Mr. Snap, I told you that everything is important.
Phil Snap:	Is there anything else?
Mr. Ross:	I don't know, Mr. Snap, is there anything else?
Phil Snap:	I don't know.
Mr. Ross:	I want to thank you for your time, Mr. Snap. We'll be in touch with you.
Phil Snap:	Oh, I got the job?
Mr. Ross:	Not exactly. If we decide on you, we will call you.
Phil Snap:	Okay.

9.2 Responding to Unlawful Questions

This exercise is designed to raise some of the unlawful questions that you don't have to answer, and provide you with some practice in developing responses that protect your privacy while maintaining a positive relationship with the interviewer. In the self-test "Can You Identify Unlawful Questions?", ten questions were presented. Assume that you did not want to answer the questions. How would you respond to each of them? One useful procedure is to write your responses and then compare them with those of other students, either in groups or with the class as a whole. Or form two-person groups and role-play the interviewer-interviewee situation. To make this realistic, the person playing the interviewer should press for an answer, while the interviewee should continue to avoid answering, yet respond positively and cordially. You will discover this is not always easy; tempers often flare in this type of interaction.

9.3 Experiencing and Analyzing Interviews

Form three-person groups, preferably among persons who do not know each other well or who have had relatively little interaction. One person should be designated the interviewer, another the interviewee, and the third the interview analyst. The interview analyst should choose one of the following situations:

1. An interview for the position of camp counselor for children with disabilities.
2. An interview for a part in a new Broadway musical.
3. A therapy interview to focus on communication problems in relating to superiors.
4. A teacher-student interview in which the teacher is trying to discover why the course taught last semester was such a dismal failure.
5. An interview between the chair of the Communication Department and a candidate for the position of instructor of Human Communication.

After the situation is chosen, the interviewer should interview the interviewee for approximately ten minutes. The analyst should observe but not interfere in any way. After the interview is over, the analyst should offer a detailed analysis, considering each of the following:

1. What happened during the interview (essentially a description of the interaction)?
2. What was well handled?
3. What went wrong? What aspects of the interview were not handled as effectively as they might have been?
4. What could have been done to make the interview more effective?

The analysts for each interview may then report their major findings to the class as a whole. A list of "common faults" or "suggestions for improving interviews" may then be developed by the instructor or group leader.

CHAPTER TEN

Small Groups

Chapter Concepts	Chapter Goals	Chapter Skills
	After completing this chapter, you should be able to	After completing this chapter, you should be able to
The Small Group	1. define *small group* and *small group communication*	recognize the norms of the groups in which you function and take these norms into consideration when interacting
The Idea-Generation Group	2. explain the purpose of brainstorming and its four rules	follow the general rules when brainstorming appropriately restimulate a brainstorming group that has lost its steam
The Personal Growth Group	3. describe the personal growth group and explain its general procedures	respond with supportiveness in consciousness-raising experiences
Information-Sharing Groups	4. describe the educational or learning group and the focus group	employ organizational structure in educational or learning groups
The Problem-Solving Group	5. explain the steps that should be followed in problem-solving discussions	follow the five steps when in group problem-solving situations make use of the wide variety of group structures available
Small Group Formats	6. define the structure and function of the round table, the panel, the symposium, and the symposium-forum	use the appropriate group format to best serve your purposes
Thinking Critically About Small Groups	7. explain the critical thinking guidelines for small groups	think critically in groups and use the six thinking hats technique to consider problems and solutions
	8. explain the six critical thinking hats technique for analyzing issues	

C onsider how many groups you are a member of. The family is the most obvious example, but you are also a member of a team, a class, a club, a sorority or fraternity, a collection of friends, and so on. Some of your most important and satisfying communications probably take place in small groups. In this chapter we first look at the small group's nature and characteristics and examine four major types of small groups.

THE SMALL GROUP

How many groups are you a member of? Why do you belong to these groups? What needs do these groups serve?

A small group is a relatively small number of individuals who are related to each other by some common purpose and share some degree of organization. It's a collection of individuals few enough in number that all may communicate with relative ease as both senders and receivers. Generally, a small group consists of approximately 5 to 12 people; in groups of this size each member is able to function as both source and receiver with relative ease. If the group is much larger than 12 this becomes difficult.

Group members are connected to one another in some way. People in a movie theater would not constitute a group, since there is no interaction directed at a common purpose. In a small group, one member's behavior is significant for all members. There must be some common purpose among the group's members. This does not mean that all members must have exactly the same purpose. But there must be some similarity in their reasons for interacting.

Group members are also connected by some structure of organizing rules. Sometimes the structure is rigid—as in groups operating under parliamentary procedure, where comments must follow prescribed rules. At other times, the structure is loose, as in a social gathering. Yet both groups have some organization and structure: Two people do not speak at the same time, a member's comments or questions are responded to, not ignored, and so on.

Society in its full sense . . . is never an entity separable from the individuals who compose it.
—*RUTH BENEDICT*

Small Group Stages

The small group develops in much the same way that a conversation develops. As in conversation, there are five stages: opening, feedforward, business, feedback, and closing. The **opening** period is usually a getting-acquainted time when members introduce themselves and engage in phatic communion. After this preliminary get-together, there is usually some **feedforward,** some attempt to identify what needs to be done, who will do it, and so on. In a formal group, the agenda (which is a perfect example of feedforward) might be reviewed and the tasks of the group identified. The **business** portion is the actual discussion of the tasks—the

A group is best defined as a dynamic whole based on interdependence rather than on similarity.
—*KURT LEWIN*

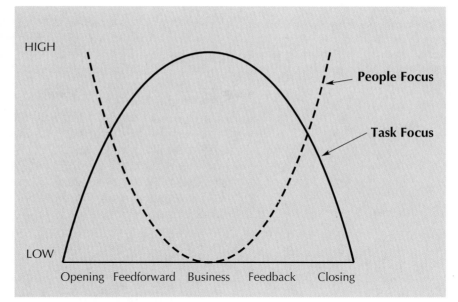

Figure 10.1 Small Group Stages and the Focus on Task and People

problem solving, the sharing of information, or whatever else the group needs to do. At the **feedback** stage, the group might reflect on what it has done and perhaps what remains to be done. Some groups may even evaluate their performance at this stage. At the **closing** stage the group members again return to their focus on individuals and will perhaps exchange closing comments—"Good seeing you again," and so on. Note that the focus of the group shifts from people to task and then again back to people. A typical pattern would look like Figure 10.1.

CULTURAL VIEWPOINT

The Small Group as a Culture

Often, a group—especially one of long standing, like a work group—develops into a kind of small culture with its own norms; these are the rules or standards identifying which behaviors are considered appropriate (willingness to take on added tasks or directing conflict toward issues rather than toward people) and which are considered inappropriate (coming late or not contributing actively). Sometimes these rules for appropriate behavior are explicitly stated in a company contract or policy: All members must attend department meetings. Sometimes the rules are implicit: Members should be well groomed. Regardless of whether norms are spelled out or not, they are powerful regulators of members' behaviors.

Norms may apply to individual members as well as to the group as a whole and, of course, will differ from one group to another (Axtell, 1990, 1993). For example, in Japan it is customary to begin meetings with what Americans would think is unnecessary socializing.

While Americans prefer to get right down to business, the Japanese prefer rather elaborate socializing before getting to the business at hand. In the United States men and women in business are expected to interact when making business decisions as well as when socializing. In Muslim and Buddhist societies, however, there are religious restrictions that prevent mixing the sexes. In the United States, Bangladesh, Australia, Germany, Finland, and Hong Kong, for example, punctuality for business meetings is very important. But in countries like Morocco, Italy, Brazil, Zambia, Ireland, and Panama, for example, time is less highly regarded, and being late is no great insult and is even expected. In the United States, and in much of Asia and Europe, meetings are held between two groups. In many Gulf states, however, the business executive is likely to conduct meetings with several different people—sometimes dealing with totally different issues—at the same time. In this situation, you have to expect to share what in the United States would be "your time" with these other parties. In the United States very little interpersonal touching goes on during business meetings; in Arab countries, however, touching (for example, hand holding) is common and is a gesture of friendship.

Norms that regulate a particular member's behavior, called **role expectations,** identify what each person in an organization is expected to do—for example, Pat has a great computer setup and so should play the role of secretary.

You are more likely to accept the norms of your group's culture when you (Napier & Gershenfeld, 1989):

- want to continue your membership in the group.
- feel your group membership is important.
- are in a group that is cohesive, when you and the other members are closely connected, are attracted to each other, and depend on each other to meet your needs.
- would be punished by negative reactions or exclusion from the group for violating the group norms.

[Next Cultural Viewpoint, page 258]

Never doubt that a small group of thoughtful, committed citizens can change the world. Indeed, it is the only thing that ever has.
—MARGARET MEAD

TEST YOURSELF
How Apprehensive Are You in Group Discussions?

Instructions Just as we are apprehensive in interpersonal conversations (Chapter 7), each of us is apprehensive to some degree in group discussions. This brief test is designed to measure your apprehension in these small group communication situations.

This questionnaire consists of six statements concerning your feelings about communication in group discussions. Indicate the degree to which each statement applies to you by marking whether you (1) strongly agree, (2) agree,

"High communication apprehensives," note Richmond and McCroskey (1992), "typically attempt to avoid small group communication or to sit rather quietly in a group if they must be present." Do you observe this tendency in yourself or in others? As a group member, how might you help reduce this apprehension?

How do your apprehension scores for group discussions and meetings compare with your score for interpersonal conversations (see pages 153–154)? How do you account for the differences?

(3) are undecided, (4) disagree, or (5) strongly disagree with each statement. There are no right or wrong answers. Do not be concerned that some of the statements are similar. Work quickly; just record your first impression.

_____ 1. I dislike participating in group discussions.
_____ 2. Generally, I am comfortable while participating in group discussions.
_____ 3. I am tense and nervous while participating in group discussions.
_____ 4. I like to get involved in group discussions.
_____ 5. Engaging in a group discussion with new people makes me tense and nervous.
_____ 6. I am calm and relaxed while participating in group discussions.

Thinking Critically About Small Group Apprehension To obtain your apprehension for group discussion score use the following formula:

18   plus scores for items 2, 4, and 6
      minus scores for items 1, 3, and 5

Scores above 18 show some degree of apprehension.

Because small groups vary so widely, you are likely to experience very different degrees of apprehension depending on the nature of the specific group. Work groups, for example, may cause greater apprehension than groups of friends. Similarly, the degree of familiarity you have with the members and the extent to which you see yourself as one of the group (rather than an outsider) will also influence your apprehension. What other factors might influence your small group apprehension?

Source: From *An Introduction to Rhetorical Communication,* 5th ed, by James C. McCroskey. Englewood Cliffs, NJ: Prentice-Hall, 1986. Reprinted by permission of the author.

THE IDEA-GENERATION GROUP

Many small groups exist solely to generate ideas. A process often used in generating ideas is **brainstorming** (Osborn, 1957; Beebe & Masterson, 1994), a technique for analyzing a problem with as many ideas as possible. The technique is also useful when you are trying to generate ideas by yourself—ideas for speeches or term papers, ideas for Saturday night, or ways to improve the student newspaper. Brainstorming is especially helpful because it lessens the inhibition of members and encourages them to exercise their creativity. It also illustrates the effectiveness of cooperative team work; members soon learn that their own ideas and creativity are sparked by the contributions of others. The technique also builds member pride in the final solution since all will have contributed to it.

Brainstorming occurs in two phases. The first is the brainstorming period proper; the second is the evaluation period. The procedures are simple. A problem is selected that is amenable to many possible solutions or ideas. Before the actual session, group members are informed of the problem so they can think about the topic. When the group meets, each person contributes as many ideas as he or she can think of. If ideas are to be recorded, a reporter is appointed or a tape recorder is set up and tested at the beginning of the session. During this idea-generating session, members follow four rules.

- No evaluation is permitted. All ideas are recorded. They are not evaluated or even discussed. Any evaluation—whether verbal or nonverbal—is criticized by the leader or members. By prohibiting evaluation, group members will more likely participate freely.
- Quantity is desired. The more ideas generated, the more likely there will be a winner.
- Combinations and extensions are desired. While members may not criticize a particular idea, they may extend or combine it. The value of a particular idea may well be in the way it stimulates another member.
- Freewheeling is desired. The wilder the idea, the better. A wild idea can be tempered easily, but it is not so easy to elaborate on a simple or conservative idea.

At times, the brainstorming session may break down with members failing to contribute new ideas. At this point, the moderator may prod members with statements such as:

- Let's try to get a few more ideas before we close this session.
- Can we piggyback any other ideas or extensions on the suggestion to . . .
- Here's what we have so far. As I read the list of contributed suggestions, additional ideas may come to mind.
- Here's an aspect we haven't focused on. Does this stimulate any ideas?

After all the ideas are generated—a period lasting no longer than 15 or 20 minutes—the entire list is evaluated. Unworkable ones are thrown out; those showing promise are retained and evaluated. During this phase, negative criticism is allowed.

THE PERSONAL GROWTH GROUP

We all need encouragement and support in the human growth process.

—DONALD SIMMERMACHER

Some personal growth groups aim to help members cope with particular problems, such as alcoholism, having an alcoholic parent, being an ex-convict, or having an overactive child or an abusive spouse. Other groups are more clearly therapeutic and are designed to change significant aspects of one's personality or behavior.

Some Popular Personal Growth Groups

The encounter group tries to facilitate personal growth and the ability to deal effectively with other people (Rogers, 1970). One of its assumptions is that members will be more effective psychologically and socially if they get to know and like themselves better. Consequently, the atmosphere of the encounter group is one of acceptance and support. Freedom to express your inner thoughts, fears, and doubts is stressed. The assertiveness training group aims to increase the willingness of its members to stand up for their rights and to act more assertively in a variety of situations (Adler, 1977).

The consciousness-raising group helps people cope with society's problems. Members all have one characteristic in common (for instance, they are all women, all unwed mothers, all new fathers, or all ex-priests). It is this commonality that leads members to join together and assist one

"I've just joined a support group for boring people."

another. In the consciousness-raising group, the assumption is that similar people are best equipped to assist each other's personal growth. Structurally, the group is leaderless. All members (usually 6 to 12 people) are equal in their control of the group and in their presumed knowledge.

A Sample Consciousness-Raising Group

Here is the way in which one consciousness-raising group operates. While in this group, the procedures are rather rigidly formulated and enforced, others operate with more flexible rules. A topic, which may be drawn from a prepared list or suggested by one of the members, is selected by majority vote. Regardless of the topic, it is always discussed from the point of view of the larger topic that brings these particular people together—let's say, women's liberation. Whether the topic is education, employment, or family, it is pursued in light of the issues and problems of the liberation of women.

After a topic is chosen, a member is selected (through some random procedure) to start. This member speaks for approximately ten minutes about his or her feelings, experiences, and thoughts. The focus is always on oneself. No interruptions are allowed. After the member has finished, other group members may ask questions for clarification. The feedback from other members is to be totally supportive.

Have you ever participated in a personal growth group? How did it compare with the one described here? What was its major purpose? Its general structure? Its major outcomes? What types of growth groups would you enjoy and profit from?

Compliance-Gaining Strategies

Compliance-gaining strategies are the tactics that influence others to do what you want them to do. Here are a few (Marwell & Schmitt, 1967, 1990; Miller & Parks, 1982):

1. **Liking.** Pat is helpful and friendly in order to get Chris in a good mood so that Chris will be more likely to comply with Pat's request.

   Pat: [*After cleaning up the living room and bedroom*] I'd really like to relax and bowl a few games with Terry. OK?

2. **Promise.** Pat promises to reward Chris if Chris complies with Pat's request.

   Pat: I'll give you anything you want if you will just give me a divorce. You can have the house, the car, the stocks, the three kids; just give me my freedom.

3. **Positive self-feelings.** Pat promises that Chris will feel better if Chris complies with Pat's request. Or **negative self-feelings** (Pat promises that Chris will feel worse if Chris does not comply with Pat's request).

   Pat: You'll see. You'll feel a lot better after the divorce. [*Or*], You'll hate yourself if you don't give me this divorce.

4. **Moral appeals.** Pat argues that Chris should comply because it is moral to comply and immoral not to comply.

   Pat: Ethical people would never stand in the way of their partner's freedom and sanity.

[Next Power Perspective, page 243]

After the questions have been answered, the next member speaks. The same procedure is followed until all members have spoken. Following the last member, there is a general discussion. During this time members may connect their own experience to the experiences of others. Or they may tell the group how they feel about some of the issues raised.

Members raise their consciousness by formulating and verbalizing thoughts on a particular topic, hearing how others feel and think about the same topic, and formulating and answering questions.

INFORMATION-SHARING GROUPS

The purpose of information-sharing groups is to acquire new information or skill through a sharing of knowledge. In most information-sharing groups, all members have something to teach and something to learn. In others, the interaction takes place because some have information and some do not.

Educational or Learning Groups

Members may follow a variety of discussion patterns. For example, a historical topic might be developed chronologically, with the discussion progressing from the past into the present and perhaps predicting the future. Issues in developmental psychology, such as a child's language development or physical maturity, might also be discussed chronologically. Other

In what ways might information-sharing groups help to improve worker morale or productivity?

Your behavior influences others
through a ripple effect. A ripple
effect works because everyone
influences everyone else.
—JOHN HEIDER

Have you ever participated in an
educational or learning group?
Was it effective? How might it have
been more effective?

The wisest mind has something yet
to learn.
—GEORGE SANTAYANA

topics lend themselves to spatial development. For example, the development of the United States might take a spatial pattern—from east to west—or a chronological pattern—from 1776 to the present. Other suitable patterns, depending on the topic and the group's needs, might be causes and effects, problems and solutions, or structures and functions.

Perhaps the most popular is the topical pattern. A group might discuss the legal profession by itemizing and discussing each of its major functions. A corporation's structure might also be considered in terms of its major divisions. Each of these topics may be further systematized by, say, listing the legal profession's functions in terms of importance or complexity and ordering the corporation's major structures in terms of decision-making power.

Focus Groups

A different type of learning group is the focus group, a kind of in-depth interview of a small group. The aim here is to discover what people think about an issue or product, for example, what do men between 18 and 25 think of the new aftershave lotion and its packaging? What do young executives earning over $70,000 think of buying a foreign luxury car?

In the focus group the leader tries to discover the beliefs, attitudes, thoughts, and feelings that members have so as to better guide decisions on changing the scent or redesigning the packaging or constructing advertisements for luxury cars. It is the leader's task to prod members to analyze their thoughts and feelings on a deeper than usual level and to use the thoughts of one member to stimulate the thoughts of others.

For example, in one study the researcher tried "to collect supplementary data on the perceptions graduates have of the Department of Communication at ABC University" (Lederman, 1990). Two major research questions, taken directly from Lederman's study, motivated this focus group:

- What do graduates of the program perceive the educational effectiveness of their major at ABC?
- What would they want implemented in the program as it exists today?

Group participants then discussed their perceptions, organized around such questions as these (Lederman, 1990):

- The first issue to discuss is what the program was like when you were a major in the department. Let's begin by going around the table and making introductions. Will you tell me your name, when you graduated from ABC, what you are doing now, and what the program was like when you were here, as you remember it?
- Based on what you remember of the program and what you have used from your major since graduating, what kinds of changes, if any, would you suggest?

THE PROBLEM-SOLVING GROUP

A problem-solving group meets to solve a problem or to reach a decision. In one sense, this is the most demanding kind of group. It requires not

In what types of problem-solving discussions do you regularly engage? Will problem-solving discussions be a part of your professional life? Your relationship life?

only a knowledge of small group communication techniques but a thorough knowledge of the particular problem. And it usually demands faithful adherence to a set of procedural rules.

The Problem-Solving Sequence

The problem-solving approach, which owes its formulation to the philosopher John Dewey's steps in reflective thinking, identifies six steps (see Figure 10.2). These steps are designed to make problem solving more efficient and effective.

Define and Analyze the Problem

In many instances the nature of the problem is clearly specified. For example, a group of designers might discuss how to package a new soap. In other instances, the problem may be vague, and it is up to the group to define it. For example, the general problem may be poor campus communications. But such a vague and general topic is difficult to tackle in a problem-solving discussion. So, for purposes of discussion, a group might be more specific and focus on how can we improve the student newspaper.

Generally, it is best to define the problem as an open-ended question ("How can we improve the student newspaper?") rather than as a statement ("The student newspaper needs to be improved") or a yes/no question ("Does the student newspaper need improvement?"). The open-ended question allows greater freedom of exploration. The problem should also be limited to a manageable area for discussion. A question such as "How can we improve the university?" is too broad and general. It would be more effective to limit the problem by focusing on one subdivision of the university. For example, you might select one of

A problem well stated is a problem half solved.
—CHARLES F. KETTERING

the following categories for discussion: the student newspaper, student-faculty relationships, registration, examination scheduling, or student advisory services.

In defining the problem, the group must analyze it—identify its dimensions. Although there are no prescribed questions that apply to all problems, appropriate questions (for most problems) seem to revolve around the following issues.

- Duration: How long has there been a problem with securing advertising? Does it look as though it will grow or lessen in importance?
- Causes: What seems to be causing the newspaper problem? Are there specific policies (editorial, advertising, or design) that might be the cause?
- Effects: What effects is this problem producing? How significant are these effects? Who is affected: students? alumni? faculty? people in the community?

The mere formulation of a problem is often far more essential than its solution, which may be a matter of mathematical or experimental skill. To raise new questions, new possibilities, to regard old problems from a new angle requires creative imagination and marks real advance in science.
—ALBERT EINSTEIN

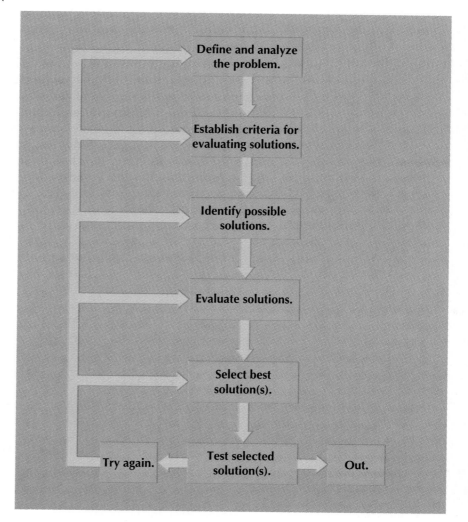

Figure 10.2 The Problem-Solving Sequence

"You know what your problem is? You don't know what your problem is. . . . That's what your problem is!!"

Cartoon by Rick Stromoski

Establish Criteria for Evaluating Solutions

Notice how different your possible solutions would be to, say, "How should convicts be treated?" depending on whether you felt your solutions should punish or rehabilitate. Therefore, before proposing any solutions, decide how you will evaluate the solutions. At this stage, then, you identify standards or criteria that you will use in evaluating the solutions or in selecting one solution over another. Generally, two types of criteria need to be considered. First, there are the practical criteria. For example, you might decide that the solutions must not increase the budget or that it must lead to a 10 percent increase in advertising revenue.

Second, are the value criteria. These are more difficult to pinpoint but might include, for example, that the newspaper must be a learning experience for all who work on it or that it must uphold the standards of free speech as established by the university.

Identify Possible Solutions

At this stage identify as many solutions as possible. Focus on quantity rather than quality. Brainstorming may be particularly useful at this point. Solutions to the student newspaper problem might include incorporating reviews of faculty publications, student evaluations of specific courses, reviews of restaurants in the campus area, outlines for new courses, and employment information.

Evaluate Solutions

After all solutions have been proposed, group members evaluate each. For example, does incorporating reviews of area restaurants meet the criteria? Would it increase the budget? Would it lead to an increase in advertising revenue? Each potential solution should be matched against the criteria for evaluation.

Select the Best Solution(s)

At this stage the best solution or solutions are selected and put into operation. Let's assume that reviews of faculty publications and outlines for new

What type of criteria would an advertising agency use in evaluating a campaign to sell soap? A university in evaluating a new multicultural curriculum? Parents in evaluating a preschool for their children?

Some problems are so complex that you have to be highly intelligent and well informed just to be undecided about them.
—LAURENCE J. PETER

Compliance-Resisting Strategies

Let's say that someone you know asks you to do something that you do not want to do, for example, lend your term paper so that this person might copy it and turn it in to another teacher. Research with college students shows that there are four major ways of responding (McLaughlin, Cody, & Robey, 1980; O'Hair, Cody, & O'Hair, 1991).

In using **identity management** you resist by trying to manipulate the image of the person making the request. For example, you might picture the person as unreasonable and say, for example, "That's really unfair of you to ask me to compromise my ethics." Or, "You know this material much better than I do; you can easily do a much better paper yourself."

When you use **non-negotiation** you refuse directly to do as requested. You might simply say, "No, I don't lend my papers out."

Resisting compliance by perhaps offering a compromise is called **negotiation** ("I'll let you read my paper but not copy it") or by offering to help the person in some other way ("If you write a first draft, I'll go over it and try to make some comments").

Justification involves justifying your refusal by citing possible consequences of compliance or noncompliance. For example, you might cite a negative consequence if you complied ("I'm afraid that I'd get caught") or you might cite a positive consequence of your not complying ("You'll really enjoy writing this paper; it's a lot of fun").

[Next Power Perspective, page 263]

courses best meet the criteria for evaluating solutions. The group might then incorporate these two new items in the newspaper's next issue. Groups use different decision-making Methods in deciding, for example, which solution to accept (see "Decision-Making methods" below). The method to be used should naturally be stated at the outset of the group discussion.

Test Selected Solution(s)

After putting the solution(s) into operation, test their effectiveness. The group might, for example, poll the students about the new newspaper or check the number of copies purchased. Or the group might analyze the advertising revenue or determine whether the readership did increase 10 percent.

If these solutions prove ineffective, the group returns to a previous stage and repeats part of the process. Often this is selecting other solutions to test. But it may also involve going further back, for example, to a reanalysis of the problem, an identification of other solutions, or a restatement of criteria.

Problem Solving at Work

Here are a few groups currently used widely in business that rely largely on the problem solving techniques discussed above.

The Nominal Group

In a typical nominal group a problem is proposed and members submit solutions in writing. The solutions are written down on a board for members to see. Members may ask for clarification but do not discuss the solutions. Instead, they work individually to rank the solutions in order of merit. Their ranked orders are collected and recorded, again for all to see. If there is agreement, the work of the nominal group is completed. If there is insufficient agreement, then the members again individually consider the solutions and again rank them. The process is continued until the group reaches some agreement.

The Delphi Method

In the Delphi method, originally developed by the RAND Corporation, a pool of experts is established but there is no interaction among them (Tersine & Riggs, 1980). Members may, in fact, be scattered throughout the world. A Delphi questionnaire is distributed to all members asking them to respond to what they feel are, for example, the communication problems the organization will have to face in the next 25 years. Members record their predictions, and the questionnaires are sent back anonymously. Responses are tabulated, recorded, and distributed to the experts, who then revise their predictions in light of the composite list. They then submit their revised predictions. These are again tabulated, recorded, and returned. The process continues until the responses no longer change significantly. The composite or final list represents the predictions or forecast of this group of experts.

Quality Circles

Quality circles are of workers whose task it is to improve some aspect of the work environment—for example, morale, productivity, or communication. The basic idea is that people who work on similar tasks will be able to devise better ways of doing things by pooling their insights and

In what types of problem-solving discussions do you regularly engage? Will they be a part of your professional life? Your relationship life? In what way?

working through common problems. The group then reports its findings—for example, ways to increase worker-management communication—to those who can do something about it.

Improvement Groups

A somewhat different type of group is the improvement group, or what is often called *kaizen,* a Japanese word that means "continual improvement" (Beebe & Masterson, 1994). These groups are based on the assumption that everything in the work environment—processes and products—can be improved. Such groups may be set up for a limited amount of time or may be permanent.

Task Groups

Often groups are formed for specific tasks—how to deal with the new administration, how to get plan XYZ accepted by the membership, or how to phase in the new computer technology. Often these groups are formed for this one specific task and are then abandoned.

Never, never rest contented with any circle of ideas, but always be certain that a wider one is still possible.

—RICHARD JEFFERIES

Decision-Making Methods

Groups may use different decision-making methods in deciding, for example, which criterion to use or which solution to accept. Generally, groups use one of three methods.

Authority

In decision making by authority, members voice their feelings and opinions but the leader, boss, or CEO makes the final decision. This is surely an efficient method; it gets things done quickly and the amount of discussion can be limited as desired. Another advantage is that experienced and informed members (for example, those who have been with the company longest) will probably exert a greater influence on the decision maker.

The great disadvantage is that members may not feel the need to contribute their insights and may become distanced from the power within the group or organization. Another disadvantage is that it may lead members to give the decision maker what they feel she or he wants to receive, a condition that can easily lead to groupthink.

Majority Rule

With this method the group agrees to abide by the majority decision and may vote on various issues as the group progresses to solve its problem. Majority rule is efficient because there is usually an option to call for a vote when the majority are in agreement. This is a useful method for issues that are relatively unimportant (which company should service the water cooler?) and where member satisfaction and commitment is not needed.

One disadvantage is that it can lead to factioning, where various minorities come to be aligned against the majority. The method may also lead to limiting discussion once a majority has agreed and a vote is called.

Consensus

The group operating under **consensus** reaches a decision only when all group members agree as, for example, in the criminal jury system. This

What decision-making method is used in your family? Are you satisfied with this? What decision-making method is used in most of your college classes? Are you satisfied with this?

method is especially important when the group wants the satisfaction and commitment of each member, to the decision and to the decision-making process as a whole (DeStephen & Hirokawa, 1988; Rothwell, 1992).

Consensus obviously takes longest and can lead to a great deal of wasted time if members wish to prolong the discussion process needlessly or selfishly. This method may also put great pressure on the person who honestly disagrees but who doesn't want to prevent the group from making a decision.

SMALL GROUP FORMATS

Small groups serve their functions in a variety of formats. Among the most popular are the round table, panel, symposium, and symposium-forum (Figure 10.3).

The Round Table

In the **round table format,** group members arrange themselves in a circular or semicircular pattern. They share information or solve the problem without any set pattern of who speaks when. Group interaction is informal and members contribute as they see fit. A leader or moderator may try to keep the discussion on the topic or encourage more reticent members to speak up.

The Panel

In the **panel,** group members are "experts" and participate in a round table format. Here, too, their remarks are informal and there is no set pattern for speakers. The difference is that there is an audience whose members may

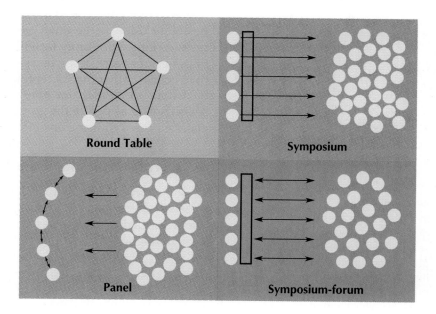

Figure 10.3 Small group formats

interject comments or ask questions. Many talk shows, such as *Donahue* and *The Oprah Winfrey Show,* use this format.

A variation is the two-panel format, with an expert panel and a lay panel. The lay panel discusses the topic but when in need of technical information, additional data, or direction, they may turn to the expert panel.

The Symposium

The **symposium** consists of a series of prepared presentations much like public speeches. All speeches are addressed to different aspects of a single topic. The leader of a symposium introduces the speakers, provides transitions from one speaker to another, and may provide periodic summaries.

The Symposium-Forum

The **symposium-forum** consists of two parts: a symposium with prepared speeches, and a forum, a general discussion largely of questions and comments from the audience. The leader introduces the speakers and moderates the question-and-answer session.

THINKING CRITICALLY ABOUT SMALL GROUPS

In approaching the study of small groups and your own participation in groups, keep the following in mind:

- The skills of small group communication are largely the skills of leadership generally. Look at this material and these skills as guides to improving your own leadership skills.
- Small groups are usually more effective in solving problems than are individuals working alone. Creative solutions emerge from a combination of thoughts. Therefore, approach small group situations with flexibility. Come to the small group with ideas and information, but resist coming with firmly formulated conclusions.
- Small groups work best when each person remains true to her or his own beliefs, rather than accepting solutions or ideas because others have done so. At the same time, small groups work best when we all see ourselves as part of the group and subordinates our own preferences for the well-being and effectiveness of the group.

The Six Critical Thinking Hats Technique

Critical thinking pioneer Edward deBono (1987) suggests using six "thinking" hats to define and analyze problems. With each hat you look at the problem from a different perspective. The technique provides a convenient and interesting way to explore a problem from a variety of different angles.

- **The fact hat** focuses on the data—the facts and figures that bear on the problem. For example, What are the relevant data on the newspaper? How can more information on the paper's history be secured? How much does it cost to print? How much advertising revenue can we get?

In what ways is your family a small group? Does it serve problem solving, idea generation, personal growth, and information sharing functions? Might any of the principles and guidelines discussed in these units be useful in your family communication?

- **The feeling hat** focuses on your feelings, emotions, and intuitions concerning the problem. How do you feel about the newspaper and about making major changes?
- **The negative argument hat** asks that you become the devil's advocate. Why might this proposal fail? What are the problems with publishing reviews of courses? What is the worst-case scenario?
- **The positive benefits hat** asks that you look at the upside. What are the opportunities that this new format will open up? What benefits will reviewing courses provide for the students? What would be the best thing that could happen?
- **The creative new idea hat** focuses on new ways of looking at the problem and can be easily combined with brainstorming techniques discussed earlier in this chapter. What other ways can you look at this problem? What other functions can a student newspaper serve? Can the student paper serve the nonacademic community as well?
- **The control of thinking hat** helps you analyze what you have done and are doing. It asks that you reflect on your own thinking processes and synthesize the results. Have you adequately defined the problem? Are you focusing too much on insignificant issues? Have you given enough attention to the possible negative effects?

Why is this six-hats technique useful in critical thinking? In what specific situations can this technique have practical value?

Feedback on Concepts and Skills

In this chapter we provided an overview of the small group's nature, the ways in which some major groups (idea generation, personal growth, information sharing, and problem solving) work, and the popular small group formats.

1. A small group is a collection of individuals, few enough for all members to communicate with relative ease as both senders and receivers. The members are related by some common purpose and have some degree of organization or structure. Most small groups develop norms or rules identifying appropriate behavior for its members.
2. The idea-generation or brainstorming group attempts to generate as many ideas as possible.
3. The personal growth group helps members to deal with personal problems and to function more effectively. Popular personal growth groups are the encounter group, the assertiveness training group, and the consciousness-raising group.
4. Information-sharing groups (for example, the educational or learning group or the focus group) attempt to acquire new information or skill through a mutual sharing of knowledge or insight.
5. The problem-solving group attempts to solve a particular problem or at least reach a decision that may be a preface to solving the problem.
6. The six steps in the problem-solving approach are: define and analyze the problem, establish criteria for evaluating solutions, identify possible solutions, evaluate solutions, select best solution(s), and test solution(s).

7. Small groups make use of four major formats: the round table, panel, symposium, and symposium-forum.
8. A useful technique in analyzing problems is the critical thinking hats technique in which you approach a problem in terms of facts, feelings, negative arguments, positive benefits, creative ideas, and overall analysis.

The skills covered in this chapter focus on our ability to effectively use the various types of small groups. Check your ability to apply these skills. Use the following scale: (1) = almost always, (2) = often, (3) = sometimes, (4) = rarely, (5) = almost never.

_____ 1. I actively seek to discover the norms of the groups in which I function and take these norms into consideration when interacting in the group.

_____ 2. I follow the general rules when brainstorming: I avoid negative criticism, strive for quantity, combine and extend the contributions of others, and contribute as wild an idea as I can.

_____ 3. I appropriately restimulate a brainstorming group that has lost its steam.

_____ 4. I respond with supportiveness in consciousness-raising experiences.

_____ 5. I employ organizational structure in educational or learning groups.

_____ 6. I follow the six steps when in group problem-solving situations: define and analyze the problem, establish the criteria for evaluating solutions, identify possible solutions, evaluate solutions, select the best solution(s), and test selected solution(s).

_____ 7. I can make use of such techniques as the nominal group, the delphi method, quality circles, improvement groups, and task groups.

_____ 8. I use the critical thinking hats technique and think about problems in terms of facts, feelings, negative arguments, positive benefits, creative ideas, and overall analysis.

Skill Development Experiences

10.1 Brainstorming

Together with a small group or with the class as a whole, sit in a circle and brainstorm one of the topics identified in Skill Development Experience 10.2. Be sure to appoint someone to write down all the contributions or use a tape recorder. After this brainstorming session, consider these questions:

1. Did any members give negative criticism (even nonverbally)?
2. Did any members hesitate to contribute really wild ideas? Why?
3. Was it necessary to restimulate the group members at any point? Did this help?

4. Did possible solutions emerge in the brainstorming session that were not considered by members of the problem-solving group?

10.2 Solving Problems in Groups

Together with four, five, or six others, form a problem-solving group and discuss one of the following questions:

- What should we do about the homeless?
- What should we do to improve student morale?
- What should we do to better prepare ourselves for the job market?
- What should we do to improve student-faculty communication?
- What should be the college's responsibility concerning AIDS?

Before beginning the discussion, each member should prepare a discussion outline, answering the following questions:

1. What is the problem? How long has it existed? What caused it? What are the effects of the problem?
2. What are some possible solutions?
3. What are the advantages and disadvantages of each of these possible solutions?
4. What solution seems best (in light of the advantages and disadvantages)?
5. How might you put this solution to a test?

CHAPTER ELEVEN

Members and Leaders in Group Communication

Chapter Concepts	Chapter Goals After completing this chapter, you should be able to	Chapter Skills After completing this chapter, you should be able to
Members in Small Group Communication	1. identify the three major types of member roles and give examples of each	participate in a small group with a group orientation, serving group task and group building and maintenance roles and avoiding dysfunction (individual) roles
Leaders in Small Group Communication	2. describe the three leadership styles and when each of these would be most appropriate	adjust your leadership style to the task at hand and the needs of group members
	3. explain at least four functions of leaders in small group communication	serve the various leadership functions as appropriate
Thinking Critically About Groupthink	4. define *groupthink* and identify its major symptoms	recognize and avoid the symptoms of groupthink

A s a group member and leader you will have the opportunity to serve a wide variety of roles and functions. In this chapter we consider your role as both member and leader in small groups. By gaining insight into these roles, you will be better able to increase your own effectiveness as group member and leader.

MEMBERS IN SMALL GROUP COMMUNICATION

Each of us serves in many roles. Javier, for example, is a part-time college student, father, bookkeeper, bowling team captain, and sometime poet. These roles represent Javier's customary and expected patterns of behavior. That is, he acts as a student—attends class, reads textbooks, takes exams, and does the things we expect of college students. Similarly, he performs those behaviors we associate with fathers, bookkeepers, and so on. In a similar way, people develop ways of behaving when participating in small groups. What are your major roles in small groups? How can you become a more effective participant?

Member Roles

Kenneth Benne and Paul Sheats (1948) proposed a classification of members' roles in small group communication that is still the best overview of this important topic. They divide members' roles into three general classes: group task roles, group building and maintenance roles, and individual roles. Each of these is served by different, specific behaviors. These roles are, of course, frequently performed by leaders as well.

Group Task Roles
Group task roles help the group to focus more specifically on achieving its goals. In performing any of these roles, you do not act as an isolated individual, but rather as a part of the larger whole. The group's needs and goals dictate the roles you will fill. As an effective group member you serve in several roles, although some people do lock into a few specific roles. For example, one person may almost always seek the opinions of others while another may concentrate on elaborating details. Usually, this single focus is counterproductive—it is better for the roles to be spread more evenly among the members and for the roles to be alternated frequently.

Group Building and Maintenance Roles
No individual or group can be task-oriented at all times. The group is a unit whose members have varied interpersonal relationships, and these need to be nourished if the group is to function effectively. Group members must be satisfied if they are to be productive. When they are not, they may become irritable when the group process gets bogged down, engage in frequent conflicts, or find the small group communication process unsatisfying.

Individual Roles

Group task roles and group building and maintenance roles are productive. They help the group achieve its goal, and they are group-oriented. Individual roles, on the other hand, are counterproductive. They hinder the group from achieving its goal and are individual rather than

TABLE 11.1 MEMBER ROLES

Member Role	Member Behavior
Group Task Roles	
Information seeker or giver/Opinion seeker or giver	Asks for or gives facts and opinions, seeks clarification of issues being discussed, presents facts and opinions to group members
Evaluator-critic	Evaluates the group's decisions; questions the logic or practicality of the suggestions and thus provides the group with both positive and negative feedback
Procedural technician or recorder	Takes care of the various mechanical duties such as distributing group materials and arranging the seating; writes down the group's activities, suggestions, and decisions and serves as the group's memory
Group Building and Maintenance Roles	
Encourager/Harmonizer	Provides members with positive reinforcement through social approval or praise for their ideas; mediates the various differences between group members
Compromiser	Tries to resolve conflict between his or her ideas and those of others; offers compromises
Follower	Goes along with members, passively accepts the ideas of others, and functions more as an audience than as an active member
Individual Roles (Dysfunctional Roles)	
Aggressor/Blocker	Expresses negative evaluation of members' actions or feelings, attacks the group or the problem being considered; provides negative feedback, is disagreeable, and opposes other members or their suggestions regardless of their merit
Recognition seeker/Self-confessor	Tries to focus attention on oneself, boasts about own accomplishments rather than the task at hand; expresses his or her own feelings and personal perspectives rather than focusing on the group
Playboy/Playgirl	Jokes around without any regard for the group process
Dominator	Tries to run the group or members by pulling rank, flattering members, or acting the role of boss

Source: The roles presented here represent an abbreviation of those proposed in the early research of Benne and Sheats (1948), a classification that is still widely used today (Lumsden & Lumsden, 1993; Beebe & Masterson, 1994).

Lord Chesterfield once advised: "Wear your learning like your watch, in a private pocket, and do not pull it out and strike it merely to show that you have one." Would this advice hold in the culture in which you were raised? That is, is modesty an expected norm?

group-oriented. Such roles, often termed dysfunctional, hinder the group's effectiveness in both productivity and personal satisfaction. Some of the major group task, building and maintenance, and individual roles are presented in Table 11.1.

Interaction Process Analysis

Another way of looking at the contributions that group members make is through **interaction process analysis** (Bales, 1950; Schultz, 1989). In this system we analyze the contributions of members in four general categories: (1) social-emotional positive contributions, (2) social-emotional negative contributions, (3) attempted answers, and (4) questions. Each of these four areas contains three subdivisions, giving us a total of twelve categories in which we can classify group members' contributions. Note that the categories under social-emotional positive are the natural opposites of those under social-emotional negative, and those under attempted

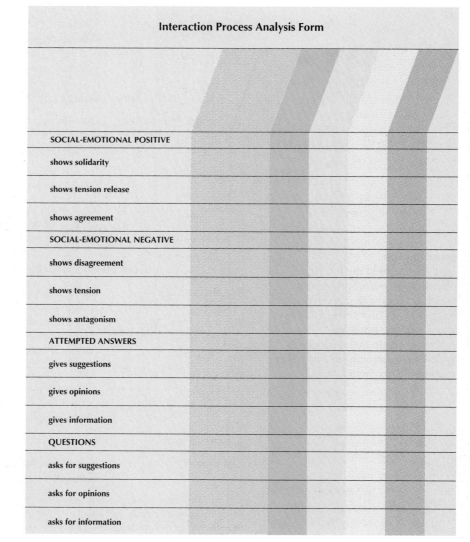

Interaction Process Analysis Form

SOCIAL-EMOTIONAL POSITIVE

shows solidarity

shows tension release

shows agreement

SOCIAL-EMOTIONAL NEGATIVE

shows disagreement

shows tension

shows antagonism

ATTEMPTED ANSWERS

gives suggestions

gives opinions

gives information

QUESTIONS

asks for suggestions

asks for opinions

asks for information

Of the four major categories identified by Bales, in which have you served most often in the last week or two of small group interaction?

Review the list of member roles. What general types of roles do you most often play in small groups (task, building and maintenance, or individual roles)? Within this general category, what more specific roles do you regularly play? What specific behaviors do you display that correspond to these roles?

answers are the natural opposites of those under questions. This table could then be used to record the contributions of individual members. Names of group members are listed across the top and a slash mark is placed in the correct box to note that this member made this specific type of contribution.

Both Benne and Sheats's classification of members' roles and Bales's interaction process analysis categories are useful in viewing the contributions that members make in small group situations. You can see, for example, if one member is locked into a particular role or if the group process breaks down because too many people are serving individual rather than group goals. These systems are designed to help us see more clearly what is going on in a group and what specific contributions may mean to the entire group process.

Member Participation

Here are several guidelines to help make your participation in small group communication more effective and enjoyable. They are an elaboration and extension of the basic characteristics of effective interpersonal communication described in Chapter 7.

Be Group-Oriented

In the small group you are a member of a team, some larger whole. Your participation is of value to the extent that it advances the group's goals and promotes member satisfaction. Pool your talents, knowledge, and

Do not wait for leaders; do it alone, person to person.
—MOTHER TERESA

Review the list of member roles. What roles do you most often play in small groups? What specific behaviors do you display that correspond to these roles?

insight so that the group arrives at a better solution than any one person could have developed. Solo performances hinder the group. This call for group orientation is not to suggest that you abandon your individuality or give up your personal values or beliefs for the group's sake. Individuality with a group orientation is advocated.

Center Conflict on Issues

Conflict in small group situations is inevitable; it is a natural part of the exchange of ideas. Don't fear or ignore it. Recognize conflict as a natural part of the small group process, but center it on issues rather than on personalities. When you disagree, make it clear that your disagreement is with the ideas expressed, and not with the person who expressed them. Similarly, when someone disagrees with you, do not take it as a personal attack. Rather, view it as an opportunity to discuss issues from an alternative point of view.

Be Critically Open-minded

If everyone is thinking alike, then somebody isn't thinking.
—GEORGE S. PATTON

When members join a group with their minds already made up, the small group process degenerates into a series of debates in which each person argues for his or her position. Instead, come to the group with information that will be useful to the discussion. Do not decide on a solution or conclusion before discussing it with the group. Advance proposed solutions or conclusions tentatively rather than with certainty. Be willing to revise your suggestions in light of the discussion. Be willing to subject all suggestions—even your own—to the various critical thinking tests discussed throughout this text.

Listen openly but critically to comments of all members. Do not accept or reject any member's suggestions without critically evaluating them. Be judiciously open-minded. Be judiciously critical of your own contributions as well as those of others.

Ensure Understanding

Make sure all participants understand your ideas and information. If something is worth saying, it is worth making it clear. When in doubt, ask: "Is that clear?" "Did I explain that clearly?" Make sure too that you fully understand other members' contributions, especially before you take issue with them. In fact, it is often wise to preface disagreement with some kind of paraphrase. For example, you might say, "As I understand you, you want to exclude freshmen from playing on the football team. Is that correct?" Then you would state your thoughts. In this way you give the other person the opportunity to clarify, deny, or otherwise alter what was said.

Evaluating Group Membership

Figure 11.1 presents an evaluation form used in my small group communication course. It summarizes members' responsibilities and also contains some general effectiveness principles covered in interpersonal effectiveness (Chapter 7). This form may be used to evaluate a small group interaction and provide the basis for a discussion of effective group membership.

Figure 11.1
Membership Evaluation Form

Group Membership Evaluation Form

Circle those roles played by the group member and indicate the specific behaviors that led to these judgments.

Member Roles:

Group task: information or opinion seeker or giver, evaluator-critic, procedural technician or recorder;

Group building/maintenance: encourager/harmonizer, compromiser, follower;

Individual: aggressor/blocker, recognition seeker/self-confessor, playboy/play-girl, and dominator.

Interaction process analysis:

shows solidarity, shows tension release, shows agreement, shows disagreement, shows tension, shows antagonism, gives suggestions, gives opinions, gives information, asks for suggestions, asks for opinions, asks for information

Group Participation

Is group-oriented	YES!	YES	yes	?	no	NO	NO!
Centers conflict on issues	YES!	YES	yes	?	no	NO	NO!
Is critically open-minded	YES!	YES	yes	?	no	NO	NO!
Ensures understanding	YES!	YES	yes	?	no	NO	NO!

Improvement Suggestions

Taboos Around the World

Not surprisingly, each culture has its own taboo topics, subjects that should be avoided, especially by visitors from other cultures. Here are several examples that Roger Axtell, in *Do's and Taboos Around the World* (1993), recommends that visitors from the United States avoid. These examples are not intended to be exhaustive, but rather should serve as a reminder that each culture defines what is and what is not an appropriate topic for discussion.

TABOOS AROUND THE WORLD

Culture	Taboos
Belgium	Politics, language differences between French and Flemish, religion
Norway	Salaries, social status
Spain	Family, religion, jobs, negative comments on bullfighting
Egypt	Middle Eastern politics
Nigeria	Religion
Libya	Politics, religion
Iraq	Religion, Middle Eastern politics
Japan	World War II
Pakistan	Politics
Philippines	Politics, religion, corruption, foreign aid
South Korea	Internal politics, criticism of the government, socialism or communism
Bolivia	Politics, religion
Colombia	Politics, criticism of bullfighting
Mexico	Mexican-American war; illegal aliens
Caribbean	Race, local politics, religion

[Next Cultural Viewpoint, page 284]

How would you characterize your leadership style? For example, are you usually more concerned with people or with task? Are you more likely to be a laissez-faire, democratic, or authoritarian leader? What major leadership functions are you most likely to serve?

LEADERS IN SMALL GROUP COMMUNICATION

In many small groups, one person serves as leader. In others, leadership may be shared by several persons. In some groups, a person may be appointed the leader or may serve as leader because of her or his position within the company or hierarchy. In other groups, the leader may emerge as the group proceeds in fulfilling its functions or may be voted as leader by the group members. In any case the role of the leader or leaders is vital to the well-being and effectiveness of the group. (Even in leaderless groups, where all members are equal, leadership functions must still be served.)

Not surprisingly, leadership has been the focus of considerable attention from researchers, who have identified a number of approaches; three of these are summarized in Table 11.2. Although contemporary theorists favor the situational approach, the traits and the functional approach continue to have merit.

The **traits approach** is valuable because it emphasizes the truism that leaders must possess certain qualities if they are to function effectively. The problem with the traits approach is that these qualities will vary with the situation, with the members, and with the culture in which the leader functions. It seems impossible to identify universal qualities that would apply to all types of groups. For example, the leaders' age or personality might be significant factors. But for some groups a youthful, humorous leader might be effective (for example, with a creative advertising team), whereas for other groups an older, more serious leader might be effective (for example,

TABLE 11.2 WHAT IS A LEADER?

Approach	Definition	Qualities Identified
Traits approach	One who possesses those characteristics (or **traits**) that contribute to leadership	Achievement, higher status, intelligence
Functional approach	One who behaves (or **functions**) as a leader	Serves task roles, ensures member satisfaction, energizes group members
Situational approach	One who balances task accomplishment and member satisfaction on the basis of the **situation**	Delegates, participates, sells, and tells depending on the members and the situation

a medical diagnosis team). Notice that even in this seemingly simple example, you can easily envision situations in which age would be irrelevant or where an older person might be more effective on the advertising team and a younger person more effective with the medical group.

The **functional approach** is significant because it helps identify what the leader should do in a given situation; it focuses on the fact that the leader needs to do certain things to merit being considered a leader. We already looked at some of these functions in our discussion of group membership, where we identified group task roles, group building and maintenance roles, and the counterproductive individual roles. These are also roles that leaders fulfill. Additional functions are examined later in this unit.

The **situational approach** deserves attention because it focuses on the two major tasks of the leader—accomplishing the task and ensuring the satisfaction of the members (concepts introduced briefly in the discussion of group stages in Chapter 10). It also merits attention because it recognizes that the leader's style must vary on the basis of the specific situation. Just as you adjust your conversational style on the basis of the specific situation, so must you adjust your leadership style on the basis of the task to be accomplished and the needs of the group members (Hersey & Blanchard, 1988).

Before examining this situational approach to leadership in more detail, you should find it interesting to analyze your own views on and style of leadership by taking the accompanying self-test, What Kind of Leader Are You?

In a thorough review of the literature on leadership, it was found that the person with the highest rate of participation in a group is the one most likely to be chosen leader (Mullen, Salas, & Driskell, 1989). Why do you suppose this relationship exists? Do you find this to be true of the groups in which you have participated?

TEST YOURSELF
What Kind of Leader Are You?

Instructions Respond by indicating YES if the statement is a generally accurate description of your leadership style and NO if it is not.

_____ 1. I would speak as a representative of the group.
_____ 2. I would settle conflicts when they occur in the group.
_____ 3. I would be reluctant to allow the others freedom of action.
_____ 4. I would decide what should be done and how it should be done.
_____ 5. I would refuse to explain my actions when questioned.
_____ 6. I would allow members complete freedom in their work.
_____ 7. I would permit the others to use their own judgment in solving problems.
_____ 8. I would let the others do their work as they think best.
_____ 9. I would allow the others a high degree of initiative.
_____ 10. I would permit the group to set its own pace.

Thinking Critically About Leadership Style These questions come from an extensive leadership test and should help you focus on some ways a leader can accomplish a task and ensure member satisfaction. Questions 1–5 are phrased so a leader concerned with completing the group's task would answer YES. Questions 6–10 are phrased so a leader concerned with ensuring that the group members are satisfied would answer YES. Think about your own style of leadership. Do you adjust your style on the basis of the group or do you have one style that you use in all situations? Consider, too, the styles of leadership that you respond to best.

Source: "T-P Leadership Questionnaire: An Assessment of Style" from J. W. Pfeiffer and J. E. Jones, _Structured Experiences for Human Relations Training._ Iowa City, Iowa: University Associates Press, 1969, pp. 9–10. Copyright by the American Educational Research Association. Reprinted by permission of the publisher.

Situational Leadership: The Concern for Task and People

Leaders must be concerned with getting the task accomplished and ensuring that members are satisfied. Groups don't work well when the leader focuses on one and neglects the other. A combined concern for both task and people satisfaction seems to work best. The general idea of situational leadership is that although both task and people are significant concerns, each situation will call for a different combination. Some situations will call for high concentration on task issues but will need little people encouragement (for example, a group of scientists working on AIDS research). On the other hand, a group of recovering alcoholics might require leadership that stresses the members' emotional needs.

Leadership Styles

In addition to looking at leadership's major concerns, we can look at leadership's three major styles: laissez-faire, democratic, and authoritarian (Shaw, 1981; Bennis & Nanus, 1985).

Laissez-Faire Leader

Laissez-faire comes from the French and means literally "allow to do." The term is often applied to a government characterized by noninterference. Applied to group communication, it refers to a leadership style in which the leader takes no initiative in directing or suggesting alternative

How would you characterize your leadership style? For example, are you usually more concerned with people or with task? Are you more likely to be a laissez-faire, democratic, or authoritarian leader? What major leadership roles are you most likely to fill? Are there any that you are likely to neglect?

Former British Prime Minister Margaret Thatcher once observed, "Being powerful is like being a lady. If you have to tell people you are, you aren't." What do you think of this?

courses of action. Rather, the leader allows the group to develop and progress on its own, even allowing it to make its own mistakes. This leader gives up or denies any real authority. The laissez-faire leader answers questions or provides relevant information, but only when asked, and gives little if any reinforcement to group members. At the same time, this leader does not punish members, so is nonthreatening.

Democratic Leader

The democratic leader provides direction but allows the group to develop and progress the way members wish. The leader encourages members to determine goals and procedures and stimulates members' self-direction and self-actualization. Unlike the laissez-faire leader, the democratic leader reinforces members and contributes suggestions for alternatives. However, this leader always allows the group to make its own decisions.

Authoritarian Leader

The authoritarian leader is the opposite of the laissez-faire leader. This leader determines the group's policies or makes decisions without consulting or securing agreement from members. This leader is impersonal. Communication goes to and from the leader, but rarely from member to member. This leader tries to minimize intragroup communication. The authoritarian leader assumes the greatest responsibility for the group's progress and wants no interference from members. Concerned with getting the group to accept his or her decisions, this leader often satisfies the group's psychological needs. He or she rewards and punishes the group much as a parent does.

Each leadership style has its place, and we should not consider one style superior to the others. Each is appropriate for a different purpose or situation. In a social group at a friend's house, any leadership other than laissez-faire would be difficult to tolerate. But when time and efficiency are critical, authoritarian leadership may be the most effective. Authoritarian leadership is also appropriate when group members continue to lack motivation despite repeated democratic efforts. When all members are about equal in their knowledge of the topic or when the members are very concerned with their individual rights, the democratic leader seems the most appropriate.

Leader's Functions: Task and People

With the situational view of leadership and the three general styles in mind, we can look at some of the major functions leaders serve. These functions are not exclusively the leader's. Nevertheless, when there is a specific leader, he or she is expected to perform them. Leadership functions are best performed unobtrusively—in a natural manner. Leaders carry out both task and people functions.

Start Group Interaction

Many groups need some prodding and stimulation to interact. Perhaps the group is newly formed and members feel uneasy. Here the leader serves an important function by stimulating the members to interact. This function is also needed when members are acting as individuals rather than as a group and the leader must make members recognize they are part of a group.

[Next Power Perspective, page 264]

"The kids want to know what's next on the agenda."

Maintain Effective Interaction

Even after the group is interacting, the leader should see that members maintain the effective interaction. When the discussion begins to drag, the leader should prod the group: "Do we have any additional comments on the proposal to eliminate required courses?" "What do you members of the college curriculum committee think about the proposal?" The leader needs to ensure that all members have an opportunity to express themselves.

Guide Members Through the Agreed-upon Agenda

This may be accomplished by asking relevant questions, by interjecting internal summaries, or by providing transitions to make clear the relationship of an issue just discussed to one about to be considered. It involves following a reasonably orderly sequence of events as identified in the agenda or formal outline of the tasks to be accomplished by the group.

Ensure Member Satisfaction

Members have different psychological needs and wants, and many people enter groups because of them. Even though a group may deal with political issues, members may have come together more for psychological than for political reasons. If a group is to be effective, it must meet not only the group's surface purposes (in this case, political), but also the underlying, or psychological, purposes that motivated many of the members to come together. One way to meet these needs is for the leader to allow digressions and personal comments, assuming they are not too frequent or overly long.

POWER PERSPECTIVE

Power from Task and Dominance Cues

Do you think you would get greater power from emphasizing your ability to do a task or from threats? Consider the results from one interesting study (Driskell, Olmstead, & Salas, 1993). In this study, task cues included maintaining eye contact, sitting at the head of the table, using a relatively rapid speech rate, speaking fluently, and gesturing appropriately. Dominance cues, on the other hand, included speaking in a loud and angry voice, pointing fingers, maintaining rigid posture, using forceful gestures, and lowering of the eyebrows. Which leader would you be more apt to follow? Results showed that most people will be more influenced by speakers using task cues. They will also see such speakers as more competent and more likable. Persons using dominance cues, on the other hand, are perceived as less competent, less influential, less likable, and more self-oriented. The implication, from at least this one study, is that if you wish to gain influence in a group (and be liked) use task cues and avoid dominance cues.

[Next Power Perspective, page 288]

Encourage Ongoing Evaluation and Improvement

All groups encounter obstacles as they try to solve a problem, reach a decision, or generate ideas. No group is totally effective. All groups have room for improvement. To improve, the group must focus on itself. Along with trying to solve some external problem, it must try to solve its own internal problems, for example, personal conflicts, failure of members to meet on time, or members who come unprepared.

Prepare Members for the Discussion

Groups form gradually and need to be eased into meaningful discussion. The leader needs to prepare members for the small group interaction as well as for the discussion of a specific issue or problem. Don't expect diverse members to discuss a problem without becoming familiar with each other. Similarly, if members are to discuss a specific problem, a proper briefing is necessary. Perhaps materials need to be distributed before the actual discussion. Or perhaps members need to read certain materials or view a particular film or television show. Whatever the preparations, the leader should organize and coordinate them.

An additional perspective can be gained by looking at the qualities derived from the leadership skills of Attila the Hun, the Mongol leader who ruled throughout much of Asia in the fifth century (see Table 11.3).

TABLE 11.3 SIX LEADERSHIP QUALITIES FROM ATTILA THE HUN

Quality	Behaviors and Examples
Empathy	Leaders must develop an appreciation for and an understanding of other cultures and the values of their members.
Courage	Leaders should be fearless and have the courage to complete their assignments; they must not complain about obstacles nor be discouraged by adversity.
Accountability	Leaders must hold themselves responsible for their own actions and for those of their members.
Dependability	Leaders must be dependable in carrying out their responsibilities; leaders must also depend upon their members to accomplish matters they themselves cannot oversee.
Credibility	Leaders must be believable to both friends and enemies; they must possess the integrity and intelligence needed to secure and communicate accurate information.
Stewardship	Leaders must be caretakers of their members' interests and well-being; they must guide and reward subordinates.

Source: These leadership qualities are paraphrased from Wes Roberts's insightful book *Leadership Secrets of Attila the Hun* (New York: Warner, 1987). Other qualities that Roberts identifies are loyalty, desire, emotional stamina, physical stamina, decisiveness, anticipation, timing, competitiveness, self-confidence, responsibility, and tenacity. You might find it profitable to review these 11 additional qualities and explain how you think they can contribute to effective small group leadership.

Figure 11.2 Leadership Evaluation Form

The Roman historian Tacitus noted that "reason and judgment are the qualities of a leader." What do you think are the defining characteristics of a leader?

Group Leadership Evaluation Form

Introductory Remarks

Opens discussion	YES!	YES	yes	?	no	NO	NO!
Explains procedures	YES!	YES	yes	?	no	NO	NO!
Gets group going	YES!	YES	yes	?	no	NO	NO!

Maintenance of Interaction

Keeps members on schedule	YES!	YES	yes	?	no	NO	NO!
Keeps to agenda	YES!	YES	yes	?	no	NO	NO!
Communication Guidance							
Encourages conflict resolution	YES!	YES	yes	?	no	NO	NO!
Ensures members' understanding	YES!	YES	yes	?	no	NO	NO!
Involves all members	YES!	YES	yes	?	no	NO	NO!
Encourages expression of differences	YES!	YES	yes	?	no	NO	NO!
Uses transitions	YES!	YES	yes	?	no	NO	NO!

Development of Effective Interpersonal Climate

Works for member satisfaction	YES!	YES	yes	?	no	NO	NO!
Builds open atmosphere	YES!	YES	yes	?	no	NO	NO!
Encourages supportiveness	YES!	YES	yes	?	no	NO	NO!

Ongoing Evaluation and Improvement

Encourages process suggestions	YES!	YES	yes	?	no	NO	NO!
Accepts disagreements	YES!	YES	yes	?	no	NO	NO!
Directs group self-evaluation	YES!	YES	yes	?	no	NO	NO!
Encourages improvement	YES!	YES	yes	?	no	NO	NO!

Concluding Remarks

Summarizes	YES!	YES	yes	?	no	NO	NO!
[Involves audience]	YES!	YES	yes	?	no	NO	NO!
Closes discussion	YES!	YES	yes	?	no	NO	NO!

Improvement Suggestions

Do you agree with social critic Eric Hoffer, who said, "Charlatanism of some degree is indispensable to effective leadership"?

Evaluating Leadership

Figure 11.2 presents a form used in my small group communication courses to evaluate the group leader's effectiveness. As with the group member evaluation form, this leadership form summarizes the wide variety of functions a group leader is expected to perform.

Factors That Work Against Small Group Effectiveness

While we need to actively use effective membership and leadership, we also need to avoid behaviors that work against small group effectiveness. Small group communication researchers have identified several important factors that limit the small group's effectiveness (Patton, Giffin, & Patton, 1989).

Procedural problems center on role conflicts (members compete for leadership positions or are unclear as to their functions), faulty problem analysis (members short-circuit the process of analyzing the problem), and faulty evaluation of proposals (members fail to agree on the criteria for judging proposals and solutions).

> Be willing to make decisions. That's the most important quality in a good leader. Don't fall victim to what I call the 'ready-aim-aim-aim-aim syndrome.' You must be willing to fire.
>
> —T. BOONE PICKENS

Drawing by Ziegler; © 1986 The New Yorker Magazine, Inc.

Process problems center on too little cohesion (members lack affiliation and may therefore leave the group) or too much cohesion (members may ignore problems to maintain harmony). Another process problem is the pressure to conform; members may be pleasant to each other and not, therefore, voice legitimate disagreements. Still another process problem occurs when members misunderstand the nature of the problem and reject accurate information.

Personality problems may occur when members are reticent to express themselves or when they take disagreements personally.

THINKING CRITICALLY ABOUT GROUPTHINK

An especially insightful perspective on thinking critically in the small group situation is provided in the concept of **groupthink**. According to Irving Janis (1983), *groupthink* is a way of thinking that group members engage in when agreement becomes all-important and overrides logical and realistic evaluation. Janis also says the term itself is meant to signal a "deterioration in mental efficiency, reality testing, and moral judgments as a result of group pressures."

Many specific behaviors of group members can lead to groupthink. One of the most significant occurs when the group limits its discussion to only a few alternative solutions. Another occurs when the group does not reexamine its decisions despite indications of possible dangers. Another happens when the group spends little time discussing why certain initial alternatives were rejected. For example, if the group rejected a certain alternative because it was too costly, members will devote little time, if any, to ways to reduce the cost.

In groupthink, members are extremely selective in the information they consider seriously. While facts and opinions contrary to the group's position are generally ignored, those that support the group's position are readily and uncritically accepted. The following symptoms should help you recognize groupthink in groups you observe or participate in:

- Group members think the group and its members are invulnerable.
- Members create rationalizations to avoid dealing with warnings or threats.
- Members believe their group is moral.
- Those opposed to the group are perceived in simplistic, stereotyped ways.
- Group pressure is applied to any member who expresses doubts or questions the group's arguments or proposals.
- Members censor their own doubts.
- Group members believe all are in unanimous agreement, whether this is stated or not.
- Group members emerge whose function it is to guard the information that gets to other members, especially when it may create diversity of opinion.

Feedback on Concepts and Skills

In this chapter we looked at membership and leadership communication in the small group. We examined the roles of members (some productive and some counterproductive), leadership, and groupthink.

1. A popular classification of small group member roles divides them into three types: group task roles, group building and maintenance roles, and individual roles.

2. Among the group task roles are information seeker or giver, opinion seeker or giver, evaluator-critic, and procedural technician or recorder; among the group building and maintenance roles are: encourager/harmonizer, compromiser, and follower; among the individual (dysfunctional) roles are: aggressor/blocker, recognition seeker/self-confessor, playboy/playgirl, and dominator.

3. Interaction process analysis categorizes contributions into four areas: social-emotional positive, social-emotional negative, attempted answers, and questions.

4. Member participation should be group-oriented, should center conflict on issues, should be critically open-minded, and should ensure understanding.

5. The situational theory views leadership as concerned with both accomplishing the task and serving the member's social and emotional needs. The degree to which either is emphasized should depend on the specific group, the unique situation.

6. Three major leadership styles are: laissez-faire, democratic, and authoritarian.

7. Among the leader's task functions are: to start the group interaction, maintain effective interaction, guide members through the agreed-on agenda, ensure member satisfaction, encourage ongoing evaluation and improvement, and prepare members for the discussion.

8. The effective leader values people, listens actively, is tactful, gives credit, is consistent, admits mistakes, has a sense of humor, and sets a good example.

9. Groupthink is "the mode of thinking that persons engage in when concurrence seeking becomes so dominant in a cohesive in-group that it tends to override realistic appraisal of alternative courses of action" (Janis, 1983).

The skills identified in this discussion center on increasing your ability to function more effectively as small group member and leader. Check your ability to use these skills. Use the following rating scale: (1) = almost always, (2) = often, (3) = sometimes, (4) = rarely, (5) = almost never.

_____ 1. I avoid playing the popular but dysfunctional individual roles in a small group: aggressor, blocker, recognition seeker, self-confessor, playboy/playgirl, dominator, help seeker, or special interest pleader.

_____ 2. In participating in a small group, I am group-, rather than individual-, oriented, center the conflict on issues rather than on personalities, am critically open-minded, and make sure that my meanings and the meanings of others are clearly understood.

_____ 3. I adjust my leadership style to the task at hand and on the needs of group members.

_____ 4. As a small group leader, I start group interaction, maintain effective interaction throughout the discussion, keep members on track, ensure member satisfaction, encourage ongoing evaluation and improvement, and prepare members for the discussion as necessary.

_____ 5. As a leader, I show that I value people, listen actively, am tactful, give credit to others, am consistent, admit mistakes, have a sense of humor, and set a good example.

_____ 6. I recognize and avoid the symptoms of groupthink and actively counter my own groupthinking tendencies as well as those evidenced in the group.

Skill Development Experiences

11.1 Using Interaction Process Analysis (IPA)

The aim of this experience is to gain some practice in using Bales's system of interaction process analysis. Five or six students should engage in a problem-solving discussion. The rest of the class should carefully observe the group interaction and, using the form on page 254, record the types of contributions each person makes. In the column under each participant's name, place a slash mark in one of the 12 categories for each contribution. An alternative procedure is to have the entire class watch a film such as _Twelve Angry Men_ or _The Breakfast Club_ and classify the characters' contributions. A general discussion should center on:

1. Does IPA enable you to identify the different types of contributions that individual members make during a discussion?
2. Can you offer suggestions for individual members based on this interaction process analysis?
3. Are members of the discussion group surprised at the types of contributions they made?

11.2 Lost on the Moon

This exercise is often used to illustrate the differences between individual and group decision making, almost always demonstrating that group decisions are much more effective and efficient than individual decisions. Of course, this is something that most people know intellectually, but this exercise dramatizes it for students in an interesting and provocative way.

The class is given the list of 15 items noted below. Each person is to visualize himself or herself as a member of a space crew stranded on the moon. Their ship is damaged and they must travel 200 miles to return to the mother ship. The 15 items have been salvaged from the crashed ship and their task is to rank the items in terms of their value in assisting them to return to the mother ship. Use number 1 for the most important item, number 2 for the next most important, and so on to 15 for the least important item.

After completing the rankings, form groups of five or six and construct a group ranking. After this is complete, correct answers and reasons should be given to students (see *Instructor's Manual*). They should then compute their individual error scores and the error score of the group decisions. The computations are made as follows: For each incorrect item, the student subtracts his or her score from the correct score, regardless of sign. This is the error score for that item. He or she does this for all 15 items and totals the error points. This is the total error score. The same procedure is followed for computing the group error score. A high error score (say, between 56 and 112) means that the student's or group's decisions were not very good ones; a low error score (say, between 0 and 45) means that the decisions were good ones or, more correctly, were similar to those responses supplied by NASA. Almost without exception the group score will be better than the individual scores.

_____ box of matches
_____ food concentrate
_____ 50 feet of nylon rope
_____ parachute silk
_____ solar-powered portable heating unit
_____ Two .45-caliber pistols
_____ 1 case dehydrated milk
_____ Two 100-pound tanks of oxygen
_____ stellar map (of moon's constellation)
_____ self-inflating life raft
_____ magnetic compass
_____ 5 gallons of water
_____ signal flares
_____ first aid kit containing injection needles
_____ solar-powered FM receiver-transmitter

Source: From "Decisions, Decisions, Decisions," by Jay Hall. Reprinted with permission from *Psychology Today Magazine*, 5:51–54, 86, 88. Copyright © 1971, Sussex Publishers, Inc.

11.3 Identifying Small Group Roles

The following dialogue was written to illustrate the general types of roles that members and leaders may serve in a small group situation. Read through the dialogue, paying special attention to the functions served by each member's comments. Then, alone or in small groups consider the questions presented following the dialogue.

Tasker: Well, we better get down to designing a package for this new aftershave lotion. Does anyone have any suggestions?

Grotask: I understand the lotion is especially addressed to men in their twenties and thirties. Is that right?

Tasker: Yes, and the manufacturer especially wants the product targeted to the young executive and middle-management types.

Greeting: Oh, right; that's important to know.

Selford: Yuppies, I can't stand yuppies.

Pearson: How do think we should attack this problem?

Selford: Yeah, I have an idea: Let's go to work for a real ad agency.

Greeting: Well, we're a great creative team; we'll come up with the right solution. I think it really has to be unique; I mean it's got to look totally different from anything else on the market.

Selford: Are we really going to be able to do this? I don't think we're going to be able to accomplish this by the end of this week. I mean it's an impossible, not to say meaningless, task.

Tasker: Let's get to the task. First, we need to define the image we want to create for the lotion and then we can consider colors, the structure of the main dispenser, the material for the dispenser, the packaging, and so on. Another team will handle the ad copy and media buying.

Pearson: Does anyone want coffee before we begin?

Tasker: I think we'd better get to the work instead of the coffee. Let's go around the group and identify what we each think would be a good image to present for the lotion. Selford, let's start with you.

Selford: How about "homelessness"?

Tasker: How about being serious and not so flippant? You know, I'm really getting tired of your always degrading what we do. If you don't want to participate, then let us know and get out.

Pearson: Tasker, you want a general type of attitude or personality characteristic. Is that right?

Tasker: Yes, that's exactly what we want.

Selford: Okay, okay. How about "intellectualism." Instead of the typical image of the strong macho type, how about appealing to the intellectual side of man?

Greeting: That's a great idea.

Grotask: I'll write that down.

Pearson: Now we're starting to get going.

Tasker: Grotask, you're next.

Grotask: How about "sensitive and brooding"?

Greeting: Yes, I like that. That's a fabulous idea.

Tasker:	Okay, Greeting, what do you think?
Greeting:	I like the two suggestions already made. Either one is good with me.
Tasker:	Greeting, you really have to contribute specific ideas or we'll never get this job done. At any rate, Pearson, what do you think?
Pearson:	I was going to say "intellectualism" myself. But I like "sensitive and brooding" too.
Tasker:	All right, let's go with "intellectualism," at least for now. The second task is to develop ideas for packaging. Let's look at color.
Grotask:	What's the name of this lotion? Isn't that going to influence the colors we use?
Tasker:	The name is chosen after the image is created and part of that image is the general packaging. Talk to me about color. Think color. What should the dominant colors of the package be?
Grotask:	How about different shades of blue? It's masculine but not too much so.
Selford:	Blue? Blue? No, blue is ugly. Anything but blue.
Greeting:	Blue is a good color, but it may be wrong.
Tasker:	Let's go through the spectrum and see what we think of each of the primary colors. Okay? ROY G BIV—the colors of the spectrum: red, orange, yellow, green, blue, indigo, and violet. Let's start at the beginning. What about red?
Selford:	Red's inappropriate; it's not masculine. Besides, red was my last boss's favorite color and I've come to hate anything red.
Grotask:	Isn't Marlboro directed at men? And that's red.
Selford:	If you people want red, pick red. But it's wrong; not intellectual.
Grotask:	What about gray?
Tasker:	Gray isn't a primary color and anyway we need to go in order. Red is the first color. How do you others feel about red?
Greeting:	I like it. But it may not be intellectual enough. But I think it's a good color.
Pearson:	That may be true. Do you want to consider orange?
Selford:	No.
Grotask:	Does anyone know the meanings for the different colors?
Tasker:	Maybe this is a good time to take lunch. I'll get the studies on the meanings of color and we can look at them after lunch. Let's meet back here at 1:30 sharp.

Thinking Critically About Small Group Roles

1. What types of roles are each of the members playing? Cite specific elements of dialogue to support your decisions. Compare your findings and conclusions with those of other analysts. On which do you agree? On which do you differ? Can you come to a general consensus?

2. If you were a member of a similar discussion group, what member would your own behavior most resemble? Least resemble?

3. Can you identify the productive and the destructive contributions of each member? How would you justify your conclusions as to which a specific behavior is productive or destructive?

4. What advice for increasing small group effectiveness would you give to each group member? Why?

CHAPTER TWELVE

Public Speaking Preparation and Delivery (Steps 1–6)

Chapter Concepts	Chapter Goals After completing this chapter, you should be able to	Chapter Skills After completing this chapter, you should be able to
Step 1: Select the Topic and Purpose	1. identify the characteristics of appropriate topics and purposes and how they may be limited	select and limit appropriate topics and purposes for public speeches
Step 2: Analyze Your Audience	2. identify the factors you would consider in audience analysis	analyze an audience to make predictions about their knowledge, attitudes, and beliefs and make appropriate adaptations in your speech
Step 3: Research Your Topic	3. explain the major sources of research and explain the computer research facilities on your campus	research varied topics, using the most relevant, efficient, and reliable sources
Step 4: Formulate Your Thesis and Identify the Major Propositions	4. explain the function of the thesis and how major propositions may be derived from it	select appropriate theses (main assertions) and expand them by asking strategic questions to develop the main ideas
Step 5: Support the Major Propositions	5. explain the nature and types of supporting materials in a public speech	support your propositions with appropriate amplifying materials and evidence
Step 6: Organize the Speech Materials	6. explain the major organizational patterns	organize the main ideas into an appropriate pattern
Thinking Critically About Public Speaking Preparation: Evaluating Research	7. explain the questions you should ask in evaluating research	evaluate research on the basis of recency, corroboration, and potential bias

Ten steps are necessary to prepare an effective public speech (Figure 12.1). Although these ten steps are presented in linear fashion (one after the other), the process of constructing a public speech seldom follows such a neat, logical sequence. You will probably not progress simply from step 1, to 2, to 3, and so on to step 10. Instead, you might go from selecting your topic and purpose (step 1) to analyzing your audience (step 2). Then, on the basis of this analysis, you may go back to step 1 and refine your purpose. Then you might go to step 3 and research your topic. So, follow all ten steps in the general order in which they are presented here, but go back and forth as you need to in order to make adjustments and refinements.

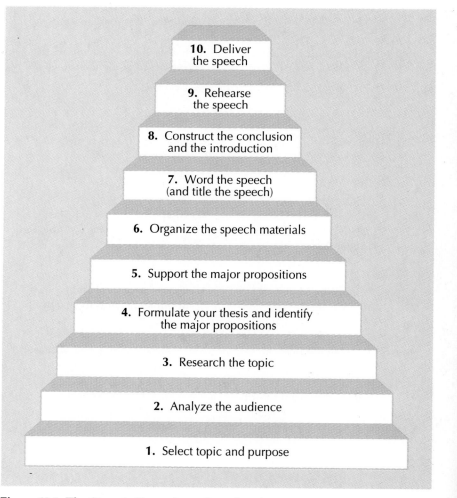

10. Deliver the speech

9. Rehearse the speech

8. Construct the conclusion and the introduction

7. Word the speech (and title the speech)

6. Organize the speech materials

5. Support the major propositions

4. Formulate your thesis and identify the major propositions

3. Research the topic

2. Analyze the audience

1. Select topic and purpose

Figure 12.1 The Steps in Preparing a Speech

STEP 1: SELECT THE TOPIC AND PURPOSE

The first step is to select the topic on which you will speak and the general and specific purposes you hope to achieve.

The Topic

Select a worthwhile topic that will prove interesting to the audience. If your first speech is to be an informative one, select a topic about which your audience probably knows little but would probably be interested in learning more. If your first speech is to be persuasive, you might select a topic about which you and the audience agree. Your aim would be to strengthen their attitudes. Or you might select a topic on which you and the audience disagree. Your aim would be to persuade them to change their attitudes in your direction.

Finding Topics

Table 12.1 offers a variety of suggestions suitable for informative or persuasive public speaking topics. In addition, you might find topics by examining surveys, news items, or by brainstorming.

TABLE 12.1   SUGGESTIONS FOR SPEECH TOPICS

Art/Music/Theater Topics

Abstract art:	meaning of; and emotion; leading artists; Kandisky; Léger; Mondrian; Picasso; Pollock; contributions of movement; values of
Entertainment:	industry; benefits; abuses; tax; functions of; and communication
Movies:	censorship; famous; making; producing; directing; acting in; history in; economics of; career training; and communication
Music:	festivals; forms; instruments; composition; styles; drama; opera; rock; punk; disco; country-western; popular; symphonic; hip hop
Theater:	Greek, Roman; commedia dell'arte; American; British; Eastern; Italian; French; performers; styles of; and television; and film; Broadway; and critics

Biological-Physiological Topics

Anesthesia:	nature of; types of; uses of; development of; dangers of
Biological:	clock; control; warfare; rhythm; sciences
Biorhythm:	nature of; predictions from; life cycles; charting
Brain:	-washing; damage; genius; intelligence; aphasia
Diseases:	major diseases of college students; prevention; detection; treatment
Food:	health; preservatives; additives; red dye; and allergies; preparation
Medicine:	preventive; forensic; and health insurance; history of; and poisoning
Nutrition:	nature of; functions of food; essential requirements; animal; human; and starvation; and diet; vitamins
Transplants:	nature of; rejection; donor selection; legal aspects; ethical aspects; religious aspects; future of; advances in

What topics would you like to hear other students speak on? What topics do you hope will be avoided? Why?

Communication Topics

Advertising: techniques; expenditures; ethical; unethical; subliminal; leading agencies

Freedom of Speech: laws protecting; and Constitution; significance of; abuses of; and censorship; and economics

Languages: artificial; sign; natural; learning of; loss of; pathologies of; sociology of; psychology of; international

Media: forms of; contributions of; abuses; regulation of; popularity of; influences of; and violence; and censorship; Nielsen ratings

Television: development of; history of; workings of; satellite; cable; commercials; propaganda; and leisure time; programming; economics

Translation: computer; missionary impetus; problems in; history of

Writing: styles; forms of; calligraphy; graphology; development of; and speech

Economic Topics

Business: cycles; associations; law; in performing arts; finance

Capitalism: nature of; economics of; development of; depression and inflation

Corporation: law; business; nature of; history; growth of the

Inflation: and deflation; causes of; effects of; types of

Investment: stocks; gold; real estate; art; restrictions on; bank; allowance

Taxation: alcohol; cigarette; history of; purposes of; historical methods of; types of

Treasury Department: monetary system; origin; functions of; and counterfeiting

Wealth: economic; distribution of; primitive economic systems; contemporary view

Philosophical Topics

Empiricism: radical; nature of; doctrines; opposition to

Existentialism: meaning of; and choice; history of; leaders in; movement

Occultism: theories of; practices; rituals; astrology; theosophy; witchcraft; divination

Phenomenology: characteristics of; principles of; growth of; development of

Relativism: philosophy; ethical; meaning of; leaders of; influence

Religion: different religions; leaders in; influence of; beliefs and agnosticism

Witchcraft: meaning of; white and black; and magic; structure of; functions of; theories of; in primitive societies; in contemporary societies

Zen: meaning of; principles of; historical development of; contemporary interest in; teachings of; influence of

Political Topics

Amnesty: in draft evasion; in criminal law; and pardons; in Vietnam War

Communism: development of; theories of; religion and; ideologies

Government: federal; state; city; powers of; abuses of; types of; democracy; socialism; communism

Imperialism: nature of; economics of; problems with; practices; history

Nationalism: nature of; history of; philosophy of; chauvinism; self-determination

Supreme Court: judicial review; decisions; makeup of; chief justices; jurisdiction

United Nations (UN): development of; functions of; agencies; and League of Nations; structure of; veto powers; Security Council

War: conduct of; financing; destruction by; causes of; debts; games; casualties

Psychological Topics

Aggression: aggressive behavior in animals; in human beings; as innate; as learned

Alcohol: alcoholism; nature of; Alcoholics Anonymous; Al Anon; physical effects of; among the young; treatment of alcoholism

Autism: nature of; treatment for; symptoms; causes

Depression: nature of; and suicide; among college students; dealing with

Guilt: causes of; symptoms of; dealing with; effects of; and suicide; and religion

Intelligence: quotient; tests; theories of; cultural differences; measuring

Love: nature of; theories of; romantic; family; and hate; and interpersonal relationships; of self; and materialism

Personality: development of; measurement of; theories of; disorders

Sociological Topics

Cities: problems of; population patterns; and crime; movement into and out of

Crime: prevention; types of; and law; and punishment

Divorce: rate; throughout world; causes of; advantages of; disadvantages of; proceedings; traumas associated with

Ethnicity: meaning of; and prejudice; theories of; and culture

Feminism: meaning of; implication of; changing concepts of; and chauvinism

Lesbian/Gay: rights, life-style; laws against; prejudice against; and religion; statistics; relationships

Prison: reform; systems; security; routine; effect on crime; personality; behavior

Racism: nature of; self-hatred; genetic theory; human rights; education; religious

Suicide: causes; among college students; laws regulating; methods; aiding the suicide of another; philosophical implications; and religion

Surveys. One excellent guideline to determine what is worthwhile, from your audience's point of view, is to look at some of the national and regional polls concerning what people think is important—the significant issues, the urgent problems. For example, a New York Times/CBS News Poll (*New York Times*, February 20, 1994, p. 3) identified the following as their biggest problems: crime and violence, health care, the economy, unemployment, the federal deficit, welfare, and war and peace. Surveys like this appear regularly in newspapers and magazines.

Naturally, all audiences are different. Yet such surveys are useful starting points to give you some insight into what others think is important and, hence, interested in listening to.

News Items. Another useful starting point is a good daily newspaper. Here you will find the important international and domestic issues, the financial issues, and the social issues all conveniently in one place. The editorial page and letters to the editor are also useful in learning what concerns people.

News magazines like *Time, Newsweek,* and such financial magazines as *Forbes, Money,* and *Fortune* will provide a wealth of suggestions. News shows like *20/20* and *60 Minutes* and the numerous talk shows often discuss the very issues that people are concerned with and hold different views on.

Brainstorming. Another useful method is to brainstorm, a procedure explained in detail in Chapter 10. You begin with your "problem," which in this case is "What will I talk about?" Then record any idea that occurs to you. Be sure to follow the four rules for effective brainstorming: avoid evaluation, strive for quantity, combine and extend ideas, and develop ideas as wild as possible. After you generate a sizable list—it should not take more than about 15 minutes—review the list and evaluate the suggestions.

Limit Your Topic

Plan to cover a limited topic in depth rather than a broad topic superficially. The limiting process is simple: repeatedly divide the topic into its significant parts. For example, divide your general topic into its component parts, then divide one of these parts into its component parts.

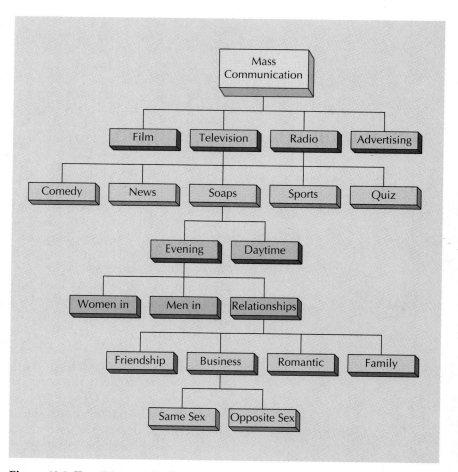

Figure 12.2 Tree Diagram for Limiting Speech Topics

Continue until the topic seems manageable, one that you can reasonably cover in some depth in the allotted time.

For example, take television programs as the first general topic area. You might divide this into such subtopics as comedy, children's programs, educational programs, news, movies, soap operas, game shows, and sports. You might then take one of these topics, say comedy, and divide it into subtopics. You might consider it on a time basis and divide television comedy into its significant time periods: pre-1960, 1961–1979, 1980 to the present. Or, you might focus on situation comedies. Here you might examine a topic such as women in television comedy, race relations in situation comedy, or families in television comedies. At this stage, the topic is beginning to look manageable. Television programs, without some limitation, would take a lifetime to cover adequately. Figure 12.2 presents a tree diagram to further illustrate this process. Notice how from the general topic of mass communication you can get to the relatively specific topic of same-sex or opposite-sex business relationships in evening television soaps.

The General Purpose

The two major kinds of speeches are the speech of information and the speech of persuasion. The informative speech creates understanding; it clarifies, enlightens, corrects misunderstandings, demonstrates how something works, or explains how something is structured. The persuasive speech, on the other hand, influences attitudes or behaviors. It may strengthen existing attitudes or change the beliefs of the audience. Or it may get the audience to respond in a particular way.

The Specific Purpose

The specific purpose of your speech identifies the information you intend to communicate (if an informative speech) or the attitude or behavior you wish to change (if a persuasive speech). For example, your specific purpose in an informative speech might be:

> to inform my audience of the parts of a computer
> to inform my audience of the new grading procedures
> to inform my audience of the new health care provisions

Your specific purpose in a persuasive speech might be:

> to persuade my audience that cigarette advertising should be abolished
> to persuade my audience that the college should establish courses in AIDS prevention
> to persuade my audience to contribute time to helping students with disabilities

Speech is power; speech is to persuade, to convert, to compel.
—RALPH WALDO EMERSON

Whether you intend to inform or persuade, your specific purpose should be narrow enough so you will be able to go into it in some depth. Your audience will benefit more from a speech that covers a

Why is it easier to strengthen than to change an audience's beliefs? Why is it easier to change an audience's beliefs from "neutral" to "favoring your position" than from "against your position" to "in favor of your position"?

"Eleven hamburgers, one frank. Eleven coffees, one tea. Eleven apple pies, one chocolate cake. . . ."

Courtesy Sieron

small area in depth than from one that covers only the surface of a broad topic.

Avoid the common pitfall of trying to accomplish too much in too short a time. For example, informing your audience about the development of AIDS and the recent testing procedures for HIV infection is actually two specific purposes. Select one and build your speech around it. Thus, informing your audience about the development of AIDS or informing your audience of the recent testing procedures for HIV infection would be more appropriate. Follow the same principle in developing your specific purpose for your persuasive speeches. For example, persuading your audience of the prevalence of AIDS in our community and that they should contribute money for AIDS services contains two specific purposes. Select one.

STEP 2: ANALYZE YOUR AUDIENCE

If you are to inform or persuade an audience, you must know who they are. What do they already know? What would they want to know more about? What are their opinions, attitudes, and beliefs? Where do they stand on the issues you wish to address? Specifically, you will want to look at the sociological characteristics (for example, age, sex, and religion) and the psychological characteristics (for example, feelings and attitudes about the speech or speaker).

Audience Sociology

Age. What is the general age of the audience? How wide is the range? Does it include different age groups that you will want to address differently? Does the age of the audience impose any limitations on the topic, the language, or the examples and illustrations you will select?

Sex. Is the audience predominantly of one sex? Do men and women view the topic differently? If so, how? Do men and women have different backgrounds, experiences, and knowledge about the topic? How will this influence the way you develop the topic?

Occupation, Income, and Status. What are the main occupations of the audience? How might this influence your speech? Does the income of the audience have any implications for your subject or the way you will develop it? What about the general status of audience members? Might this influence the speech in any way?

How might the religion and religiousness of your audience figure into your next speech?

Religion and Religiousness. What is the dominant religious affiliation of the audience? What are the implications of this for the speech? What is the strength of their belief? How might this relate to the topic?

How would you describe your human communication class as an audience for an informative speech on the changing job market in the next three years? For a persuasive speech entitled "The Need to Build Homeless Shelters in This Community"?

Context. Will the context influence what you discuss or the way you will present your speech? Are there facilities for showing slides? Is there a chalkboard? Is there adequate light? Are there enough seats? Is there a podium? Is a microphone necessary?

Other Factors. What other factors will influence the way you prepare and present your speech? Is marital status relevant? Does the audience have special interests you might note in your speech?

How might cultural factors influence the way you develop a speech on the need to change immigration laws?

CULTURAL VIEWPOINT

Culture and the Audience

Nationality, race, and cultural identity and identification are crucial in audience analysis. Largely because of different training and experiences, the interests, values, and goals of different cultural groups will also differ. In analyzing cultural factors, ask yourself at least the following questions:

1. *Are the differences within cultures relevant to your topic and purpose?* Speakers who fail to demonstrate an understanding of these differences will be distrusted. Speakers—especially if they are seen as outsiders—who imply that all African Americans are athletic and all lesbians are masculine will quickly lose credibility. Avoid any implication that you are stereotyping audience members (or groups to which they belong). It is sure to work against your achieving your purpose.

2. *Are the attitudes, beliefs, and values held by different cultures relevant to your topic and purpose?* Find out what these are. For example, the degree to which listeners are loyal to family members, feel responsibility for the aged, and believe in the value of education will vary from one culture to another. Build your appeals around *your* specific audience's attitudes, beliefs, and values.

3. *Will the various cultures differ in their goals or the way they view suggestions to change their lives?* For example, groups that have experienced recent oppression may be more concerned with immediate goals and with more immediate means of effecting changes in their lives. Many want revolutionary rather than evolutionary change. They may have little patience with the more conservative posture of the majority, which tells them to be content with small gains.

4. *Will the cultures have different views toward education, employment, and life in general?* Oppressed groups often cannot afford the luxury of idealism. Pragmatic appeals will work best with formerly and currently oppressed members. Some cultures values formal education and take great pride in their members' graduating from college and earning advanced degrees. Other cultures may place greater value on practical experience, on hard work, or on living for the pleasure of the moment.

[Next Cultural Viewpoint, page 307]

Drawing by Leo Cullum; © 1992 The New Yorker Magazine, Inc. Reprinted by permission.

Audience Psychology

Focus your psychological analysis of the audience on three questions:

How Willing Is Your Audience? If you face an audience willing (even anxious) to hear your speech, you will have a relatively easy time relating your speech to them. If, however, your audience is listening unwillingly, consider the following suggestions:

- Secure their interest and attention as early in your speech as possible.
- Reward the audience for their attendance and attention.
- Relate your topic and supporting materials directly to your audience's needs and wants.
- Show the audience why they should listen to your speech.
- Involve the audience directly in your speech.
- Use supporting materials that gain attention and secure interest.
- Focus on a few (even one) very strong issues.

How Favorable Is Your Audience? If you face an audience that has unfavorable attitudes toward your topic or your purpose or even toward you, consider these suggestions:

- Build on commonalities; emphasize not the differences but the similarities.
- Build your speech from areas of agreement, through areas of slight disagreement, up to the major differences.
- Strive for small gains.

How would you describe the attitudes and beliefs of members of your human communication class as an audience for an information speech on how to get the job you want? for a persuasive speech on the need to build homeless shelters in this community?

How Knowledgeable Is Your Audience? Listeners differ greatly in the knowledge they have. Some listeners will be quite knowledgeable about the topic. Others will be almost totally ignorant. Mixed audiences are the really difficult ones. If your audience knows little about your topic, consider these suggestions:

- Do not talk down to these members of your audience.
- Do not confuse a lack of knowledge with a lack of intelligence.

If your audience knows a great deal about your topic, consider these suggestions:

- Let the audience know that you are aware of their knowledge and expertise.
- Emphasize your credibility, especially your competence in this general subject area (see Chapter 15).

It's [success in the media] in the preparation—in those dreary pedestrian virtues they taught you in seventh grade and you didn't believe.

—DIANE SAWYER

STEP 3: RESEARCH YOUR TOPIC

Research is essential if your speech is to be worthwhile and if you and the audience are to profit from it. First read from a general source—an article in an encyclopedia or magazine. You might pursue some of the references

Today, more and more research is being conducted via computer. Data bases, containing vast amounts of information on just about any topic, can be easily accessed in many college libraries. What data bases will prove most useful in preparing your next speech? For what personal or professional interest might you access a computer data base? Which one(s) would you access?

in the article or seek books on the topic in the library catalog. You might also consult one or more of the guides to periodical literature for recent articles in journals, magazines, and newspapers. For some topics, you might want to consult individuals. Professors, politicians, physicians, or others with specialized information might prove useful.

Computer Searches

Many college libraries now provide access to computer searches, such as those on CD-ROM (Compact Disk Read-Only Memory), which make research both enjoyable and efficient. These systems enable you to access a wide variety of specialized data bases. For example, the ABI/INFORM data base covers more than 500 periodicals in business; ERIC indexes more than 775 major journals as well as convention papers, dissertations, and curriculum materials in education and communication; and PERIODICAL ABSTRACTS indexes more than 250 journals covered by the *Reader's Guide to Periodical Literature*. With such systems you can access an annotated bibliography built around just about any topic.

One of the great advantages is that you can request references that deal with specific topics, for example, teenage drug abuse in schools, integrating multiculturalism into the college curriculum, or AIDS prevention programs in elementary schools. No longer do you have to look up, for example, drug abuse and then search each article to see if it deals with teenagers in school. The computer program will search the articles for you and indicate which of the articles deals with both drug abuse and teenagers in a school setting (as major topics). The program will not—unless you direct it to do so—access articles that merely contain the words *drug abuse* or *teenagers in school*. Most systems allow you to print out the bibliography or download it to your own computer disk.

Since these information retrieval systems vary so much from one library to another and since they are changing and expanding so rapidly, it is best to investigate the specific resources of your college or local library. Table 12.2 presents some helpful research sources.

STEP 4: FORMULATE YOUR THESIS AND IDENTIFY THE MAJOR PROPOSITIONS

The thesis is the main idea that you want to convey to the audience. The thesis of Lincoln's Second Inaugural Address was that Northerners and Southerners should work together for the good of the entire country. The thesis of the *Rocky* movies was that the underdog can win.

Let's say, for example, you are planning to deliver a persuasive speech in favor of Senator Winters. Your thesis statement might be: "Winters is the best candidate." This is what you want your audience to believe, what you want your audience to remember even if they forget everything else. In an informative speech, on the other hand, the thesis statement focuses on what you want your audience to learn. For example, for a speech on jealousy, a suitable thesis might be: "Two main theories of jealousy exist."

The ultimate goal of all research is not objectivity, but truth.
—HELENE DEUTSCH

Today, more and more research is being conducted via computer. Data bases, containing vast amounts of information on just about any topic, can be easily and efficiently accessed in many college libraries. Which data bases will prove most useful in preparing your next speech? For what personal or professional interest might you access a computer data base? Which one(s) would you access?

Expert Power

You possess **expert power** over another person if he or she regards you as having expertise or knowledge. Most often you have expertise and knowledge and others see this in you and therefore attribute expert power to you. Of course, there are instances in which expert power is attributed to those who are neither expert nor knowledgeable.

Your expert power increases when you are seen as unbiased, with nothing to gain personally from influencing others. It decreases as you are seen to be biased or as having something to gain from persuading the other people.

An excellent way to increase your expert power is to carefully research and integrate that research into your speech. A few suggestions:

- Mention the sources in your speech by citing at least the author and, if helpful, the publication and the date: "In their book *Confidence and Public Speaking,* communication professors Paul Nelson and Judy Pearson call this the oral footnote."
- Provide smooth transitions between your words and the words of the author you are citing. Avoid such expressions as "I have a quote here" or "I want to quote an example." These expressions give the impression that the research is something apart from your speech rather than an integral piece.

TABLE 12.2 SOME RESEARCH SOURCES

The Card/On-Line Catalog

	Has given way to the computer catalog in many libraries. Contains "cards" of three types: title, subject, and author. The cards give the following information about each book: number of pages; whether there are illustrations, bibliographies, or index; date of publication; publisher; and identifying number, which tells where the book can be found in your library.

Encyclopedias

Encyclopaedia Britannica	The most comprehensive and authoritative; 33 volumes
Collier's Encyclopedia	Distinguished by its illustrations and clarity of style; 24 volumes
Encyclopedia Americana	Especially useful for American topics; 30 volumes
Columbia Encyclopedia, Random House Encyclopedia	Useful one-volume encyclopedias
The New Catholic Encyclopedia, Encyclopaedia Judaica, Encyclopedia of Islam, Encyclopedia of Buddhism, McGraw-Hill Encyclopedia of Science and Technology, International Encyclopedia of the Social Sciences	More specialized works representing the wide variety of available encyclopedias
Grolier Multimedia Encyclopedia, Compton's Interactive Encyclopedia, and *Microsoft Encarta*	Some of the available choices for CD-ROM encyclopedias

Biographical Material

Biographical Index	An index to biographies appearing in various sources
Dictionary of National Biography (DNB)	Articles on famous dead British men and women
Concise Dictionary of National Biography	Short edition of DNB
Dictionary of American Biography (DAB)	Articles on famous dead Americans
The Concise Dictionary of American Biography	Short edition of DAB

• It sometimes helps to mention the qualifications of the person or reference work you are citing (if the audience is unfamiliar with this): "*Statistical Abstracts of the United States,* the most recent and reliable source of statistics available, reports that . . . "

[Next Power Perspective, page 305]

Dictionary of Canadian Biography (DCB)	Articles on those who have contributed significantly to Canada
Current Biography	A periodical containing articles, most with photographs, on living individuals
Directory of American Scholars, International Who's Who, Who's Who in America, Who's Who, Dictionary of Scientific Biography, American Men and Women of Science	Representative of the specialized biographical sources available

Newspaper, Magazine, and Journal Indexes

The New York Times Index	Published since 1913, indexes all sorts of its articles
Reader's Guide to Periodical Literature	Published from 1900, indexes more than 100 popular magazines
Education Index	Articles from journals and magazines relevant to education
The Catholic Periodical and Literature Index, The Social Science and Humanities Index, Business Periodicals Index, Art Index, Applied Science and Technology Index	Specialized indexes
Psychological Abstracts, Sociological Abstracts, Language and Language Behavior Abstracts, Communication Abstracts	Brief summaries of articles in these areas of study. (Many such indexes and abstracts are available on CD-ROM.)

Almanacs

The World Almanac & Book of Facts	Published since 1868, the most popular and probably the best almanac, containing information on just about every subject, including the arts, science, governments, population, geography, religion, and just about every conceivable topic. Also available on CD-ROM.
Information Please Almanac, Reader's Digest Almanac and Yearbook, The New York Times Encyclopedia Almanac, Universal Almanac	Similar in style and purpose
Whitaker's Almanac	Focuses on Great Britain
Canadian Almanac and Directory	Focuses on Canada
Statistical Abstracts of the United States	Summarizes all types of facts and figures

What was the thesis of the last film you saw? the last novel, play, or short story you read?

What main ideas might you generate from these theses: (1) College athletics should be expanded, (2) students need to be educated about AIDS, and (3) the personal computer is a useful household product?

Limit your thesis statement to one central idea. Statements such as "We should support Winters and the entire Democratic Party" contain not one but two basic ideas.

Use your thesis statement to generate your main ideas. Once you phrase the thesis statement, the main divisions of your speech will suggest themselves. Let's say you are giving a speech to a group of high school students on the values of a college education. Your thesis is "A college education is valuable." You then ask yourself, "Why is it valuable?" From these answers you generate your major propositions. You might first brainstorm the question and identify as many answers as you can. Don't evaluate them, just generate as many as possible. Your list might look something like this:

A college education is valuable because:

1. It helps you get a job.
2. It increases your potential to earn a good salary.
3. It gives you greater job mobility.
4. It helps you secure more creative work.
5. It helps you appreciate the arts more fully.
6. It helps you understand an extremely complex world.
7. It helps you understand different cultures.
8. It helps you avoid taking a regular job for a few years.
9. It helps you meet lots of people and make friends.
10. It helps you increase personal effectiveness.

For purposes of illustration, let's stop at this point. You have ten possible main points—too many to cover in a short speech. Further, not all are equally valuable or relevant to your audience. Look over the list to make it shorter and more meaningful. Here are some suggestions:

Eliminate Points That Seem Least Important to Your Thesis

You might want to eliminate, say, number 8, since it's inconsistent with the positive values of college.

Combine Points That Have a Common Focus

Notice, for example, that the first four points center on jobs. You might, therefore, consider grouping them under a general heading: A college education will help you secure a better job.

This might be one of your major propositions, which you can develop by defining what you mean by "better job." You might also use some of the ideas you generated in your brainstorming session. This main point and its elaboration might look like this:

I. A college education will help you secure a better job.
   A. College graduates earn higher salaries.
   B. College graduates have more creative jobs.
   C. College graduates have greater job mobility.

Note that A, B, and C are all aspects or subdivisions of "a better job."

Select Points That Are Most Relevant to Your Audience

Ask yourself what will interest the audience most. On this basis, you might drop items 5 and 7 on the assumption that your audience, high school students, will not consider learning about the arts or different cultures to be particularly exciting. Further, you might conclude that high school students care most about increasing personal abilities. So you might include this point as your second major proposition:

I. A college education will help you increase your personal effectiveness.

Much as you developed the subordinate points in your first proposition by defining what you meant by a "good job," you would define what you mean by "personal effectiveness":

I. A college education will help you increase your personal effectiveness.
   A. A college education will help you increase your ability to communicate.
   B. A college education will help you acquire learning skills.
   C. A college education will help you acquire coping skills.

You then follow the same procedure used to generate these subordinate points (A, B, and C) to develop the subheadings. For example, you might divide A into two major subheads:

I. A college education will improve your ability to communicate.
   A. A college education teaches writing skills.
   B. A college education teaches speech skills.

How would you develop the assertion that a college education will help you understand other cultures?

Use Two, Three, or Four Main Points at Most

Remember, your aim is not to cover every aspect of a topic but to emphasize selected parts. Further, you want to have enough time to amplify and support the points you present. With too many propositions this becomes impossible. Also, you don't want to present too much information.

Phrase Your Propositions in Parallel Style

Use similar wording in your major propositions.

NOT THIS:

Mass Media Functions
   I.   The media entertain.
   II.   The media function to inform their audiences.
   III.   Creating ties of union is a major media function.
   IV.   The conferral of status is a function of all media.

THIS:

Mass Media Functions
   I.   The media entertain.
   II.   The media inform.

III. The media create ties of union.
IV. The media confer status.

Develop Your Main Points So They Are Separate and Distinct

Do not overlap your main points.

NOT THIS:

 I. Color and style are important in clothing selection.

THIS:

 I. Color is important in clothing selection.
 II. Style is important in clothing selection.

ETHICAL ISSUE

Speaker Ethics

Ethics is an essential aspect of all forms of communication. Here are four guidelines to stimulate you to start thinking about the ethical responsibilities of the public speaker. Which of these do you agree with? Which do you disagree with? What additional guides would you propose?

Truth
Present truth as you understand it. Be truthful also about the sources of your materials. Avoid defaming others—an act which is illegal as well as unethical. Defamation occurs when a speaker falsely attacks the reputation of another person that causes damage to this person. When this occurs in print or in pictures it is called *libel* and when it occurs in spoken form, it is called *slander*. So be careful of your facts, especially in speaking against another person.

Knowledge
As a speaker, you have the ethical responsibility to know what you are talking about, to have prepared yourself as thoroughly as possible.

Audience-Centered
An ethical speaker has the audience's interests in mind and avoids exploiting audiences for his or her own gain. This doesn't mean that the speaker cannot also gain—the politician seeking votes is seeking self-gain, but ideally is also concerned with the audience's interests. It is also unethical (and illegal) to present a "clear and present danger," for example, a speech that proves dangerous to the welfare of the people and the country, by causing people to riot.

Preparation
The audience has the right to expect that the speaker has done his or her best in preparing. This doesn't mean perfection; it means that reasonable preparation be made before engaging the attention of the audience.

[Next Ethical Issue, page 343]

False words are not only evil in themselves, but they infect the soul with evil.

—PLATO

STEP 5: SUPPORT THE MAJOR PROPOSITIONS

Now that you have identified your thesis and your major propositions, you need to support each. Tell the audience what it needs to know about color and style in clothing selection. Or, in the persuasive speech example, convince them that a college education will help them get better jobs.

In the informative speech, your support primarily amplifies—describes, illustrates, defines, exemplifies—the concepts you discuss. You want the "color in clothing" to come alive to the audience. Amplification accomplishes this. Specifically, you might use examples, illustrations, and the testimony of various authorities. Definitions especially help to breathe life into abstract or vague concepts. Statistics (summary figures) that explain various trends are essential for certain topics. Audiovisual aids—charts, maps, objects, slides, films, tapes, CDs, and so on—help clarify vague concepts. These forms of amplification are covered in detail in Chapter 14, "The Informative Speech."

In a persuasive speech your support is proof—material that offers evidence, argument, and motivational appeal and that establishes your credibility and reputation. To persuade your audience to buy Brand X, in part by demonstrating that it is cheaper, you must give proof that this is true. You might compare the price of Brand X to other brands. Or you might demonstrate that the same amount of Brand X will do twice the work of other brands selling at the same price.

You support your propositions with reasoning from specific instances, from general principles, from analogy, and from causes and effects. These may be thought of as logical support. Also, you support your position with motivational appeals. You might appeal to the audience's desire for status, financial gain, or increased self-esteem: "No one wants to be at the low end of the hierarchy. Our new management seminar will help you climb that corporate ladder faster and easier than you ever thought possible." You also add persuasive force through your personal reputation or credibility. If audience members see you as competent, highly moral, and charismatic, they are more likely to believe you. These forms of support are covered in depth in Chapter 15, "The Persuasive Speech."

What kinds of supporting materials would you expect a speaker to use in a speech on *the types of gambling*? On *the need to legalize gambling*?

STEP 6: ORGANIZE THE SPEECH MATERIALS

You must organize your material if the audience is to understand and remember it (Whitman & Timmis, 1975). Here are six patterns you might use to organize the body of a speech.

Time Pattern

Organizing major issues on the basis of some temporal relationship is a popular pattern for informative speeches. Generally, when this pattern is used, the speech is organized into two or three major parts. You might begin with the past and work up to the present or future, or begin with the present or future and work back to the past. You might organize a speech on a child's development of speech and language in a time or temporal pattern. Major propositions might look like this:

I.   Babbling is the first stage.
II. Lallation is the second stage.
III. Echolalia is the third stage.
IV. Communication is the fourth stage.

Most historical topics lend themselves to organization by a time pattern. Events leading to the Civil War, steps toward a college education, and the history of writing will all yield to temporal patterning.

Spatial Pattern

Similar to temporal patterning is patterning the main points of a speech on the basis of space. Both temporal and spatial patterns are especially appropriate for informative speeches. Most physical objects fit well into spatial patterns. Similarly, the structure of a hospital, school, skyscraper, or even a dinosaur might be appropriately described using a spatial pattern. Here a spatial pattern is used in a speech on places to visit in Central America.

I.   Your first stop is Guatemala.
II. Your second stop is Honduras.
III. Your third stop is Nicaragua.
IV. Your fourth stop is Costa Rica.

Topical Pattern

Perhaps the most popular pattern of organization is the topical pattern, which divides the speech into major topics. This pattern is an obvious one for organizing a speech on, say, the branches of government. Here the divisions are clear:

I.   The legislative branch is controlled by Congress.
II. The executive branch is controlled by the President.
III. The judicial branch is controlled by the courts.

Speeches on problems facing the college graduate, great works of literature, and the world's major religions all lend themselves to a topical organizational pattern.

Problem-Solution Pattern

A popular pattern for organizing the persuasive speech is to present the main ideas in terms of problem and solution. The speech is divided into two parts. One part deals with the problem and the other with the solution. Let's say you are trying to persuade an audience that home health aides should be given higher salaries and increased benefits. Here a problem-solution pattern might be appropriate. In the first part of the speech, you might discuss some of the problems confronting home health aides: industry luring away the most qualified graduates of the leading universities, many health aides leaving the field after two or three years, and the low status of the occupation in many undergraduates' minds. In the second part, you would consider the possible solutions: making health aides' salaries competitive with those in private industry, making benefits as attractive as those offered by industry, and raising the status of the health aide profession.

The speech, in outline form, would look like this:

I. Three major problems confront home health care.
   A. Industry lures away the most qualified graduates.
   B. Numerous excellent health aides leave the field after two or three years.
   C. Home health care is currently a low-status occupation.
II. Three major solutions to these problems exist.
   A. Increase salaries for home health aides.
   B. Make benefits for health aides more attractive.
   C. Raise the status of the home health care profession.

Cause-Effect/Effect-Cause Pattern

Similar to the problem-solution pattern of organization is the cause-effect or effect-cause pattern. Both are especially appropriate for persuasive speeches. Here you divide the speech into two major sections—causes and effects. For example, a speech on the reasons for highway accidents might fit into a cause-effect pattern. In such a speech you would first consider the causes of highway accidents and then some of the effects—the number of deaths, the number of accidents, and so on. Similarly, illnesses or low self-esteem can be explained with a cause-effect pattern. An outline of the causes and effects of low self-esteem might look something like this:

I. Low self-esteem is caused by two main factors.
   A. A history of criticism can contribute to low self-esteem.
   B. Perfectionistic and unrealistic goals can contribute to low self-esteem.
II. Low self-esteem has two main effects.
   A. Depression is a frequent effect of low self-esteem.
   B. An unwillingness to socialize with others is a frequent effect of low self-esteem.

The Motivated Sequence

The motivated sequence is a pattern of arranging your information to motivate your audience to respond positively to your purpose (Gronbeck, McKerrow, Ehninger, & Monroe, 1994). In the motivated sequence there are five steps: (1) attention, (2) need, (3) satisfaction, (4) visualization, and (5) action. This pattern is appropriate for both informative and persuasive speeches.

(1) Attention Make the audience give you their undivided attention. If you execute this step effectively, your audience should be anxious to hear what you have to say. You can gain audience attention through a variety of means (see p. 312).

For example, let's say you were giving an informative speech about the workings of home computers. In this attention step you might say: "By the time you graduate, there will be more home computers than automobiles." You might then explain the phenomenal growth of computers in education until you have the complete attention of your audience.

(2) Need Here you would prove that a need exists. The audience should feel that they need to learn or do something because of this need. You can establish need by:

1. stating the need or problem as it exists or will exist;
2. illustrating the need with specific examples, illustrations, statistics, testimony, and other forms of support; and
3. pointing to how this need affects your specific listeners—for example, their financial status, career goals, or individual happiness.

In a speech on home computers, you might say in this step: "Much as it is now impossible to get around without a car, it will be impossible to get around the enormous amount of information without a home computer." You might then explain how knowledge is expanding so rapidly that without computer technology, it will be impossible to keep up with any field.

(3) Satisfaction Here you would present the "solution" to satisfying the need that you demonstrated in step 2. The audience should believe that what you are informing them about or persuading them to do will satisfy the need. Here you would answer the question "How will the need be satisfied by what I am asking the audience to learn, believe, or do?" This step usually contains two types of information:

1. a clear statement (with examples and illustrations if necessary) of what you want the audience to learn, believe, or do; and
2. a statement of how or why what you are asking them to learn, believe, or do will lead to satisfying the need identified in step 2.

For example, you might say: "Learning a few basic principles of home computers will enable you to process your work more efficiently, in less time, and more enjoyably." You might then explain the various steps your listeners could take to satisfy the needs you have identified.

(4) Visualization Visualization intensifies the audience's feelings or beliefs. It takes the audience beyond the present place and time and helps them imagine the situation as it would be if the need were satisfied as suggested in step 3. You can accomplish this by (1) demonstrating the positive benefits to be derived if this advocated proposal is put into operation or (2) demonstrating the negative consequences that will occur if your plan is not put into operation.

Of course, you could combine the two methods and demonstrate both the positive benefits of your plan and the negative effects of the existing plan or of some competing proposal. For example, you might say: "With these basic principles firmly in mind (and a home computer), you'll be able to stay at home and do the library research for your next speech by just punching in the correct code." You might then demonstrate the speech research process so your listeners will visualize exactly the advantages of computer research.

Talk that does not end in any kind of action is better suppressed altogether.

—THOMAS CARLYLE

(5) Action Here you would tell the audience what they should do to satisfy the need. You want to move the audience in a particular direction. For example, you might want them to speak for Farrington or against

Williamson, to attend the next student government meeting, or to work for a specific political candidate. Here are a few ways to accomplish this step.

1. State exactly what audience members should do.
2. Appeal to your listeners' emotions.
3. Give the audience guidelines for future action.

For example, you might say: "Supplement these few principles by further study. Probably the best way is to enroll in a computer course. Also, read the brief paperback, *The Home Computer for the College Student.*" You might then identify the computer courses that would be appropriate for a beginning student. Further, you might identify a few other books or distribute a brief list of books suitable for your listeners.

Notice that an informative speech could have stopped after the satisfaction step. You accomplish the goal of informing the audience about some principles of home computers with the satisfaction step. In some cases, though, you may feel it helpful to complete the steps to emphasize your point.

In a persuasive speech, on the other hand, you must go at least as far as visualization (if you limit your purpose to strengthening or changing attitudes or beliefs) or to the action step (if you aim to get your listeners to behave in a certain way).

Additional Thought Patterns

The six thought patterns just considered are the most common and are useful for many public speeches. But other patterns might be appropriate for different topics. Here are several:

Structure-Function

The structure-function pattern is useful in informative speeches in which you want to discuss how something is constructed (its structural aspects) and what it does (its functional aspects). This pattern might be useful, for example, in a speech in which you explain what an organization is and what it does, the parts of a university and how they operate, or the sensory systems of the body and their various functions. This pattern might also be useful in discussing the nature of a living organism: its anatomy (structures) and its physiology (functions).

Comparison and Contrast

Arranging your material in a comparison-and-contrast pattern is useful in informative speeches when you want to analyze two different theories, proposals, departments, or products in terms of their similarities and differences. In this type of speech you would explain each theory or proposal but would focus primarily on how they are similar and how they are different.

Pro and Con, Advantages and Disadvantages

The pro-and-con pattern, sometimes called the advantages-disadvantages pattern, is useful in informative speeches in which you want to explain objectively the advantages (the pros) and the disadvantages (the cons) of different plans, methods, or products.

Can you use the motivated sequence to analyze an advertisement appearing in newspapers or on television?

Both the comparison-and-contrast and the pro-and-con patterns might be developed by focusing on the several qualities or aspects of each plan or product. For example, if you were comparing two health plans, your major propositions might center on such topics as outpatient care, hospital care, and home health care. Under each of these major propositions, you would show what Health Plan 1 provides and then what Health Plan 2 provides. Both of these patterns are also useful in persuasive speeches in which you want to highlight the weaknesses in one plan or product and the strengths of another, much like advertisers do when they compare their product with Brand X.

Claim and Proof

This pattern is especially useful in a persuasive speech in which you want to prove the truth or usefulness of a particular proposition. It is the pattern that you see frequently in trials, when the claim made by the prosecution is that the defendant is guilty and the proof is the various pieces of evidence: the defendant had a motive; the defendant had the opportunity; the defendant had no alibi. In this pattern your speech would consist of two major parts. In the first part you would explain your claim (tuition must not be raised, library hours must be expanded, courses in AIDS education must be instituted). In the second part you would offer your evidence or proof as to why tuition must not be raised, for example.

Multiple Definition

This pattern is useful for informative speeches in which you want to explain the nature of a concept (What is a born-again Christian? What is a scholar? What is multiculturalism?). In this pattern each major heading would consist of a different type of definition or way of looking at the concept. A variety of definition types are discussed in Chapter 14.

Who What Why Where When

This is the pattern of the journalist and is useful in informative speeches when you wish to report or explain an event, for example, a robbery, political coup, war, or trial. Here you would have five major parts to your speech, each dealing with the answers to one of these five questions.

Because your thought pattern serves primarily to help your listeners follow your speech, you might want to tell your listeners (in your introduction or as a transition between the introduction and the body of your speech) what pattern you will be following. Here are just a few examples:

- In our discussion of language development, we'll follow the baby from the earliest sign of speech through true communication.
- In touring Central America, we'll travel from north to south.
- I'll first explain the problems with raising tuition and then propose a workable solution.
- First, we'll examine the causes of hypertension and then its effects.

THINKING CRITICALLY ABOUT PUBLIC SPEAKING PREPARATION: EVALUATING RESEARCH

In using research in your own speeches and in listening to the research in the speeches of others, be sure that you also critically evaluate it. Here are a few questions you might ask of all types of evidence.

- Is the support recent? We live in a world of rapid change. Economic strategies that worked for your parents will not work for you. As the world changes, so must your strategies for coping with it. And what is true of economics is also true of other areas. Therefore, other things being equal, supporting materials are best when they are recent.
- Is there corroborative support? Support is best when it comes from different directions. For example, in considering accounting as a major, your evidence should come not only from educational authorities attesting to the value of your college's program, but also from government statistics on the need for accountants, from economic forecasts concerning probable earnings, and so on. Conclusions gathered from diverse sources of evidence are more likely to be true.
- Are the sources unbiased? Ask yourself how biased the sources are and in what directions they are biased. Do not treat a tobacco company report on the connection between smoking and lung cancer with the same credibility as a report by an impartial medical research institute. Question research conducted or disseminated by any special-interest group.

Feedback on Concepts and Skills

In this chapter we began explaining the steps in preparing a public speech.

1. The preparation of a public speech involves ten steps: (1) select the subject and purpose, (2) analyze the audience, (3) research the topic, (4) formulate the thesis and identify the major propositions, (5) support the major propositions, (6) organize the speech materials, (7) word the speech, (8) construct the conclusion and the introduction, (9) rehearse the speech, and (10) deliver the speech. The first six of these were discussed in this chapter; the remaining four are discussed in Chapter 13.
2. Speech topics should deal with significant issues that interest the audience. Subjects and purposes should be limited in scope.
3. In analyzing the audience, consider age; sex; cultural factors; occupation, income, and status; religion and religiousness; the occasion; and the specific context.
4. Research the topic, beginning with general sources and gradually exploring more specific and specialized sources.
5. Formulate the thesis of the speech and develop your major propositions by asking relevant questions about this thesis.
6. Support the major propositions with a variety of materials that amplify and provide evidence.
7. Organize the speech materials in a clear, easily identifiable thought pattern. Suitable patterns include: time, space, topical, problem-solution, cause-effect/effect-cause, motivated sequence, structure-function, comparison and contrast, pro and con, claim and proof, multiple definition, and who what why where when.

In this discussion we covered the first six steps necessary in preparing a public speech, which entail a variety of specific skills. Check your ability to use these skills. Use the following rating scale: (1) = almost always, (2) = often, (3) = sometimes, (4) = rarely, (5) = almost never.

_____ 1. In preparing a public speech, I follow a logical progression of steps such as that outlined here.

_____ 2. I select appropriate topics and purposes and narrow them to manageable proportions.

_____ 3. I analyze my audience in terms of its sociological and psychological characteristics and adapt the speech on the basis of these findings.

_____ 4. I research topics effectively and efficiently.

_____ 5. After selecting my thesis, I expand it by asking strategic questions to develop my main ideas or propositions.

_____ 6. After generating my possible major propositions, I eliminate those points that seem least important to my thesis, combine those that have a common focus, and select those most relevant to my audience.

_____ 7. I support my propositions with amplifying materials such as examples, statistics, and visual aids and with logical, emotional, and ethical proof.

_____ 8. In organizing the speech's main points, I select a thought pattern appropriate to the subject matter, purpose, and audience.

Skill Development Experiences

12.1 Limiting Your Speech Topic

For one of the following, narrow the topic sufficiently for a five-minute informative or persuasive speech. Once you have selected a suitably limited subject, formulate a specific purpose.

history	film
emotions	energy
family	television
communication problems	health
psychology	work
education	play
mass media	economics
nonverbal communications	conflict
politics	love
religion	literature
the United States	health care
war	drugs
entertainment	transportation
philosophy	vegetables
language	science

12.2 Identifying Theses

Every communication has a thesis. Select at least three different communication forms—for example, a soap opera, a situation comedy, a play, a film, a novel, a short story, or a public speech—and identify their theses. Share these in small groups or with the whole class. From this brief experience, the following should be clear:

1. The thesis is the central idea—the main assertion—of the communication.
2. Although people will state the thesis differently, there should be a fair degree of agreement.
3. Identifying the thesis makes the work as a whole more understandable and meaningful.
4. Any communication work revolves around a central thesis; the examples, illustrations, behaviors of the characters, and even the music, support or elaborate the thesis.

12.3 Predicting Audience Attitudes

Try to predict the attitudes of your class members toward each of the following propositions by indicating how you think the majority of the class members feel about each. Record F for favorable, N for neutral, and U for unfavorable.

_____ 1. Marijuana should be legalized for all persons over 21.

_____ 2. All required college courses should be abolished.

_____ 3. X-rated movies (even XXX movies) should be shown on television without time restrictions.

_____ 4. Members of groups that have been discriminated against should be given preferential treatment in entrance into graduate and professional schools.

_____ 5. The death penalty should be law in all states.

_____ 6. Lesbians and gay men should be allowed the same adoption rights as heterosexuals.

_____ 7. "Hate speech" should not be covered by the first amendment's protection of free speech.

_____ 8. Tenure for college teachers should be eliminated.

_____ 9. Gambling should be legalized in all states.

_____ 10. Puerto Rico should be made the fifty-first state.

After all members have recorded their responses, discuss:

- the accuracy of your predictions; take a class poll and see how many accurately predicted the class attitudes
- the cues (verbal and nonverbal) used in making the predictions
- the adaptations you would make as a speaker addressing your class on one or more of the propositions presented above

CHAPTER THIRTEEN

Public Speaking Preparation and Delivery (Steps 7–10)

Chapter Concepts	Chapter Goals	Chapter Skills
	After completing this chapter, you should be able to	After completing this chapter, you should be able to
Step 7: Word the Speech	1. define oral style	use oral style in wording your speeches
	2. explain the role of clarity, vividness, appropriateness, personal style, forcefulness, and sentence structure in public speaking style	word your speeches so they are clear, vivid, appropriate, personal, and forceful
		construct sentences that are short, direct, active, positive, and varied
Step 8: Construct the Conclusion and Introduction	3. explain the functions of the conclusion and the introduction	construct conclusions that effectively summarize and close your speech
	4. explain the use of transitions	construct introductions that gain attention and orient the audience
Step 9: Rehearse the Speech	5. define and explain the methods for controlling speaker apprehension	manage your speaker apprehension
	6. explain the major goals of public speaking rehearsal and some specific rehearsal suggestions	rehearse your speech effectively and efficiently
	7. define the three general methods of delivery	effectively use the extemporaneous method of delivery
Step 10: Deliver the Speech	8. explain volume, rate, pitch, articulation, and pronunciation and the problems associated with each	deliver your speech with appropriate and varied voice, pausing, and body action
	9. explain the guidelines for use of eye contact, facial expression, posture, gestures, and movement	deliver your speech with appropriate eye contact, facial expressions, posture, gestures, and body movements
Thinking Critically About Public Speaking Preparation and Evaluation	10. explain the guidelines for expressing critical evaluations	be positive, specific, objective, constructive, and keep in mind the irreversibility of communication

A t this point, you are probably deep into your preparation. You have your topic limited and adapted to your audience; it is well researched and organized. In this chapter we continue with the process of preparing a speech and consider how to word the speech, how to conclude and introduce the speech, how to rehearse it, and finally how to deliver the completed public speech.

STEP 7: WORD THE SPEECH

Speaking and writing need to be different largely because listening and reading are different. In listening you hear a speech only once; therefore, it must be instantly intelligible. In reading you can reread an essay or look up an unfamiliar word. Temporary attention lapses may force you to reread a sentence or paragraph, but in listening you can never make up for such lapses.

Researchers who have examined a great number of speeches and writings have found several important differences (DeVito, 1965, 1981; Akinnaso, 1982). Generally, spoken language consists of shorter, simpler, and more familiar words than does written language. There is more qualification in speech than in writing. For example, when you speak, you generally make greater use of such expressions as *although, however,* and *perhaps.* When you write, you probably edit these out as you are writing. Spoken language also contains a greater number of self-reference terms—*I, me, my.* And it contains more expressions that incorporate the speaker as part of the observation ("it seems to me that . . . ," "as I see it . . . ").

For most speeches, an "oral style" is appropriate. These specific suggestions will help you style a speech that will retain the best of the oral style while maintaining comprehension and persuasion.

Clarity

Clarity in speaking style should be your primary goal. Here are some guidelines to help you make your speech clear.

Be Economical

Don't waste words. Two important ways to achieve economy are to avoid redundancies (unnecessary repetition) and meaningless words. Notice the redundancies in the following expressions and how a more economical and clearer style results when you eliminate the italicized terms:

- *more* unique
- at 9 A.M. *in the morning*
- we *first* began the discussion
- the full *and complete* report

The most valuable of all talents is that of never using two words when one will do.

—THOMAS JEFFERSON

- I *myself personally*
- blue *in color*
- *over*exaggerate
- you, *members of the audience*
- about *approximately* 9 inches *or so*

Use Specific Terms and Numbers

Picture these terms:

- living thing
- animal
- dog
- poodle

Notice that as the terms get more specific, the picture gets clearer and more detailed. Be specific so your audience will see what you want them to see. Don't say *car* when you want them to picture a limousine, and don't say *movie* when you want them to think of *The Flintstones*.

The same is true of numbers. Don't say "earned a good salary" if you mean "earned $90,000 a year." Don't say "taxes will go up" when you mean "taxes will increase 22 percent." Don't say "their defense budget was enormous" when you mean "the defense budget was 17 billion dollars."

Use Short, Familiar, and Commonly Used Terms

Favor the short word over the long, the familiar term over the unfamiliar. Say "help" instead of "assist," say "show" instead of "indicate," say "harmless" instead of "innocuous."

[Next Power Perspective, page 349]

Drawing by Barsotti, © 1981 The New Yorker Magazine, Inc.

Vividness

Select words to help make your ideas come alive in the listeners' minds.

Use Active Verbs

Favor verbs that communicate activity rather than passivity. The verb *to be* in all its forms—*is, are, was, were,* and *will be*—is relatively inactive. Try replacing such forms with action verbs. Instead of saying "Management will be here tomorrow," consider "Management will descend on us (or jets in) tomorrow."

Use Figures of Speech

One of the best ways to achieve vividness is to use figures of speech. Table 13.1 presents a few you might use.

TABLE 13.1 FIGURES OF SPEECH

Figure	Definition	Examples
Alliteration	Repetition of the same initial consonant sound in two or more words close to one another	Fifty famous flavors
Hyperbole	Use of extreme exaggeration	I'm so hungry I could eat horsemeat.
Metaphor	Comparison of two unlike things	She's a lion when she wakes up. He's a real bulldozer.
Metonymy	Substitution of a name for a title with which it is closely associated	City Hall issued the following new release ("City Hall" is used instead of "the city council").
Personification	Attribution of human characteristics to inanimate objects	This room cries for activity. My car is tired and needs water.
Simile	Comparison of two unlike objects using the word *like* or *as*	He takes charge like a bull. The teacher is as gentle as a lamb.
Rhetorical Question	A question used to make a statement or produce some desired effect rather than to secure an answer that is obvious	Do you want to be popular? Do you want to get well? Do you want to pass the next exam?

How might you make more vivid such bland sentences as "The children played in the yard," "The soldiers took the hill," and "The singer sang three songs"?

Use Imagery

Appeal to the audience's senses, especially their visual, auditory, and tactile senses. Make them see, hear, and feel what you are talking about.

- *Visual Imagery.* Describe people or objects to create images the audience can see. When appropriate, describe visual qualities such as height, weight, color, size, shape, length, and contour. Let your audience see the sweat pouring down the faces of coal miners, and the short, overweight executive in a pin-striped suit smoking an enormous cigar.
- *Auditory Imagery.* Use terms that describe sounds to appeal to the audience's sense of hearing. Let listeners hear the car screeching, the wind whistling, the bells chiming, and the angry professor roaring.
- *Tactile Imagery.* Use terms referring to temperature, texture, and touch to create tactile imagery. Let listeners feel the cool water running over their bodies, the fighter's punch, the rough-as-sandpaper clothing, and a lover's soft caress.

CULTURAL VIEWPOINT

High- and Low-Context Cultures

Is your native culture a high-context culture or a low-context culture (Hall & Hall, 1987)? A high-context culture (Japanese, Arabic, Latin American, Thai, Korean, Apache, and Mexican are examples) is one in which much of the information in communication is in the context or in the person—for example, information that is shared through previous communications, through assumptions about each other, and through shared experiences. The information is not explicitly stated in the verbal message. A low-context culture (German, Swedish, Norwegian, and the United States are examples) is one in which most information is explicitly stated in the verbal message, and in formal transactions in written (contract) form.

To appreciate the distinction between high and low context, consider giving directions ("Where's the recycling center?"). To someone who knows the neighborhood (a high-context situation) you can assume the person knows the local landmarks. So, you can give directions such as "next to the laundromat on Main Street" or "the corner of Albany and Elm." To the newcomer (a low-context situation), you cannot assume the person shares any information with you. So, you would have to use only those directions that even a stranger would understand, for example, "make a left at the next stop sign" or "go two blocks and then turn right."

Members of low-context cultures are usually direct in their reactions to others. This directness is generally appreciated by other low-context culture members. But it may prove insulting, insensitive, or unnecessary to the high-context cultural member. Conversely, to the low-context member, the high-context cultural member may appear vague, underhanded, or dishonest in his or her reluctance to be explicit or engage in communication that a low-context member would consider open and direct.

Another frequent source of misunderstanding that can be traced to the distinction between high- and low-context cultures can be seen in face-saving. High-context cultures place a great deal more emphasis on saving face. For example, in high-context cultures criticism should only take place in private to enable the person to save face. Low-context cultures may not make this public-private distinction. This cultural difference may well create problems in your own class. For example, part of the process of learning public speaking is learning to express criticism of others' efforts. Some members, because of their cultural training, may resist this and feel it is not quite proper to voice criticism of a peer in a public setting. How should you deal with this?

[Next Cultural Viewpoint, page 352]

Appropriateness

Appropriate language is consistent in tone with your topic, your audience, and your own self-image. It's language that does not offend anyone or make anyone feel uncomfortable. It's language that seems natural to the situation. Here are some guidelines to help you choose appropriate language.

Speak at the Appropriate Level of Formality

Although public speaking usually takes place in a relatively formal situation, relatively informal language seems to work best. One way to achieve an informal style is to use contractions: *don't* instead of *do not*, *I'll* instead of *I shall*, and *wouldn't* instead of *would not*. Contractions give a public speech the sound and rhythm of conversation—a quality to which listeners generally react favorably.

Avoid Written-Style Expressions

Avoid expressions that are more familiar in writing such as "the former" or "the latter" as well as such expressions as "the argument presented above." These make listeners feel you are reading to them rather than talking with them.

Avoid Unfamiliar Terms

Be careful to avoid terms the audience does not know. Avoid foreign and technical terms unless you are certain the audience is familiar with them. Similarly, avoid jargon (the technical vocabulary of a specialized field) unless you are sure its meaning is clear to your listeners. Some acronyms (NATO, UN, NOW, and CORE) are probably familiar to most audiences; most, however, are not. When you use these terms, explain their meaning.

Avoid Slang, Vulgar, and Offensive Expressions

Be careful not to offend your audience with language that embarrasses or makes them think you have little respect for them. Although your listeners may use such expressions, they generally resent their use by public speakers.

Avoid terms that might be interpreted as sexist, heterosexist, or racist. Do not use the masculine pronoun to refer to all persons. Change your sentences so you can use the plural *they* or *them,* or say "he and she" or "her and him." Refer to professions or positions with gender-neutral terms, for example, *chairperson, police officer,* and *repairperson.* Don't imply that the hypothetical doctor or lawyer is male by using sex identifiers such as *woman doctor* or *female lawyer.* Similarly, do not imply that all couples or relationships consist of a man and a woman. Avoid qualifying terms indicating affectional orientation, as in *the lesbian politician* or *the gay swimmer.*

Personal Style

Audiences favor speakers who use a personal rather than an impersonal style—who speak with them rather than at them.

Use Personal Pronouns

Say "I," "me," "he," "she," and "you." Avoid such expressions as the impersonal "one" (as in, "One is led to believe that. . . "), "this speaker," or "you, the listeners." These expressions distance the audience and create barriers rather than bridges.

Direct Questions to the Audience

Involve the audience by asking them questions. With a small audience, you might even briefly take responses. With larger audiences, you might ask the question, pause to allow the audience time to consider their

WIZARD OF ID by Parker © 1992/Creators Syndicate

responses, and then move on. When you direct questions to your listeners, they feel part of a public speaking transaction.

Create Immediacy

Immediacy is a connectedness, a relatedness, and a oneness with your listeners. Create immediacy by using the "you approach." Say "you'll enjoy reading . . . " instead of "everyone will enjoy reading . . . " Refer to commonalities between you and the audience. Say, for example, "We are all children of immigrants" or "We all want to see our team in the playoffs." Refer also to shared experiences and goals. Say, for example, "We all need a more responsive PTA." Finally, recognize and refer to audience feedback. Say, for example, "I can see from your expressions that we're all here for the same reason."

Sentence Construction

Effective public speaking style also requires careful attention to the construction of sentences. Here are some guidelines.

Favor Short over Long

Short sentences are more forceful and economical. They are easier to understand and to remember. Listeners do not have the time or inclination to unravel long and complex sentences.

Favor Direct over Indirect

Direct sentences are easier to understand. They are also more forceful. Instead of saying "I want to tell you of the three main reasons why we should not adopt the Bennett Proposal," say, "We should not adopt the Bennett Proposal. Let me give you three good reasons."

Favor Active over Passive

Active sentences are easier to understand. They also make your speech livelier and more vivid. Instead of saying "The lower court's original decision was reversed by the Supreme Court," say, "The Supreme Court reversed the lower court's decision." Instead of saying "The proposal was favored by management," say, "Management favored the proposal."

Favor Positive over Negative

Positive sentences are easier to comprehend and to remember (DeVito, 1976; Clark, 1974). Notice how sentences (a) and (c) are easier to understand than (b) and (d).

(a) The committee rejected the proposal.
(b) The committee did not accept the proposal.
(c) This committee works outside the normal company hierarchy.
(d) This committee does not work within the normal company hierarchy.

Vary the Type and Length

The advice to use short, direct, active, and positive sentences is valid most of the time. But too many sentences of the same type or length will make your speech boring. Use variety while generally following the guidelines given above.

Personal style is not always the most effective style to use. When might a more formal, impersonal style be more effective?

---

1. Never use a metaphor, simile, or other figure of speech which you are used to seeing in print.
2. Never use a long word when a short one will do.
3. If it is possible to cut a word out, always cut it out.
4. Never use the passive when you can use the active.
5. Never use a foreign phrase, a scientific word, or a jargon word if you can think of an everyday English equivalent.
6. Break any of these rules sooner than say anything outright barbarous.

—George Orwell

STEP 8: CONSTRUCT THE CONCLUSION AND INTRODUCTION

Your conclusion and introduction need special care because they will determine, in large part, the effectiveness of your speech.

The Conclusion

Devote special care to this brief but crucial part of your speech. In your conclusion summarize and close.

Summarize

You may summarize your speech in a variety of ways.

Restate Your Thesis. Restate the essential thrust of your speech—your thesis or perhaps the purpose you hoped to achieve.

Restate Its Importance. Tell the audience again why your topic or thesis is so important. Here is how one speaker used this type of conclusion: "If we do not move to restore our universities and improve the educational infrastructure in Canada, we will be unilaterally withdrawing from the future. We will be condemning ourselves to the economic vassaldom of those who do perceive education and brains as the only real resource and, in fact, the ultimate resource of any nation" (Light, 1984).

Restate Your Major Propositions. Simply reiterate your two, three, or four major propositions.

Close

The conclusion's second function is to provide closure—to give the speech a crisp and definite end. Don't leave your audience wondering whether you have finished. Two popular ways of achieving closure are using a quotation and posing a challenge.

Use a Quotation. One that summarizes your thesis or provides an interesting perspective on your point of view often provides effective closure. Do make sure that it is clearly and directly related to your speech purpose; otherwise, the audience will spend their time trying to discover the connection.

Pose a Challenge or Question. You may wish to end your speech with a provocative question or challenge. Here, for example, a speaker concludes his speech by posing a question and answering it (Styles, 1985): "What does that mean for Canada? Weighed in the global balance, as well as our trade balance, we have a working partnership with what is still the most powerful nation on earth. It's imperative that we maintain it and (with our, at times, somewhat different points of view) vital that we continue to work hard at explaining our interests, so that for both of us the best possible results are achieved."

True eloquence consists in saying all that should be said, and that only.

—LA ROCHEFOUCAULD

Any authentic work of art must start an argument between the artist and his audience.

—DAME REBECCA WEST

The Introduction

Construct the introduction after you have constructed the body and the conclusion to your speech. Try to accomplish two goals in your introduction: Gain attention and orient the audience as to what you will talk about.

Gain Attention

In your introduction focus the audience's attention on your topic. And try to maintain that attention throughout your speech.

Ask a Question. Questions are effective because they are a change from normal statements and involve the audience. They tell the audience that you are talking directly to them and care about their responses.

Refer to Specific Audience Members. Involving members directly makes them perk up and pay attention.

Refer to Recent Happenings. Being familiar with such events, the audience will pay attention to your approach.

Use an Illustration or Dramatic or Humorous Story. We are all drawn to illustrations and stories about people—they make your speech vivid and concrete. Use them to secure audience attention in the introduction and to maintain it throughout.

Use Audiovisual Aids. These will engage attention because they are new and different. In Chapter 14 lots of specific examples are given.

Orient the Audience

The introduction, or preview, should orient the audience and help them follow your thoughts more closely. You can orient the audience in several ways.

Give the Audience a General Idea of Your Subject. Say, for example, "Tonight I want to discuss the proposed tax revision," "I'm going to focus on gender differences in communication," or "I'll cover the pros and cons of the Brommel proposal for dealing with atomic waste."

Give a Detailed Preview of Your Main Propositions. Identify the propositions you will discuss, for example, "In this brief talk I will cover four major attractions of New York City: the night life, theater, restaurants, and museums."

Identify the Goal You Hope to Achieve. A librarian addressing my public speaking class oriented the audience by stating goals in this way: "Pay attention for the next few minutes and you'll be able to locate anything we have in the library by using the new touch-screen computer access system."

Some Common Faults with Conclusions and Introductions

Avoid these common faults made by many beginners

Don't Apologize. A common fault is to apologize for something in your speech. Don't. Your inadequacies—whatever they are—will be clear enough to any discerning listener. Do not point them out. Having given this advice, it should be noted that this would not hold in all cultures. For example, in Iran a speaker would be expected to use self-deprecating terms to symbolize his or her humility and modesty (Keshavarz, 1988). In the United States, then, avoid such expressions as: "I am not an expert on this topic," "I wanted to illustrate these ideas with a videotape but I couldn't get my hands on a VCR," or "I didn't do as much reading on this topic as I should have." And never start a speech with "I'm not very good at giving public speeches."

Don't Preface Your Introduction. Don't begin with such common but ineffective statements as: "I'm really nervous, but here goes," "Before I begin my talk, I want to say. . . ," or "I hope I can remember everything I want to say."

Don't Introduce New Material in Your Conclusion. Instead, reinforce what you have already said, summarize your essential points, or give new expression to ideas already covered.

Don't Drag Out the Conclusion. End crisply and just once. Don't preface each sentence of the conclusion with terms that indicate the end. "In summary," "in conclusion," and similar expressions will lead the audience to expect an ending. When you are ready to end, end.

Transitions and Internal Summaries

Connect parts of your speech to each other so their relationships are clear to you and to the audience. Remember, your audience will hear your speech only once.

Transitions are words, phrases, or sentences used to connect the various parts of your speech. They provide guideposts that help the audience follow the development of your thoughts and arguments. Some examples of transitional expressions you may find useful are: "My next point . . . ," "A second example (argument, fact) . . . ," "If you want further evidence, consider . . . ," "First, . . . , second, . . . ," "Furthermore, . . . ," "So, as you can see . . . ," "Not only should we . . . , but we should also . . . ," "Given this situation, what should we do?" Use transitions in at least the following places:

- between the speech's introduction and its body
- between the body and the conclusion, and
- between the speech's main points

Also make use of "nonverbal transitions." For example, pause between main points; move to the other side of the room; step forward or backward; stand still if you are moving or move if you are standing still; or lean forward. These movements, especially when combined with verbal transitions, will help signal that you are going from one idea to another.

*Therefore, since brevity is the soul of wit,
and tediousness the limbs and outward flourishes,
I will be brief.*
—POLONIUS IN SHAKESPEARE'S HAMLET

Every speech ought to be put together like a living creature, with a body of its own, so as to be neither without head, nor without feet, but to have both a middle and extremities, described proportionately to each other and to the whole.

—PLATO, PHAEDRUS

Internal Summaries

Closely related to the transition is the internal summary—a statement summarizing what you have discussed, usually a major subdivision of your speech. Incorporate internal summaries into the transitions connecting the major arguments or issues. Say, for example, "Now that we've seen how a college education will help you get a better job, let's look at how college can increase your personal effectiveness."

Internal summaries remind your listeners of what they have just heard and preview what they will hear. The clear connection that internal summaries create will help listeners follow your speech despite any lapses in attention or noise.

Before the Introduction and After the Conclusion

Think of your speech as beginning as soon as the audience focuses on you. Similarly, think of it ending not after you have spoken the last sentence but only after the audience directs its focus away from you. Here are a few suggestions.

Display enthusiasm (not signs of discomfort or displeasure) when you get up from your seat and walk to your speaking position. People much prefer listening to a speaker who looks like she or he wants to speak.

Don't start your speech as soon as you get up from your seat or even as soon as you get to the front. Survey your audience; make eye contact and engage their attention. Stand in front of the audience with a sense of control. Pause briefly, then begin.

Begin low, speak low;
Take fire, rise higher;
When most impressed
Be self-possessed;
At the end wax warm,
And sit down in a storm.
—JOHN LEIFCHILD

If a question period follows your speech and you are in charge of this, pause after completing your conclusion. Ask audience members if they have any questions. If there is a chairperson who will ask for questions, pause after your conclusion, and then nonverbally signal to the chairperson that you are ready. If there are to be no questions, pause after your last statement, maintain audience eye contact, and then walk (do not run) to your seat. Show no signs of relief. Focus your attention on whatever activity is taking place.

The Preparation Outline

Here is a relatively detailed outline similar to the ones you might prepare in constructing your speech. The sidenotes should clarify both the content and the format of a full sentence outline.

Generally the title, thesis, and purpose of the speech are prefaced to the outline. When the outline is an assignment that is to be handed in, additional information may be requested.

Note the general format for the outline; note that the headings are clearly labeled and that the indenting helps you to see clearly the relationship that one item bears to the other. For example, in Introduction II, the outline format helps you to see that A, B, C, and D are explanations (amplification, support) for II.

Have You Ever Been Culture Shocked?

Thesis: Culture shock can be described in four stages.

Purpose: To inform my audience of the four phases of culture shock

Introduction

I. Many of you have or will experience culture shock.

    A. Many people experience culture shock, that reaction to being in a culture very different from what you were used to.

    B. By understanding culture shock, you'll be in a better position to deal with it if and when it comes.

II. Culture shock occurs in four stages (Oberg, 1960).

    A. The Honeymoon occurs first.

    B. The Crisis occurs second.

    C. The Recovery occurs third.

    D. The Adjustment occurs fourth.

[Let's follow the order in which these four stages occur and begin with the first stage, the honeymoon.]

Body

I. The Honeymoon occurs first.

    A. The Honeymoon is the period of fascination with the new people and culture.

    B. You enjoy the people and the culture.

        1. You love the people.

            a. For example, the people in Zaire spend their time very differently from the way New Yorkers do.

            b. For example, my first 18 years living on a farm was very different from life in a college dorm.

        2. You love the culture.

            a. The great number of different religions in India fascinated me.

            b. Eating was an especially great experience.

[But like many relationships, life is not all honeymoon; soon there comes a crisis.]

II. The Crisis occurs second.

    A. The Crisis is the period when you begin to experience problems.

        1. One third of American workers abroad fail because of culture shock (Samovar & Porter, 1991, p. 232).

Note that the introduction, body, and conclusion are clearly labeled and separated visually.

The speaker assumes that the audience knows the general nature of culture shock and so does not go into detail as to its definition. But just in case some audience members do not know and to refresh the memory of others, the speaker includes a brief definition.

Note that references are integrated throughout the outline just as they would be in a term paper. In the actual speech, the speaker might say: "Anthropologist Kalervo Oberg who coined the term culture shock said it occurs in four stages."

The introduction serves the two functions noted: It gains attention (by involving the audience and by stressing the importance of the topic to the audience's desire to gain self-understanding) and it orients the audience as to what is to follow. This particular orientation identifies both the number of stages and their names. If this speech were a much longer and more complex one, the orientation might also have included brief definitions of each stage.

Another function often served by the introduction is to establish a relationship between yourself as the speaker, the topic, and the audience. In this particular speech, this function might have been served by your telling the audience how you experienced culture shock and how knowing the stages helped you cope with the difficulties. You might then tell the audience that the same would be true for them and thus connect all three major elements of the speech.

This transition cues the audience into a four-part presentation. Also, the numbers repeated throughout the outline will further aid the audience in keeping track of where you are in the speech. Most important, it tells the audience that the speech will follow a temporal thought pattern.

Notice the parallel structure throughout the outline. For example, note that I, II, III, and IV in the body are all phased in exactly the same way. Although this may seem unnecessarily redundant, it will help your audience follow your speech more closely and will also help you in logically structuring your thoughts.

Notice that there are lots of examples in this speech. These examples are identified only briefly in the outline and would naturally be elaborated on in the speech.

Notice too the internal organization of each major point. Each main assertion in the body contains a definition of the stage (IA, IIA, IIIA, and IVA) and examples (IB, IIB, IIIB, and IVB) to illustrate the stage.

Because this is a specific fact, some style manuals require that the page number should be included.

2. The personal difficulties are also great.

B. Life becomes difficult in the new culture.

1. Communication is difficult.

2. It's easy to offend people without realizing it.

[As you gain control over the various crises, you begin to recover.]

III. The Recovery occurs third.

A. The Recovery is the period where you learn how to cope.

B. You begin to learn intercultural competence (Lustig & Koester, 1993).

1. You learn how to communicate.

   a. Being able to go to the market and make your wants known was a great day for me.

   b. I was able to ask for a date.

2. You learn the rules of the culture.

   a. The different religious ceremonies each have their own rules.

   b. Eating is a ritual experience in lots of places throughout Africa.

[Your recovery leads naturally into the next and final stage, the adjustment.]

IV. The Adjustment occurs fourth.

A. The Adjustment is the period where you come to enjoy the new culture.

B. You come to appreciate the people and the culture.

[Let me summarize, then, the stages you go through in experiencing culture shock.]

Conclusion

I. Culture shock can be described in four stages.

A. The Honeymoon is first.

B. The Crisis is second.

C. The Recovery is third.

D. The Adjustment is fourth.

Note that each statement in the outline is a complete sentence. You can easily convert this outline into a phrase or key word outline for use in delivery. The full sentences, however, will help you see more clearly relationships among items.

The transitions are inserted between all major parts of the speech. Although they may seem too numerous in this abbreviated outline, they will be appreciated by your audience because the transitions will help them follow your speech.

Notice that these four points correspond to I, II, III, and IV of the body and to I A, B, and C of the conclusion. Notice how the similar wording adds clarity.

II. By knowing the four stages, you can better understand the culture shock you may now be experiencing on the job, at school, or in your private life.

This step provides closure; it makes it clear that the speech is finished. It also serves to encourage reflection on the part of the audience as to their own culture shock.

References

Lustig, M. W., & Koester, J. (1993). *Intercultural competence: Interpersonal communication across cultures*. New York: HarperCollins.

Oberg, K. (1960). Culture shock: Adjustment to new cultural environments. *Practical Anthropology*, 7:177–182.

Samovar, L. A., & Porter, R. E. (1991). *Communication between cultures*. Belmont, CA: Wadsworth.

This reference list includes just those sources that appear in the completed speech. APA citation form is used here. Check with your instructor for the recommended style manual.

The Skeletal Outline

Here is a skeletal outline—a kind of template for structuring a speech. This particular outline would be appropriate for a speech using a time, spatial, or topical organization pattern. Note that in this skeletal outline there are three major propositions (I, II, and III in the Body). These correspond to the II A, B, and C in the introduction (where you would orient the audience) and to the I A, B, and C in the conclusion (where you would summarize your major propositions). The transitions are signaled by square brackets. As you review this outline—the watermarks will remind you of the functions of each outline item—you will be able to see how it can be adapted for use with other organization patterns, for example, problem-solution, cause-effect, or the motivated sequence.

Thesis: _____*your main assertion; the core of your speech*_____ .

Specific Purpose: _____*what you hope to achieve from this speech*_____ .

Introduction

    I. _____*gain attention*_____ .

    II. _____*orient audience*_____ .

        A. _____*first major proposition; same as I in body*_____ .

        B. _____*second major proposition; same as II in body*_____ .

        C. _____*third major proposition; same as III in body*_____ .

[Transition: _____ *connect the introduction to the body* _____]

Body

I. _____ *first major proposition* _____ .

    A. _____ *support for I (the first major proposition)* _____ .

    B. _____ *further support for I* _____ .

[Transition: _____ *connect the first major proposition to the second* _____]

II. _____ *second major proposition* _____ .

    A. _____ *support for II (the second major proposition)* _____ .

    B. _____ *further support for II* _____ .

[Transition: _____ *connect the second major proposition to the third* _____]

III. _____ *third major proposition* _____ .

    A. _____ *support for III* _____ .

    B. _____ *further support for III* _____ .

[Transition: _____ *connect the third major proposition (or all major propositions) to the conclusion* _____]

Conclusion

I. _____ *summary* _____ .

    A. _____ *first major proposition; same as I in body* _____ .

    B. _____ *second major proposition; same as II in body* _____ .

    C. _____ *third major proposition; same as III in body* _____ .

II. _____ *closure* _____ .

The Delivery Outline

In the extemporaneous method, you use a delivery outline to assist you in delivering the speech. Do not use your preparation outline as you may read from the outline which is not an effective way to give a speech. Instead, construct a brief delivery outline. Here are some guidelines.

- *Be brief.* Don't allow the outline to stand in the way of speaker-audience contact. Use key words to trigger in your mind the ideas you wish to discuss.
- *Be delivery-minded.* Include any delivery guides you might wish to remember while you are speaking, for example, "pause," or "show VA."
- *Rehearse your speech with this outline.* In your rehearsals, use this outline only. Make your rehearsal as close to the real thing as possible.

Below is a sample delivery outline constructed from the preparation outline on culture shock, presented on pages 314–317. Note these features in the following sample outline.

- It is brief enough so that you will be able to use it effectively without losing eye contact with the audience. It uses abbreviations (for example, CS for culture shock) and phrases rather than complete sentences.
- It is detailed enough to include all essential parts of your speech, including transitions.
- It contains delivery notes specifically tailored to your own needs, for example, pause suggestions and guides to using visual aids.
- It is clearly divided into introduction, body, and conclusion and uses the same numbering system as the preparation outline.

PAUSE!

LOOK OVER THE AUDIENCE!

[INTRODUCTION]

  I. Many experience CS
    A. CS: the reaction to being in a culture very different from your own
    B. By understanding CS, you'll be better able to deal with it

PAUSE—SCAN AUDIENCE

  II. CS occurs in 4 stages (WRITE ON BOARD)
    A. Honeymoon
    B. Crisis
    C. Recovery
    D. Adjustment

[Let's examine these stages of CS]

PAUSE/STEP FORWARD

[BODY]

I. Honeymoon

    A. fascination w/people and culture

    B. enjoyment of people and culture

        1. Zaire example

        2. farm to college dorm

[But life is not all honeymoon—the Crisis]

II. Crisis

    A. problems arise

        1. 1/3 Am workers fail abroad

        2. personal difficulties

    B. life becomes difficult

        1. communication

        2. offend others

[As you gain control over the crises, you learn how to cope]

PAUSE

III. Recovery

    A. period of learning to cope

    B. you learn intercultural competence

        1. communication becomes easier

        2. you learn the culture's rules

[As you recover, you adjust]

IV. Adjustment

    A. learn to enjoy (again) the new culture

    B. appreciate people and culture

[These then are the four stages; let me summarize]

PAUSE

[CONCLUSION]

I. CS occurs in 4 stages: honeymoon, crisis, recovery, & adjustment

II. By knowing the 4 stages, you can better understand the culture shock you may now be experiencing on the job, at school, or in your private life.

PAUSE

ASK FOR QUESTIONS

STEP 9: REHEARSE THE SPEECH

Let's start the discussion of rehearsal by dealing with what is probably your number one concern—stage fright, or what is now called speaker apprehension.

Dealing with Speaker Apprehension

Of all public speaking issues, speaker apprehension (or "stage fright") is probably your most important concern. In fact, "communication apprehension is probably the most common handicap that is suffered by people in contemporary American society" (McCroskey & Wheeless, 1976). Approximately 20 percent of the general population suffers from communication apprehension (Richmond & McCroskey, 1989). Take the accompanying apprehension test to measure your own fear of public speaking.

The human brain starts working the moment you are born and never stops until you stand up to speak in public.
—GEORGE JESSEL

TEST YOURSELF

How Apprehensive Are You of Public Speaking?

Instructions This questionnaire consists of six statements concerning your feelings about public speaking. Indicate the degree to which each statement applies to you by marking whether you (1) strongly agree, (2) agree, (3) are undecided, (4) disagree, or (5) strongly disagree with each statement. There are no right

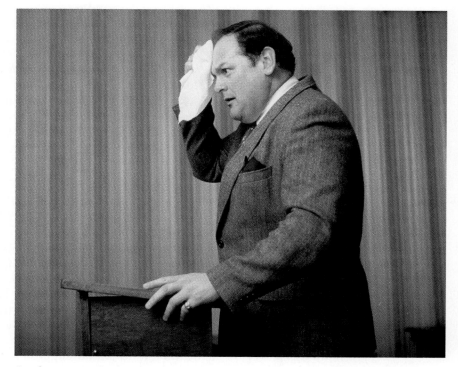

In what communication situations are you most apprehensive? Least apprehensive? What accounts for these differences?

or wrong answers. Do not be concerned that some of the statements are similar to others. Work quickly; just record your first impression.

_____ 1. I have no fear of giving a speech.
_____ 2. Certain parts of my body feel very tense and rigid while giving a speech.
_____ 3. I feel relaxed while giving a speech.
_____ 4. My thoughts become confused and jumbled when I am giving a speech.
_____ 5. I face the prospect of giving a speech with confidence.
_____ 6. While giving a speech, I get so nervous that I forget facts I really know.

Thinking Critically About Public Speaking Apprehension To obtain your public speaking apprehension score, use the following formula:

18 plus scores for items 1, 3, and 5;
minus scores for items 2, 4, and 6.

A score above 18 shows some degree of apprehension. Most people score above 18, so if you scored relatively high, you are among the vast majority of people. You may find it interesting to compare your several apprehension scores (Chapters 7, 9, and 11). Most people would score highest on public speaking and the job interview and relatively low on conversations and group discussions.

Source: From An Introduction to Rhetorical Communication, 5th ed., by James C. Mc-Croskey. Englewood Cliffs, NJ: Prentice-Hall, 1986. Reprinted by permission of the author.

Five factors especially influence students' public speaking anxiety (Beatty, 1988). Understanding these factors will help you control them and your fear of speaking.

1. *Perceived novelty.* New and different situations make us anxious. Therefore, gaining as much experience in public speaking as you can will lessen your anxiety.
2. *Subordinate status.* When you feel that others are better speakers or that they know more than you do, your anxiety increases. Thinking positively about yourself and being thorough in your preparation reduces this particular cause of anxiety.
3. *Conspicuousness.* When you are the center of attention, as you normally are in public speaking, your anxiety increases. Therefore, try thinking of public speaking as a type of conversation. If you are comfortable talking in small groups, then visualize your audience as an enlarged small group.
4. *Dissimilarity.* When you feel you have little in common with your listeners, you feel anxious. Try emphasizing your similarity with your listeners as you plan your speeches as well as during the actual presentation.
5. *Prior history.* When you have a prior history of apprehension, you are more likely to become anxious. Positive public speaking experiences will help reduce this cause of anxiety.

Here are a few additional suggestions to deal with and control speaker apprehension (Beatty, 1988; Richmond & McCroskey, 1992; Watson & Dodd, 1984):

- Prepare and practice thoroughly. Inadequate preparation—not having rehearsed the speech enough, for example—is reasonable cause for anxiety. Since much fear is a fear of failure, preparation will lessen the possibility of failure and the accompanying apprehension.
- Familiarize yourself with the public speaking context. Try, for example, to rehearse in the room in which you will give your speech. Or, stand in the front of the room before the actual presentation, as if you were giving your speech.
- Gain experience. Experience will help speakers who suffer moderate degrees of apprehension. It will show you that a public speech can be effective despite your fears and anxieties; give you feelings of accomplishment; and convince you that public speaking can be intellectually rewarding as well as enjoyable.
- Put apprehension in perspective. Fear increases when you feel that the audience's expectations are very high (Ayres, 1986). So maintain realistic expectations. Compete with yourself. Your second speech does not have to be better than that of the previous speaker, but it should be better than your own first one. Your audience does not expect perfection, either.
- Use physical activity and deep breathing. Anxiety is generally lessened by physical activity—large body movements as well as small movements of the hands, face, and head. Try including some chalkboard writing or a demonstration that requires movement. By breathing deeply a few times before getting up to speak, you will help your body relax. This may help you overcome your initial fear of walking to the front of the room.

Methods of Delivery

Speakers vary widely in delivery methods. Some speak "off the cuff" with no apparent preparation. Others read their speeches from manuscript. Others construct a detailed outline and compose the speech at the moment of delivery. These represent the three general methods of delivery: impromptu, manuscript, and extemporaneous.

The Impromptu Method

The impromptu method involves speaking without preparation. You and the topic meet for the first time, and the speech begins. On some occasions, you cannot avoid impromptu speaking. In a classroom, you might be asked to comment on the speaker and speech you just heard: in effect, you give an impromptu speech of evaluation. At meetings, people are often asked for impromptu comments on various issues. You can greatly improve impromptu speaking by cultivating public speaking ability in general. The more proficient you are as a speaker, the better you will be impromptu.

The Manuscript Method

In the **manuscript** method, you write out the speech and read it. This is the safest method when exact timing and wording are required. It could be disastrous if a political leader did not speak from manuscript on sensitive

How might communication rehearsal (usually discussed only in reference to public speaking) also be helpful in interpersonal, interviewing, and group situations?

Why is it dangerous to memorize your entire speech? What are some of the problems that memorizing a speech may create?

issues. An ambiguous word, phrase, or sentence that proved insulting, belligerent, or conciliatory might cause serious problems. With a manuscript speech, you can control style, content, organization, and all other elements. A variation of the manuscript method involves writing out the speech and then memorizing it. You would then recite the entire speech from memory, much as an actor recites a part in a play. The great disadvantages of the manuscript method are that the speech doesn't sound natural and there is no opportunity to adjust the speech on the basis of audience feedback.

The Extemporaneous Method

The **extemporaneous** method is useful when exact timing and wording are not required. College teachers who practice good lecturing use this method. They have prepared thoroughly, know what they want to say, and have the lecture's organization clearly in mind. But they are not committed to exact wording. This method allows greater flexibility for feedback. Should a point need clarification, you can elaborate when it will be most effective. It is also easy to be natural, because you are being yourself. And you may move about and interact with the audience.

The major disadvantage of this method is that you may stumble and grope for words. If you have rehearsed the speech several times, however, this is unlikely. While you cannot give the precise attention to style that you can in the manuscript and memorized methods, you can memorize certain key phrases.

Overall, the extemporaneous method gives the greatest advantages with the fewest disadvantages. However, consider the advantages of memorizing these parts of your speech:

- your opening and closing lines—perhaps the first and last two or three sentences; this will help you focus your attention on the audience at the two most important moments of your speech
- the major propositions and the order in which you will present them; after all, if you expect your audience to remember these points, they will expect you to remember them as well

Rehearsal Procedures

Rehearsal should enable you to see how the speech will flow as a whole and to make any necessary changes and improvements. It will also enable you to time your speech so that you stay within the allotted limit. The following procedures should help you use your rehearsal time most effectively.

- Rehearse the speech from beginning to end rather than in parts. Be sure to include all the examples and illustrations (and audiovisual aids, if any).
- Time the speech during each rehearsal. Adjust your speech—both what you say and your delivery rate—on the basis of this timing.
- Rehearse the speech under conditions as close as possible to those under which you will deliver it. If possible, rehearse in the room in which you will present the speech and in front of a few supportive listeners. Get together with two or three other students in an empty classroom where you can each serve as speaker and listener.
- Rehearse the speech in front of a full-length mirror to help you see how you will appear to the audience. This will be difficult at first, and you may have to force yourself to watch yourself. Practice your eye contact, your movements, and your gestures in front of the mirror.
- Do not interrupt your rehearsal to make notes or changes; do these between rehearsals. If possible, record your speech (ideally, on videotape) so you can hear exactly what your listeners will hear.
- Rehearse at least three or four times or as long as your speech continues to improve.

STEP 10: DELIVER THE SPEECH

Your voice and body are a great part of the message that the audience will receive. Use these tools to complement your verbal messages.

Voice

Your voice is the major tool in delivering your message. Let's look at how to use your voice more effectively by considering five voice dimensions: volume, rate, pitch, articulation and pronunciation, and pauses. Manipulation of these elements will enable you to control your voice to maximum advantage.

Volume

Volume refers to your voice's relative intensity (loudness or softness). In an adequately controlled voice, volume varies according to such factors as the distance between you and your listeners, the competing noise, and the emphasis you wish to give an idea. An obvious problem is a voice that is too low. If listeners have to strain to hear, they will soon tire of listening. On the other hand, a too loud voice will prove disturbing because it intrudes on the listeners' psychological space. Vary your volume to best reflect your ideas—perhaps increasing volume for key words or phrases and lowering volume when talking about something extremely serious. Be especially careful not to fade away at the ends of sentences.

My basic rule is to speak slowly and simply so that my audience has an opportunity to follow and think about what I am saying.
—MARGARET CHASE SMITH

Rate

Rate refers to the speed at which you speak. About 140 words per minute is average for speaking as well as for reading aloud. If you talk too fast, you deprive your listeners of the time they need to digest what you are saying. If your rate is too slow, your listeners' thoughts will wander. Therefore, speak at a pace that engages but doesn't bore and allows listeners time for reflection. Vary your rate during the speech; this calls attention to certain points and adds variety.

Pitch

Pitch refers to the relative highness or lowness of your voice as perceived by your listeners. If your vocal cords vibrate rapidly, listeners will perceive a high pitch. If they vibrate slowly, they will perceive a low pitch. Changes in pitch often signal changes in meanings. The most obvious is the difference between a statement (where the pitch falls) and a question (where the pitch rises). Problems of pitch include levels that are too high, too low, or too predictable. Neither of the first two is common in speakers with otherwise normal voices. With practice, you can correct a pitch pattern that may be too predictable or monotonous. Also with experience, pitch changes will come naturally from the sense of what you are saying.

Everyone who speaks American English speaks a dialect (regional or social variety) of that language.
—ROBERT G. KING AND
ELEANOR M. DIMICHAEL

Articulation and Pronunciation

Articulation refers to movements of the speech organs as they modify and interrupt the air stream you send from the lungs. Different movements (for example, of the tongue, lips, teeth, palate, or vocal cords) produce different sounds. **Pronunciation** refers to the production of syllables or words according to some accepted standard, such as that of a dictionary. Our concern here is to identify and correct some of the most common problems associated with faulty articulation and pronunciation.

Articulation: Errors of Omission.
Omitting sounds or even syllables is a major articulation problem but one easily overcome with concentration and practice. Here are some examples:

Incorrect	Correct
gov-a-ment	gov-ern-ment
hi-stry	hi-sto-ry
wanna	want to
studyin	studying
a-lum-num	a-lum-i-num
comp-ny	comp-a-ny
vul-ner-bil-ity	vul-ner-a-bil-ity
mis-chiév-ious	mís-chie-vous
com-pár-a-ble	cóm-par-a-ble

Articulation: Errors of Substitution.
Substituting an incorrect sound for the correct one is also easy to correct. Among the most popular substitutions are [d] for [t] and [d] for [th], for example, *wader* for *waiter*, *dese* for *these*, *bedder* for *better*, or *ax* for *ask*. Other prevalent substitution errors include *ekcetera* for *etcetera*, *ramark* for *remark*, and *lenth* for *length*.

Articulation: Errors of Addition.
These errors involve adding sounds where they do not belong. Some examples include:

Incorrect	Correct
acrost	across
athalete	athlete
Americer	America
idear	idea
filim	film
lore	law

If you make any of these errors, you can easily correct them by following these steps:

1. Become conscious of your own articulation patterns (and the specific errors you are making).
2. Listen carefully to the articulation of prominent speakers (for example, broadcasters).
3. Practice the correct patterns until they become part of your normal speech behavior.

Pronunciation: Errors of Accent.
The following words are often accented incorrectly: New Orléans, ínsurance, and orátor for the correct New Órleans, insúrance, órator.

Pronunciation: Errors of Adding Sounds.
For some words, many people add sounds that are not part of the acceptable pronunciation. In the first three examples, the error is pronouncing letters that are a part of

the word but should remain silent. In the last three examples, sounds are inserted where they do not belong.

Incorrect	Correct
homage	omage
Illinois	Illinoi
evening	evning
athalete	athlete
airaplane	airplane
burgalar	burglar

The best way to correct pronunciation problems is to check a word's pronunciation in a dictionary. Learn to read your dictionary's pronunciation key.

Pauses

Filled pauses are those in the stream of speech that you fill with vocalizations such as -er, -um, and -ah. Even expressions such as *well* and *you know*, when used just to fill up silence, are filled pauses. These pauses are ineffective and weaken the strength of your message. They will make you appear hesitant, unprepared, and unsure.

Unfilled pauses, silences interjected into the stream of speech, can be especially effective if used correctly. Here are a few examples of places where unfilled pauses—silences of a few seconds—should prove effective.

- Pause at transitional points. This will signal that you are moving from one part of the speech or from one idea to another. It will help listeners separate the main issues you are discussing.
- Pause at the end of an important assertion. This will let the audience think about its significance.
- Pause after asking a rhetorical question. This will give the audience time to think about how they would answer.
- Pause before an important idea. This will help signal that what comes next is especially significant.
- Pause before you begin your speech (to scan the audience and gather your thoughts) and after you finish it (to allow your audience to sink in and to dispel any idea that you are anxious to leave your audience).

Body Action

Your body is a powerful instrument in your speech. You speak with your body as well as with your mouth. The total effect of the speech depends not only on what you say but also on the way you present it. The five aspects of body action especially important in public speaking are eye contact, facial expression, posture, gestures, and movement.

Eye Contact

Avoid the major eye contact problems: not enough and eye contact that does not cover the audience fairly. Speakers who do not maintain sufficient eye contact appear distant, unconcerned, and less trustworthy than speakers who look directly at their audience. And, of course, without eye contact, you will not be able to secure that all-important audience feed-

Newscaster Ted Koppel once said: "Look . . . ours is a business of appearances, and it's terribly important to appear to be self-confident. The minute you give evidence of doubt, people are going to eat you alive." Do you agree with this?

back. Communicate equally with members on the left and on the right, in the back and the front.

Facial Expression

If you believe in your thesis you will probably display your meanings appropriately and effectively. Nervousness and anxiety, however, can prevent you from relaxing enough so that your emotions come through. But time and practice will allow you to relax, and your feelings will reveal themselves appropriately and automatically.

Posture

When delivering your speech stand straight but not stiff. Try to communicate a command of the situation but not any nervousness you may feel. Avoid putting your hands in your pockets or leaning on the desk or chalkboard. With practice you will feel more at ease and will communicate this in the way you stand before the audience.

Gestures

Gestures help illustrate your verbal messages. To be effective, body action should be spontaneous and natural. If you feel relaxed and comfortable with yourself and your audience, you will generate natural body action without conscious and studied attention.

Movement

Speakers who move too little may appear fearful or distant. Too much movement may lead the audience to concentrate on the movement itself, wondering where you will wind up next. Movement that is too patterned will cause the audience to become bored.

Use movement to emphasize transitions and to introduce important assertions. For example, when making a transition, you might step forward to signal that something new is coming. Similarly, use this type of movement to signal an important assumption, bit of evidence, or closely reasoned argument.

Using Notes

Effective delivery depends on the smooth use of notes during the speech. A few simple guidelines may help you avoid some common errors (McCroskey, 1982; Kesselman-Turkel & Peterson, 1982).

* Use only your delivery notes when you deliver your speech. One side of a 3-by-5-inch index card, or at most an 8½-by-11-inch page, should be sufficient for most speeches. This will relieve anxiety over forgetting your speech but not be extensive enough to prevent meaningful speaker-audience interaction.
* Know your notes intimately. Rehearse at least twice with the same notes you will take to the speaker's stand.
* Use your notes with "open subtlety." Don't make them more obvious then necessary, but don't try to hide them. Don't gesture with them, but don't turn away from the audience to steal a glance at them, either.

THINKING CRITICALLY ABOUT PUBLIC SPEAKING PREPARATION AND EVALUATION

Part of your function in learning public speaking is learning to evaluate the finished, delivered speech. As a beginning guide to speech evaluation, focus on the following questions, which come from topics covered in this chapter and the previous one. Use these questions to check your own speeches as well as a guide to evaluating the speeches of others.

The Subject and Purpose
1. Is the subject worthwhile? Relevant? Interesting to the audience and speaker?
2. What is the speech's general purpose (to inform, to persuade)?
3. Is the topic narrow enough to be covered in some depth?
4. Is the specific purpose clear to the audience?

The Audience
5. Has the speaker considered the age; sex; cultural factors; occupation, income, and status; and religion of the audience? How does the speech deal with these factors?
6. Has the speaker considered and adapted to the willingness, favorableness, and knowledge of the audience?

Research
7. Is the speech adequately researched? Are the sources reliable and up to date?
8. Does the speaker seem thoroughly to understand the subject?

The Thesis and Major Propositions
9. Is the speech's thesis clear and limited to one main idea?
10. Are the speech's main propositions clearly related to the thesis?
11. Are there an appropriate number of major propositions in the speech (not too many, not too few)?

Supporting Materials
12. Is each major proposition adequately and appropriately supported?
13. Do the supporting materials amplify what they purport to amplify? Do they prove what they purport to prove?

Organization
14. How is the body of the speech organized? What is the organization pattern?
15. Is the organization pattern appropriate to the speech topic? To the audience? Does it help the audience follow the speech?

Wording
16. Does the language help the audience to understand clearly and immediately what the speaker is saying? For example, are the words simple rather than complex, concrete rather than abstract?
17. Are the sentences short, direct, active, positive, and varied?

The Conclusion, Introduction, and Transitions

18. Does the conclusion effectively summarize and close the speech?
19. Does the introduction gain the audience's attention and provide a clear orientation to the speech?
20. Are there adequate transitions? Do the transitions help the audience better understand the speech's development?

Delivery

21. Does the speaker maintain eye contact with the audience?
22. Are the volume and rate appropriate to the audience, occasion, and topic?
23. Are the voice and body actions appropriate to the speaker, subject, and audience?

Speech Evaluation

It is helpful to have a form to record your evaluation of a particular speech. Presented here is an evaluation form that is open-ended and encourages comment on the effectiveness of the various steps. While providing some reminders of areas to look at, it also provides a rating system for evaluating essential areas and some reminders of areas to work on.

Speech Evaluation Form

Evaluation Key: 1 = excellent; 2 = good; 3 = fair; 4 = needs improvement; 5 = needs lots of improvement. Circle or underscore items the speaker needs to work on; write in additional items requiring attention.

Subject and Purpose
Work on: selecting more worthwhile subject, relating to audience, clarifying purpose, making purpose clear to audience

Audience Analysis and Adaption
Work on: Relating topic and support to specific audience, occasion, and context

Research
Work on: doing more extensive research, using more convincing sources, integrating sources into speech

(continued)

Thesis and Major Propositions

Work on: clarifying your thesis, stating propositions more clearly, relating propositions to thesis

Supporting Materials

Work on: using more support, using more varied support, relating support more directly to your propositions, establishing your credibility

Organization

Work on: using a clear thought pattern, making pattern clear to audience

Wording

Work on: clarity, vividness, appropriateness, personal style, forcefulness

Conclusion

Work on: summary, closure

Introduction

Work on: gaining attention, orienting audience

Transitions

Work on: including more transitions, integrating transitions more smoothly into speech

Delivery

Work on: volume, rate, pitch, quality, articulation, pronunciation, pauses, eye contact, facial expressions, posture, gestures, movement

General Evaluation

Expressing Your Evaluation

The major purpose of classroom evaluation is to improve your public speaking technique. Through constructive criticism you, as a speaker and as a listener-critic, will more effectively learn the principles of public speaking. You will be shown what you do well and what you can improve.

For all its benefits, however, evaluation is often resisted. The main source of resistance seems to be that evaluations are often expressed in a manner that encourages defensiveness. Suggestions for improvement

Anyone can be accurate and even profound, but it is damned hard work to make criticism charming.

—H. L. Mencken

often appear as personal attacks. The following suggestions should help to make critical evaluations a more effective part of the total learning process.

Before reading the specific suggestions for expressing criticism, take the following test, which asks you to identify what's wrong with selected critical comments.

TEST YOURSELF

What's Wrong with These Comments?

Instructions Examine each of the following critical comments. For the purpose of this exercise assume that each comment represents the critic's complete evaluation. What's wrong with each?

1. I loved the speech. It was great. Really great.
2. The introduction didn't gain my attention.
3. You weren't interested in your own topic. How do you expect us to be interested?
4. Nobody was able to understand you.
5. The speech was weak.
6. The speech didn't do anything for me.
7. Your position was unfair to those of us on athletic scholarships; we earned those scholarships.
8. I found four things wrong with your speech. First, ...
9. You needed better research.
10. I liked the speech; we need more police on campus.

The discussion below offers suggestions for making your critical evaluations more effective and will illustrate why each of these ten comments is ineffective. You might try to put yourself into the position of a speaker who receives comments such as these and ask yourself if you would find these helpful.

I love criticism just as long as it's unqualified praise.
—NOEL COWARD

Say Something Positive

Egos are fragile and public speaking is extremely personal. Positive feedback is particularly important in itself, but it is almost essential as a preface to any negative comments. There are always positive characteristics, and it is more productive to concentrate on these first. Thus, instead of saying—as in our self-test—"The speech didn't do anything for me," tell the speaker what you liked first. Then bring up a weakness and suggest how it might be corrected.

Be Specific

Criticism is most effective when it is specific. Statements such as "I thought your delivery was bad" or "I thought your examples were good" or, as in our self-test, "I loved the speech . . . Really great" and "The speech was weak" are poorly expressed evaluations. These statements do not specify what the speaker might do to improve delivery or to capitalize on the examples used. In commenting on delivery, refer to such specifics as eye contact, vocal volume, or whatever else is of consequence. In commenting on the examples, tell the speaker why they were good. Were they realistic? interesting? dramatically presented?

Be Objective

When evaluating a speech, transcend your own biases as best you can, unlike the self-test example: "Your position was unfair . . . We earned those scholarships." Examine the speech from the point of view of the detached critic. Evaluate, for example, the validity of the arguments and their suitability to the audience, the language, the supporting materials. Analyze, in fact, all the ingredients that went into the preparation and presentation of the speech.

Limit Criticism

Cataloging a speaker's weak points, as in "I found four things wrong with your speech," will overwhelm, not help, the speaker. If you are the sole critic, your criticism naturally will need to be more extensive. If you are one of many critics, limit your criticism to one or perhaps two points.

Be Constructive

Criticism should be constructive. Your primary goal should be to provide the speaker with insight that you feel will prove useful in future public speaking transactions. For example, to say "The introduction didn't gain my attention" doesn't tell the speaker how he or she might have gained your attention. Instead, you might say, "The example about the computer crash would have more effectively gained my attention in the introduction."

Focus on Behavior

Focus criticism on what the speaker said and did during the actual speech. Try to avoid the very natural tendency to mind-read the speaker, to assume that you know why the speaker did one thing rather than another. Instead of saying "You weren't interested in your topic" (a comment that attacks the speaker), say, "I would have liked to have seen greater variety in your delivery. It would have made me feel you were more interested." Instead of saying, "You didn't care about your audience," say "I would have liked it if you looked more directly at us while speaking."

Own Your Own Criticism

In giving criticism own your comments. Take responsibility for your criticism. The best way to express this ownership is to use I-messages rather than you-messages. Instead of saying "You needed better research," say "I would have been more persuaded if you used more recent research."

I-messages will also prevent you from using "should messages," a type of expression that almost invariably creates defensiveness and resentment. When you say "you should have done this" or "you shouldn't have done that," you assume a superior position and imply that what you are saying is correct and that what the speaker did was incorrect. When you own your evaluations and use I-messages, on the other hand, you are giving your perception. It is then up to the speaker to do something about them or to reject them.

Feedback on Concepts and Skills

In this chapter we looked at the last four steps in the public speaking process: wording the speech, constructing the conclusion and the introduction, rehearsing, and delivering the speech.

1. Compared with written style, oral style contains shorter, simpler, and more familiar words; greater qualification; and more self-referential terms.

2. Clarity may be best achieved by being economical and specific. Use guide phrases—short, familiar, and commonly used terms.

3. Vividness may be best achieved by using active verbs, strong verbs, figures of speech, and imagery.

4. Make your style appropriate to your audience by speaking on a suitable level of formality, and by avoiding unfamiliar, foreign, and technical terms; jargon; acronyms; slang; and vulgar and offensive terms.

5. Personal style may be best achieved by using personal pronouns, asking questions, and creating immediacy.

6. Forcefulness may be achieved by eliminating weakeners, avoiding clichés, and varying intensity as appropriate.

7. In constructing sentences for public speeches, favor short, direct, active, and positively phrased sentences. Vary the type and length.

8. The impromptu method involves speaking without any specific preparation. The manuscript method involves writing out the entire speech and reading it to the audience. The extemporaneous method involves thorough preparation, and memorizing the main ideas and their order of appearance, without a commitment to exact wording.

9. Regulate your voice for greatest effectiveness. Adjust your volume on the basis of the distance between you and your audience and the emphasis you wish to give certain ideas, for example. Adjust your rate on the basis of time constraints, the speech's content, and the listening conditions. Adjust your pitch (the relative highness or lowness of the voice) on the basis of the meanings you wish to communicate.

10. Avoid the major problems of articulation and pronunciation: errors of omission, substitution, addition, accent, and adding sounds.

11. Use pauses to signal a transition between the major parts of the speech, to allow the audience time to think, to allow the audience to ponder a rhetorical question, and to signal the approach of a particularly important idea.

12. Use rehearsal to time your speech; perfect your volume, rate, and pitch; incorporate pauses and other delivery notes; and perfect your bodily action.

13. Effective body action involves maintaining eye contact with your entire audience, allowing your facial expressions to convey your feelings, using your posture to communicate command of the public speaking interaction, gesturing naturally, and moving around a bit.

14. In expressing critical evaluations try to say something positive, be specific, be objective, limit your criticism, be constructive, focus on behavior, and own your own criticism.

Several significant skills for style and delivery were stressed in this chapter. Check your mastery of these skills, using the following scale: (1) = almost always, (2) = often, (3) = sometimes, (4) = rarely, and (5) = almost never.

_____ 1. I word my speech so it is clear, vivid, appropriate, personal, and forceful.

_____ 2. I construct sentences that are short, direct, active, and positive, and I vary the type and length of sentences.

_____ 3. In general, I use the extemporaneous method of delivery.

_____ 4. I vary my vocal volume, rate, and pitch so as to best reflect and reinforce my verbal messages. I avoid the common problems with volume, rate, and pitch.

_____ 5. I avoid the articulation and pronunciation errors of omission, substitution, addition, accent, and pronouncing sounds that should be silent.

_____ 6. I use pauses to signal transitions, to allow listeners time to think, and to signal the approach of a significant idea.

_____ 7. I rehearse my speech often, perfect my delivery, rehearse the speech as a whole, time the speech at each rehearsal, approximate the specific speech situation as much as possible, see and think of myself as a public speaker, and incorporate any delivery notes that may be of value during the actual speech presentation.

_____ 8. During the speech delivery, I maintain eye contact with the entire audience, allow my facial expressions to convey my feelings, gesture naturally, and incorporate purposeful body movements.

_____ 9. In expressing critical evaluations of the speeches of others I try to say something positive, be specific, be objective, limit criticism, be constructive, focus on behavior, and own my own criticism.

Skill Development Experiences

13.1 Getting Specific

One of the major skills in public speaking is learning to make your ideas specific so that your listeners will understand exactly what you want them to understand. Rewrite each of the following ten sentences to make the italicized terms more specific.

1. The *woman* walked up the *hill* with her *children*.
2. The *teacher* was discussing *economics*.
3. The *player scored*.
4. The *teenager* was listening to a *CD*.
5. No one in the *city* thought the *mayor* was doing anything useful.
6. The *girl* and the *boy* each received lots of *presents*.
7. I read the *review* of the *movie*.
8. The *couple* rented a *great car*.
9. The *detective* wasn't much help in solving the *crime*.
10. The *children* were playing an *old game*.

13.2 Climbing Up and Down the Abstraction Ladder

The "abstraction ladder" shows that there are degrees of verbal abstraction. Notice in the chart (see page 338) that as we go from *animal* to *pampered white toy poodle* we are descending to lower levels of abstraction; that is, we are getting more and more specific. And as we do so, we communicate our meanings more clearly and hold the listener's attention more easily.

For each term listed, indicate at least four possible terms that are increasingly specific.

13.3 Constructing Conclusions

Prepare a conclusion to a hypothetical speech on one of the topics listed, making sure that you (1) review the speech's main points and (2) provide closure. Be prepared to explain the methods you used to accomplish each of these functions.

1. Undergraduate degree programs should be five-year programs.
2. Proficiency in a foreign language should be required of all college graduates.

3. Children should be raised and educated by the state.
4. All wild-animal killing should be declared illegal.
5. Properties owned by churches and charitable institutions should be taxed in the same way as other properties are taxed.
6. History is bunk.
7. Suicide and its assistance by others should be legalized.
8. Teachers—at all levels—should be prevented from going on strike.
9. Gambling should be legalized by all states.
10. College athletics should be abolished.

13.4 Constructing Introductions

Prepare an introduction to one of the topics listed, making sure that you (1) secure the audience's attention and interest and (2) orient the audience as to what is to follow. Be prepared to explain the methods you used to accomplish each of these aims.

1. College is not for everyone.
2. It is better never to love than to love and lose.
3. Tenure should be abolished.
4. Maximum sentences should be imposed even for first offenders of the drug laws.

Level 1	Level 2; more specific than level 1	Level 3; more specific than level 2	Level 4; more specific than level 3	Level 5; more specific than level 4
animal	dog	poodle	toy poodle	pampered white toy poodle
house				
goal				
desire				
car				
toy				
sports				
machine				
message				

5. All alcoholic beverages should be banned from campus.
6. Abortion should be declared illegal.
7. Psychotherapy is a waste of time and money.
8. Television should be censored for violence and sex.
9. Euthanasia should be legalized by the federal government.
10. Religion is the hope (opiate) of the people.

CHAPTER FOURTEEN

The Informative Speech

Chapter Concepts	Chapter Goals	Chapter Skills
	After completing this chapter, you should be able to	After completing this chapter, you should be able to
Guidelines for Informative Speaking	1. explain the principles for informative speaking	follow the principles of informative speaking
Types of Informative Speeches	2. discuss the speech of description, definition, and demonstration and the strategies to use in each	develop the speech of information, following the suggestions for descriptive, definitional, and demonstration speeches
Amplifying Materials	3. define *examples* and *illustrations*, *testimony*, *definitions*, and *audiovisual aids*	select a variety of amplifying materials: examples, illustrations, testimony, audiovisual aids, and statistics and use these effectively in public speeches
	4. explain the ways in which you can use examples and illustrations, testimony, definitions, statistics, and audiovisual aids to amplify your speech	
Thinking Critically About the Informative Speech	5. analyze and evaluate an informative speech with the standards discussed in this chapter	offer positive and constructive speech evaluations

In whatever occupation you find yourself, you will be asked to communicate information to others: to describe the new pension system, to demonstrate the new computer program, or to define your company goals. The higher up you go in your organization's hierarchy, the more often you will be informing others.

In this chapter we cover speeches of information (in which you tell your listeners something they didn't know before), and in the next chapter we cover speeches of persuasion (in which you change your listeners' attitudes or beliefs or get them to do something). The informative speech is the easier one and so we start with it and with the principles that are useful in developing this type of speech.

Drawing by Martin; © 1992 The New Yorker Magazine, Inc.

"Have you noticed ethics creeping into some of these deals lately?"

Listener Ethics

Most discussions of ethics focus exclusively on the speaker (see Ethical Issue in Chapter 12). Public speaking, however, is a two-way process. Both speaker *and* listener share in the success or failure of the interaction. So too, both share in the moral implications of the public speaking exchange. Two major principles should govern your behavior as a listener.

An Honest Hearing First, as a listener, give the speaker an honest hearing. Listen fully and openly. Try to put aside prejudices and pre-conceptions so you can evaluate the speaker's message fairly. Then, accept or reject the speaker's ideas on the basis of the information offered, and not on the basis of some bias. Of course, you will see any given topic from your own point of view. As a listener, however, try to see the topic, and particularly the specific purpose, from the speaker's point of view as well.

Empathize with the Speaker You don't have to agree with the speaker. Try, however, to understand emotionally as well as intellectually what the speaker means. Only after you have achieved empathic understanding should you evaluate the speaker, the speech, or the purpose.

Honest Responses Second, just as the speaker should be honest with the listener, the listener should be honest with the speaker. This means giving open and honest feedback to the speaker. It means reflecting honestly on the questions that the speaker raises. It means providing an appropriate evaluation and critique. Much as the listener has a right to expect an active speaker, the speaker has the right to expect an active listener. The speaker has a right to expect a listener who will actively deal with, rather than just passively hear, the message.

[Next Ethical Issue, page 379]

GUIDELINES FOR INFORMATIVE SPEAKING

When you communicate information, you tell your listeners something they did not know before. Regardless of the type of information, the following guidelines should help.

Limit the Amount of Information

Information is defined as any input that the person attends to for the purposes of reducing uncertainty or confirming prior knowledge.

—Blaine Goss

Don't overload your listeners with information; limit the amount you communicate. It is better to present two new items of information with examples, illustrations, and descriptions than to present five without amplification.

Stress Usefulness

Listeners will best remember information they see as useful to their own needs or goals. If you want the audience to listen, relate your speech to their needs, wants, or goals. For example, you might say:

> We all want financial security. We all want to be able to buy those luxuries we read so much about in magazines and see every evening on television. Wouldn't it be nice to be able to buy a car without worrying about where to get the down payment or how to make the monthly payments? Actually, that is not an unrealistic goal as I'll demonstrate in this speech. In fact, I will show you three ways you can invest your money to increase your income by at least 20 percent.

There should be little doubt that this speaker will have a most attentive and willing audience.

Do the lecturers you prefer follow these principles for informative speaking? Can you give specific examples of how they follow these rules?

Relate New Information to Old

Listeners will learn information more easily and retain it longer when you relate it to what they already know. To describe what something new looks or tastes like, compare it to something familiar: "The jicama is a Mexican potato. It looks like a brown-skinned turnip. It has a white inside and tastes something like crispy water chestnuts." Relate the new to the old, the unfamiliar to the familiar, the unseen to the seen, the untasted to the tasted.

All we do is done with an eye to something else.

—Aristotle

Present Information Through Several Senses

Listeners best remember information they receive through several senses—hearing, seeing, smelling, tasting, feeling. Use as many senses as you can. If you are describing a football field's layout (presenting information through hearing), also show a picture of the field (presenting information through seeing as well). If you are giving a speech on stress and you are talking about muscular tension, make the audience feel their own muscle tension by asking them to tighten their leg or stomach muscles.

What are the major mistakes that speakers make in lecturing? Can you identify specific principles of informative speaking that they frequently violate? What one suggestion for improvement would you offer to a hypothetical college teacher?

TYPES OF INFORMATIVE SPEECHES

In informative speeches, you will focus on describing, demonstrating, and defining terms and processes. You might do all three in one speech or you might devote your entire speech to just one. Let's look at each type.

The Speech of Description

In a descriptive speech, you explain an object or person, an event, or process. Here are a few examples:

Describing an Object or Person

The structure of the brain	A shopping center
The inventions of Thomas Edison	The skeletal structure of the body
The parts of a telephone	A houseboat
The layout of Philadelphia	The library
The college hierarchy	A television station

Describing an Event or Process

The process of digestion	Tooth decay
The events leading to World War II	Buying stock
Organizing a body-building contest	Predicting the weather
Putting on a parade	Writing a book
Printing money	The workings of an artificial heart

Strategies for Describing

Here are some suggestions for describing objects and people, events and processes.

1. Consider using a spatial or a topical organization when describing objects and people. Consider using a temporal pattern when describing events and processes. You might use a spatial pattern in describing a museum and start from the first floor and work up to the top floor. To describe the inventions of Thomas Edison, you might select three or four major inventions and discuss each equally, using a topical pattern. A temporal pattern would also be appropriate to describe how a hurricane develops, how a bodily process works, or how the Berlin Wall came to be torn down.

2. Use a variety of categories to describe the object or event. Use physical categories and ask yourself such questions as: What color is it? How big is it? What is it shaped like? How much does it weigh? How long or short is it? What is its volume? How attractive or unattractive is it? Also consider, for example, friendliness/unfriendliness, warmth/coldness, rich/poor, aggressive/meek, and pleasant/unpleasant.

3. Consider using audiovisual aids. Show pictures of the brain, the inside of a telephone, the skeleton of the body. In describing an event or process, create a diagram or flow chart to illustrate stages: in buying stock, publishing a newspaper, or putting a parade together.

What descriptive categories might you use to describe this book? Does this book have psychological as well as physical characteristics that might be useful in describing it?

Developing the Speech of Description

You might construct a speech of description as in this example. Here the speaker describes the four steps in reading a textbook. Each main point covers one of the major steps. The organizational pattern is a temporal one; the speaker discusses the main points in the order they would normally occur. The outline form for the body of such a speech might appear like this:

Specific purpose: to describe the four steps in reading a textbook.
Thesis: You can increase your textbook-reading effectiveness. (How can you increase your textbook-reading effectiveness?)

I. Preview the text.
II. Read for understanding.
III. Read for retention.
IV. Review the text.

In delivering such a speech, the speaker might begin:

There are four major steps in reading a textbook: preview the text, read for understanding, read for retention, and review what you have read. Let's look at each of these steps in more detail.

The first step is to preview the text. Start at the beginning and look at the table of contents. How is the book organized? What are the major parts? Each part consists of several units. Let's look at how a unit is organized.

The Speech of Definition

What is leadership? What is a born-again Christian? What is the difference between sociology and psychology? What is safe sex? These are all suitable topics for informative speeches of definition.

A definition is a statement of a concept's meaning. Use definitions to explain difficult or unfamiliar concepts or to make a concept more vivid or forceful. In defining a term or giving an entire speech of definition you may focus on a term, system, or theory, or the similarities and differences between them. The subject may be new to the audience or a familiar one presented in a new and different way. Here are some examples:

Defining a Term

sexual harassment	ESP
bull market	etiquette
drug addiction	sexual ethics
censorship	gay rights
free speech	mysticism

Defining a System or Theory

what is socialism?	Freudian theory
Confucianism: its major beliefs	ten-step programs
the nature of "argumentativeness"	codependency
creative thinking	Marxism

Defining Similar and Dissimilar Terms or Systems

communism and socialism: some similarities and differences
what do Catholics and Protestants have in common?
Oedipus and Electra: how do they differ?
neurosis and psychosis
football versus soccer

To define is to exclude and negate.
—JOSÉ ORTEGA Y GASSET

The beginning of wisdom is the definition of terms.
—SOCRATES

Strategies for Defining

1. Use a variety of definitions. See the discussion of definitions under "Amplifying Materials" on pages 349–350.
2. Use credible sources when defining by authority. When you use an authority to define a term, make sure the person is in fact an authority on that topic. And be sure to tell the audience who the authority is and the basis for the person's expertise.
3. Proceed from the known to the unknown. Start with what your audience knows and work up to what is new or unfamiliar. Let's say you wish to define *phonemics* (with which your audience is unfamiliar). The specific idea you wish to get across is that each phoneme stands for a unique sound. You might begin your definition like this:

> *We all know that in the written language each letter of the alphabet stands for a unit of the written language. Each letter is different from every other letter. A* t *is different from a* g *and a* g *is different from a* b, *and so on. Each letter is called a* grapheme. *In English we have 26 such letters.*
>
> *We can look at the spoken language in much the same way. Each sound is different from every other sound. A* t *sound is different from a* d *sound and a* d *sound is different from a* k *sound, and so on. Each individual sound is called a* phoneme.

How would you define a computer to people who never heard of one but who do know about typewriters?

Developing the Speech of Definition

Here is an example of how you might go about constructing a speech of definition. The speaker selects three major types of lying and arranges them in a topical pattern.

Specific purpose: to define lying by explaining the major types.
Thesis: There are three major kinds of lying. (What are the three major kinds of lying?)

I. Concealment is hiding the truth.
II. Falsification is presenting false information as if it were true.
III. Misdirection is acknowledging a feeling but misidentifying its cause.

In delivering such a speech, the speaker might begin:

> *A lie is a lie is a lie. True? Well, not exactly. Actually, we lie in lots of ways. We can lie by concealing the truth. We can lie by falsification—by presenting false information as if it were true. And we can lie by misdirection—by acknowledging a feeling but misidentifying its cause. Let's look at the first type—the lie of concealment.*

> *That which so describes its object as to distinguish it from all others; it is no definition of any one thing if its terms are applicable to any one other.*
>
> —EDGAR ALLAN POE

The Speech of Demonstration

How would you outline a speech on the definition of an effective leader?

In using demonstration (or in a speech devoted entirely to demonstration), you show your listeners how to do something or how something works. Here are some examples:

Demonstrating How to Do Something

giving mouth-to-mouth resuscitation

balancing a checkbook

piloting a plane

driving defensively

how to criticize without offending

conducting an interview

saving for retirement

how to complain and get results

Demonstrating How Something Operates

how the body maintains homeostasis

how dialysis works

how a piano works

how the stock market works

how a computer accesses information

Strategies for Demonstrating

In demonstrating how to do something or how something operates, consider the following guidelines.

1. Use a temporal organizational pattern (in most cases). Demonstrate each step in the sequence in which it is to be performed. Do not skip steps even if you think they are familiar to the audience. They may not be.

   Connect the steps with appropriate transitions. For instance, in explaining the Heimlich maneuver, you might say: "Now that you have your arms around the choking victim's chest, your next step is to . . . "

   Label the steps clearly by saying, for example, "the first step," "the second step," and so on.

2. Consider presenting a broad overview and then the individual steps. When demonstrating, it is often helpful to first give a broad general picture and then present each step in detail. For example, let's say you were talking about how to prepare a wall for painting. You might begin by giving your listeners a general idea of how you will demonstrate the process:

   In preparing the wall for painting, make sure the wall is smoothly sanded, free of dust, and dry. Sanding a wall is not like sanding a block of wood. Let's look at the proper way to sand a wall.

3. Use visual aids that show the steps in sequence. A good example is the restaurant sign demonstrating the Heimlich maneuver. These signs demonstrate each step with pictures as well as words, making it easy to understand this important process.

Developing the Speech of Demonstration

How would you outline a speech of demonstration on registering at college?

In this example of a demonstration speech, the speaker demonstrates how to listen actively.

Specific purpose: to demonstrate three techniques of active listening.
Thesis: We can learn active listening. (How can we learn active listening?)

   I. Paraphrase the speaker's meaning.
  II. Express understanding of the speaker's feelings.
 III. Ask questions.

If this chapter were an informative speech, which type would it be (primarily)? Can you illustrate how this chapter contains elements of all three types of informative speeches?

In delivering the speech, you might begin:

> *Active listening is a special kind of listening. It's listening with total involvement, with a concern for the speaker. It's probably the most important type of listening you can engage in. Active listening involves three techniques: paraphrasing the speaker's meaning, expressing understanding of the speaker's feelings, and asking questions.*
>
> *Your first step in active listening is to paraphrase the speaker's meaning. What is a paraphrase? A paraphrase is a restatement in your own words of the speaker's meaning.*

AMPLIFYING MATERIALS

Once you have identified your specific purpose and your main assertions or propositions (the statements given Roman numerals in your speech outline), devote your attention to **amplifying** (making more understandable, meaningful, and relevant) these assertions. Develop them so the audience will understand each more easily and fully. In this section we explain five ways to amplify your assertions: examples and illustrations, testimony, definitions, statistics, and audiovisual aids.

POWER PERSPECTIVE

Information or Persuasion Power

Information or **persuasion power** is power that you get from being seen as someone who can communicate logically and persuasively. If someone sees you as having the ability to communicate effectively, they will be more likely to believe and follow you. Generally, persuasion power is attributed to people who are seen as possessing significant information and the ability to use that information in presenting a well reasoned argument. Information or persuasion power is also enhanced by the use of powerful speech (discussed in the power perspectives in chapters 5 and 13).

[Next Power Perspective, page 383]

What types of informative speeches might you be called upon to deliver in your professional life? Will the types of such speeches change as you go up the organizational hierarchy?

Examples and Illustrations

Examples and illustrations are specific instances in varying degrees of detail. A relatively brief specific instance is an example. A longer, more detailed example told in narrative, or storylike, form is an illustration.

Examples and illustrations make an idea vivid and real in the listeners' minds. To talk in general terms about starvation throughout the world might have some effect on listeners. But an example or illustration of a 6-year-old girl roaming the streets eating garbage would make the idea vivid and real.

Examples and illustrations may be factual or imaginary. Thus, in explaining friendship, you might tell about an actual friend's behavior. Or you might formulate a composite of an ideal friend and describe how this person would act in a particular situation. Both types are useful, both effective. David Rockefeller (1985) uses a particularly effective, real example to illustrate how people can make charitable contributions in creative ways.

> *One of the most fascinating ventures along these lines has been the actor Paul Newman's venture into salad oil. Some three years ago— as a lark—he and a friend started a company to market his homemade salad oil and other products such as Newman's Own Indus-*

Whose testimony would you find especially useful to amplify the following assertions: (1) crime is increasing in the major cities throughout the world, (2) computer literacy is being integrated in elementary schools, and (3) business needs will change drastically in the next ten years?

trial Strength Venetian Spaghetti Sauce, and then donate any profits to charity. Last year the company netted some $1.19 million, which it gave to support 80 different nonprofit groups!

Testimony

Testimony refers to experts' opinions or to witnesses' accounts. Testimony supports your ideas by adding a note of authority. You might, for example, want to state an economist's predictions concerning inflation and recession. Or you might cite an art critic's evaluation of a painting or art movement.

In the following excerpt, U.S. Congresswoman Shirley Chisholm addresses the Independent Black Women's Caucus of New York City and uses the testimony of noted psychologist Rollo May to bolster her argument that black women must assume political power rather than wait for it to be given to them.

> *As Rollo May has put it: "Power cannot, strictly speaking, be given to another, for then the recipient still owes it to the giver. It must in some sense be assumed, taken, asserted, for unless it can be held against opposition, it is not power and will never be experienced as real on the part of the recipient."*
>
> *And those of us in this room know all too well that whatever is given to us is almost always a trap.*

How would you describe the use of testimonials by advertisers? Do they restrict themselves to experts and eyewitnesses?

You might also consider using an eyewitness's testimony. You might, for example, cite the testimony of an eyewitness to an accident, the inmate who spent two years in a maximum-security prison, or the patient who underwent an operation.

One way to present testimony is to use direct quotations. Although often useful, they can be cumbersome. Therefore, unless the quotation is short, easily understood, and related directly to the point you are trying to make, use your own words. Paraphrase the essence of the testimony. Note, of course, that the ideas are borrowed from your authority or source.

Definitions

There is nothing so stupid as an educated man, if you get off the thing that he was educated in.
—WILL ROGERS

Definitions are almost always helpful in an informative speech. Here are some types of definitions that may prove useful. One method is to define by **etymology,** to explain the term's origin. For example, to define the word *communication,* you might note that it comes from the Latin *communis,* meaning "common." In communicating, you seek to establish a commonness, a sameness, a similarity with another person.

A definition by **authority** cites some well-known authority's perspective on the meaning of the term. You might, for example, use the authority of satirist Ambrose Bierce and define *love* as nothing but "a temporary insanity curable by marriage" and *friendship* as "a ship big enough to carry two in fair weather, but only one in foul."

Defining by **operations** involves describing how you would construct the object. For example, in defining a chocolate cake, you would provide the recipe.

Using each of the four types of definitions discussed in this chapter, how would you define friendship? A healthy diet? Teacher? Economic recession?

When you define by **direct symbolization,** you show your listeners the actual item or a model or picture of it. For example, to describe clothing throughout history, you might show actual samples or drawings and photographs of such clothing.

Definitions are especially useful when they are needed and when they add to your audience's understanding your meaning. They are distracting when not needed and when they only add to audience confusion.

CULTURAL VIEWPOINT

Language Variations

Perhaps the most obvious cultural difference in communication is the variation from one language to another. Linguists estimate that there are between 5000 and 6000 different languages spoken throughout the world. Mandarin Chinese is by far the most widely spoken language, with some 885 million speakers. English (450 million), Hindi (367 million), Spanish (352 million), and Russian (294 million) complete the five most common languages in the world (Johnson, 1994).

There are also numerous dialects spoken within many of these languages. Some dialects are **regional**; speakers from Arkansas, Wisconsin, and Massachusetts, for example, will speak differently but, perhaps with some small effort, will be able to understand each other. In fact, mutual intelligibility is the yardstick that distinguishes language differences from dialect differences. People who speak different languages are mutually unintelligible; people who speak different dialects of the same language are mutually intelligible. Thus, Mandarin and Cantonese are classified as separate languages rather than as dialects of Chinese because their speakers cannot understand each another.

Social dialects, on the other hand, are variations based on sociological factors such as class or ethnic background or occupation. Thus, the Harvard professor and the sharecropper will speak a different dialect, though they too will generally be mutually intelligible. A clear example of social dialects is heard in the language of teenagers. Depending on your age, you may or may not know the meaning of such terms as *fat pockets* (someone with lots of money), *kicks* (sneakers), *shoot the gift* (engage in conversation), *livin' large* (living in financial comfort), and *think it ain't* (I totally agree with you). But, for the most part and with such obvious exceptions, teenagers and older people can understand each other's language.

On the basis of these simple concepts, a few suggestions for the public speaker may be offered:

• Avoid trying to speak the dialect of your audience when that dialect is not your own. Although the intention is often to appear to be one of the group, it will probably backfire and mark you as an outsider trying to pretend to be someone you're not.

- When using terms that are unique to your dialect, explain them. Better, use terms that are common to both your speech and your audience's speech dialect.
- When addressing audiences consisting of members who have learned your language as a second language, avoid using idioms—expressions whose meanings cannot be figured out from the individual words used. These will prove especially difficult for second-language learners.

[Next Cultural Viewpoint, page 372]

Audiovisual Aids

When you plan a speech, consider using an **audiovisual aid**—a visual or auditory means for clarifying important ideas (Kemp & Dayton, 1985; Heinrich, 1983). At the start, ask yourself if you should use an audiovisual

"And now I'd like to introduce our county's new tax collector."

NATIONAL ENQUIRER

Cartoon by W. Engleman

What type of visual aid might you develop for a speech on how to make great coffee?

aid. How would the aid make your speech more effective? What type of aid should you use? Charts? Slides? Models? How should you go about creating it? What principles should you follow to make sure your aid helps you achieve your public speaking purpose? How should you use the aid?

Audiovisual aids are not added frills. They are integral parts of your speech and serve important functions. Here are a few of their more important functions.

- *Audiovisuals gain attention and maintain interest.* We perk up when the speaker says, "I want you to look at this chart showing the employment picture for the next five years" or "Listen to the way Springsteen uses vocal variety."
- *Audiovisuals add clarity.* Let's say you want to illustrate the growth of the cable television industry in the United States over the last thirty years. You could say, "In 1952 there were 14,000 subscribers, in 1955 there were 150,000 subscribers. . . " This gets pretty boring and you

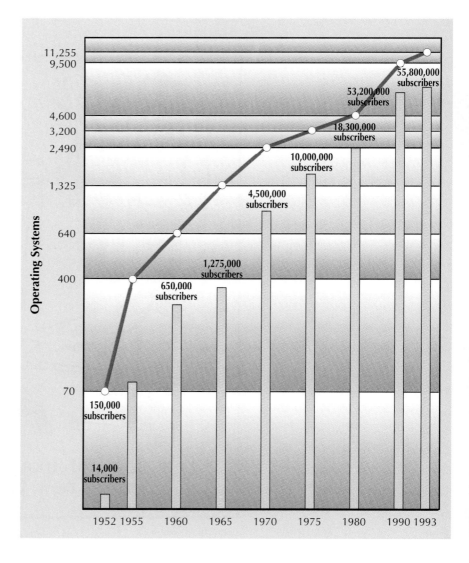

Figure 14.1
Bar Graph Visual Aid

Can you select a speech topic and illustrate how you might use each of these audiovisual aids?

still haven't covered the 1960s, 1970s, and 1980s. Note how much easier this same information is communicated in the bar graph in Figure 14.1. At a glance we can see the rapid growth from practically nothing to more than 53 million subscribers.

- *Audiovisuals help the audience to remember.* A great deal of the information we have in our minds is stored in visual form. For example, you probably picture the map of the United States in answering the question "Where is Colorado in relation to California?" In a similar way, if you provide your audience with such visual cues, they will be able to more easily recall your speech.

- *Audiovisuals reinforce your message.* Audiovisuals add the redundancy that listeners need to understand and remember what you have said. An audiovisual aid allows you to present the same information in two different ways—verbally and audiovisually. This one-two punch helps the audience to understand more clearly and to remember more accurately what you have said.

Types of Audiovisual Aids

Let's say you are convinced of the value of using an audiovisual aid. But what kind? Some of the more popular aids are presented in Table 14.1.

TABLE 14.1 SOME POPULAR AUDIOVISUAL AIDS

Type	Comments
Actual object	The best audiovisual aid; integrate it into your speech if you can.
Models	Replicas of the actual object are useful when explaining complex structures like the vocal mechanism or the brain. Models clarify the size of structures, their position, and interface.
Chalkboard	Useful for recording key terms or important definitions. Be careful not to lose the audience's attention by turning your back.
Word charts	Help highlight key points. (Figure 14.2)
Organizational charts	Show how an organization is structured.
Flow charts	Help clarify processes like the steps in learning a skill or in performing a complex set of behaviors. Figure 14.3 identifies the stages a child goes through in learning language.
Flip charts	Large pads of paper mounted on a stand. As you deliver your speech, you flip the pages to reveal visuals.
Bar, line graphs	Useful for showing differences over time (see Figure 14.1).
Pie charts	Useful for showing how a whole is divided into parts.
Maps	Useful for showing geographical elements and changes throughout history. Maps can illustrate population density, immigration patterns, economic conditions, and the location of resources.
Slides and pictures	Useful for showing scenes or graphics you cannot easily describe. They help maintain attention but only if easily seen. Do not pass pictures around the room since they draw your listeners' attention away from what you are saying.
Records and tapes	Useful for many topics other than music, for example, radio and television advertising, and to present actual excerpts by people you mention in your speech.

Do your college instructors use audiovisual aids? What suggestions concerning audiovisual aids would you offer them?

Some Tips on Using Audiovisual Aids

Use the aid only when it is relevant. Show it when you want the audience to concentrate on it and then remove it. If you do not remove it, the audience's attention may remain focused on the visual when you want to continue.

Know your aids intimately. This is especially true when you are planning to use several. Be sure you know in what order they are to be used and what you will say when you introduce them. Know exactly what goes where and when.

Test the aids before using them. Be certain they can be easily seen or heard from all parts of the room.

Rehearse your speech with the audiovisual aids. Practice the actual movements with the actual aids. Decide how you are going to use a chart. Will it stand by itself? Will you tape it to the board (and do you have tape with you)? Will you ask another student to hold it? Will you hold it yourself?

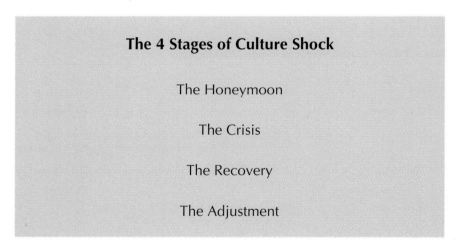

Figure 14.2
Word Chart Visual Aid

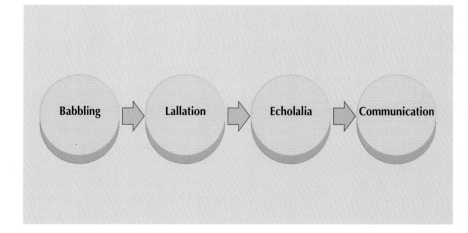

Figure 14.3
Flow Chart Visual Aid

Do not talk to your audiovisual aid. Both you and the aid should be focused on the audience. Talk to your audience at all times. Know your aids so well that you can point to what you want without breaking eye contact with your audience.

Statistics

Statistics are summary-type numbers. Statistics help us to see at a glance the important characteristics of an otherwise complex set of numbers. For a teacher to read off 50 grades on the last examination would not help you to grasp where your score fell in relation to the others in your class. In such cases, statistical information is much more helpful.

Measures of central tendency tell you the general pattern of a group of numbers or scores. The *mean* is the arithmetic average; it is the sum of the scores divided by the number of scores. Means are useful for communicating an idea as to what is average. For example, knowing that the mean on the last test was 89 gives you a good idea as to how the entire class did and also how well you did relative to the rest of the class.

The *median* is the middle score; 50 percent of the cases fall above the median and 50 percent fall below it. For example, if the median score on the midterm was 78 it means that half the class scored higher than 78 and half scored lower. The median thus gives you some idea as to how the scores are distributed and also gives you an idea as to how far above or below the middle you scored.

The *mode* is the most frequently occurring score. It is the single score that most people received. If the mode of the midterm was 85 it means that more students received 85 than any other single score.

Measures of correlation tell you how closely two or more things are related. You might say, for example, that there is a high correlation between smoking and lung cancer or between poverty and crime. Recognize that high correlations do not mean causation. The fact that two things vary together (that is, are highly correlated) does not mean that one causes the other. They may both be caused by some third factor.

Measures of difference tell you the extent to which scores differ from the average or from each other. For example, the *range* tells us how far the lowest score is from the highest score. The range is computed by subtracting the lowest from the highest score. If the lowest score on the midterm was 76 and the highest was 99, the range was 23 points. Generally, a high range indicates great diversity, whereas a low range indicates great similarity.

Percentiles are useful for specifying the percentage of scores that fall below a particular score. For example, if you scored 700 on the College Entrance Examination Board test, you were approximately in the ninety-seventh percentile. This means that 97 percent of those taking the test scored lower than 700. Generally, the twenty-fifth, fiftieth, and seventy-fifth percentiles (also called, respectively, the first, second, and third quartiles) are distinguished. The second quartile, or fiftieth percentile, is also the median, since exactly half the scores are above and half are below.

In the following excerpts the speakers use statistical figures to make their assertions more vivid and more meaningful. Ernest L. Boyer (1978), then U.S. commissioner of Education, used the arithmetic mean to demonstrate that children are avid television viewers.

Averages and relationships and trends and graphs are not always what they seem. There may be more in them than meets the eye, and there may be a good deal less.

—DARRELL HUFF

How would you use statistics to illustrate the increase in school violence, the rate of inflation, the cost of war, and the rise in drug use in corporations?

> *Young children—2 to 5 years old—now watch television over 4*
> *hours every day, nearly 30 hours a week. That's more than 1500*
> *hours every year. And by the time a youngster enters first grade he*
> *or she has had 6000 hours of television viewing.*

To stress the prevalence of emotional problems and suicide among college students, Patricia Ann Hayes, a student, uses statistics effectively.

> *Dr. Dana Farnsworth, a leading expert in the field of student mental*
> *health, lists some rather ominous nationwide statistics for colleges.*
> *He stresses that of each 10,000 students 1000 will have emotional*
> *conflicts severe enough to warrant professional help, 300 to 400 will*
> *have feelings of depression deep enough to impair efficiency, 5 to 10*
> *will attempt suicide, and 1 to 3 will succeed in taking his own life.*
> *If these statistics are true, my university should encounter 15 to 45*
> *suicide attempts of which 3 to 6 will be successful.*

Keep in mind that the audience will ask essentially the same questions that a good researcher would ask in analyzing statistics: Are the statistics based on a large enough sample? Is the sample a fair representation of the entire population? Is the statistic based on a recent sampling? Are the statistics collected and analyzed by an unbiased source? Answer these questions for your audience. For example, stress the unbiased nature of the source who collected and analyzed the statistics, the representativeness of the sample, and the recency of the statistical collections and computations.

Further, make the statistics clear to listeners who will hear the figures only once. Round off figures so they are easy to comprehend and retain. Don't say that the median income of workers in this city is $12,347. This may be accurate, but it will be difficult to remember. Instead, say that it is "around $12,300" or even "a bit more than $12,000."

Make explicit the connection between the statistics and what they show. To say, for example, that college professors make an average of $42,000 per year needs to be related specifically and to the proposition that teachers' salaries should be raised or lowered—depending on your point of view.

Here, for example, Geneva Johnson (1991) uses statistics to dramatize the rapid population growth of the elderly:

Figures won't lie, but liars will figure.
—GENERAL CHARLES H. GROSVENOR

> *Today's population is growing at a steady rate of 1 percent per year*
> *and now includes 6 million elderly. By 2030, we will have 17 million*
> *and by 2050, 26 million. Implication, today, is that 1 in 40 people are*
> *80 or older. By 2050, 1 in 12 will be 80 or older.*

Other Forms of Amplification

Other ways you can amplify a statement or proposition include the following:

- *Quotations.* Short, directly relevant, and clear quotations work best. If they are long, it is probably best to paraphrase them. Be sure to connect these quotations to your own words as smoothly as possible. Always give credit to the source, whether you quote directly or paraphrase.

- *Facts.* A series of factual statements often makes a point especially vivid. For example, you might cite a series of population increases to show the growth of a geographical area. Make sure your facts are reliable, recent, and accepted by your audience.
- *Questions.* A series of questions often helps to gain attention and focus the audience's attention on a specific issue or proposition. The questions may be rhetorical or actual questions that you want your audience to think about.
- *Narration.* A short story or anecdote often helps to illustrate a point. The parables in many religious works are good examples of narration used to illustrate a general principle. Be sure to include only those details that are needed to understand the point you are making. Often it is this story that listeners will remember most clearly, so be sure to connect your story very explicitly to the proposition in your speech.

THINKING CRITICALLY ABOUT THE INFORMATIVE SPEECH

Here is an informative speech delivered by a college student, Joey Callow. Along with the speech is a series of questions to provide some initial structure for thinking critically about informative speeches. The questions are numbered to make it easier to refer to these in small group or general class discussions. The questions focus on a variety of critical thinking skills:

- **Identification** or **discovery** questions ask you to examine a portion of the speech and identify the means used by the speaker to accomplish some aim, for example, How did the speaker gain attention? What thought pattern did the speaker use? What forms of reasoning did the speaker rely on?
- **Evaluation** questions are both specific and general. **Specific evaluation** questions ask that you examine a particular section and evaluate how effectively the speaker handled a task, for example, How effectively did the speaker support an argument? How effective was the orientation? Did the speaker effectively relate the topic to the specific audience? **General evaluation** questions ask you to make an overall assessment of the speech, for example, Did the speaker accomplish his or her aim? Was the speech an effective one?
- **Problem-solving** or **application** questions ask that you place yourself in the role of the speaker and consider how you would deal with specific issues, for example, If this speech was addressed to your class, what changes would the speaker have to make in the examples used? Would the organizational pattern the speaker used prove effective with your class?

The following suggestions will help you get the most out of your reading and thinking:

1. First, read the speech all the way through, ignoring the questions on the right.

2. After you have read through the entire speech, quickly read through the questions to give yourself a broad overview of the areas focused on.
3. Read the speech in brief sections and respond to the questions keyed to these sections.
4. Think too about some general issues that will also prove useful:

- What principle is the speaker following or violating?
- How might the speaker have accomplished his aim more effectively?
- What adjustments or changes would the speaker have had to make if he was speaking to other audiences, say, for example, to your class?
- What rhetorical devices or techniques can you identify that might prove useful to you as a public speaker?

The most important thing to remember here is that your aim should be to use this speech as a learning tool, as a model. What can you learn from this speech that will help you in your own public speaking?

Informative Speech

Joey Callow, *Miami University*

One of the primary functions of the introduction is to gain attention and to focus it on the topic of the speech. (1) What method did Callow use to gain attention? (2) How effectively was this done?

Remember the old saying, "Little things mean a lot"? The one that's become associated with the cheapest presents? [laughter] Or the hugs and handshakes of friends instead of sweaters and Swatches on our birthday? [laughter] Well, no more, for today little things do mean a lot. In fact some little things mean a multibillion dollar industry in the next few years. Things capable of repairing electrical circuits, creating safer nuclear power plants, and changing medicine and medical technology as we know it today. Little things called micromachines. Miniaturized mechanical devices such as heaters, springs, tongs, (unintelligible) even electrical motors built to the size of one-fifth the width of a human hair. According to Dr. George Hazelring of the National Science Foundation, micromachines have people walking around bug-eyed thinking about what the future holds. The electronics revolution of the '70s and '80s can be copied—and even surpassed—by the micromechanical revolution of the 1990s and beyond. Little things do mean a great deal. And it's time for us to put our eyes back in our sockets and turn to the microscope [laughter] to explore this fascinating world of micromachines. First we're going to simply look at the basis and excitement surrounding these devices. Second, focus on some commercial applications of micromachines that are already prevalent in our daily lives. Finally, turn our microscope into a time machine and view some slides to see what the future holds for all

The second major function is to create a speaker-audience-topic connection. (3) Did the speaker do this?

(4) How would you evaluate this topic if the speech were given in your class? (5) Is it worthwhile? Appropriate to your class? Sufficiently narrow in scope?

The third major function is to orient the audience. (6) What method does Callow use to accomplish this orientation? How effectively does Callow accomplish this?

of us. Only then will we truly realize the revolution that is under way and grasp the big picture created by these little machines.

Basically, micromachines are simply machines built at the microscopic level. [laughter] In our quest to change cumbersome computers into portable PCs, engineers have discovered a technology which makes common, everyday devices to sizes of 15/100 microns of a micro—or 1/10 of a millimeter at best. At such measurements, micromachines operate and function though they may be invisible to the naked eye.

Machines such as mechanical gears, built with a special process using silicon, so small individual red blood cells can fit between these mechanical teeth. A larger, but still simple pair of tongs, barely big enough to grasp onto a human hair, will be the standard. What makes these micromachines even more impressive, according to *Popular Mechanics*, July 1988, is that each micromachine can cost less than 1/10 of a cent to produce. In actuality, thousands of micromachines can fit into a square inch and cost only a few dollars.

Adding to the excitement surrounding these micromachines is the development of a micromotor, tiny turbines run by static electricity. While rubbing a rubber comb on wool seems insignificant to us, according to Ken Gabriel of AT&T Laboratories right here in Hofield, New Jersey, at the micro level it is enough power to run simple circuitry, start the rotary engine that will spin at half the speed of sound, and it will be in 1/10 of a millisecond. With their size, cost, and new power source, micromachines are creating a whole new line of products with a varying degree of functions, and will allow operations to take place on scales that until recently were not possible.

Perhaps the idea of living with invisible machines sounds, well, ominous, complicated. But all of us have already been affected by these amazing devices. Micromachines have done many commercial applications—medical equipment, automotive operations, and nuclear power plants. According to Kirk Peterson, executive vice-president of [unintelligible] of Fremont, California, millions of micromachines are in use everywhere, in blood pressure–measuring devices, in air intake systems, and electronically fuel-injected cars. In both cases, the micromachines serve as sensors, measuring changes in air pressure that causes either the mercury, the column, or the gas intake in your engine to function accordingly. The automobile industry is not stopping there.

(7) What is the thesis of this speech? Would this thesis be appropriate for your class as an audience? Does Callow explicitly identify his thesis or does he leave it only implied?

(8) What is the specific purpose? Is this purpose sufficiently narrow for a speech of this length? (9) Did the speaker accomplish his purpose (assume you were a member of the audience)?

(10) What are the major propositions of this speech? How effectively are they derived from the thesis? Are they effectively highlighted?

(11) What organizational pattern does Callow use? Is this effective? Would you have used the same pattern for your class?

(12) Were the sources used sufficient to support the propositions the speaker advances? What types of source material would you have liked to see used more extensively?

(13) What types of supporting materials would you have used?

(14) What means does Callow use to involve his audience? How does he relate his speech directly to the needs and wants of his audience?

(15) How does Callow try to communicate an excitement about micromachines? How effectively does he do this?

(16) Does Callow use language effectively? Is his language clear? Personal? Vivid? Forceful? Immediate? Can you supply examples to support your conclusions about Callow's use of language? Would you offer any suggestions for using language more effectively?

(17) How effectively did Callow use humor? Is the humor relevant, brief, spontaneous in appearance, tasteful, and appropriate? Do you have any suggestions for making Callow's humor more effective?

(18) Does Callow establish the credibility of his sources?
(19) What is the most important dimension of credibility for sources such as Callow uses, that is, competence, moral character, or charisma?

They're adapting these same micromachines in the new air bag systems as well. According to July 7, 1988, *New York Times,* it's the micromachines that will automatically determine when the air bags open whenever there is a specific drop in acceleration. And as is the case with the air bag system, protect the driver from serious injuries. When I spoke to Dr. George Hazenbake of the National Science Foundation, he explained to me how German scientists are adapting these same micromachines to create safer nuclear power plants. They separate lighter forms of uranium used in creating nuclear power from the heavier forms of the element that only causes destabilization at the reactor core. Surprisingly enough, micromachines that we've never seen are monitoring, aiding, and protecting the personal health and safety of millions of people that take their blood pressure, drive new cars, and [unintelligible]. And yet these micromachines are the most basic types available. Static electric motors as a new power source are instigating the more important movable micromechanical revolution in the next 12 months alone, especially in the personal, industrial, and medical fields. Because of their relative cost, micromachines will have a major impact on the personal housegoods, from watches that cost less than a penny to produce to major household appliances reduced in both size and cost. Rodney Brooks, of MIT's Artificial Intelligence Laboratory, is working on a micromechanical vacuum, about 4 to 6 inches in length, and all the power of today's larger appliance. Until you drop it on the floor and the independent machine seeks and vacuums. [laughter] Sort of like a giant, silvery, mechanical roach that can roam around your house without your knowledge, yet with more of a fairly useful purpose. [laughter] Well while we're not asking for further roaches to stay underground, according to Neal Flynn, presenter of the microbotic workshop in November 1987, these micromachines have some industrial applications as well. According to Flynn, underground electrical cables, that can sometimes take days to find and fix, can be sought out and repaired by our friends in only a few hours. The microrobot measures current using its mechanical legs. When it reaches the break, it extends its body across the fault, reestablishing the connection and literally becoming a piece of that electric wire.

But however impressive these applications in personal households and industries may seem, perhaps the most important application is coming in the medical field in the next year. Hundreds of micromachines can fit into a capsule the size of an aspirin and can be simply swallowed—no incision, and no [unintelligible]. Once inside the body, they can be programmed to come up anywhere they're needed—insulin regulators and nitroglycerine patches, for diabetes and heart patients will be fixed internally, as needed when a micromachine performs the appropriate functions. The November 30, 1987, *Newsweek* points out that tiny scissors with electronic eyes just like an electronic pac-man, will travel through your arteries, [laughter] chomping away cholesterol and other forms of impurities that cause heart attacks and other problems. With the help of a computer mouse-like hookup doctors can perform surgical techniques more accurately than any fiberoptic technologies medically. With the help of those electronic eyes, doctors will actually be inside the body, cutting away polyps from the colon, [unintelligible] and removing cancerous tumors from the brain. The silicon that I mentioned earlier, that all micromachines are made of, is also inert to all biological systems. Translated into common terms, just as a microrobot can extend itself to repair an electrical wire, micromachines can extend themselves to repair ulcers of the stomach, broken arterial walls, or even tissues of the human heart with no adverse effects on the rest of the body. Long hospital stays and large hospital bills are a thing of the past. Micromachines work just as effectively by lying in the soft [unintelligible] for a few hours, giving new meaning to the doctor's phrase "Take two pills and call me in the morning." [laughter] Medical technology as we know it today will be completely transformed by our micromechanical applications.

From measuring of blood pressure to cleaning out the buttresses, from preventing injuries from automobiles, to deaths from heart attacks and cancer, micromachines are only beginning to establish themselves as the most important development of the 1990s and beyond. After examining their basis, focusing on some commercial applications, and viewing some slides of what the future holds for all of us, it seems clear that these little things will soon be having a big, big impact. Because little things can mean a lot.

This speech won as best informative speech in the 1989 National Forensic Association's Individual Events Tournament. It is reprinted from 1989 Championship Debates and Speeches, *© 1989 American Forensic Association, ed. Christina L. Reynolds and Larry G. Schnoor (Fargo, ND: North Dakota State University, 1991), pp. 70–72. Reprinted by permission of the American Forensic Association.*

(20) Did Callow establish his own credibility? How? For example, does he establish his competence, moral character, or charisma? (21) Which is the most important aspect of credibility in this situation?

This speech is not titled. (22) What would you title it?

(23) How effectively does Callow follow the principles of informative speaking? (24) Does he limit the amount of information he presents? (25) Does he stress relevance and usefulness? (26) Does he present information on the appropriate level (use your own class as the target audience in answering this question)? (27) Does he relate new information to old? (28) Does he present information through several senses? (29) Does he vary the level of abstraction appropriately?

One of the two major functions of the conclusion (in an informative speech) is to summarize the thesis or major points of the speech. (30) Does Callow do this effectively? The other function is to bring the speech to a definite close. (31) Does Callow do this effectively?

(32) What is your overall evaluation of this speech? That is, if this speech were given in your class, what grade would you give it? (33) What is the major strength of this speech as you see it? (34) What is the major weakness? How might this weakness have been corrected?

Feedback on Concepts and Skills

In this chapter we covered the nature of the informative speech and ways you can most effectively communicate information.

1. Three general types of informative speeches are speeches of description, speeches of definition, and speeches of demonstration.
2. In preparing informative speeches, observe the guidelines for informative speaking: limit the amount of information, stress the information's usefulness, relate new information to information the audience already knows, and present information through several senses.
3. Use amplifying materials to make your ideas clear to your audience: examples and illustrations, testimony, definitions, statistics, and audiovisual aids.

Effective public speakers need to master a variety of informing skills. Check your own use of these skills. Use the following rating scale: (1) = almost always, (2) = often, (3) = sometimes, (4) = rarely, (5) = almost never.

_____ 1. In my informative speeches, I follow the principles of informative speaking: limit the amount of information, stress its relevance and usefulness to the audience, and relate any new information to what the audience already knows.

_____ 2. In developing the speech of information, I follow the suggestions for descriptive, definitional, and demonstration speeches.

_____ 3. In my informative speeches, I select a variety of amplifying materials: examples, illustrations, testimony, audiovisual aids, and statistics.

Skill Development Experiences

14.1 Amplifying Statements

Here are some rather broad statements. Select one and amplify it using at least three different methods of amplification. Identify each method used. Since the purpose of this exercise is to provide greater insight into amplification forms and methods, you may, for this exercise, invent facts, figures, illustrations, examples, and the like. In fact, it may benefit you to go to extremes in constructing these forms of support.

1. Significant social and political contributions have been made by college students.
2. The Sears Tower in Chicago is the world's tallest building.
3. Dr. Kirk is a model professor.
4. My grandparents left me money in their will.
5. The college I just visited seems ideal.

6. The writer of this article is an authority.
7. I knew I was marrying into money as soon as I walked into the house.
8. Considering what that individual did, punishment to the fullest extent of the law would be mild.
9. The fortune teller told us good news.
10. The athlete lived an interesting life.

14.2 Critically Evaluating Testimony

For each of the numbered propositions presented below, consider what the person's ideal qualifications would be before you would accept his or her testimony or alternatively, if you were presenting testimony on these issues, how would you establish the person's qualifications so that your audience would accept what he or she says?

1. a report of an accident
2. the importance of a proper diet
3. improve your communication skills
4. follow an astrologer's advice
5. buy real estate now
6. how to read the stock market page
7. the nature of manic depression
8. how to feed your pet
9. writing a book
10. how to rise in the corporation

CHAPTER FIFTEEN

The Persuasive Speech

Chapter Concepts	Chapter Goals	Chapter Skills
	After completing this chapter, you should be able to	After completing this chapter, you should be able to
Guidelines for Persuasive Speaking	1. explain the guidelines for persuasive speaking	appropriately apply the principles of persuasion in speeches
Types of Persuasive Speeches	2. describe the two types of persuasive speeches and the strategies to use in each	develop persuasive speeches that seek to strengthen or change existing attitudes or move to action
Logical Appeals	3. define the major types of reasoning and common fallacies to avoid	develop and adapt arguments to your audience

detect reasoning fallacies and avoid them in your own speeches |
Psychological Appeals	4. discuss the role of psychological appeals in motivating behavior	develop and adapt psychological appeals to your audience
Credibility Appeals	5. explain speaker credibility	establish your competence, character, and charisma
Thinking Critically About the Persuasive Speech	6. identify the standards for evaluating a persuasive speech	critically evaluate persuasive speeches

Like the ability to inform, you will find yourself in a wide variety of situations where you will have to rely on your persuasive abilities: to accept or reject the union proposal, to change over to a new bookkeeping system, or to donate blood or money or time. The higher up you go in your organization's hierarchy, the more often you will be informing and persuading others.

In this chapter we cover the speech of persuasion (in which you change your listeners' attitudes or beliefs or get them to do something). The speeches of politicians, advertisers, and religious leaders are perhaps the clearest examples of persuasive speeches. In many of your own speeches, you too will aim at persuasion.

GUIDELINES FOR PERSUASIVE SPEAKING

Your success in strengthening or changing attitudes or beliefs and in moving your listeners to action will depend on your use of the principles of persuasion (Smith, 1982; Bettinghaus & Cody, 1994; Littlejohn & Jabusch, 1987). Let's look at three major principles.

Using Selective Exposure

Audiences follow the **law of selective exposure.** It has two parts.

1. Listeners actively seek information that supports their opinions, beliefs, values, decisions, and behaviors.
2. Listeners actively avoid information that contradicts their existing opinions, beliefs, attitudes, values, and behaviors.

If you want to persuade an audience that holds different attitudes from your own, anticipate selective exposure. Therefore, proceed inductively; that is, hold back on your thesis until you present your evidence and argument. Then relate this evidence and argument to your initially contrary thesis.

Let's say you are giving a speech on the need to reduce spending on college athletic programs. If your audience agrees with you and wants to cut athletic spending, you might lead with your thesis. If, however, your audience strongly favors the existing athletic programs, then lead with your evidence and hold off stating your thesis until the end of your speech.

Using Audience Participation

Persuasion is greatest when the audience participates actively, as in paraphrasing or summarizing. Speakers who arouse huge crowds often have them chant slogans, repeat catch phrases, and otherwise participate actively. The implication is simple: persuasion is a transactional process. It involves both speaker and listeners. You will be more effective if you can get the audience to actively participate.

Using the Magnitude of Change Principle

The greater and more important the change you want to produce in your audience, the more difficult your task will be. People normally demand numerous reasons and convincing evidence before they make important decisions—career changes, moving families to another state, or investing life savings in certain stocks. People change gradually and in small degrees. Persuasion, therefore, is most effective when it strives for small changes and works over a period of time.

TYPES OF PERSUASIVE SPEECHES

In persuasive speeches, you try to achieve either of two goals: (1) to strengthen (or reinforce) or change your listeners' attitudes and beliefs or (2) to motivate them to do something.

Betty Friedan in her 1963 book, The Feminine Mystique, *challenged assumptions about women's roles that most had simply accepted, and she raised issues that are still being debated. If you were to write a book in a similar tradition, what existing assumptions (about women and men, race, national and international relations, education, sexual behavior, religion, etc.) would you challenge? What arguments might you offer in support of your challenge?*

Speeches to Strengthen or Change Attitudes or Beliefs

Many speeches seek to strengthen existing attitudes or beliefs. For example, people who listen to religious speeches are usually already believers, so these speeches aim to strengthen their attitudes and beliefs. Here the audience is favorably inclined to the speaker's purpose and willing to listen. Speeches designed to change attitudes or beliefs are more difficult. Most people resist change. When you try to change beliefs or attitudes, you are fighting an uphill battle.

Depending on the audience's initial position, you can view the following examples as topics for speeches to strengthen or change attitudes or beliefs:

Legalize marijuana.
Television shows are mindless.
Tapes and CDs should be rated for excessive sex and violence.
Make Puerto Rico the fifty-first state.

Strategies for Strengthening or Changing Attitudes and Beliefs

When you try to strengthen or change attitudes and beliefs, consider the following principles:

1. Carefully estimate your listeners' attitudes and beliefs. If your goal is to strengthen these attitudes and beliefs, state your thesis as early in your speech as you wish. Since your listeners basically agree with you, your thesis statement will create a bond of agreement. If, however, you wish to change their attitudes, reserve your thesis until after you have provided your evidence.
2. Seek change in small increments. When addressing an audience that opposes your position, limit your purpose to small changes. Let's say, for example, that your ultimate goal is to get an anti-abortion group to favor abortion on demand. Obviously, this goal is too great to achieve in one speech. Therefore, strive for small changes. Try, for example, to get the audience to see that some abortions should be legalized.
3. Give your audience good reasons for believing what you want them to believe. Give them hard evidence and arguments. Show them how such attitudes and beliefs relate directly to their own goals and motives.

Developing the Speech to Strengthen or Change Attitudes and Beliefs

The following speech focuses on attitudes and beliefs. In this example, the speaker uses a problem-solution organizational pattern, first presenting the problems created by cigarette smoking, and then the solution.

Specific purpose: To persuade my audience that cigarette advertising should be banned from all media.
Thesis: Cigarette advertising should be abolished. (Why should it be abolished?)

How would you develop a speech to move to action if your specific purpose was to persuade your listeners to enroll in a course on AIDS education?

I. Cigarette smoking is a national problem.
   A. Cigarette smoking causes lung cancer.
   B. Cigarette smoking pollutes the air.
   C. Cigarette smoking raises the cost of health care.
II. Cigarette smoking will be lessened if advertisements are prohibited.
   A. Fewer people would start to smoke.
   B. Smokers would smoke less.

In delivering such a speech, you might begin like this:

I think we all realize that cigarette smoking is a national problem that affects each and every one of us. No one escapes the problems caused by cigarette smoking—not the smoker and not the nonsmoker. Cigarette smoking causes lung cancer. Cigarette smoking pollutes the air. And cigarette smoking raises the cost of health care for you and me.

Let's look first at the most publicized of all smoking problems: lung cancer. There can be no doubt—the scientific evidence is overwhelming—that cigarette smoking causes lung cancer.

Speeches to Move to Action

The persuasive speech designed to motivate a specific behavior may focus on just about any behavior. Here are some examples:

Vote (Do not vote) for Smith.
Give money to the American Cancer Society.
Major in economics.
Buy American.

My only concern was to get home after a hard day's work.
—ROSA PARKS

Strategies for Moving Listeners to Action

When designing a speech to get listeners to do something, keep the following principles in mind.

1. Be realistic about what you want the audience to do. Remember you have only 10 or 15 minutes and in that time you cannot move the proverbial mountain. So ask for small, easily performed behaviors—to sign a petition, to vote in the next election, to donate a small amount of money.
2. Demonstrate your own willingness to do the same. As a general rule, never ask the audience to do what you have not done yourself.
3. Stress the specific advantages of these behaviors to your audience. Don't ask your audience to engage in behaviors because of only abstract reasons. Give them concrete, specific reasons why they will benefit from the actions.

Developing the Speech to Move to Action

Here is an example of a speech to move to action in which the speaker tries to persuade the audience to buy a personal computer.

Specific purpose: To persuade my audience to buy a personal computer.

Thesis: Personal computers are useful. (Why are personal computers useful? or How are personal computers useful?)
   I. Personal computers are useful for word processing.
       A. You can type faster with a word processor.
       B. You can revise documents easily with a word processor.
  II. Personal computers are useful for bookkeeping.
 III. Personal computers are useful for research.

In delivering such a speech, you might say:

> *Have you ever added up all the hours spent typing your college papers? Have you ever tried to keep your finances in order only to lose the little pieces of paper you wrote your figures on? And then you had to start all over again. Have you ever gone to our college library and not found what you were looking for?*
>
> *Typing, bookkeeping, and research are a computer's three greatest strengths. After I show you how a computer can do these things, you'll want to buy a personal computer of your own.*

CULTURAL VIEWPOINT

Ethnocentrism

One problem that hinders intercultural communication is the tendency to see others and their behaviors through your own cultural filters. *Ethnocentrism* is the tendency to evaluate the values, beliefs, and behaviors of your own culture as being more positive, logical, and natural than those of other cultures. Ideally, you would see both yourself and others as different but equal, with neither being inferior nor superior.

Ethnocentrism exists on a continuum. People are not either ethnocentric or not ethnocentric; rather, most are somewhere between these polar opposites. And, of course, your degree of ethnocentrism varies depending on the group on which you focus. For example, if you are Greek American, you may have a low degree of ethnocentrism when dealing with Italian Americans but a high degree when dealing with Turkish Americans or Japanese Americans. Most important for our purposes is that your degree of ethnocentrism (and we are all ethnocentric to at least some degree) will influence your interpersonal, group, public, and mass communication behaviors.

The accompanying table, drawing from a number of researchers (Lukens, 1978; Gudykunst & Kim, 1992; Gudykunst, 1994), summarizes some of the interconnections. In this table five degrees of ethnocentrism are identified; in reality, of course, there are as many degrees as there are people. The "communication distances" are general terms that highlight the attitude that dominates that level of ethnocentrism. Under "communications" are some of the major ways people might interact given their particular degree of ethnocentrism.

The more I traveled the more I realized that fear makes strangers of people who should be friends.
—SHIRLEY MACLAINE

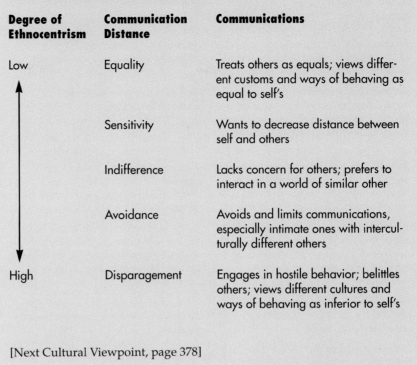

The Ethnocentrism Continuum

Degree of Ethnocentrism	Communication Distance	Communications
Low	Equality	Treats others as equals; views different customs and ways of behaving as equal to self's
	Sensitivity	Wants to decrease distance between self and others
	Indifference	Lacks concern for others; prefers to interact in a world of similar other
	Avoidance	Avoids and limits communications, especially intimate ones with interculturally different others
High	Disparagement	Engages in hostile behavior; belittles others; views different cultures and ways of behaving as inferior to self's

[Next Cultural Viewpoint, page 378]

LOGICAL APPEALS

An argument consists of evidence (for example, facts) and a conclusion. Evidence together with the conclusion that it supports equal an argument, a logical appeal. Reasoning is the process of forming conclusions on the basis of evidence. For example, you might reason that because college graduates earn more money than nongraduates (evidence), Jack and Jill should go to college if they wish to earn more money (conclusion).

Throughout this discussion we approach the forms of reasoning from the point of view of the speaker using them in a speech. But these forms of reasoning are equally valuable for the listener. That is, you must analyze the validity of the reasoning you use not only as a speaker but also as a listener.

In addition to the four major types of reasoning to be discussed below, there are a variety of fallacies that you need to guard against as speaker and listener. Ten of these are presented in Table 15.1.

Reasoning from Specific Instances to Generalizations

In reasoning from specific instances, you examine several items and then conclude something about the whole. This form of reasoning is useful when you want to develop a general principle or conclusion but cannot examine the whole. For example, you sample a few communication courses and con-

Table 15.1   Fallacies and Critical Thinking

Fallacy	Examples	Critical Thinking
Name Calling: the speaker gives an idea, a group of people, or an ideology a derogatory name	The proposal is antilabor. He's an atheist, what do you expect?	This technique tries to make you condemn the idea or person without analyzing the evidence
Glittering Generality (the opposite of name calling) occurs when the speaker tries to gain your acceptance of an idea by associating it with things you value highly	True democracy requires us to . . . It's the American way.	Respond to the reality and not to such "virtue words" (words that denote highly respected qualities); often the speaker is trying to get you to ignore the evidence and approve the idea without evaluation
Transfer occurs when the speaker associates his or her idea with something you respect to gain your approval or with something you dislike to gain your rejection	The proposal is in the best tradition of equality and democracy. The proposed change is just another form of apartheid.	Remember that not all language aims to describe or objectively present the facts; much language is emotive and appeals to your emotions and not your reason
Testimonial involves a speaker using the authority or image of some positively evaluated person to gain your approval or of some negatively evaluated person to gain your rejection.	Recall Ed McMahon for American Publishing, Michael Jordan for BVDs, and, of course, the glamorous models and television and film stars for everything from cereal to shampoo	Recall that the person usually has little to do with the product and is no more an authority on the product than you are; also recall that these people are getting paid millions to endorse these products
Plain folks is used when the speaker identifies himself or herself and the proposal with the audience	We're all middle class and we need a break. As parents—and I'm a parent just like you—we know . . .	Often the speaker is one of the audience, but that has nothing to do with the validity of the proposal
In **card stacking** the speaker selects only the evidence and arguments that build a case (even falsifies evidence and distorts the facts)	See almost any political campaign speech	Most issues are too complex to have all the arguments on one side; usually, if an issue is presented with only one side, you can be pretty sure that another side is being hidden
The **band wagon** technique involves the speaker trying to persuade you to accept or reject an idea because "everybody is doing it," or the "right" people are doing it	Economists agree that . . . The entire faculty agrees that . . .	Wide agreement is probably a good sign that there may be some validity in a proposition, but it is not proof; most people once thought the world was flat or that women could never be body builders
Granfallon (a term coined by novelist Kurt Vonnegut) refers to the tendency of people to see themselves as constituting a cohesive and like-minded group because they are given a label	As Christians (Jews, Muslims) we know that . . . Those of us who are "workers" will naturally resent the . . .	This fallacy has the effect of dividing the world into "we" and "they," a form of polarization (see Chapter 5) that inevitably simplifies and ignores individual differences
In **agenda-setting** the speaker argues that XYZ is the issue and that others are unimportant	Balancing the budget is the key to our city's survival. There is only one issue confronting elementary education in New York City and that is violence; if the schools are not made safe, education cannot take place.	In almost all situations, there are many issues and many sides to each issue; often the person proclaiming "X is the issue" really means "I'll have an advantage if you focus solely on X and ignore the other issues"
Attack involves accusing another person (usually an opponent) of some serious wrongdoing so that the issue under discussion never gets examined	How can we support a candidate who has been unfaithful and has lied?	Although a person's personal reputation and past behavior are often relevant, more often personal attack is used to draw attention away from other issues

The first seven fallacies were originally identified for the Institute for Propaganda Analysis (Lee & Lee, 1972), but are now recognized as common to all forms of persuasion (Albrecht, 1980; Ruggiero, 1990). The last three are presented by Pratkanis and Aronson (1991; Goleman, 1992).

Can you describe recent advertisements that use any of these ten fallacious reasoning techniques?

clude something about communication courses in general. You visit several Scandinavian cities and conclude something about all of Scandinavia.

Critically analyze reasoning from specific instances by asking these questions.

1. Were enough specific instances examined? Two general guidelines will help determine how much is enough. First, the larger the group you wish to cover by your conclusion, the greater the number of specific instances you should examine. If you want to draw a conclusion about your college's entire student body, you will need to examine a much larger sample than if you limit your conclusion to members of your Human Communication class.

    Second, the greater the differences among items or people in the group you want to draw a conclusion about, the more specific instances you will have to examine. For example, if you want to draw conclusions about students throughout the world, your sample would have to be much larger than if you limit your conclusion to students in the United States.

2. Were the specific instances representative? If you want to draw conclusions about your school's student body, you cannot simply survey physics or art majors. Rather, you have to examine a representative sample.

3. Are there significant exceptions? When you examine specific instances and draw a conclusion about the whole, consider the exceptions. If you examine a number of Venusians and discover that 70 percent have incomes in the top 25 percent of the galaxy, you might conclude that Venusians are rich. But what about the 30 percent who have incomes in the bottom 10 percent? You have to consider these significant exceptions.

Reasoning from Analogy

In reasoning from analogy, you compare like things and conclude that since they are alike in so many respects, they are also alike in some other respect. Analogies may be literal or figurative. In a literal analogy the items compared are from the same class—foods, cars, people, countries, cities, or whatever.

In a figurative analogy, the items compared are from different classes. These analogies are useful for amplification but are not logical proof. A figurative analogy might compare, for example, children with birds. You might note that, as birds are free to roam all over the world, children need to be free to roam all over their new and unexplored universe.

In critically analyzing the adequacy of an analogy—here of literal analogies—ask yourself two general questions.

1. Are the two cases alike in essential respects? A difference in significant respects will weaken your analogy's strength.

2. Do the differences make a difference? In any analogy, regardless of how literal, compared items will be different: No two things are exactly the same. But in reasoning with analogies, ask yourself if the differences make a difference. Obviously, not all do.

How would you use reasoning by analogy to persuade an audience that college core requirements should be eliminated?

" 'The subway was late' is an excellent excuse for tardiness, however, there are no subways in Iowa!"

NATIONAL ENQUIRER

Cartoon by Art Bouthillier

Reasoning from Causes and Effects

You may either reason from cause to effect or from effect to cause. Causal reasoning goes like this:

X results from Y
since X is undesirable
Y should be eliminated

In an actual speech, the reasoning might be presented like this:

All the available evidence shows unmistakably that cancer [X] results from smoking [Y]. Smoking is personally destructive [X]; we have no choice but to do everything we can to eliminate smoking entirely [Y].

Alternatively, of course, you might argue that X results from Y; and since X is desirable, Y should be encouraged. In a speech, you might say:

We know that general self-confidence [X] results from positively reinforcing experiences [Y]. Therefore, if you want to encourage the development of self-confidence in your children [X], give them positively reinforcing experiences [Y].

It is difficult, if not impossible, for most people to think otherwise than in the fashion of their own period.

—GEORGE BERNARD SHAW

In critically analyzing reasoning from cause to effect or from effect to cause, ask yourself these questions.

1. Might other causes be producing the observed effect? If you observe a particular effect (say, high crime), ask if causes other than the one you are postulating might be producing it. Thus, you might assume that poverty leads to crime, but other factors might be actually causing the high crime rate. Or poverty might be one cause but not the most important.

2. Is the causation in the predicted direction? If two things occur together, it is often difficult to determine which is the cause and which the effect. For example, you see in the same person a lack of interpersonal intimacy and of self-confidence; the person who lacks self-confidence seldom has intimate relationships. But which is the cause and which the effect? The lack of intimacy might cause low self-confidence. However, low self-confidence might also cause a lack of intimacy. Or maybe some other cause (a history of negative criticism, for example) is producing both.

3. Is there evidence for a causal rather than merely a time-sequence relationship? Although two things might occur together, they may not be related in a cause-effect relationship. Divorce frequently results after repeated infidelities, but infidelity itself may not be the cause. Rather, some other factor (for example, boredom or the desire for change) may be leading to both infidelity and divorce.

Reasoning from Sign

Medical diagnosis is a good example of reasoning by sign. The general procedure is simple. If a sign and a condition are frequently paired, the sign's presence is taken as proof of the condition's presence. Thus tiredness, extreme thirst, and overeating are signs of hyperthyroidism since they frequently accompany the condition. When these signs (or symptoms) disappear after treatment, it is taken as a sign that the thyroid disease is arrested. Critically analyze reasoning from sign by asking yourself:

1. Do the signs necessitate the conclusion? Given the extreme thirst, overeating, and the like, how certain can you be of the hyperthyroid conclusion? With most medical and legal matters you can never be absolutely certain. You can only be certain beyond a reasonable doubt.

2. Are there other signs that point to the same conclusion? In the thyroid example, other factors could have caused the extreme thirst and similarly, the overeating. Yet taken together they pointed to only one reasonable diagnosis. Generally, the more signs that point toward the conclusion, the more confidence you can have that it is valid or correct.

3. Are there contradictory signs? Let's say, for example, that Higgins, suspected of murder, had a motive and a history of violence (signs that support the conclusion that Higgins was the murderer). But if Higgins also had an alibi for the time of the murder (a contradictory sign), the conclusion of guilt would have to be discarded.

How dangerous it always is to reason from insufficient data.
—SHERLOCK HOLMES

PSYCHOLOGICAL APPEALS

When you use psychological appeals, you aim at your listeners' needs and desires. Psychological appeals focus on motives—those forces that energize a person to develop, change, or strengthen particular attitudes or behaviors. Some of the motives to which you might address your appeals are discussed here.

Power, Control, and Influence

We want power, control, and influence. We want power over ourselves and others, to control events and things in the world, and to be influential. You will motivate your listeners when you enable them to increase these factors by learning what you have to say or doing as you suggest.

In a commencement address at Ohio University, Vincent Ryan Ruggiero (1987) appeals to his listeners' desire to control their lives more efficiently:

> People often ask me how I have managed to stay abreast of the research in several disciplines, write articles and books, and maintain an active speaking and consulting schedule, usually while teaching a full course load. . . .
>
> I decided that by being thrifty with time and investing it with the same care wealthy people exercise in investing their money, I could, in effect, lengthen my life. So I set about developing some rules that would help me live more efficiently. I'd like to share with you the six I have found most helpful.

Self-Esteem and Approval

He who gives food to the people will win.

—Lech Walesa

We all want to see ourselves positively, in the best possible light. We want to see ourselves as worthy and contributing human beings. Inspirational speeches—of the "you are the greatest" type—never seem to lack receptive audiences. In relating to your audience's desire for approval, avoid being too obvious. Few people want to be told that they need or desire approval.

CULTURAL VIEWPOINT

Fear and Intercultural Communication

In considering emotions in persuasion, it seems appropriate to consider how the role of emotions—particularly that of fear—relates to intercultural communication. There is little doubt that fear stands in the way of mastering intercultural communication (Stephen & Stephen, 1985; Gudykunst, 1994). You may wish to think of your responses to the self-test "How Open Are You Interculturally?" in Chapter 1 (page 34) as you consider these specific types of fear.

You may fear for your self-esteem. You may become anxious about your ability to control the intercultural situation or you may worry about your own level of discomfort.

You may fear that you will be taken advantage of by the member of this other culture. Depending on your own stereotypes you may fear being lied to, financially duped, or made fun of.

You may fear that members of this other group will react to you negatively. They may not like you or may disapprove of your attitudes or beliefs or they may even reject you as a person. Conversely, you may fear negative reactions from members of your own group. They might, for example, disapprove of your socializing with the interculturally different.

These fears—coupled with the greater effort that intercultural communication takes and the ease with which you communicate with those who are culturally similar—can easily create sufficient anxiety to make some people give up.

Achievement

We want to achieve. As students you want to be successful. As a teacher and writer I too want to be successful. We want to achieve as friends, as parents, as lovers. This is why we read books and listen to speeches that tell us how to be more successful.

To use the achievement motive, explicitly state how your ideas and recommendations will contribute to the listeners' achievements. If you tell your listeners how they can increase their potential, earn better grades, secure more prestigious jobs, and become more popular with friends, you will have a highly motivated audience.

Financial Gain

Other motives frequently mentioned as effective in persuasion are altruism, fear, individuality and conformity, love and affiliation, and status. How might these be used in a speech on helping the homeless?

The desire for financial gain motivates many people. If you show an audience that what you advocate will make them money, they will listen with interest. In a speech designed to motivate action against certain proposed budget cuts, Cyril F. Brickfield appeals to the financial motive of his senior citizen audience:

> Congress is now considering freezing Social Security COLAs [cost-of-living adjustments]. Congress is willing to force more than a half million of us into poverty. But the defense budget is exempt from any freeze.
> Ladies and gentlemen, let me ask you, is it fair that older Americans must lose their inflation protection while the Pentagon doesn't?

ETHICAL ISSUE

Fear and Emotional Appeals

One of the most widely discussed ethical issues in communication is the legitimacy of appeals based on fear and emotion. This issue is raised frequently in connection with attempts to change attitudes, beliefs, and behaviors. The case of a real estate broker appealing to your desire for status, a friend who wants a favor appealing to your desire for social approval, and a salesperson appealing to your desire for sexual rewards are all familiar examples. The political candidates' promises in campaign speeches that are aimed at getting votes and not at what is good for the community. The question they all raise is simply, "Is this type of appeal justified?"

Many arguments can be advanced on both sides of the issue. The "everyone is doing it" argument is perhaps the most familiar, but it does not address the question of whether such appeals are justified. Another argument is that since people are composites of logic and emotion, effective appeals must be based in part on emotions. Again, however, this does not answer the question of whether emotional appeals are ethical; it merely states that they are effective.

Here are some questions to get you thinking about the ethical aspects involved in the use of fear and emotional appeals in persuasion:

- Is it ethical for parents to use fear appeals to dissuade their teenage children from engaging in sexual relationships? Is the parent's motive relevant in deciding whether such appeals are ethical or unethical?
- Is it ethical to use fear appeals in public speeches or in advertisements to prevent sexually transmitted diseases? Is it ethical to use the same appeals if the motive is to sell condoms?
- How would you evaluate the rhetoric of the pro- and anti-abortion groups in terms of their use of fear and emotional appeals?
- What is the dominant mode of religious rhetoric on television? Advertisements? Political rhetoric? Talk shows?
- What ethical guidelines would you propose for the use of fear and emotional appeals in persuasion?

CREDIBILITY APPEALS

How believable are you as a speaker—apart from any evidence or argument you might advance? What is there about you as a person that makes others believe or not believe you? We call this quality of believability **speaker credibility** (McCroskey, 1986; Riggio, 1987). Before reading about credibility, you may wish to take the self-test "How Credible Are You?"

TEST YOURSELF
How Credible Are You?

Instructions Respond to each of the following phrases as you think members of this class (your audience) see you when you deliver a public speech. Use the following scale:

7 = Very true
6 = Quite true
5 = Fairly true
4 = Neither true nor untrue
3 = Fairly untrue
2 = Quite untrue
1 = Very untrue

_____ 1. knowledgeable about the subject matter
_____ 2. experienced
_____ 3. confident
_____ 4. informed about the subject matter
_____ 5. fair in the presentation of material (evidence and argument)
_____ 6. concerned with the audience's needs
_____ 7. consistent over time on the issues addressed in the speech
_____ 8. similar to the audience in attitudes and values
_____ 9. positive rather than negative
_____ 10. assertive in personal style
_____ 11. enthusiastic about the topic and in general
_____ 12. active rather than passive

Thinking Critically About Your Credibility This test focuses on the three qualities of credibility: competence, character, and charisma, and it is based on a large body of research (e.g., McCroskey, 1986; Riggio, 1987). Items 1 through 4 refer to your perceived competence: How competent or capable does the audience see you when you give a public speech? Items 5 through 8 refer to your perceived character: Does the audience see you as a person of good and moral character? Items 9 through 12 refer to your perceived charisma: Does the audience see you as dynamic and active rather than as static and passive? You may wish to consider what specific steps you can take to change any audience perception with which you may be unhappy.

Credibility is important to the politician because it influences how people vote. It is important in education, since it influences a teacher's impact on a class. Credibility influences every communication situation.

We can identify three major qualities of credibility: **competence,** the knowledge and expertise the audience thinks the speaker has; **character,** the speaker's intentions and values as seen by the audience; and **charisma,** the audience's evaluation of the speaker's personality and dynamism.

Competence

The more knowledge and expertise the audience perceives you to have, the more likely they will believe you. For example, you believe a teacher to the extent that you think he or she is knowledgeable on the subject. Here are some methods to demonstrate your competence to your audience.

1. Tell the audience of special experience or training that qualifies you to speak on this specific topic. At the same time, do not call attention to your inadequacies or to any gaps in your knowledge. Avoid such statements as "I know I'm not an expert, but . . . "

It's not whether you really cry. It's whether the audience thinks you are crying.

—INGRID BERGMAN

How would your class evaluate your credibility in general? Your competence? Character? Charisma?

You will always find a few Eskimos ready to tell the Congolese how to cope with the heat.

—STANISLEC LEE

"The 'Post' did an unflattering piece on me."

Drawing by M. Twohy; © 1993 The New Yorker Magazine, Inc.

2. Cite a variety of research sources. Make it clear that you have thoroughly researched the topic—mention books you have read, persons you have interviewed, articles you have consulted. Weave these throughout your speech.
3. Stress particular competencies of your sources if your audience is not aware of them. Instead of saying, "Senator Smith thinks . . . ," establish the senator's credibility early by saying something like: "Senator Smith, who headed the finance committee for three years and was formerly professor of economics at MIT, thinks . . . "

Character

Character concerns the speaker's honesty and basic nature. We want to know if we can trust the speaker. We believe a speaker we trust. As a speaker, demonstrate qualities of character that will increase your credibility. Here are some suggestions.

1. Stress your fairness. When delivering a persuasive speech, stress that you have examined both sides of the issue and that your presentation is accurate and fair.
2. Stress your concern for enduring values. Make it clear to the audience that your position—your thesis—is related to higher-order values. Show them exactly how this is true.

   Notice how President George Bush (1988) stressed his concern for such enduring values as family, religion, tradition, and individual power in his speech accepting the Republican nomination:

POWER PERSPECTIVE

Credibility as Personal Power

Credibility gives you power to influence others. If you are seen to have credibility, others will believe what you say and are more likely to do as you ask. Here are a few general guidelines for increasing your credibility.

1. Although research shows that people believe those they think are competent and not necessarily those who really are competent, it helps if you develop the qualities that you want to project.
2. Use a variety of methods to establish your credibility. Relying totally on your competence, character, or charisma is not likely to produce the same results as would a demonstration of all three characteristics.
3. Demonstrate your possession of these qualities clearly but at the same time exercise moderation. Don't emphasize your competence so much that the audience concludes that you therefore must be incompetent. "Doubt the man," advises Louise Colet, "who swears to his devotion."

Which of these three credibility qualities would most influence you in buying a new car? In choosing a doctor? In selecting a graduate school? In choosing a relationship partner? Why?

If you were former Surgeon General Joycelyn Elders's speech advisor, what kinds of persuasive appeals (logical, psychological, or credibility) would you suggest she emphasize in delivering a speech to your class on the need for teaching about AIDS and safe sex in elementary schools? What would your advice be if she were addressing Congress on this same topic? If she were addressing a conference of principals of religious schools?

At the bright center is the individual. And radiating out from him or her is the family, the essential unit of closeness and of love. For it is the family that communicates to our children—to the twenty-first century—our culture, our religious faith, our traditions and history.

From the individual to the family to the community, and so out to the town, to the church and school and, still echoing out, to the country, the state, the nation—each doing only what it does well, and no more. And I believe that power must always be kept close to the individual, close to the hands that raise the family and run the home.

3. Stress your similarity with the audience, particularly your beliefs, attitudes, values, and goals. The more similar you are to your listeners, the more likely they will perceive you as credible. At the same time, make it clear that the audience's interests are foremost in your mind.

Charisma

We favor the dynamic speaker over the hesitant, nonassertive one. We perceive the shy, introverted, soft-spoken individual as less credible than the extroverted and forceful individual. Some suggestions for demonstrating charisma are:

1. Demonstrate a positive attitude to the entire speech encounter. Stress your pleasure at addressing the audience. Stress hope rather than despair, happiness rather than sadness.
2. Demonstrate assertiveness. Show the audience that you are a person who will stand up for your rights. Show them that you will not back off simply because the odds may be against you.
3. Be enthusiastic. The lethargic speaker who plods through the speech is the very opposite of the charismatic speaker. Try viewing a film of Martin Luther King, Jr. or Billy Graham speaking. They are totally absorbed with the speech and the audience. They are excellent examples of the enthusiasm that makes speakers charismatic.

THINKING CRITICALLY ABOUT THE PERSUASIVE SPEECH

Here is a persuasive speech delivered by a college student, Shelley Schnathorst. As is the informative speech in Chapter 14, this speech is accompanied by a series of questions designed to give structure to your thinking critically about persuasive speeches in general and this speech in particular. Recall that the questions are of different types (see Chapter 14, page 359).

- **Identification** or **discovery**
- **Evaluation**
- **Problem-solving** or **application**

Of all the speeches included here this is the most difficult. It deals, in a relatively sophisticated way, with a topic about which most people know very little. (1) If this speech were given in your class, would you consider this too complex? If so, what would you do to make it simpler and easier to understand?

(2) What type of introduction did Schnathorst use? Does this introduction gain your attention? Establish a speaker-audience-topic connection? Orient the audience?

Persuasive Speech

Shelley Schnathorst, *University of Northern Iowa*

In Roman times the Latin phrase "caveat emptor" or "let the buyer beware" was an appropriate warning to the citizens of that time. In the United States today we pride ourselves on a system which protects consumers from dangerous products. And while we understand that we still have responsibilities in our own protection, we have come to trust the safety of the products we must use. But for thousands of people each year that trust is misplaced. They are the ones who use medical devices ranging from x-rays to incubators and pacemakers to prostheses.

There are over 1600 different types of medical devices in use today by virtually every patient who enters a doctor's office for tests or a hospital for operations. Although the range of medical devices may seem broad, they are all subject to the medical regulatory system.

The Food and Drug Administration, or the FDA, has been given responsibility to approve medical devices. Yet Representative Henry Waxman of California stated on May 4th of 1987 that "only a handful have actually been so approved." Because most devices have not gone through rigorous approval processes, they present enormous hazards to us. In testifying before the House of Representatives on May 5th of last year, Stephen Ferguson, president of one of the world's largest manufacturers of medical devices, stated, "Everyone in this room will someday want one of the devices we have under development, as the best available choice for yourselves or someone you know." So that we can improve the safety of those choices, we need to look at the importance of regulating medical devices, flaws in current regulations, and finally workable solutions to insure that we are adequately protected.

Adequate regulation is essential for two reasons. First and foremost, medical devices are often critical to the health and survival of individuals. By definition, a medical device is any instrument or apparatus intended to prevent, diagnose, or treat a human illness or disorder. And of course, when we seek the help of a doctor or a hospital, we hope that the devices they use will make us better, and we trust that they will not make us worse. Yet sometimes devices that are considered life supporting become life threatening.

John Villforth an FDA administrator reported in a May 1986 *FDA Consumer* that a heart resuscitation unit failed when the machine, like many of its type, had no warning device to indicate that the batteries powering units were defective. In addition, a July 2, 1987, segment of *20/20* reported that investigators discovered a flaw in the Therac 25, a radiation machine used in the treatment of cancer. Each of the three patients interviewed complained of being burned by the machine. After the loss of two lives, investigations led to the discovery of a computer program error which had given some patients forty-five times the amount of radiation requested. As amateurs in health care, we cannot be expected to have a clear understanding of every medical device and its hazards. Yet, our lives are at stake.

A second reason for adequate regulation was described by Representative Waxman, who is chairman of the House Subcommittee on Medical Devices. He stated that unlike a consumer product such as a child's toy, or even a Toyota, which can be recalled, it is more difficult to deal with medical

(3) Does Schnathorst avoid the common faults of introductions: apology, hollow promises, pretending, prefacing?

(4) In what way does Schnathorst establish the importance of the topic? How would you have done this?

(5) What is the thesis of this speech? Would this thesis be appropriate for your class?

(6) What is the general purpose? What is the specific purpose? Would the specific purpose be appropriate if this speech was given in your class? Is the specific purpose sufficiently narrow in scope? Does the speaker accomplish her aim?

(7) What organizational pattern is used in this speech? Is this pattern effective given the speaker's purpose? (8) Does Schnathorst use primacy or recency? (9) Climax or anticlimax order? Were the orders selected effective in achieving the speaker's purpose?

How effectively does Schnathorst apply the principles of persuasion? (10) Does she use the credibility principle? (11) The audience participation principle? (12) The inoculation principle? (13) The magnitude of change principle?

(14) What forms of reasoning does the speaker use? Specific instances? Analogy? Causes and effects? Sign? Is the reasoning sound? Does the evidence pass the tests for validity?

(15) What kinds of motivational appeals are used here? Are these effective?

(16) How effectively are the statistics used in this speech? (17) What other forms of supporting material are used? Are these effective in supporting Schnathorst's thesis? (18) Would you have preferred other types of supporting materials? Why?

(19) Are transitions used effectively? Where might more transitions be used? (20) What about internal summaries? How effective is this internal summary?

devices, for oftentimes they have been implanted into a human body. Consider the case of Constance Walters, who testified in a videotape before House hearings. To correct a curvature in her spine, she had an operation in which a medical device called a Weiss spring was implanted into her back in February of last year. By April she was experiencing tremendous pain. The Weiss spring which had never been submitted for testing snapped inside her. As Walters said, "It is worse now, I can't be anybody. Do something so that someone else's life is not totally ruined like this."

According to Waxman, the best solution is to have a system that provides reasonable assurance that devices are both safe and effective. Well, there is a law intended to provide such an assurance. However, that law, the Medical Device Amendment of 1976, is flawed itself.

In his May 4, 1987 testimony, Dr. Sidney Wolf, Director of the Public Citizen Health Research Group, outlined three specific flaws in current regulation. First, legislation requires that most devices meet FDA performance standards. The catch is the FDA has never devised any standards, and thus cannot regulate the devices.

In the absence of standards, the FDA relies upon Article (510K) of the Medical Device Amendment. (510K) allows a manufacturer to introduce a new device on the market simply by claiming it is substantially equivalent to devices on the market in 1976. There is no need to claim that the devices are any better than the devices in 1976, and the claims that are made go untested. Dr. Wolf stated that this second flaw is perhaps the biggest loophole in the law.

In fact, Representative Waxman noted that well over 98 percent of the new medical devices that enter the market each year do so by claiming substantial equivalence rather than going through premarket safety tests and reviews. What this means is that Americans continue to serve as guinea pigs for new medical devices. Constance Walters was a guinea pig, for the Weiss spring had never been submitted for testing.

Now the question that some of you may be asking is how common is such a problem. The third flaw in this system insures that we will never know the answer, for complete, systematic reporting of defects is not required. Now the law requires that manufacturers report defects directly to the FDA. But, hospitals, doctors, distributors, those who actually work with the devices are not mandated to report the defects to anyone. And for the information that is reported, a General Accounting Office study published in December of 1986 found that there is a funneling effect. They examined what happened to nearly 1200 reports of medical device problems and found that because of the informality of the process and lack of required reporting, less than one percent of those problems ever reached FDA files.

Failure to develop standards, reliance on an equivalent standard instead, and finally incomplete reporting all combine to create inadequate protection. It is protection which Tama and James Jackson wish they had had when their firstborn baby, a baby boy, developed jaundice. The baby was placed in an illuminated hospital incubator, which rid the child's body of the yellow coloration. The next day the incubator was empty. Their baby was found in intensive care with a fever of 106 degrees. The next morning, the Jackson's firstborn died. The cause of death, the incubator. With a broken thermostat and alarm and a defective on-off switch, the incubator literally became an oven. To prevent such horrors, immediate action needs to be taken. As is evident, current regulation must be modified.

First, the FDA should be required to develop the standards called for 12 years ago, so that the design of the device will be safe to begin with. For none of the examples that I have provided is an isolated malfunction, but rather a flaw in the design itself.

Second, establishing design standards will close the (510K) loophole, and products won't be approved only because they are equivalent to devices in 1976. For as you well know, since 1976, improvements in medical technologies have occurred. Therefore, we should demand that such technologies be incorporated into new medical devices.

Third, reporting of defects should be mandated. Not just by manufacturers, but of course by doctors, hospitals, and distributors. This again should be standardized format of reporting. Now this proposal will work, for when reports of problems do reach the FDA they have been proven to be quite effective in protecting our interest. For example, when the FDA received reports of faulty sleep apnea monitors, which help children prone to sudden infant death syndrome, they [were] able to respond quite quickly. The FDA received reports that faulty monitors had electrocuted one child and burned several others. With this information, the FDA was able to issue safety alerts to health care profession-

(21) The example of the Jackson baby is a good example of mixing the levels of abstraction considered in Unit 21. How effective is this example in supporting Schnathorst's thesis?

(22) Does Schnathorst establish her credibility? How? Is this sufficient? What suggestions would you offer for increasing speaker credibility?

(23) Would you characterize the language of the speech as direct or indirect? Abstract or concrete? Objective or subjective? Formal or informal? Accurate or inaccurate? What specific elements can you identify to support your conclusions?

(24) Is the language used clear? Vivid? Appropriate to the audience (assume an audience like your class members) and topic? Personal? Forceful?

(25) What do you remember most after reading this speech? What do you think you will remember from this speech next week? Next month? (26) What public-speaking principle might you derive on the basis of what you remember now and what you think you'll remember later from this speech?

als, home users, sleep apnea support groups, and of course the manufacturers who could improve the device.

Currently, there is a bill before the House Subcommittee on Health, Environment and Energy. Although not yet in its final form, this bill will insure that necessary alterations be made in FDA regulations. It is this bill, HR 2595, which you should encourage your legislators to support.

Again, although we cannot be expected to know everything about every medical device, there are times that we or someone we know will be using one. Therefore we need to trust the proverb, "let the buyer beware," and become more informed about such devices.

The 1976 bill was well-intentioned. However, after a decade of talk and no action, it is time that Congress with our assistance take serious steps in regulating this multibillion dollar medical device industry. With timely action we can discover and correct what otherwise might be a fatal flaw. But we must act. For as Helen Keller once wrote, "Science may have found a cure for most evils, but it has found no remedy for the worst of them all, the apathy of human beings."

(27) What type of conclusion did Schnathorst use? Was this effective? (28) How effective was the quotation from Helen Keller? Did it effectively bring the speech to a crisp and definite close?

(29) What is your overall evaluation of this speech? That is, if this speech were given in your class, what grade would you give it? (30) What is the major strength of this speech as you see it? (31) What is the major weakness? How might this weakness have been corrected?

This speech won as best persuasive speech in the 1988 American Forensic Associations' sponsored National Individual Events Tournament. From 1988 Championship Debates and Speeches. *Copyright © 1988 by the American Forensic Association. Reprinted by permission.*

Feedback on Concepts and Skills

In this chapter we covered the nature of the persuasive speech and ways you can most effectively change attitudes and behaviors.

1. The major types of persuasive speeches are (1) those that aim to strengthen or change attitudes or beliefs and (2) those that aim to actuate or move the listeners to action.
2. In preparing your persuasive speeches, consider the following guidelines for persuasive speaking: the selective exposure principle, the audience participation principle, and the magnitude of change principle.
3. Argument refers to a reason or series of reasons that lead to or support a conclusion. Evidence plus the conclusion it supports equal an argument.
4. In critically analyzing reasoning fallacies be alert to such techniques as name calling, glittering generalities, transfer, testimonial, plain folks, card stacking, band wagon, granfalloon, agenda-setting, and attack.

5. In reasoning from specific instances to a generalization, we examine several specific instances and then conclude something about the whole.

6. In reasoning from analogy, we compare like things and conclude that since they are alike in so many respects, they are also alike in some unknown or unexamined respect. Analogies may be literal or figurative.

7. In reasoning from causes and effects, we may go in either of two directions: We can reason from known or observed cause to unobserved effect, or from observed or known effect to some unobserved cause.

8. In reasoning from sign, we deduce that if a sign and an object, event, or condition are repeatedly or frequently paired, the sign's presence is taken as evidence or proof that the object, event, or condition is present.

9. Psychological or motivational appeals are directed at an individual's needs and desires such as fear; power, control, and influence; self-esteem and approval; achievement; and financial gain.

10. Credibility refers to that quality of persuasiveness that depends on the audience's perception of the speaker's competence, character, and charisma.

As an effective public speaker you need to master a variety of persuading skills. Check your own use of these skills. Use the following rating scale: (1) = almost always, (2) = often, (3) = sometimes, (4) = rarely, (5) = almost never.

_____ 1. In my persuasive speeches, I apply (where relevant) the principles of persuasion: selective exposure, audience participation, and magnitude of change.

_____ 2. In my persuasive speeches, I critically analyze reasoning from specific instances to generalizations, analogy, causes and effects, and sign.

_____ 3. In listening to persuasive attempts, I detect such fallacies as name calling, glittering generalities, transfer, testimonial, plain folks, card stacking, band wagon, granfalloon, agenda-setting, and attack.

_____ 4. To motivate my audience I use psychological appeals—for example, fear; power, control, and influence; achievement; and financial gain.

_____ 5. In my speeches, I seek to establish my credibility by displaying competence, high moral character, and dynamism or charisma.

Skill Development Experiences

15.1 Constructing Arguments

Construct an argument (from specific instances to generalizations, analogy, causes and effects, and sign) for or against any one of the following propositions. Since the purpose of this experience is to familiarize you with constructing arguments, use hypothetical (even fanciful) data to build your arguments.

1. AIDS prevention should be (should not be) a required course in colleges.
2. Tenure for college teachers should be (should not be) abolished.
3. Church property should be (should not be) taxed.
4. The death penalty should be (should not be) abolished in all states.
5. Tapes, cassettes, and CDs should be (should not be) labeled for sexual content and violence.

15.2 Constructing Motivational Appeals

Here are some fears that many people say they have:

- fear of losing money or not making enough
- fear of losing jobs
- fear of ill health, of getting a disease
- fear of looking bad, of negative personal appearance
- fear of interpersonal unhappiness—for example, relationship difficulties, not having enough friends
- fear of lack of self-confidence

Select one of the specific purposes and audiences noted below and develop a motivational appeal based on one or more of these fears. After constructing these appeals, share your results with others, either in small groups or the class as a whole. In your discussion you may wish to consider some or all of the following questions.

1. How effective do you think such an appeal would be if actually presented to such an audience?
2. Might some of the appeals backfire and stimulate audience resentment? Why might such resentment develop? What precautions might be taken by the speaker to prevent such resentment?
3. What are the ethical implications of using these motivational appeals?

Purposes
1. Marijuana should (not) be made legal for those over 18 years of age.
2. Cigarette smoking should (not) be banned in all public places.
3. Capital punishment should (not) be law in all states.
4. Social Security benefits should be increased (decreased) by at least one-third.
5. Retirement should (not) be mandatory at age 65 for all government employees.
6. National health insurance should (not) be instituted.
7. Athletic scholarships should (not) be abolished.
8. Property taxes should be lowered (increased) by 50 percent.
9. Required courses in college should (not) be abolished.
10. Teachers should (not) be paid according to performance; they should (not) be paid according to seniority, degrees earned, or publications.

Audiences
1. Senior citizens of Metropolis
2. Senior Club of your high school
3. Small Business Operators Club of Anytown

4. Council for Better Housing
5. Veterans of Vietnam
6. Los Angeles Society of Interior Designers
7. Catholic Women's Council
8. National Council of African-American Artists
9. Parent-Teachers Association of elementary schools in your community
10. Society for the Rehabilitation of Former Drug Addicts

15.3 Building Credibility in 60 Seconds

Write a brief introduction (approximately one minute in length or about 150 words) about yourself for someone else to use in introducing you and your next speech. Mention at least three specific details that would help establish your competence, character, and/or charisma.

15.4 Persuading with Compliance-Gaining Strategies

Here are a few strategies for getting others to do as you wish (Marwell & Schmitt, 1967, 1990; Miller & Parks, 1982). Review the strategies and try to think of ways in which you might use these in persuasive speeches.

Promise. Pat promises to reward Chris if Chris complies with Pat's request.

Pat: I'll give you anything you want if you will just give me a divorce. You can have the house, the car, the stocks, the three kids; just give me my freedom.

Threat. Pat threatens to punish Chris for noncompliance.

Pat: If you don't give me a divorce, you'll never see the kids again.

Expertise. Pat promises that Chris will be rewarded for compliance (or punished for noncompliance) because of "the nature of things."

Pat: It will be a lot easier for everyone involved if you don't contest the divorce.

Self-feelings. Pat promises that Chris will feel better if Chris complies with Pat's request and worse if Chris does not.

Pat: You'll see. You'll feel a lot better if you donate blood during the blood drive.

Altercasting. Pat casts Chris in the role of the "good" person (or "bad" person) and argues that Chris should comply because a person with "good" qualities would comply while a person with "bad" qualities would not.

Pat: Any intelligent person would vote for additional funding for the homeless. *(Or):* Only a cruel and selfish tightwad would deny the homeless additional funding.

Esteem. Pat tells Chris that people will think more highly of Chris (relying on the need for approval of others) if Chris complies with Pat's request or people will think less if Chris does not comply.

Pat: Everyone will respond to your decision to volunteer at the homeless shelter. *(Or):* Everyone will think you're lazy and selfish if you don't volunteer your free time.

How would you use any one of these strategies to persuade others and accomplish each of the following five goals?

* to persuade a friend to cut classes and go to the movies
* to persuade a group to vote in favor of building a senior citizen center
* to persuade an audience to reaffirm their faith in the government
* to persuade an audience to manage their time more efficiently
* to persuade an audience to change their telephone company to Expand-a-Phone

15.5 Comparing Credibility

Credibility judgments are made both absolutely and comparatively. Thus, for example, you may judge the credibility of a witness at a trial or a newspaper reviewer or a local religious leader on the basis of some absolute standards you may have. But even in making this absolute judgment, you are probably also comparing this person with similar others and are probably positioning this person somewhere on a scale along with these others. Similarly, you may make a comparison credibility judgment of the three candidates running for Mayor and vote for the one to whom you attribute the highest credibility. So your judgment for Senator Smith is made not just absolutely but also in comparison with the others in the race.

This exercise emphasizes this concept of comparative credibility judgments and asks you to rank order the following people, roles, and institutions; use 3 for the highest credibility and 1 for the lowest.

After completing these ratings, consider, for example:

* What reasons did you use in constructing your rankings? That is, what qualities of credibility did you consider in your ranking? Why did you single out these particular qualities?
* Do any of your rankings illustrate the notion that credibility depends on the subject matter? Are there certain qualities that make you believe someone regardless of the subject matter?
* Which of the three characteristics of credibility (competence, character, charisma) would you consider the most important for: (a) a family physician, (b) a college professor, (c) a divorce lawyer, (d) a romantic-life partner, (e) a best friend?
* Are any of your credibility judgments gender-related? That is, do you attribute higher credibility to women on some issues and to men on others? Are any of your credibility judgments culture-related? That is, might you attribute high or low credibility ratings to people or products or institutions because of their culture?

1. Talk-show hosts on the causes of divorce
   _____ Oprah Winfrey
   _____ Phil Donahue
   _____ Geraldo Rivera
2. United States politicians on the role of the politician in today's world
   _____ Bill Clinton
   _____ Ross Perot
   _____ Newt Gingrich
3. Actors on the art of acting
   _____ Robert DeNiro
   _____ Meryl Streep
   _____ James Earl Jones
4. Periodicals on international business
   _____ *Money Magazine*
   _____ *The Wall Street Journal*
   _____ *The Washington Post*
5. Newscasters
   _____ Barbara Walters
   _____ Ted Koppel
   _____ Connie Chung
6. Speaker on minority rights
   _____ military speaker
   _____ religious speaker
   _____ political speaker
7. Authors of exercise books on the proper way to exercise
   _____ Richard Simmons
   _____ Jane Fonda
   _____ Arnold Schwarzenegger
8. Sources of accurate and up-to-date information on film and television stars
   _____ *Entertainment Tonight*
   _____ *The National Enquirer*
   _____ *People* Magazine
9. Scholar on the meaning of life
   _____ philosopher
   _____ minister/priest/rabbi
   _____ scientist
10. Professionals on giving buyers the most for their money
    _____ car dealer
    _____ lawyer
    _____ dentist

Glossary

A word is dead When it is said, Some say. I say it just begins to live.
—EMILY DICKINSON

Included here are definitions of the major concepts covered in *Essentials of Human Communication*. Also defined are additional terms that may logically be used throughout an introduction to communication course. For a more extensive glossary see Joseph A. DeVito, *The Communication Handbook: A Dictionary* (Harper-Collins 1986).

Abstraction A general concept derived from a class of objects; a part representing some whole.

Abstraction process The process by which a general concept is derived from specifics; the process of the senses perceiving some (never all) characteristics of an object, person, or event.

Accent The stress or emphasis placed on a syllable when pronounced.

Acculturation The processes by which contact with or exposure to another culture modifies or changes a person's culture.

Active listening A process of combining into some meaningful whole the listener's understanding of the speaker's total message—verbal and nonverbal, thoughts and feelings.

Adaptors Nonverbal behaviors that serve some kind of need and occur in their entirety when emitted in private or in public without being seen—for example, scratching one's head until the itch is eliminated.

Adjustment principle The principle of verbal interaction that claims communication can take place only to the extent that the communicating parties share the same system of signals.

Affect displays Movements of the facial area and body that convey emotional meaning such as anger, fear, and surprise.

Affinity-seeking strategies Behaviors designed to increase your interpersonal attractiveness and make another person like you more.

Agapic love Compassionate, self-giving, spiritual, and altruistic love.

Agenda setting A persuasive technique in which the speaker identifies his or her agenda as the significant issue and others as insignificant.

Allness The assumption that all can be known or is known about a given person, issue, object, or event.

Altercasting A statement that places the listener in a specific role for a specific purpose and asks that the listener consider the question or problem from this role's perspective.

Ambiguity The condition in which a word or phrase may be interpreted as having more than one meaning.

Appeals for the suspension of judgment A type of disclaimer in which the speaker asks listeners to delay their judgments until they have heard the entire message.

Appraisal interview A type of interview in which management or more experienced colleagues assess the interviewee's performance.

Arbitrariness The feature of human language that refers to the fact that there is no real or inherent relationship between a word's form and its meaning. If we do not know anything of a particular language, we could not examine a word's form and discover its meaning.

Argot A kind of sublanguage, generally of an underworld or criminal class, which is difficult and sometimes impossible for outsiders to understand.

Argumentativeness A willingness to argue for a point of view, to speak one's mind.

Articulation The physiological movements of the speech organs as they modify and interrupt the air stream emitted from the lungs.

Artifactual communication Communication that takes place through the wearing and arrangement of various artifacts—for example, clothing, jewelry, buttons, or the furniture in your house and its arrangement.

Assertiveness A willingness to stand up for your rights but with respect for the rights of others.

Assimilation The process of message distortion in which you rework messages to conform to your attitudes, prejudices, needs, and values.

Attention The process of responding to a stimulus or stimuli.

Attitude A predisposition to respond for or against an object.

Attraction The state or process by which you are drawn to another, by having a highly positive evaluation of that other person.

Attractiveness The degree to which one is perceived to be physically attractive and to possess a pleasing personality.

Attribution A process through which you attempt to understand the reasons or motivations for the behaviors of others (as well as your own).

Audience participation principle The principle of persuasion that states persuasion is achieved more effectively when the audience participates actively.

Authoritarian leader A group leader who determines group policies or makes decisions without consulting or securing agreement from members.

Avoidance An unproductive conflict strategy in which you take mental or physical flight from the actual conflict.

Bandwagon A persuasive technique in which the speaker tries to gain compliance by saying that "everyone is doing it" and urges you to jump on the bandwagon.

Barriers to communication Those factors (physical or psychological) that prevent or hinder effective communication.

Behavioral synchrony The similarity in the behavior, usually nonverbal, of two people. Generally, behavioral synchrony is an index of mutual liking.

Belief Confidence in the existence or truth of something; conviction.

Beltlining The unproductive conflict strategy in which one person hits another with insults or attacks below his or her level of tolerance—that is, below the belt.

Blame The unproductive conflict strategy in which the conflict's cause is attributed to the other person; the concentration on discovering who is the cause of a conflict or difficulty, and the avoidance of confronting the issues causing the conflict.

Blindering A misevaluation in which a label prevents you from seeing as much of an object as you might; a process of concentrating on the verbal level while neglecting nonverbal levels; a form of *intensional orientation*.

Blind self The part of yourself that contains information about you that is known to others but not to you.

Boundary markers Markers separating territories—such as the armrests in a theater that separate one person's space from another's.

Brainstorming A technique for generating ideas among people.

Breadth The number of topics about which individuals in a relationship communicate.

Cant A kind of sublanguage; the conversational language of any nonprofessional (usually noncriminal) group, which is generally understood only by members of that culture; distinguished from *argot*.

Card stacking A persuasive technique in which the speaker selects only the evidence and arguments that build a case and omits or distorts any contradictory evidence.

Central markers A type of marker which consists of an item placed in a territory to reserve it—for example, a jacket left on a library chair.

Certainty An attitude of closed-mindedness that creates a defensiveness among communication participants; opposed to provisionalism.

Channel The vehicle or medium through which signals pass.

Cherishing behaviors Small behaviors that you enjoy receiving from a relational partner—for example, a kiss, a smile, or a gift of flowers.

Chronemics The study of the communicative nature of time—how you treat and use time to communicate. Two general areas of chronemics are *cultural time* and *psychological time*.

Civil inattention Polite ignoring of others so as not to invade their privacy.

Clichés Overused phrases that have lost their novelty and part of their meaning, and that call attention to themselves because of their overuse.

Closed-mindedness An unwillingness to receive certain communication messages.

Code A set of symbols used to translate a message from one form to another.

Cognitive disclaimer A disclaimer in which the speaker seeks to confirm his or her cognitive capacity, for example, "You may think I'm drunk, but I'm as sober as anyone here."

Cohesiveness The property of togetherness. Applied to group communication situations, it refers to the mutual attractiveness among members; a measure of the extent to which individual group members work together.

Colloquy A small group format in which a subject is explored through the interaction of two panels (one asking and one answering questions) or through panel members responding to questions from audience members.

Communication (1) The process or act of communicating; (2) the actual message or messages sent and received; and (3) the study of the processes involved in the sending and receiving of messages. The term *communicology* (q.v.) is suggested for the third definition.

Communication network The pathways of messages; the organizational structure through which messages are sent and received.

Communicology The study of communication, particularly that subsection concerned with human communication.

Competence In communication, the rules of the more social or interpersonal dimensions of communication, often used to refer to those qualities that make for effectiveness in interpersonal communication.

Complementary relationship A relationship in which one person's behavior stimulates complementary behavior in the other; in complementary relationships, behavior differences are maximized.

Compliance-gaining strategies Tactics that are directed to gain the agreement of others; behaviors designed to persuade others to do as you wish.

Compliance-resisting strategies Tactics used to resist or refuse to do as asked. Nonnegotation, negotiation, identity management (positive or negative), and justification are four types of compliance-resisting strategies.

Confidence The absence of social anxiety; the communication of comfortableness in social situations; one of the qualities of effective interpersonal communication.

Confirmation A communication pattern that acknowledges another person's presence and communicates an acceptance of the person, the person's definition of self, and your relationship as defined or viewed by this other person. Opposed to disconfirmation.

Conflict A disagreement between or among individuals.

Connotation The feeling or emotional aspect of meaning, generally viewed as consisting of evaluative (for example, good/bad), potency (strong/weak), and activity (fast/slow) dimensions; the associations of a term. See *denotation*.

Congruence A condition in which both verbal and non-verbal behaviors reinforce each other.

Consensus A principle of attribution through which you attempt to establish whether other people react or behave in the same way as the person on whom you are now focusing. If this is so, you seek reasons for the behavior outside the individual; if the person is not acting in accordance with the general consensus, then you seek reasons that are internal to the individual.

Consistency (1) A perceptual process that influences you to maintain balance among your perceptions; a process that influences you to see what you expect to see and to be uncomfortable when your perceptions contradict your expectations; (2) a principle of attribution through which you attempt to establish whether a per-

son behaves the same way in similar situations. If there is consistency, you are likely to attribute the behavior to the person, to some internal motivation; if there is no consistency, you are likely to attribute the behavior to some external factor.

Contamination A form of territorial encroachment that renders another's territory impure.

Content and relationship dimensions A principle of communication that messages refer both to content (the world external to both speaker and listener) and to relationship dimensions (the relationship existing between the individuals interacting).

Context of communication The physical, social-psychological, cultural, and temporal environment in which communication takes place.

Controllability One of the factors you consider in judging whether or not a person is responsible for his or her behavior. If the person is in control, then you judge that he or she is responsible.

Conversational turns The changing (or maintaining) of the speaker or listener role during a conversation. These turns are generally signaled nonverbally. Speaker cues include turn-maintaining cues that allow the speaker to maintain the speaker role and turn-yielding cues that let the listener know the speaker wishes to give up the speaker role. Listener cues include turn-requesting cues that let the speaker know the listener would like to speak, turn-denying cues that let the speaker know the listener does not wish to say anything, and backchanneling cues that communicate agreement or involvement in the conversation without any desire to exchange speaker and listener roles.

Cooperation An interpersonal process by which individuals work together for a common end; the pooling of efforts to produce a mutually desired outcome.

Cooperation, principle of An implicit agreement between speaker and listener to cooperate in trying to understand what each is communicating.

Counseling interview A type of interview in which the interviewer tries to learn about the interviewee in an attempt to provide some form of guidance, advice, or insight.

Credentialing A type of disclaimer in which the speaker acknowledges that what is about to be said may reflect poorly on himself or herself, but he or she will say it nevertheless (usually for quite positive reasons).

Credibility The degree to which a receiver perceives the speaker to be believable.

Cultural time The communication function of time as regulated and perceived by a particular culture. Generally, the three types of cultural time are technical time, referring to precise scientific time; formal time, referring to a culture's divisions of time (for example, dividing a semester into 14 weeks); and informal time, referring to the loose use of such time terms as *immediately, soon,* and *right away.*

Cultural transmission The feature of language referring to the fact that human languages (at least in their outer surface form) are learned. Unlike various forms of animal language, which are innate, human languages are transmitted traditionally or culturally. This feature does not deny the possibility that certain language aspects may be innate.

Culture The relatively specialized life-style of a group of people—their values, beliefs, artifacts, ways of behaving, and ways of communicating—that is passed from one generation to the next.

Culture shock The psychological reaction you experience when placed in a culture very different from your own or from what you are used to.

Date An extensional device used to emphasize the notion of constant change and symbolized by a subscript: for example, John Smith$_{1972}$ is not John Smith$_{1996}$.

Decoder That which takes a message in one form (for example, sound waves) and translates it into another code (for example, nerve impulses) from which meaning can be formulated. In human communication, the decoder is the auditory mechanism; in electronic communication, the decoder is the telephone earpiece. See *encoder.*

Decoding The process of extracting a message from a code—for example, translating speech sounds into nerve impulses. See *encoding.*

Defensiveness An attitude of an individual or an atmosphere in a group characterized by threats, fear, and domination; messages evidencing evaluation, control, strategy, neutrality, superiority, and certainty are assumed to lead to defensiveness. Opposed to *supportiveness.*

Democratic leader A group leader who stimulates self-direction and self-actualization of members.

Denial One of the obstacles to expressing emotion; the process by which you deny your emotions to yourself or to others.

Denotation Referential meaning; the objective or descriptive meaning of a word. See *connotation.*

Depenetration A reversal of penetration; a condition where the breadth and depth of a relationship decreases.

Depth The degree to which the inner personality—the inner core of an individual—is penetrated in interpersonal interaction.

Dialogue A form of communication in which each person is both speaker and listener; communication characterized by involvement, concern, and respect for the other person; opposed to *monologue.*

Disconfirmation A communication pattern in which you ignore the other person as well as this person's communications. Opposed to *confirmation.*

Distinctiveness A principle of attribution in which you ask whether a person reacts in similar ways in different situations. If the person does, there is low distinctiveness and you are likely to conclude there is an internal cause or motivation for the behavior; if there is high distinctiveness, you are likely to seek the cause in some external factors.

Double-bind message A particular kind of contradictory message possessing the following characteristics: (1) The persons interacting share a relatively intense relationship; (2) two messages are communicated at the same time, demanding different and incompatible responses; (3) at least one person in the double bind cannot escape from the contradictory messages; (4) there is a threat of punishment for noncompliance.

Dyadic communication Two-person communication.

Dyadic consciousness An awareness of an interpersonal relationship or pairing of two individuals, distinguished from situations in which two individuals are together but do not perceive themselves as being a unit or twosome.

Dyadic effect The tendency for the behavior of one person in a dyad to influence a similar behavior in the other person. Used most often to refer to the reciprocal nature of self-disclosure.

Ear markers A type of marker consisting of identifying marks that indicate that the territory or object belongs to a particular person—for example, initials on an attaché case.

Effect The outcome or consequence of an action or behavior; communication is assumed always to have some effect.

Emblems Nonverbal behaviors that directly translate words or phrases—for example, the hand signs for "okay" and "peace."

Empathy A quality of effective interpersonal communication that refers to the ability to feel another's feelings as that person does and to communicate that similarity of feeling.

Employment interview A type of interview in which the interviewee is questioned to ascertain his or her suitability for a particular job.

Encoder Something that takes a message in one form (for example, nerve impulses) and translates it into another form (for example, sound waves). In human communication, the encoder is the speaking mechanism; in electronic communication the encoder is the telephone mouthpiece. See *decoder.*

Encoding The process of putting a message into a code—for example, translating nerve impulses into speech sounds. See *decoding*.

Enculturation The process of transmitting culture from one generation to another.

E-Prime A form of the language that omits the verb *to be* except when used as an auxiliary or in statements of existence. Designed to eliminate the tendency toward projection, or assuming that characteristics that one attributes to a person (for example, "Pat is brave") are actually in that person instead of in the observer's perception of that person.

Equality A quality of effective interpersonal communication in which personalities are recognized as equal, and both individuals are seen as worthwhile, valuable contributors to the total interaction.

Equity theory A theory claiming that you experience relational satisfaction when rewards and costs are equally distributed between the two persons in the relationship.

Erotic love A sexual, physical love; a love that is ego-centered and given because of an anticipated return.

Etc. (et cetera) An extensional device used to emphasize the notion of infinite complexity; since you can never know all about anything, any statement about the world or an event must end with an explicit or implicit etc.

Ethics The branch of philosophy that deals with the rightness or wrongness of actions; the study of moral values.

Ethnocentrism The tendency to see others and their behaviors through your cultural filters, often as distortions of your behaviors; the tendency to evaluate the values and beliefs of your culture more positively than those of another culture.

Euphemism A polite word or phrase substituted for a more direct, but taboo or otherwise offensive, term.

Evaluation The process of placing a value on some person, object, or event.

Exit interview A type of interview designed to establish why an employee (the interviewee) is leaving the organization.

Expressiveness A quality of effective interpersonal communication referring to the skill of communicating genuine involvement in the interpersonal interaction.

Extemporaneous speech A speech that is thoroughly prepared and organized in detail and in which certain aspects of style are predetermined.

Extensional devices Linguistic devices proposed by Alfred Korzybski for keeping language as a more accurate means for talking about the world. The extensional devices include the etc., date, and index (the working devices); and the hyphen and quotes (the safety devices).

Extensional orientation A point of view in which the primary consideration is given to the world of experience and only secondary consideration is given to the labels. See *intensional orientation*.

Fact-inference confusion A misevaluation in which you make an inference, regard it as a fact, and act upon it as if it were a fact.

Factual statement A statement made by the observer after observation, and limited to the observed. See *inferential statement*.

Fear appeal The appeal to fear to persuade an individual or group of individuals to believe or to act in a certain way.

Feedback Information given back to the source. Feedback may come from the source's own messages (as when you hear what you are saying) or from the receiver(s) in the form of applause, yawning, puzzled looks, questions, letters to a newspaper editor, increased or decreased magazine subscriptions, and so forth.

Feedforward Information sent prior to the regular messages telling the listener something about future messages.

Field of experience The total of your experiences, which influences your ability to communicate. In some communication views, two people can communicate only to the extent that their fields of experience overlap.

Force An unproductive conflict strategy in which you attempt to win an argument by physical force or threats of force.

Forum A small group format in which group members answer questions from the audience; often follows a symposium.

Free information Information about a person that you can see or that he or she drops into the conversation, and that can serve as a topic of conversation.

Friendship An interpersonal relationship between two persons that is mutually productive, established and maintained through perceived mutual free choice, and characterized by mutual positive regard.

General Semantics The study of the relationships among language, thought, and behavior.

Glittering generality A persuasive technique in which the speaker tries to gain acceptance of any idea by associating it with things the audience values highly.

Granfallon The tendency of people to see themselves as constituting a cohesive and like-minded group because they are given a label.

Group A collection of individuals related to each other with some common purpose and structure.

Groupthink A tendency in some groups to make agreement among members more important than the issues at hand.

Gunnysacking An unproductive conflict strategy in which you store up grievances against the other person and unload them during a conflict encounter.

Haptics Touch or tactile communication.

Hedge A type of disclaimer in which the speaker disclaims the importance of what he or she is about say.

Heterosexist language Language that assumes all people are heterosexual and thereby denigrates lesbians and gay men.

Hidden self The part of yourself that contains information about you that is known to you but unknown to and hidden from others.

Home field advantage The increased power that comes from being in your own territory.

Home territories Territories for which individuals have a sense of intimacy and over which they exercise control—for example, a child's clubhouse.

Hyphen An extensional device used to illustrate that what may be separated verbally may not be separable on the event or nonverbal level; although you may talk about body and mind as if they were separable, in reality they are better referred to as body-mind.

Illustrators Nonverbal behaviors that accompany and literally illustrate the verbal messages—for example, upward motions that accompany the verbalization "It's up there."

I-messages Messages in which the speaker accepts responsibility for personal thoughts and behaviors; messages in which the speaker's point of view is stated explicitly. Opposed to *you-messages*.

Immediacy A quality of effective interpersonal communication referring to a feeling of togetherness and oneness with another person.

Implicit personality theory A personality theory that each individual maintains, complete with rules or systems, through which others are perceived.

Impromptu speech A speech given without any prior preparation.

Inclusion, principle of In verbal interaction, the principle that all members should be a part of (included in) the interaction.

Index An extensional device used to emphasize the notion of nonidentity (no two things are the same) and symbolized by a subscript—for example, politician$_1$ is not politician$_2$.

Indiscrimination A misevaluation caused by categorizing people, events, or objects as members of a particular class and responding to specific members only as members of that class; a failure to recognize each individual as an individual and unique; a failure to apply the index.

Inevitability A communication principle referring to the fact that communication cannot be avoided; all behavior in an interactional setting is communication.

Inferential statement A statement that anyone can make at anytime, and is not limited to the observed. See *factual statement*.

Information That which reduces uncertainty.

Information overload That condition in which the amount of information is too great to be dealt with effectively; or the number or complexity of messages is so great that the individual or organization is not able to deal with them.

Informative interview A type of interview in which the interviewer asks the interviewee, usually a person of some reputation and accomplishment, questions designed to elicit his or her views, predictions, perspectives, and the like on specific topics.

In-group talk Talk about a subject or in a vocabulary that only certain people understand, often in the presence of someone who does not belong to this group and therefore does not understand.

Inoculation principle A persuasion principle that states persuasion will be more difficult to achieve when previously challenged beliefs and attitudes are attacked, because the individual has built up defenses in a manner similar to biological inoculation.

Insulation A reaction to territorial encroachment in which you erect some sort of barrier between yourself and the invaders.

Intensional orientation A point of view in which you give primary consideration to the way things are labeled and only secondary consideration (if any) to the world of experience. See *extensional orientation*.

Interaction management A quality of effective interpersonal communication referring to the ability to control the interaction to the satisfaction of both participants.

Interaction process analysis A content analysis method that classifies messages into four general categories: social emotional positive, social emotional negative, attempted answers, and questions.

Intercultural communication Communication between persons of different cultures or who have different cultural beliefs, values, or ways of behaving.

Interethnic communication Communication between members of different ethnic groups.

International communication Communication between nations.

Interpersonal communication Communication between two persons or among a small group and distinguished from public or mass communication; communication of a personal nature and distinguished from impersonal communication; communication between or among intimates or those involved in a close relationship; often, intrapersonal, dyadic, and small group communication in general.

Interpersonal conflict A conflict or disagreement between two persons; a conflict within an individual caused by his or her relationships with other people.

Interpersonal perception The perception of people; the processes through which you interpret and evaluate people and their behavior.

Interracial communication Communication between members of different races.

Interview The interpersonal communication in which two persons interact largely by question-and-answer format to achieve specific goals.

Intimate distance The shortest proxemic distance, ranging from touching to 6 to 18 inches.

Intrapersonal communication Communication with yourself.

Invasion The unwarranted entrance into another's territory that changes the territory's meaning. See *territorial encroachment*.

Irreversibility A communication principle referring to the fact that communication cannot be reversed; once something has been communicated, it cannot be uncommunicated.

Jargon A sublanguage, often of a professional class, which is unintelligible to individuals not belonging to the group; the "shoptalk" of the group.

Johari window A visualization of one's four selves, based on the information about the self that is known or unknown to self and others.

Kinesics The study of the communicative dimension of face and body movements.

Laissez-faire leader A group leader who allows the group to develop, progress, or make mistakes on its own.

Leadership That quality by which one individual directs or influences the thoughts and/or the behaviors of others. See *laissez-faire leader*, *democratic leader*, and *authoritarian leader*.

Leveling A process of message distortion in which a message is repeated, but the number of details is reduced, some details are omitted entirely, and some details lose their complexity.

Level of abstraction The relative distance of a term or statement from the actual perception; a low-order abstraction would be a description of the perception, whereas a high-order abstraction would consist of inferences about inferences about descriptions of a perception.

Linguistic collusion A reaction to in which you speak in a language unknown to the intruders and thus separate yourself from them.

Listening The process of receiving, understanding, remembering, evaluating, and responding to a message.

Looking-glass self The self-concept that results from the image of yourself that others reveal to you.

Loving An interpersonal process in which you feel a closeness, caring, warmth, and an excitement for another person.

Ludus love Love as a game, as fun; the position that love is not to be taken seriously and is to be maintained only as long as it remains interesting and enjoyable.

Magnitude of change principle The persuasion principle that the greater and more important the change desired by the speaker, the more difficult it will be to achieve.

Manic love Love characterized by extreme highs and extreme lows; obsessive love.

Manipulation An unproductive conflict strategy that avoids open conflict; instead, attempts are made to divert the conflict by being especially charming and getting the other person into a noncombative frame of mind.

Manuscript speech A speech designed to be read verbatim from a script.

Markers Devices you use to signal others that a particular territory belongs to you; three types of markers are usually distinguished: boundary, central, and ear markers.

Mass communication Communication addressed to an extremely large audience, mediated by audio and/or visual transmitters, and processed by gatekeepers before transmission.

Matching hypothesis The assumption that persons date and mate people who are approximately the same in terms of physical attractiveness.

Meaningfulness A perception principle that refers to your assumption that people's behavior is sensible, stems from some logical antecedent, and is consequently meaningful rather than meaningless.

Mere exposure hypothesis The theory that repeated or prolonged exposure to a stimulus may change the attitude toward the stimulus object, generally in the direction of increased positiveness.

Message Any signal or combination of signals that serve as stimuli for a receiver.

Metacommunication Communication about communication.

Metalanguage Language used to talk about language.

Metamessage A message that communicates about another message.

Micromomentary expressions Extremely brief movements that are not consciously perceived and that are thought to reveal a person's real emotional state.

Mindfulness and mindlessness States of relative awareness. In a mindful state, you are aware of the logic and rationality of your behaviors and the logical connections among elements. In a mindless state, you are unaware of this logic and rationality.

Minimization An unproductive conflict strategy in which you make light of the other person's disagreements or of the whole conflict.

Model A physical or verbal representation of an object or process.

Monologue A communication form in which one person speaks and the other listens: there is no real interaction among participants; opposed to dialogue.

Motivated sequence An organizational pattern for arranging the information in a discourse to motivate an audience to respond positively to your purpose.

Name calling A persuasive technique in which the speaker gives an idea a derogatory name.

Negative feedback Feedback that serves a corrective function by informing the source that his or her message is not being received in the way intended. Negative feedback serves to redirect the source's behavior. Looks of boredom, shouts of disagreement, letters critical of newspaper policy, and the teacher's instructions on how to better approach a problem are examples of negative feedback. See *positive feedback.*

Neutrality A response pattern lacking personal involvement; encourages defensiveness; opposed to *empathy.*

Noise Anything that distorts or interferes with the message in the communication system. Noise is present to the extent that the message sent differs from the message received. Physical noise interferes with the physical transmission of the signal or message—for example, the static in radio transmission. *Psychological noise* refers to distortions created by such processes as prejudice and biases. *Semantic noise* refers to distortions created by a failure to understand each other's words.

Nonallness An attitude or point of view which recognizes that you can never know all about anything and that what you know, say, or hear is only a part of what there is to know, say, or hear.

Nonnegotiation An unproductive conflict strategy in which the individual refuses to discuss the conflict or disagreement, or to listen to the other person.

Nonverbal communication Communication without words.

Olfactory communication Communication by smell.

Openness A quality of effective interpersonal communication that refers to the willingness (1) to engage in appropriate self-disclosure, (2) to react honestly to incoming stimuli, and (3) to own your feelings and thoughts.

Open self The part of yourself that contains information about you that is known to you and to others.

Oral style The style of spoken discourse that, when compared with written style, consists of shorter, simpler, and more familiar words; more qualification, self-reference terms, allness terms, verbs and adverbs; and more concrete terms and terms indicative of consciousness of projection—for example, "as I see it."

Other-orientation A quality of effective interpersonal interaction referring to your ability to adapt to the other person's needs and desires during the interpersonal encounter.

Other talk Talk about the listener or some third party.

Owning feelings The process by which you take responsibility for your feelings instead of attributing them to others.

Panel or round table A small group format in which participants seated together speak without any set pattern.

Paralanguage The vocal (but nonverbal) aspect of speech. Paralanguage consists of voice qualities (for example, pitch range, resonance, tempo), vocal characterizers (for example, laughing or crying, yelling or whispering), vocal qualifiers (for example, intensity, pitch height), and vocal segregates (for example, "uh-uh" meaning "no," or "sh" meaning "silence").

Passive listening Listening that is attentive and supportive but occurs without talking or directing the speaker in any nonverbal way; also used negatively to refer to inattentive and uninvolved listening.

Pauses Silent periods in the normally fluent stream of speech. Pauses are of two major types: filled pauses (interruptions in speech that are filled with such vocalizations as "-er" or "-um") and unfilled pauses (silences of unusually long length).

Perception The process of becoming aware of objects and events from the senses.

Perceptual accentuation A process that leads you to see what you expect and want to see; for example, you see people you like as better looking and smarter than people you do not like.

Personal distance The second-shortest proxemic distance, ranging from 18 inches to 4 feet.

Personal rejection An unproductive conflict strategy in which the individual withholds love and affection, and seeks to win the argument by getting the other person to break down under this withdrawal.

Persuasion The process of influencing attitudes and behavior.

Persuasion interview A type of interview in which the interviewer attempts to change the interviewee's attitudes or behavior.

Phatic communion Primarily social communication designed to open the communication channels rather than to communicate something about the external world; "Hello," and "How are you?" in everyday interaction are common examples.

Pitch The highness or lowness of the vocal tone.

Plain folks A persuasive technique in which the speaker identifies himself or herself and the proposal with the audience.

Polarization A form of fallacious reasoning that considers only the two extremes; also referred to as "either-or" thinking.

Positive feedback Feedback that supports or reinforces behavior along the same lines as it is proceeding—for example, applause during a speech. See *negative feedback*.

Positiveness A quality of effective interpersonal communication referring to the communication of positiveness toward the self, the other, and the communication situation generally, and willingness to stroke the other person as appropriate.

Pragmatic love Practical love; love based on compatibility; love that seeks a relationship that will satisfy each person's important needs and desires.

Primacy effect The condition by which what comes first exerts greater influence than what comes later.

Primary affect displays The communication of the six primary emotions: happiness, surprise, fear, anger, sadness, and disgust/contempt. See *affect displays*.

Process Ongoing activity; nonstatic; communication is referred to as a process to emphasize that it is always changing and in motion.

Productivity The feature of language that makes possible the creation and understanding of novel utterances. With human language you can talk about matters you have never talked about before, and understand utterances you have never heard before. Also referred to as *openness*.

Progressive differentiation A relational problem caused by the exaggeration or intensification of differences or similarities between individuals.

Projection A psychological process whereby you attribute your characteristics or feelings to others; often used to refer to the process whereby you attribute your faults to others.

Pronouncements Authoritative statements that imply that the speaker is in a position of authority and the listener is in a childlike or learner role.

Pronunciation The production of syllables or words according to some accepted standard, such as in a dictionary.

Provisionalism An attitude of open-mindedness that leads to the creation of supportiveness; opposite of certainty.

Proxemics The study of the communicative function of space; the study of how people unconsciously structure their space—the distance between people in their interactions, the organization of space in homes and offices, and even the design of cities.

Proximity As a principle of perception, the tendency to perceive people or events that are physically close as belonging together or representing some unit; physical closeness; one of the qualities influencing interpersonal attraction.

Public communication Communication in which the source is one person and the receiver is an audience of many persons.

Public distance The longest proxemic distance, ranging from 12 to more than 25 feet.

Public speaking Communication that occurs when a speaker delivers a relatively prepared, continuous address in a specific setting to a relatively large audience.

Punctuation of communication The breaking up of continuous communication sequences into short sequences with identifiable beginnings and endings, or stimuli and responses.

Pupillometrics The study of communication through changes in the size of the pupils of the eyes.

Psychological time The importance that you place on past time, in which particular regard is shown for the past and its values and methods; present time, in which you live in the present for the enjoyment of the present; and future time, in which you devote your energies to planning for the future.

Purr words Highly positive words that express the speaker's feelings rather than refer to any objective reality; opposite of *snarl words*.

Pygmalion effect The condition in which you make a prediction and then proceed to fulfill it; a type of self-fulfilling prophecy but one that refers to others and to your evaluation of others rather than to yourself.

Quotes An extensional device used to emphasize that a word or phrase is being used in a special sense and should therefore be given special attention.

Racist language Language that denigrates a particular race.

Rapid fading The evanescent or impermanent quality of speech signals.

Rate The speed with which you speak, generally measured in words per minute.

Receiver Any person or thing that takes in messages. Receivers may be individuals listening to or reading a message, a group of persons hearing a speech, a television audience, or a machine that stores information.

Recency effect The condition in which what comes last (that is, most recently) exerts greater influence than what comes first.

Recurrence, principle of The principle of verbal interaction that individuals will repeat many times and in many ways who they are, how they see themselves, and in general what they think is important and significant.

Redefinition An unproductive conflict strategy in which you give the conflict another definition so that the conflict's source disappears.

Redundancy A message's quality that makes it totally predictable and therefore lacking in information. A message of zero redundancy would be completely unpredictable; a message of 100 percent redundancy would be completely predictable. All human languages contain some degree of built-in redundancy, generally estimated at about 50 percent.

Reflexiveness The language feature that refers to the fact that human language can be used to refer to itself; that is, you can talk about your talk and create a metalanguage—a language for talking about language.

Regulators Nonverbal behaviors that regulate, monitor, or control another person's communications.

Reinforcement or packaging, principle of The principle of verbal interaction holding that in most interactions, messages are transmitted simultaneously through a number of different channels that normally reinforce each other; messages come in packages.

Rejection A response to an individual that rejects or denies the validity of an individual's self-view.

Relational communication Communication between or among intimates or those in close relationships; term used by some theorists as synonymous with interpersonal communication.

Relational deterioration The stage of a relationship during which the connecting bonds between the partners weaken and the partners begin drifting apart.

Resemblance As a principle of perception, the tendency to perceive people or events that are similar in appearance as belonging together.

Response Any bit of overt or covert behavior.

Rigid complementarity The inability to change the type of relationship between yourself and another even though the individuals, the context, and many other variables have changed.

Role The part an individual plays in a group; an individual's function or expected behavior.

Selective exposure principle The persuasion principle holding that listeners will actively seek out information that supports their opinions, beliefs, attitudes, and values and actively avoid information that contradicts them.

Self-acceptance Your satisfaction with yourself, your virtues and vices, and your abilities and limitations.

Self-attribution A process through which you seek to account for and understand the reasons and motivations for your behavior.

Self-concept Your self-evaluation; self-appraisal.

Self-disclosure The process of revealing something significant about yourself to another individual or to a group—something that would not normally be known by them.

Self-fulfilling prophecy The situation in which you make a prediction or prophecy and fulfill it yourself—for example, expecting a class to be boring and then fulfilling this expectation by perceiving it as boring.

Self-monitoring The manipulation of the image that you present to others in your interpersonal interactions. High self-monitors carefully adjust their behaviors on the basis of feedback from others so that they can project the desired image. Low self-monitors do not consciously manipulate their images.

Self-serving bias A bias that operates in the self-attribution process that leads you to take credit for the positive consequences and to deny responsibility for the negative consequences of your behavior.

Self-talk Talk about oneself.

Semantics The area of language study concerned with meaning.

Sexist language Language derogatory to one sex, generally women.

Sharpening A process of message distortion in which the details of messages, when repeated, are crystallized and heightened.

Shyness The discomfort and uneasiness in interpersonal situations.

Signal and noise, relativity of The principle of verbal interaction that holds that what is signal (meaningful) and what is noise (interference) is relative to the communication analyst, the participants, and the context.

Signal reaction A conditioned response to a signal; the response is immediate rather than delayed.

Silence The absence of vocal communication; often misunderstood to refer to the absence of any and all communication.

Silencers Unproductive conflict strategies that literally silence the other person—for example, crying, or feigning emotional or physical disturbance.

Similarity A principle of attraction holding that you are attracted to qualities similar to those you possess and to people who are similar to you; opposed to complementarity.

Sin licenses A disclaimer in which the speaker acknowledges that he or she is about to break some normally operative rule; the speaker asks for a license to sin (that is, to break a social or interpersonal rule).

Slang The language used by special groups that is not considered proper by the general society; the language made up of the argot, cant, and jargon of various groups.

Small group communication Communication among a collection of individuals, few enough in number that all may interact with relative ease as both senders and receivers, whose members are related to each other by some common purpose and some degree of organization or structure.

Snarl words Highly negative words that express the speaker's feelings rather than refer to any objective reality; opposite of *purr words*.

Social comparison processes The processes by which you compare yourself (for example, your abilities, opinions, and values) with others and then assess and evaluate yourself.

Social distance The third proxemic distance, ranging from 4 to 12 feet; the distance at which business is usually conducted.

Social exchange theory A theory claiming that you develop and maintain relationships in which the rewards or profits are greater than the costs.

Social penetration theory A theory concerned with relationship development from the superficial to intimate levels and from few to many areas of interpersonal interaction.

Source Any person or thing that creates messages. A source may be an individual speaking, writing, or gesturing or a computer solving a problem.

Speaker apprehension A fear of engaging in communication transactions; a decrease in the frequency, strength, and likelihood of engaging in communication transactions.

Speech Messages utilizing a vocal-auditory channel.

Spontaneity The communication pattern in which you verbalize what you are thinking without attempting to develop strategies for control; encourages supportiveness; opposed to strategy.

Static evaluation An orientation that fails to recognize that constant change characterizes the world; an attitude that sees people and events as fixed rather than constantly changing.

Status The relative level you occupy in a hierarchy; status always involves a comparison, and thus your status is relative only to another's status. In this culture, occupation, financial position, age, and educational level are significant determinants of status.

Stereotype In communication, a fixed impression of a group of people through which you then perceive specific individuals; stereotypes are most often negative (Martians are stupid, uneducated, and dirty), but may also be positive (Venusians are scientific, industrious, and helpful).

Storge love Love based on companionship, similar interests, and mutual respect; love that is lacking in great emotional intensity.

Strategy The use of some plan to control other members of a communication interaction that guides your communications; encourages defensiveness.

Stroking Verbal or nonverbal acknowledgment of another person; positive stroking consists of compliments and rewards and, in general, behaviors you look forward to or take pride in receiving; negative stroking is punishing and includes criticisms, expressions of disapproval, or even physical punishment.

Sublanguage A variation from the general language, used by a particular group of people; argot, cant, and jargon are particular sublanguages.

Superiority A point of view or attitude that assumes that others are not equal to you; encourages defensiveness; opposed to *equality*.

Supportiveness A quality of effective interpersonal communication in which you are descriptive rather than evaluative, spontaneous rather than strategic, and provisional rather than certain.

Symmetrical relationship A relationship between two or more persons in which one's behavior stimulates the same type of behavior in the other person(s). Examples include situations in which one person's anger encourages or stimulates anger in another person, or in which one person's critical comment leads the other to respond in like manner.

Symposium A small group format in which each member delivers a relatively prepared talk on some aspect of the topic. Often combined with a *forum*.

Taboo Forbidden; culturally censored. Taboo language is frowned upon by "polite society." Themes and specific words may be considered taboo—for example, death, sex, certain forms of illness, and various words denoting sexual activities and excretory functions.

Tactile communication Communication by touch; communication received by the skin.

Territorial encroachment The trespassing on, use of, or appropriation of one's territory by another. The major types of territorial encroachment are violation, invasion, and contamination.

Territoriality A possessive or ownership reaction to an area of space or to particular objects.

Testimonial A persuasive technique in which the speaker uses the authority or image of some positively evaluated person to gain your approval or of some negatively evaluated person to gain your rejection.

Theory A general statement or principle applicable to a number of related phenomena.

Thesis The main assertion of a message—for example, the theme of a public speech.

Touch avoidance The tendency to avoid touching and being touched by others.

Transactional The relationship among elements in which each influences and is influenced by each other element; communication is a transactional process, since no element is independent of any other element.

Transfer A persuasive technique in which the speaker associates his or her idea with something you respect to gain your approval or with something you dislike to gain your rejection.

Turf defense The most extreme reaction to territorial encroachment through which you defend your territory and expel the intruders.

Two-valued orientation A point of view in which you see events or evaluate questions in terms of two values—for example, right or wrong, good or bad. Often referred to as the fallacy of polarization.

Universal of communication A feature of communication common to all communication acts.

Unknown self That part of you that contains information about you that is unknown to you and to others, but that is inferred to exist on the basis of various projective tests, slips of the tongue, dream analyses, and the like.

Value Relative worth of an object; a quality that makes something desirable or undesirable; ideals or customs about which you have emotional responses, whether positive or negative.

Violation Unwarranted use of another's territory. See *territorial encroachment*.

Voice qualities Aspects of paralanguage, specifically: pitch range, vocal lip control, glottis control, pitch control, articulation control, rhythm control, resonance, and tempo.

Volume The relative loudness of the voice.

Withdrawal (1) A reaction to territorial encroachment in which you leave the territory. (2) A tendency to close yourself off from conflicts rather than confront the issues.

Written style See *oral style*.

You-messages Messages in which the speaker denies responsibility for his or her thoughts and behaviors; messages that attribute what is really the speaker's perception to another person; messages of blame; opposed to *I-messages*.

Bibliography

> It is the vice of scholars to suppose that there is no knowledge in the world but that of books. Do you avoid it, I conjure you; and thereby save yourself the pain and mortification that must otherwise ensue from finding out your mistake continually!
> —WILLIAM HAZLITT

Adams, Dennis M., & Hamm, Mary E. (1990). *Cooperative learning: Critical thinking and collaboration across the curriculum.* Springfield, IL: Charles C. Thomas.

Adams, Linda with Lenz, Elinor. (1989). *Be your best.* New York: Putnam.

Adler, Ronald B. (1977). *Confidence in communication: A guide to assertive and social skills.* New York: Holt, Rinehart and Winston.

Adler, Ronald B., Rosenfeld, Lawrence B., & Towne, Neil. (1992). *Interplay: The process of interpersonal communication* (4th ed.) New York: Holt, Rinehart and Winston.

Akinnaso, F. Niyi. (1982). On the differences between spoken and written language. *Language and Speech, 25,* Part 2, 97–125.

Albrecht, Karl. (1980). *Brain power: Learn to improve your thinking skills.* Englewood Cliffs, NJ: Prentice-Hall/Spectrum.

Alessandra, Tony. (1986). How to listen effectively, *Speaking of Success* (Video Tape Series). San Diego, CA: Levitz Sommer Productions.

Altman, Irwin, & Taylor, Dalmas. (1973). *Social penetration: The development of interpersonal relationships.* New York: Holt, Rinehart and Winston.

Andersen, Peter A., and Leibowitz, Ken. (1978). The development and nature of the construct of touch avoidance. *Environmental Psychology and Nonverbal Behavior, 3,* 89–106.

Argyle, Michael. (1988). *Bodily communication* (2nd ed). New York: Methuen.

Argyle, Michael, & Henderson, M. (1985). *The anatomy of relationships: And the rules and skills needed to manage them successfully.* London: Heinemann.

Argyle, Michael, & Ingham, R. (1972). Gaze, mutual gaze and distance. *Semiotica, 1,* 32–49.

Aronson, Elliot, Wilson, Timothy D., & Akert, Robin M. (1994). *Social psychology: The heart and the mind.* New York: HarperCollins.

Asch, Solomon. (1946). Forming impressions of personality. *Journal of Abnormal and Social Psychology, 41,* 258–290.

Authier, Jerry, & Gustafson, Kay. (1982). Microtraining: Focusing on specific skills. In Eldon K. Marshall, P. David Kurtz, & Associates, *Interpersonal helping skills: A guide to training methods, programs, and resources* (pp. 93–130). San Francisco: Jossey-Bass.

Axtell, Roger E. (1990). *Do's and taboos of hosting international visitors.* New York: Wiley.

Axtell, Roger E. (1991). *Do's and taboos of public speaking: How to get those butterflies flying in formation.* New York: Wiley.

Axtell, Roger E. (1993). *Do's and taboos around the world,* 3rd ed. New York: Wiley.

Aylesworth, Thomas G., & Aylesworth, Virginia L. (1978). *If you don't invade my intimate zone or clean up my water hole, I'll breathe in your face, blow on your neck, and be late for your party.* New York: Condor.

Ayres, Joe. (1986). Perceptions of speaking ability: An explanation for stage fright. *Communication Education, 35,* 275–287.

Ayres, Joe, Ayres, Debbie M., & Sharp, Diane. (1993). A progress report on the development of an instrument to measure communication apprehension in employment interviews. *Communication Research Reports, 10,* 87–94.

Bach, George R., & Deutsch, Ronald M. (1979). *Stop! You're driving me crazy.* New York: Berkley.

Bach, George R., & Wyden, Peter. (1968). *The intimate enemy.* New York: Avon.

Bales, Robert F. (1950). *Interaction process analysis: A method for the study of small groups.* Cambridge, MA: Addison-Wesley.

Barker, Larry L. (1990). *Communication,* 5th ed. Englewood Cliffs, NJ: Prentice-Hall.

Barker, Larry, Edwards, R., Gaines, C., Gladney, K., & Holley, F. (1980). An investigation of proportional time spent in various communication activities by college students. *Journal of Applied Communication Research, 8,* 101–109.

Barna, LaRay M. (1985). Stumbling blocks in intercultural communication. In Larry A. Samovar & Richard E. Porter (Eds.), *Intercultural communication: A reader* (4th ed.). (pp. 330–338). Belmont, CA: Wadsworth.

Barnlund, Dean C. (1970). A transactional model of communication. *Language behavior: A book of readings in communication*, compiled by J. Akin, A. Goldberg, G. Myers, and J. Stewart. The Hague: Mouton.

Barnlund, Dean C. (1975). Communicative styles in two cultures: Japan and the United States. In A. Kendon, R. M. Harris, & M. R. Key (Eds.), *Organization of behavior in face-to-face interaction*. The Hague, Netherlands: Mouton.

Barnlund, Dean C. (1989). *Communicative styles of Japanese and Americans*. Belmont, CA: Wadsworth.

Baron, Robert A., & Byrne, Donn. (1984). *Social psychology: Understanding human interaction* (4th ed.). Boston: Allyn & Bacon.

Bartholomew, Kim. (1990). Avoidance of intimacy: An attachment perspective. *Journal of Social and Personal Relationships, 7*, 147–178.

Bavelas, Janet Beavin. (1990). Can one not communicate? Behaving and communicating: A reply to motley. *Western Journal of Speech Communication, 54*, 593–602.

Baxter, Leslie A. (1983). Relationship disengagement: An examination of the reversal hypothesis. *Western Journal of Speech Communication, 47*, 85–98.

Baxter, Leslie A., & Wilmot, William W. (1984). "Secret tests": Social strategies for acquiring information about the state of the relationship. *Human Communication Research, 11*, 171–201.

Beach, Wayne A. (1990–1991). Avoiding ownership for alleged wrongdoings. *Research on Language and Social Interaction, 24*, 1–36.

Beatty, Michael J. (1988). Situational and predispositional correlates of public speaking anxiety. *Communication Education, 37*, 28–39.

Beck, A. T. (1988). *Love is never enough*. New York: Harper & Row.

Beebe, Steven A., & Masterson, John T. (1994). *Communicating in small groups: Principles and practices* (4th ed.). New York: HarperCollins.

Beier, Ernst. (1974, October). How we send emotional messages. *Psychology Today*, 53–56.

Bell, Robert A., & Buerkel-Rothfuss, Nancy L. (1990). S(he) loves me, s(he) loves me not: Predictors of relational information-seeking in courtship and beyond. *Communication Quarterly, 38*, 64–82.

Bell, Robert A., & Daly, John A. (1984). The affinity-seeking function of communication. *Communication Monographs, 51*, 91–115.

Benne, Kenneth D. & Sheats, Paul. (1948). Functional roles of group members. *Journal of Social Issues, 4*, 41–49.

Bennis, Warren, & Nanus, Burt. (1985). *Leaders: The strategies for taking charge*. New York: Harper & Row.

Berg, John H., & Archer, Richard L. (1983). The disclosure-liking relationship. *Human Communication Research, 10*, 269–281.

Berger, Charles R., & Calabrese, Richard J. (1975). Some explorations in initial interaction and beyond: Toward a theory of interpersonal communication. *Human Communication Research, 1*, 99–112.

Berger, Charles R., & Bradac, James J. (1982). *Language and social knowlege: Uncertainty in interpersonal relations*. London: Edward Arnold.

Berger, Charles R., & Chaffee, Steven H. (Eds.). (1987). *Handbook of communication science*. Newbury Park, CA: Sage.

Berman, J. J., Murphy-Berman, V., & Singh, P. (1985). Cross-cultural similarities and differences in perceptions of fairness. *Journal of Cross-Cultural Psychology, 16*, 55–67.

Bernstein, W. M., Stephan, W. G., & Davis, M. H. (1979). Explaining attributions for achievement: A path analytic approach. *Journal of Personality and Social Psychology, 37*, 1810–1821.

Berscheid, Ellen, & Walster, Elaine Hatfield. (1978). *Interpersonal attraction* (2nd ed.). Reading, MA: Addison-Wesley.

Bettinghaus, Erwin P., & Cody, Michael J. (1994). *Persuasive communication* (5th ed.). New York: Holt, Rinehart and Winston.

Birdwhistell, Ray L. (1970). *Kinesics and context: Essays on body motion communication*. New York: Ballantine.

Blumstein, Philip, & Schwartz, Pepper. (1983). *American couples: Money, work, sex*. New York: Morrow.

Bochner, Arthur. (1978). On taking ourselves seriously: An analysis of some persistent problems and promising directions in interpersonal research. *Human Communication Research, 4*, 179–191.

Bochner, Arthur. (1984). The functions of human communication in interpersonal bonding. In Carroll C. Arnold & John Waite Bowers (eds.), *Handbook of rhetorical and communication theory*. Boston: Allyn & Bacon.

Bochner, Arthur, & Kelly, Clifford. (1974). Interpersonal competence: Rationale, philosophy, and implementation of a conceptual framework. *Communication Education, 23*, 279–301.

Bok, Sissela. (1978). *Lying: Moral choice in public and private life*. New York: Pantheon.

Bok, Sissela. (1983). *Secrets*. New York: Vintage.

Borisoff, Deborah, & Merrill, Lisa. (1985). *The power to communicate: Gender differences as barriers*. Prospect Heights, IL: Waveland.

Bosmajian, Haig. (1974). *The language of oppression*. Washington, DC: Public Affairs Press.

Bourland, D. David, Jr. (1965–66). A linguistic note: Writing in E-prime. *General Semantics Bulletin*, 32 & 33.

Boyer, Ernest. (1978). *Vital speeches of the day*, 44.

Brody, Jane F. (1991, April 28). How to foster self-esteem. *New York Times Magazine* 26–27.

Brownell, Judi. (1987). Listening: The toughest management skill. *Cornell Hotel and Restaurant Administration Quarterly, 27*, 64–71.

Brougher, Toni. (1982). *A way with words*. Chicago, IL: Nelson-Hall.

Bruneau, Tom. (1985). The time dimension in intercultural communication. In Larry A. Samovar & Richard E. Porter (Eds.), *Intercultural communication: A reader* (4th ed.) (pp. 280–289). Belmont, CA: Wadsworth.

Bruneau, Tom. (1990). Chronemics: The study of time in human interaction. In Joseph A. DeVito and Michael L. Hecht (Eds.), *The nonverbal communication reader* (pp. 301–311). Prospect Heights, IL: Waveland.

Bugental, J., & Zelen, S. (1950). Investigations into the 'Self-Concept,' I. The W-A-Y technique. *Journal of Personality, 18*, 483–498.

Burgoon, Judee K., & Hale, Jerold L. (1988). Nonverbal expectancy violations: Model elaboration and application to immediacy behaviors. *Communication Monographs, 55*, 58–79.

Burgoon, Judee K., Buller, David B., & Woodall, W. Gill. (1989). *Nonverbal communication: The unspoken dialogue*. New York: Harper & Row.

Butler, Pamela E. (1981). *Talking to yourself: Learning the language of self-support*. New York: Harper & Row.

Camden, Carl, Motley, Michael T., & Wilson, Ann. (1984). White lies in interpersonal communication: A taxonomy and preliminary investigation of social motivations. *Western Journal of Speech Communication, 48*, 309–325.

Cappella, Joseph N. (1987). Interpersonal communication: Definitions and fundamental questions. In Charles R. Berger & Steven H. Chaffee (Eds.). *Handbook of communication science* (pp. 184–238). Newbury Park, CA: Sage.

Cappella, Joseph N. (1993). The facial feedback hypothesis in human interaction: Review and speculation. *Journal of Language and Social Psychology, 12*, 13–29.

Cate, R., Henton, J., Koval, J., Christopher, R., & Lloyd, S. (1982). Premarital abuse: A social psychological perspective. *Journal of Family Issues, 3*, 79–90.

Cialdini, Robert T. (1984). *Influence: How and why people agree to things*. New York: Morrow.

Clark, Herbert. (1974). The power of positive speaking. *Psychology Today, 8*, 102, 108–111.

Clement, Donald A., & Frandsen, Kenneth D. (1976). On conceptual and empirical treatments of feedback in human communication. *Communication Monographs, 43*, 11–28.

Cline, M. G. (1956). The influence of social context on the perception of faces. *Journal of Personality, 2*, 142–185.

Cody, Michael J. (1982). A typology of disengagement strategies and an examination of the role intimacy, reaction to inequity, and relational problems play in strategy selection. *Communication Monographs, 49*, 148–170.

Cody, Michael J., Marston, Peter J., & Foster, Myrna. (1984). Paralinguistic and verbal leakage of deception as a function of attempted control and timing of questions. In R. M. Bostrom (Ed.), *Communication yearbook 7* (pp. 464–490). Newbury Park, CA: Sage.

Collier, Mary Jane. (1991). Conflict competence within African, Mexican, and Anglo American friendships. In Stell Ting-Toomey & Felipe Korzenny (Eds.), *Cross-cultural interpersonal communication* (pp. 132–154). Newbury Park, CA: Sage.

Cook, Mark. (1971). *Interpersonal perception*. Baltimore: Penguin.

Cooley, Charles Horton. (1922). *Human nature and the social order* (Rev. ed.). New York: Scribner's.

Cozby, Paul. (1973). Self-disclosure: A literature review. *Psychological Bulletin, 79*, 73–91.

Cragan, John F., & Wright, David W. (1986). *Communication in small group discussions: A case study approach* (2nd ed.). St. Paul, MN: West.

Daly, John A., Richmond, Virginia P., & Leth, S. (1979). Social communicative anxiety and the personal selective process: Testing the similarity effect in selection decisions. *Human Communication Research, 6*, 18–32.

Davis, Murray S. (1973). *Intimate relations*. New York: Free press.

Davitz, Joel R. (Ed.). (1964). *The communication of emotional meaning*. New York: McGraw-Hill.

Deal, James E., & Wampler, Karen Smith. (1986). Dating violence: The primacy of previous experience. *Journal of Social and Personal Relationships, 3*, 457–471.

deBono, Edward. (1987). *The six thinking hats*. New York: Penguin.

Derlega, Valerian J., Winstead, Barbara A., Wong, Paul T. P., & Greenspan, Michael. (1987). Self-disclosure and relationship development: An attributional analysis. In Michael E. Roloff & Gerald R. Miller (Eds.), *Interpersonal processes: New directions in communication research* (pp. 172–187). Newbury Park, CA: Sage.

Derlega, Valerian J., Winstead, Barbara, Wong, Paul T. P., & Hunter, Susan. (1985). Gender effects in an initial encounter: A case where men exceed women in disclosure. *Journal of Social and Personal Relationships, 2*, 25–44.

DeStephen, R., & Hirokawa, R. (1988). Small group consensus: Stability of group support of the decision, task process, and group relationships. *Small Group Behavior, 19*, 227–239.

Deturck, Mark A. (1987). When communication fails: Physical aggression as a compliance-gaining strategy. *Communication Monographs, 54,* 106–112.

DeVito, Joseph A. (1965). Comprehension factors in oral and written discourse of skilled communicators. *Communication Monographs, 32,* 124–128.

DeVito, Joseph A. (1969). Some psycholinguistic aspects of active and passive sentences. *Quarterly Journal of Speech, 55,* 401–406.

DeVito, Joseph A. (1974). *General semantics: Guide and workbook* (Rev. ed.). DeLand, FL: Everett/Edwards.

DeVito, Joseph A. (1976). Relative ease in comprehending yes/no questions. In Jane Blankenship & Herman G. Stelzner (Eds.), *Rhetoric and communication* (pp. 143–154). Urbana: University of Illinois Press.

DeVito, Joseph A. (1981). *The psychology of speech and language: An introduction to psycholinguistics.* Washington, DC: University Press of America.

DeVito, Joseph A. (1986). *The communication handbook: A dictionary.* New York: Harper & Row.

DeVito, Joseph A. (1986). Teaching as relational development. In Jean Civikly (Ed.), *Communicating in college classrooms: New directions for teaching and learning* No. 26 (pp. 51–60). San Francisco, CA: Jossey-Bass.

DeVito, Joseph A., & Hecht, Michael L. (Eds.). (1990). *The nonverbal communication reader.* Prospect Heights, IL: Waveland Press.

Diener, E., & Walbom, M. (1976). Effects of self-awareness on antinormative behavior. *Journal of Research in Personality, 10,* 107–111.

Dindia, Kathryn, & Baxter, Leslie A. (1987). Strategies for maintaining and repairing marital relationships. *Journal of Social and Personal Relationships, 4,* 143–158.

Dindia, Kathryn, & Fitzpatrick, Mary Anne. (1985). Marital communication: Three approaches compared. In Steve Duck & Daniel Perlman (Eds.), *Understanding personal relationships: An interdisciplinary approach* (pp. 137–158). Newbury Park, CA: Sage.

Dodd, Carley H. (1982). *Dynamics of intercultural communication.* Dubuque, IA: Brown.

Dreyfuss, Henry. (1971). *Symbol sourcebook.* New York: McGraw-Hill.

Driskell, James, Olmstead, Beckett, & Salas, Eduardo. (1993). Task cues, dominance cues, and influence in task groups. *Journal of Applied Psychology, 78,* 51–60.

Duck, Steve. (1986). *Human relationships.* Newbury Park, CA: Sage.

Duck, Steve, & Gilmour, Robin. (Eds.). (1981). *Personal relationships. 1: Studying personal relationships.* New York: Academic.

Duncan, Barry L., & Rock, Joseph W. (1991). *Overcoming relationship impasses.* New York: Plenum.

Egan, Gerard. (1970). *Encounter: Group processes for interpersonal growth.* Belmont, CA: Brooks/Cole.

Ekman, Paul. (1965). Communication through nonverbal behavior: A source of information about an interpersonal relationship. In S. S. Tomkins & C. E. Izard (Eds.), *Affect, cognition and personality.* New York: Springer.

Ekman, Paul. (1975). The universal smile: Face muscles talk every language. *Psychology Today, 9,* 35–39.

Ekman, Paul. (1985). *Telling lies: Clues to deceit in the marketplace, politics, and marriage.* New York: W. W. Norton.

Ekman, Paul, & Friesen, Wallace V. (1969). The repertoire of nonverbal behavior: Categories, origins, usage, and coding. *Semiotica, 1,* 49–98.

Ekman, Paul, Friesen, Wallace V., & Ellsworth, Phoebe. (1972). *Emotion in the human face: Guidelines for research and an integration of findings.* New York: Pergamon.

Ekman, Paul, Friesen, Wallace V., & Tomkins, S. S. (1971). Facial affect scoring technique: A first validity study. *Semiotica, 3,* 37–58.

Ellis, Albert. (1988). *How to stubbornly refuse to make yourself miserable about anything, Yes anything.* Secaucus, NJ: Lyle Stuart.

Ellis, Albert, & Harper, Robert A. (1975). *A new guide to rational living.* Hollywood: Wilshire.

Elmes, Michael B., & Gemmill, Gary. (1990). The psychodynamics of mindlessness and dissent in small groups. *Small Group Research, 21,* 28–44.

Ennis, Robert H. (1987). A taxonomy of critical thinking dispositions and abilities. In Joan Boykoff Baron & Robert J. Sternberg (Eds.), *Teaching thinking skills: Theory and practice* (pp. 9–26). New York: Freeman.

Exline, R. V., Ellyson, S. L., & Long, B. (1975). Visual behavior as an aspect of power role relationships. In P. Pliner, L. Krames, & T. Alloway (Eds.), *Nonverbal communication of aggression.* New York: Plenum.

Fay, Allen. (1988). *PQR: Prescription for a Quality Relationship.* New York: Multimodal.

Festinger, Leon. (1954). A theory of social comparison processes. *Human Relations, 7,* 117–140.

Fiske, Susan T., & Taylor, Shelley E. (1984). *Social cognition.* Reading, MA: Addison-Wesley.

Fitzpatrick, Mary Anne. (1983). Predicting couples' communication from couples' self-reports. In R. N. Bostrom (Ed.), *Communication yearbook 7* (pp. 49–82). Newbury Park, CA: Sage.

Floyd, James J. (1985). *Listening: A practical approach.* Glenview, IL: Scott, Foresman.

Folger, Joseph P., & Poole, Marshall Scott. (1984). *Working through conflict: A communication perspective.* Glenview, IL: Scott, Foresman.

Fraser, Bruce. (1990). Perspectives on politeness. *Journal of Pragmatics, 14*, 219–236.

Furnham, Adrian, & Bochner, Stephen. (1986). *Culture shock: Psychological reactions to unfamiliar environments.* New York: Methuen.

Galvin, Kathleen, & Brommel, Bernard J. (1991). *Family communication: Cohesion and change* (3rd ed.). Glenview, IL: Scott, Foresman.

Garner, Alan. (1981). *Conversationally speaking.* New York: McGraw-Hill.

Gelles, R. (1981). The myth of the battered husband. In R. Walsh & O. Pocs (Eds.), *Marriage and family 81/82.* Dushkin: Guildford.

Gelles, R., & Cornell, C. (1985). *Intimate violence in families.* Newbury Park, CA: Sage.

Gibb, Cecil A. (1969). Leadership. In G. Lindsey & E. Aronson (Eds.), *The handbook of social psychology: Vol. 4* (2nd ed., pp. 205–282). Reading, MA: Addison-Wesley.

Gibb, Jack. (1961). Defensive communication. *Journal of Communication, 11*, 141–148.

Glucksberg, Sam, & Danks, Joseph H. (1975). *Experimental psycholinguistics: An introduction.* Hillsdale, NJ: Erlbaum.

Goffman, Erving. (1967). *Interaction ritual: Essays on face-to-face behavior.* New York: Pantheon.

Goffman, Erving. (1971). *Relations in public: Microstudies of the public order.* New York: Harper Colophon.

Goleman, Daniel. (1992, October 27). Voters assailed by unfair persuasion. *New York Times*, pp. C1, C8.

Gonzalez, Alexander, & Zimbardo, Philip G. (1985, March). Time in perspective. *Psychology Today, 19*, 20–26.

Goodall, D. B., & Goodall, H. L. Jr. (1982). The employment interview: A selective review of the literature with implications for communication research. *Communication Quarterly, 30*, 116–123.

Gordon, Thomas. (1975). *P.E.T.: Parent effectiveness training.* New York: New American Library.

Goss, Blaine, Thompson, M., & Olds, S. (1978). Behavioral support for systematic desensitization for communication apprehension. *Human Communication Research, 4*, 158–163.

Gottman, John. (1994, March/April). What makes marriage work? *Psychology Today, 27*, 38–43, 68.

Graham, Jean Ann, Bitti, Pio Ricci, & Argyle, Michael. (1975). A cross-cultural study of the communication of emotion by facial and gestural cues. *Journal of Human Movement Studies, 1*, 68–77.

Graham, Jean Ann, & Argyle, Michael. (1975). The effects of different patterns of gaze combined with different facial expressions, on impression formation. *Journal of Movement Studies, 1*, 178–182.

Gratus, Jack. (1988). *Successful interviewing: How to find and keep the best people.* New York: Penguin.

Gronbeck, Bruce E., McKerrow, Raymie E., Ehninger, Douglas, & Monroe, Alan H. (1994). *Principles and types of speech communication* (12th ed.) New York: HarperCollins.

Gross, Larry. (1991). The contested closet: The ethics and politics of outing. *Critical Studies in Mass Communication, 8* (September), 352–388.

Gross, Ronald. (1991). *Peak learning.* Los Angeles: Jeremy P. Tarcher.

Gu, Yueguo. (1990). Polite phenomena in modern Chinese. *Journal of Pragmatics, 14*, 237–257.

Gudykunst, William B., & Kim, Young Yun. (1992), eds. *Readings on communication with strangers: An approach to intercultural communication.* New York: McGraw-Hill.

Gudykunst, William B., & Ting-Toomey, Stella with Chua, Elizabeth. (1988). *Culture and interpersonal communication.* Thousand Oaks, CA: Sage.

Gudykunst, William B., & Kim, Young Yun. (1992). *Communicating with strangers: An approach to intercultural communication* (2nd ed.). New York: McGraw-Hill.

Gudykunst, William B. (Ed.). (1983). *Intercultural communication theory: Current perspectives.* Thousand Oaks, CA: Sage.

Gudykunst, William B. (1994). *Bridging differences: Effective intergroup communication* (2nd ed.). Thousand Oaks, CA: Sage.

Gudykunst, William B. (1989). Culture and the development of interpersonal relationships. In J. A. Andersen (Ed.), *Communication Yearbook: Vol. 12* (pp. 315–354). Thousand Oaks, CA: Sage.

Gupta, U., & Singh, P. (1982). Exploratory studies in love and liking and types of marriages. *Indian Journal of Applied Psychology, 19*, 92–97.

Hackman, Michael Z., & Johnson, Craig E. (1991). *Leadership: A communication perspective.* Prospect Heights, IL: Waveland Press.

Hall, Edward T. (1959). *The silent language.* Garden City, NY: Doubleday.

Hall, Edward T. (1963). System for the notation of proxemic behavior. *American Anthropologist, 65*, 1003–1026.

Hall, Edward T. (1966). *The hidden dimension.* Garden City, NY: Doubleday.

Hall, Edward T., & Hall, Mildred Reed. (1987). *Hidden differences: Doing business with the Japanese.* New York: Doubleday.

Hall, Judith A. (1984). *Nonverbal sex differences.* Baltimore: Johns Hopkins.

Hambrick, Ralph S. (1991). *The management skills builder: Self-directed learning strategies for career development.* New York: Praeger.

Hamlin, Sonya. (1988). *How to talk so people listen.* New York: Harper & Row.

Haney, William. (1973). *Communication and organizational behavior: Text and cases* (3rd ed.). Homewood, IL: Irwin.

Hart, Roderick P., & Burks, Don M. (1972). Rhetorical sensitivity and social interaction. *Communication Monographs, 39,* 75–91.

Hart, Roderick P., Carlson, Robert E., & Eadie, William F. (1980). Attitudes toward communication and the assessment of rhetorical sensitivity. *Communication Monographs, 47,* 1–22.

Hatfield, Elaine, & Traupman, Jane. (1981). Intimate relationships: A perspective from equity theory. In Steve Duck & Robin Gilmour (Eds.), *Personal Relationships. 1: Studying Personal Relationships* (pp. 165–178). New York: Academic.

Hayakawa, S. I., & Hayakawa, Alan R. (1990). *Language in thought and action* (5th ed.). New York: Harcourt Brace Jovanovich.

Hecht, Michael L. (1978a). The conceptualization and measurement of interpersonal communication satisfaction. *Human Communication Research, 4,* 253–264.

Hecht, Michael L. (1978b). Toward a conceptualization of communication satisfaction. *Quarterly Journal of Speech, 64,* 47–62.

Hecht, Michael L., & Ribeau, Sidney. (1984). Ethnic communication: A comparative analysis of satisfying communication. *International Journal of Intercultural Relations, 8,* 135–151.

Heinrich, Robert, et al. (1983). *Instructional media: The new technologies of instruction.* New York: Wiley.

Heiskell, Thomas L., & Rychlak, Joseph F. (1986). The therapeutic relationship: Inexperienced therapists' affective preference and empathic communication. *Journal of Social and Personal Relationships, 3,* 267–274.

Hendrick, Clyde, & Hendrick, Susan. (1990). A relationship—specific version of the love attitudes scale. In J. W. Heulip (Ed.), *Handbook of Replication Research in the Behavioral and Social Sciences* [Special Issue]. *Journal of Social Behavior and Personality, 5,* 239–254.

Henley, Nancy M. (1977). *Body politics: Power, sex, and nonverbal communication.* Englewood Cliffs, NJ: Prentice-Hall.

Hersey, Paul, & Blanchard, Ken. (1988). *Management of organizational behavior: Utilizing human resources.* Englewood Cliffs, NJ: Prentice-Hall.

Hess, Ekhard H. (1975). *The tell-tale eye.* New York: Van Nostrand Reinhold.

Hess, Ursula, Kappas, Arvid, McHugo, Gregory J., Lanzetta, John T., et al. (1992). The facilitative effect of facial expression of the self-generation of emotion. *International Journal of Psychophysiology, 12,* 251–265.

Hewitt, John, & Stokes, Randall. (1975). Disclaimers. *American Sociological Review, 40,* 1–11.

Hickson, Mark L., & Stacks, Don W. (1989). *NVC: Nonverbal communication: Studies and applications* (2nd ed.). Dubuque, IA: Wm. C. Brown.

Hocker, Joyce L., & Wilmot, William W. (1985). *Interpersonal conflict* (2nd ed.). Dubuque, IA: Wm. C. Brown.

Hopper, Robert, Knapp, Mark L., & Scott, Lorel. (1981). Couples' personal idioms: Exploring intimate talk. *Journal of Communication, 31,* 23–33.

Hupka, Ralph. (1981). Cultural determinants of jealousy. *Alternative Lifestyles, 4,* 310–356.

Infante, Dominic A. (1988). *Arguing constructively.* Prospect Heights, IL: Waveland.

Infante, Dominic A., & Rancer, Andrew S. (1982). A conceptualization and measure of argumentativeness. *Journal of Personality Assessment, 46,* 72–80.

Infante, Dominic A., Rancer, Andrew S., & Womack, Deanna F. (1993). *Building communication theory* (2nd ed.). Prospect Heights, IL: Waveland.

Infante, Dominic A., Riddle, Bruce L., Horvath, Cary L., & Tumlin, S. A. (1992). Verbal aggressiveness: Messages and reasons. *Communication Quarterly, 40,* 116–126.

Infante, Dominic A., Sabourin, T. C., Rudd, J. E., & Shannon, E. A. (1990). Verbal aggression in violent and nonviolent marital disputes. *Communication Quarterly, 38,* 361–371.

Infante, Dominic A., & Wigley, C. J. (1986). Verbal aggressiveness: An interpersonal model and measure. *Communication Monographs, 53,* 61–69.

Insel, Paul M., & Jacobson, Lenore F. (Eds.). (1975). *What do you expect? An inquiry into self-fulfilling prophecies.* Menlo Park, CA: Cummings.

Jaksa, James A., & Pritchard, Michael S. (1994). *Communication ethics: Methods of analysis* (2nd ed.). Belmont, CA: Wadsworth.

Janis, Irving. (1983). *Victims of group thinking: A psychological study of foreign policy decisions and fiascoes* (2nd ed.). Boston: Houghton Mifflin.

Jensen, J. Vernon. (1985). Perspectives on nonverbal intercultural communication. In Larry Samovar & Richard E. Porter (Eds.), *Intercultural communication: A reader* (4th ed.) (pp. 256–272). Belmont, CA: Wadsworth.

Johannesen, Richard L. (1991). *Ethics in human communication* (4th ed.). Prospect Heights, IL: Waveland Press.

Johnson, C. E. (1987). An introduction to powerful and powerless talk in the classroom. *Communication Education, 36,* 167–172.

Jones, E. E., et al. (1984). *Social stigma: The psychology of marked relationships.* New York: W. H. Freeman.

Jones, E. E., & Davis, K. E. (1965). From acts to dispositions: The attribution process in person perception. In L. Berkowitz (Ed.), *Advances in experimental social psychology* (Vol. 2) (pp. 219–266). New York: Academic.

Jones, Stanley. (1986). Sex differences in touch communication. *Western Journal of Speech Communication, 50,* 227–241.

Jones, Stanley, & Yarbrough, A. Elaine. (1985). A naturalistic study of the meanings of touch. *Communication Monographs, 52,* 19–56.

Jourard, Sidney M. (1971a). *Self-disclosure.* New York: Wiley.

Jourard, Sidney M. (1971b). *The transparent self* (Rev. ed.). New York: Van Nostrand Reinhold.

Jourard, Sidney M. (1966). An exploratory study of body-accessibility. *British Journal of Social and Clinical Psychology, 5,* 221–231.

Jourard, Sidney M. (1968). *Disclosing man to himself.* New York: Van Nostrand Reinhold.

Joyner, Russell. (1993). An auto-interview on the need for E-prime. *Etc.: A Review of General Semantics, 50,* 317–325.

Kanner, Bernice. (1989, April 3). Color schemes. *New York Magazine,* 22–23.

Kelley, H. H. (1967). Attribution theory in social psychology. In D. Levine (Ed.), *Nebraska symposium on motivation* (pp. 192–240). Lincoln: University of Nebraska Press.

Kelley, H. H. (1973). The process of causal attribution. *American Psychologist, 28,* 107–128.

Kelley, H. H. (1979). *Personal relationships: Their structures and processes.* Hillsdale, NJ: Erlbaum.

Kelley, H. H., & Thibaut, J. W. (1978). *Interpersonal relations: A theory of interdependence.* New York: Wiley/Interscience.

Kemp, Jerrold E., & Dayton, Deane K. (1985). *Planning and producing instructional media* (5th ed.). New York: Harper & Row.

Kennedy, C. W., & Camden, C. T. (1988). A new look at interruptions. *Western Journal of Speech Communication, 47,* 45–58.

Keshavarz, Mohammad Hossein. (1988). Forms of address in post-revolutionary Iranian Persian: A sociolinguistic analysis. *Language in Society, 17,* 565–575.

Kesselman-Turkel, Judi, & Peterson, Franklynn. (1982). *Note-taking made easy.* Chicago: Contemporary Books.

Kim, Hyun J. (1991). Influence of language and similarity on initial intercultural attraction. In Stella Ting-Toomey & Felipe Korzenny (Eds.), *Cross-cultural interpersonal communication* (pp. 213–229). Newbury Park, CA: Sage.

Kim, Young Yun. (Ed.). (1986). *Interethnic communication: Current research.* Newbury Park, CA: Sage.

Kim, Young Yun. (1988). Communication and acculturation. In Larry A. Samovar & Richard E. Porter (Eds.), *Intercultural communication: A reader* (5th ed.) (pp. 344–354). Belmont, CA: Wadsworth.

Kim, Young Yun. (1991). Intercultural communication competence. In Stella Ting-Toomey and Felipe Korzenny (Eds.), *Cross-cultural interpersonal communication* (pp. 259–275). Newbury Park, CA: Sage.

Kim, Young Yun & Gudykunst, William B. (Eds.). (1988). *Theories in intercultural communication.* Newbury Park, CA: Sage.

Kleinke, Chris L. (1978). *Self-perception: The psychology of personal awareness.* San Francisco, CA: Freeman.

Kleinke, Chris L. (1986). *Meeting and understanding people.* New York: W. H. Freeman.

Knapp, Mark L. (1984). *Interpersonal communication and human relationships.* Boston: Allyn & Bacon.

Knapp, Mark L., & Hall, Judith. (1992). *Nonverbal communication in human interaction* (3rd ed.). New York: Harcourt Brace Jovanovich.

Knapp, Mark L., Hart, Roderick P., Friedrich, Gustav W., & Shulman, Gary M. (1973). The rhetoric of goodbye: Verbal and nonverbal correlates of human leave-taking. *Communication Monographs, 40,* 182–198.

Knapp, Mark L., & Vangelista, Anita L. (1992). *Interpersonal communication and human relationships* (2nd ed.). Boston: Allyn & Bacon.

Kochman, Thomas. (1981). *Black and white: Styles in conflict.* Chicago: University of Chicago Press.

Komarovsky, M. (1964). *Blue collar marriage.* New York: Random House.

Korda, M. (1975). *Power! How to get it, how to use it.* New York: Ballantine.

Korzybski, A. (1933). *Science and sanity.* Lakeville, CT.: The International Non-Aristotelian Library.

Kramarae, Cheris. (1981). *Women and men speaking.* Rowley, MA: Newbury House.

Kramer, Ernest. (1963). Judgment of personal characteristics and emotions from nonverbal properties. *Psychological Bulletin, 60,* 408–420.

Krivonos, P. D., & Knapp, M. L. (1975). Initiating communication: What do you say when you say hello? *Central States Speech Journal, 26,* 115–125.

Laing, Ronald D., Phillipson, H., & Lee, A. Russell (1966). *Interpersonal perception.* New York: Springer.

Langer, Ellen J. (1978). Rethinking the role of thought in social interaction. In J. H. Harvey, W. J. Ickes, & R. F. Kidd (Eds.), *New directions in attribution research* (vol. 2) (pp. 35–38). Hillsdale, NJ: Erlbaum.

Langer, Ellen J. (1989). *Mindfulness.* Reading, MA: Addison-Wesley.

Larsen, Randy J., Kasimatis, Margaret, & Frey, Kurt. (1992). Facilitating the furrowed brow: An unobtrusive test of the facial feedback hypothesis applied to unpleasant affect. *Cognition and Emotion, 6,* 321–338.

Larson, Charles U. (1992). *Persuasion: Reception and responsibility* (6th ed.). Belmont, CA: Wadsworth.

Leathers, Dale G. (1986). *Successful nonverbal communication: Principles and applications.* New York: Macmillan.

Lederer, William J. (1984). *Creating a good relationship.* New York: Norton.

Lederman, Linda. (1990). Assessing educational effectiveness: The focus group interview as a technique for data collection. *Communication Education, 39,* 117–127.

Lee, Alfred McClung, & Lee, Elizabeth Briant. (1972). *The fine art of propaganda.* San Francisco: International Society for General Semantics.

Lee, John Alan. (1973). Styles of loving. *Psychology Today, 8,* 43–51.

Lee, John Alan. (1976). *The colors of love.* New York: Bantam.

Leeds, Dorothy. (1988). *Powerspeak.* New York: Prentice Hall.

Leung, Kwok. (1988). Some determinants of conflict avoidance. *Journal of Cross Cultural Psychology, 19,* 125–136.

LeVine, R., & Bartlett, K. (1984). Pace of life, punctuality and coronary heart disease in six countries. *Journal of Cross-Cultural Psychology, 15,* 233–255.

Lewis, David. (1989). *The secret language of success.* New York: Carroll and Graf.

Light, Walter F. (1984, July 15). *Vital speeches of the day, 50.*

Littlejohn, Stephen W. (1992). *Theories of human communication* (4th ed.). Belmont, CA: Wadsworth.

Littlejohn, Stephen W., & Jabusch, David M. (1987). *Persuasive transactions.* Glenview, IL.: Scott, Foresman.

Luft, Joseph. (1969). *Of human interaction.* Palo Alto, CA: Mayfield.

Luft, Joseph. (1970). *Group processes: An introduction to group dynamics* (2nd ed.). Palo Alto, CA: Mayfield.

Luft, Joseph. (1984). *Group processes: An introduction to group dynamics* (3rd ed.). Palo Alto, CA: Mayfield Publishing.

Lujansky, H., & Mikula, G. (1983). Can equity theory explain the quality and stability of romantic relationships? *British Journal of Social Psychology, 22,* 101–112.

Lukens, J. (1978). Ethnocentric speech. *Ethnic Groups, 2,* 35–53.

Lumsden, Gay, & Lumsden, Donald. (1993). *Communicating in groups and teams.* Belmont, CA: Wadsworth.

Lustig, Myron W., & Koester, Jolene. (1993). *Intercultural competence: Interpersonal communication across cultures.* New York: HarperCollins.

Lyman, Stanford M., & Scott, Marvin B. (1967). Territoriality: A neglected sociological dimension. *Social Problems, 15,* 236–249.

MacLachlan, John. (1979, November). What people really think of fast talkers. *Psychology Today,* 113–117.

Malandro, Loretta A., Barker, Larry, & Barker, Deborah Ann. (1989). *Nonverbal communication* (2nd ed.). New York: Random House.

Malinowski, Bronislaw. (1923). The problem of meaning in primitive languages. In C. K. Ogden & I. A. Richards (Eds.), *The meaning of meaning* (pp. 296–336). New York: Harcourt Brace Jovanovich.

Marshall, Evan. (1983). *Eye language: Understanding the eloquent eye.* New York: New Trend.

Marshall, Linda L., & Rose, Patricia. (1987). Gender, stress and violence in the adult relationships of a sample of college students. *Journal of Social and Personal Relationships, 4,* 299–316.

Marwell, Gerald, & Schmitt, David R. (1967). Dimensions of compliance-gaining behavior: An empirical analysis. *Sociometry, 39,* 350–364.

Marwell, Gerald, & Schmitt, David R. (1990). An introduction. In James Price (Ed.) *Seeking compliance: The production of interpersonal influence messages* (pp. 3–5). Scottsdale, AZ: Gorsuch Scarisbrick.

Matsumoto, David (1991). Cultural influences on facial expressions of emotion. *Southern Communication Journal, 56,* 128–137.

Maynard, Harry E. (1963). How to become a better premise detective. *Public Relations Journal, 19,* 20–22.

McCroskey, James C. (1986). *An introduction to rhetorical communication* (5th ed.). Englewood Cliffs, NJ: Prentice-Hall.

McCroskey, James C., & Wheeless, Lawrence. (1976). *Introduction to human communication.* Boston: Allyn & Bacon.

McGill, Michael E. (1985). *The McGill Report on male intimacy.* New York: Harper & Row.

McLaughlin, Margaret L. (1984). *Conversation: How talk is organized.* Newbury Park, CA: Sage.

McLaughlin, Margaret L., Cody, Michael L., & Robey, C. S. (1980). Situational influences on the selection of strategies to resist compliance-gaining attempts. *Human Communication Research, 1,* 14–36.

Medley, H. Anthony. (1978). *Sweaty palms: The neglected art of being interviewed.* Belmont, CA: Wadsworth Lifetime Learning Publications.

Mehrabian, Albert. (1976). *Public places and private spaces.* New York: Basic Books.

Merton, Robert K. (1957). *Social theory and social structure.* New York: Free Press.

Midooka, Kiyoski (1990). Characteristics of Japanese style communication. *Media Culture and Society, 12*, 47–49.

Miller, Gerald R. (1978). The current state of theory and research in interpersonal communication. *Human Communication Research, 4*, 164–178.

Miller, Gerald R., & Parks, Malcolm R. (1982). Communication in dissolving relationships. In Steve Duck (Ed.), *Personal relationships 4: Dissolving personal relationships.* New York: Academic Press.

Moghaddam, Fathali M., Taylor, Donald M., & Wright, Stephen C. (1993). *Social psychology in cross-cultural perspective.* New York: W. H. Freeman.

Molloy, John. (1975). *Dress for success.* New York: P. H. Wyden.

Molloy, John. (1977). *The woman's dress for success book.* Chicago: Follet.

Molloy, John. (1981). *Molloy's live for success.* New York: Bantam.

Montagu, Ashley. (1971). *Touching: The human significance of the skin.* New York: Harper & Row.

Morris, Desmond. (1977). *Manwatching: A field guide to human behavior.* New York: Abrams.

Morris, Desmond, Collett, Peter, Marsh, Peter, & O'Shaughnessy, Marie. (1979). *Gestures: Their origins and distribution.* New York: Stein and Day.

Motley, Michael T. (1990a). On whether one can(not) not communication: An examination via traditional communication postulates. *Western Journal of Speech Communication, 54*, 1–20.

Motley, Michael T. (1990b). Communication as interaction: A reply to Beach and Bavelas. *Western Journal of Speech Communication, 54*, 613–623.

Mullen, Brian, Salas, Edwardo, & Driskell, James. (1989). Salience, motivation, and artifact as contributions to the relation between participation rate and leadership. *Journal of Experimental Social Psychology, 25*, 545–559.

Naifeh, Steven, & Smith, Gregory White. (1984). *Why can't men open up? Overcoming men's fear of intimacy.* New York: Clarkson N. Potter.

Naisbitt, John. (1984). *Megatrends: Ten new directions transforming our lives.* New York: Warner.

Napier, Rodney W., & Gershenfeld, Matti K. (1981). *Groups: Theory and experience* (2nd ed.). Boston: Houghton Mifflin.

Neugarten, Bernice. (1979). Time, age, and the life cycle. *American Journal of Psychiatry, 136*, 887–894.

Ng, Sik Hung, & Bradac, James J. (1993). *Power in language: Verbal communication and social influence.* Thousand Oaks, CA: Sage.

Nickerson, Raymond S. (1987). Why teach thinking? In Joan Boykoff Baron & Robert J. Sternberg. (Eds.), *Teaching thinking skills: Theory and practice* (pp. 27–37). New York: W. H. Freeman.

Nierenberg, Gerald, & Calero, Henry. (1973). *Metatalk.* New York: Simon and Schuster.

Oberg, Kalervo. (1960). Cultural shock: Adjustment to new cultural environments. *Practical Anthropology, 7*, 177–182.

O'Hair, Mary John, Cody, Michael J., & O'Hair, Dan. (1991). The impact of situational dimensions on compliance-resisting strategies: A comparison of methods. *Communication Quarterly, 39*, 226–240.

Osborn, Alex. (1957). *Applied imagination* (rev. ed.). New York: Scribners.

Patton, Bobby R., Giffin, Kim, & Patton, Eleanor Nyquist. (1989). *Decision-making group interaction* (3rd ed.). New York: Harper & Row.

Patton, Michael Quinn. (1980). *Qualitative evaluation methods.* Thousand Oaks, CA: Sage.

Pearce, Barnett, & Sharp, Stewart M. (1973). Self-disclosing communication *Journal of Communication, 23*, 409–425.

Pearson, Judy C. (1980). Sex roles and self-disclosure. *Psychological Reports, 47*, 640.

Pearson, Judy C. (1989a). *Communication in the family.* New York: Harper & Row.

Pearson, Judy C. (1989b). *Gender and communication.* Dubuque, IA: Wm. C. Brown.

Pearson, Judy C. (1993). *Communication in the family* (2nd ed.). New York: HarperCollins.

Pearson, Judy C., & Spitzberg, B. H. (1990). *Interpersonal communication: Concepts, components, and contexts* (2nd ed.). Dubuque, IA: Wm. C. Brown.

Pease, Allen. (1984). *Signals: How to use body language for power, success and love.* New York: Bantam.

Penfield, Joyce (Ed.). (1987). *Women and language in transition.* Albany: State University of New York Press.

Perlman, Daniel, & Peplau, Letitia Anne. (1981). Toward a social psychology of loneliness. In Steve Duck & Robin Gilmour (Eds.), *Personal Relationships 3: Personal Relationships in Disorder* (pp. 31–56). New York: Academic.

Pfeiffer, J. W., & Jones, J. E. (1969). *Structured experiences for human relations training.* Iowa City, IA: University Associates Press.

Pilkington, Constance J., & Richardson, Deborah R. (1988). Perceptions of risk in intimacy. *Journal of Social and Personal Relationships, 5*, 503–508.

Pittenger, Robert E., Hockett, Charles F., & Danehy, John J. (1960). *The first five minutes.* Ithaca, NY: Paul Martineau.

Pratkanis, Anthony, & Aronson, Elliot. (1991). *Age of propaganda: The everyday use and abuse of persuasion.* New York: W. H. Freeman.

Pryor, J. B. (1980). Self-reports and behavior. In D. M. Wegner & R. R. Vallacher (Eds.), *The self in social psychology*. New York: Oxford University Press.

Qubein, Nido R. (1986). *Get the best from yourself*. New York: Berkley.

Rankin, Paul. (1929). Listening ability. Proceedings of the Ohio State Educational Conference's Ninth Annual Session.

Reed, Warren H. (1985). *Positive listening: Learning to hear what people are really saying*. New York: Franklin Watts.

Rich, Andrea L. (1974). *Interracial communication*. New York: Harper & Row.

Richards, I. A. (1951). Communication between men: The meaning of language. In Heinz von Foerster (Ed.), *Cybernetics: Transactions of the Eighth Conference*.

Richmond, Virginia, McCroskey, James, & Payne, Steven. (1987). *Nonverbal behavior in interpersonal relationships*. Englewood Cliffs, NJ: Prentice-Hall.

Richmond, Virginia P., & McCroskey, James C. (1989). *Communication: Apprehension, avoidance, and effectiveness* (2nd ed.). Scottsdale, AZ: Gorsuch Scarisbrick.

Richmond, Virginia P., & McCroskey, James C. (1992). *Communication: Apprehension, avoidance, and effectiveness* (3rd ed.). Scottsdale, AZ: Gorsuch Scarisbrick.

Riggio, Ronald E. (1987). *The charisma quotient*. New York: Dodd, Mead.

Robinson, W. P. (1972). *Language and social behavior*. Baltimore: Penguin.

Rockefeller, David. (1985). *Vital speeches of the day, 51*, September 15.

Rodriguez, Maria. (1988). Do blacks and Hispanics evaluate assertive male and female characters differently? *Howard Journal of Communication, 1*, 101–107.

Rogers, Carl. (1970). *Carl Rogers on encounter groups*. New York: Harrow Books.

Rogers, Carl, & Farson, Richard. (1981). Active listening. In Joseph A. DeVito (Ed.), *Communication: Concepts and processes* (3rd ed.) (pp. 137–147). Englewood Cliffs, NJ: Prentice-Hall.

Rosenfeld, Lawrence. (1979). Self-disclosure avoidance: Why I am afraid to tell you who I am. *Communication Monographs, 46*, 63–74.

Rosenthal, Robert, & Jacobson, L. (1968). *Pygmalion in the classroom*. New York: Holt, Rinehart and Winston.

Rothwell, J. Dan. (1982). *Telling it like it isn't: Language misuse & malpractice: What we can do about it*. Englewood Cliffs, NJ: Prentice-Hall.

Rothwell, J. Dan. (1992). *In mixed company: Small group communication*. Fort Worth, TX: Harcourt Brace Jovanovich.

Ruben, Brent D. (1985). Human communication and cross-cultural effectiveness. In Larry A. Samovar & Richard E. Porter (Eds.), *Intercultural communication: A reader* (4th ed.) (pp. 338–346). Belmont, CA: Wadsworth.

Ruben, Brent D. (1988). *Communication and human behavior* (2nd ed.). New York: Macmillan.

Rubenstein, Carin, & Shaver, Philip. (1982). *In search of intimacy*. New York: Delacorte.

Rubin, Alan. (1979). Television use by children and adolescents. *Human Communication Research, 5*, 109–120.

Rubin, Rebecca B., & Nevins, Randi. (1988). *The road trip: An interpersonal adventure*. Prospect Heights, IL: Waveland.

Rubin, Rebecca B., Fernandez-Collado, Carlos. (1992). A cross-cultural examination of interpersonal communication motives in Mexico and the United States. *International Journal of Intercultural Relations, 16*, 145–157.

Rubin, Zick, & McNeil, Elton B. (1985). *Psychology: Being human* (4th ed.). New York: Harper & Row.

Ruesch, Jurgen, & Bateson, Gregory. (1951). *Communication: The social matrix of psychiatry*. New York: Norton.

Ruggiero, Vincent Ryan. (1987). *Vital speeches of the day, 53*, August 15.

Ruggiero, Vincent Ryan. (1990). *The art of thinking: A guide to critical and creative thought* (3rd ed.). New York: HarperCollins.

Samovar, Larry A., & Porter, Richard E. (Eds.). (1988). *Intercultural communication: A reader* (5th ed.). Belmont, CA: Wadsworth.

Samovar, Larry A., Porter, Richard E., & Jain, Nemi C. (1981). *Understanding intercultural communication*. Belmont, CA: Wadsworth.

Sargent, J. F., & Miller, Gerald R. (1971). Some differences in certain communication behaviors of autocratic and democratic leaders. *Journal of Communication, 21*, 233–252.

Schafer, R. B., & Keith, P. M. (1980). Equity and depression among married couples. *Social Psychology Quarterly, 43*, 430–435.

Schatski, Michael. (1981). *Negotiation: The art of getting what you want*. New York: New American Library.

Scherer, K. R. (1986). Vocal affect expression. *Psychological Bulletin, 99*, 143–165.

Schultz, Beatrice G. (1989). *Communicating in the small group: Theory and practice*. New York: Harper & Row.

Seidler, Ann, & Bianchi, Doris. (1988). *Voice and diction fitness: A comprehensive approach*. New York: Harper & Row.

Seidman, I. E. (1991). *Interviewing as qualitative research: A guide for researchers in education and the social sciences*. New York: Teachers College, Columbia University.

Shannon, Jacqueline. (1987). Don't smile when you say that. *Executive female, 10,* 33, 43.

Shaw, Marvin. (1981). *Group dynamics: The psychology of small group behaviors* (3rd ed.). New York: McGraw-Hill.

Shimanoff, Susan. (1980). *Communication rules: Theory and research.* Newbury Park, CA: Sage.

Sillars, Alan L., & Scott, Michael D. (1983). Interpersonal perception between intimates: An integrative review. *Human Communication Research, 10,* 153–176.

Sincoff, Michael Z., & Goyer, Robert S. (1984). *Interviewing.* New York: Macmillan.

Singer, Marshall R. (1987). *Intercultural communication: A perceptual approach.* Englewood Cliffs, NJ: Prentice-Hall.

Skopec, Eric William. (1986). *Situational interviewing.* Prospect Heights, IL: Waveland.

Smith, Mary John. (1982). *Persuasion and human action.* Belmont, CA: Wadsworth.

Snyder, Mark. (1986). *Public appearances, private realities.* New York: Freeman.

Sommer, Robert. (1969). *Personal space: The behavioral basis of design.* Englewood Cliffs, NJ: Prentice-Hall/Spectrum.

Spitzberg, Brian H. (1991). Intercultural communication competence. In Larry A. Samovar & Richard E. Porter (Eds.), *Intercultural communication: A reader* (pp. 353–365). Belmont, CA: Wadsworth.

Spitzberg, Brian H., & Cupach, William R. (1984). *Interpersonal communication competence.* Beverly Hills, CA: Sage.

Spitzberg, Brian H., & Cupach, William R. (1989). *Handbook of interpersonal competence research.* New York: Springer-Verlag.

Spitzberg, Brian H., & Hecht, Michael L. (1984). A component model of relational competence. *Human Communication Research, 10,* 575–599.

Sprague, Jo, & Stuart, Douglas. (1988). *The speaker's handbook* (2nd ed.) San Diego: Harcourt Brace Jovanovich.

Steil, Lyman K., Barker, Larry L., & Watson, Kittie W. (1983). *Effective listening: Key to your success.* Reading, MA: Addison-Wesley.

Steiner, Claude. (1981). *The other side of power.* New York: Grove.

Stephen, W. G., & Stephen, C. W. (1985). Intergroup anxiety. *Journal of Social Issues, 41,* 157–176.

Sternberg, Robert J. (1987). Questions and answers about the nature and teaching of thinking skills. In Joan Boykoff Baron & Robert J. Sternberg (Eds.), *Teaching thinking skills: Theory and practice* (pp. 251–259). New York: W. H. Freeman.

Stewart, Charles J., & Cash, William B. Jr. (1988). *Interviewing: Principles and practices* (5th ed.). Dubuque, IA: Wm. C. Brown.

Styles, R. P. (1985, October 1). *Vital speeches of the day, 51.*

Swan, W. B., Jr. (1987). Identity negotiation: Where two roads meet. *Journal of Personality and Social Psychology, 53,* 1038–1051.

Tannen, Deborah. (1994a). *Gender and discourse.* New York: Oxford University Press.

Tannen, Deborah. (1994b). *Talking from 9 to 5: How women's and men's conversational styles affect who gets heard, who gets credit, and what gets done at work.* New York: William Morrow.

Taylor, Dalmas A., & Altman, Irwin. (1987). Communication in interpersonal relationships: Social penetration processes. In M. E. Roloff & G. R. Miller (Eds.), *Interpersonal processes: New directions in communication research* (pp. 257–277). Newbury Park, CA: Sage.

Tersine, Richard J., & Riggs, Walter E. (1980). The Delphi technique: A long-range planning tool. In Stewart Ferguson & Sherry Devereaux Ferguson (Eds.), *Intercom: Readings in organizational communication* (pp. 366–373). Rochelle Park, NJ: Hayden Book.

Thibaut, John W., & Kelley, Harold H. (1986). *The social psychology of groups.* New Brunswick, NJ: Transaction Books.

Thorne, Barrie, Kramarae, Cheris, & Henley, Nancy (Eds.) (1983). *Language, gender and society.* Rowley, MA: Newbury House.

Trager, George L. (1958). Paralanguage: A first approximation. *Studies in Linguistics, 13,* 1–12.

Trager, George L. (1961). The typology of paralanguage. *Anthropological Linguistics, 3,* 17–21.

Veenendall, Thomas L., & Feinstein, Marjorie C. (1990). *Let's talk about relationships: Cases in study.* Prospect Heights, IL: Waveland.

Wade, Carole, & Tavris, Carol. (1990). *Learning to think critically: The case of close relationships.* New York: HarperCollins.

Walker, Charles J., & Blaine, Bruce. (1991). The virulence of dread rumors: A field experiment. *Language and Communication, 11,* 291–297.

Walster, Elaine, Walster, G. W., & Berscheid, Ellen. (1978). *Equity: Theory and research.* Boston: Allyn & Bacon.

Watson, Arden K., & Dodd, Carley H. (1984). Alleviating communication apprehension through rational emotive therapy: A comparative evaluation. *Communication Education, 33,* 257–266.

Watzlawick, Paul. (1977). *How real is real? Confusion, disinformation, communication: An anecdotal introduction to communications theory.* New York: Vintage.

Watzlawick, Paul. (1978). *The language of change: Elements of therapeutic communication.* New York: Basic Books.

Watzlawick, Paul, Beavin, Janet Helmick, & Jackson, Don D. (1967). *Pragmatics of human communication: A study of interactional patterns, pathologies, and paradoxes.* New York: Norton.

Weinberg, Harry L. (1959). *Levels of knowing and existence.* New York: Harper & Row.

Weinstein, Eugene A., & Deutschberger, Paul. (1963). Some dimensions of altercasting. *Sociometry, 26,* 454–466.

Wells, Theodora. (1980). *Keeping your cool under fire: Communicating non-defensively.* New York: McGraw-Hill.

Whitman, Richard F., & Timmis, John H. (1975). The influence of verbal organizational structure and verbal organizing skills on select measures of learning. *Human Communication Research, 1,* 293–301.

Wiemann, John M. (1977). Explication and test of a model of communicative competence. *Human Communication Research, 3,* 195–213.

Wiemann, John M., & Backlund, P. (1980). Current theory and research in communicative competence. *Review of Educational Research, 50,* 185–199.

Wilmot, William W. (1987). *Dyadic communication* (3rd ed.). New York: Random House.

Wilson, R. A. (1989). Toward understanding E-prime. *Etc.: A Review of General Semantics, 46,* 316–319.

Won-Doornink, Myong Jin. (1991). Self-disclosure and reciprocity in South Korean and U.S. male dyads. In Stella Ting-Toomey & Felipe Korzenny (Eds.), *Cross-cultural interpersonal communication* (pp. 116–131). Thousand Oaks, CA: Sage.

Wood, Julia T. (1982). Communication and relational culture: Bases for the study of human relationships. *Communication Quarterly, 30,* 75–83.

Wood, Julia T. (1994). *Gendered lives: Communication, gender, and culture.* Belmont, CA: Wadsworth.

Yun, Hum. (1976). The Korean personality and treatment considerations. *Social Casework, 57,* 173–178.

Zima, Joseph P. (1983). *Interviewing: Key to effective management.* Chicago, IL: Science Research Associations, Inc.

Zimmer, Troy A. (1986). Premarital anxieties. *Journal of Social and Personal Relationships, 3,* 149–159.

Zincoff, M. Z., & Goyer, Robert S. (1984). *Interviewing.* New York: Macmillan.

Zunin, Leonard M., & Zunin, Natalie B. (1972). *Contact: The first four minutes.* Los Angeles, CA: Nash.

Credits

Index

Movement, 329

Name calling, 374
Narration, 359
Negotiation, 243
Neutrality, 222–223
Noise, 12
Nominal group, 243
Nonverbal communication, 121–141
    artifactual messages in, 125,
        131–133
    body movement in, 122–123
    culture and, 125, 130, 133, 134,
        137–138, 140–141
    eye movements in, 126–127
    facial movements in, 123–125, 329
    feedforward and, 12
    listening and, 87
    metacommunication in, 10–11
    paralanguage in, 135–137
    rules of, 9
    spatial distances in, 128–130,
        162, 193
    in speeches, 125, 126, 328–329
    territoriality and, 131
    time in, 137–141
    touch in, 134–135, 234
Norms, small group, 233–234
Notes, for speeches, 319–320, 329

Objectivity, 84–85, 334
Offensive expressions, 308–309
Office decor, 133
Openness, 159–160, 221, 222
    to intercultural communication,
        33–34
    in listening process, 85–86
    in small groups, 256
Operations, definition by, 351
Opinions, 154
Organization, 54
    speech, 293–298
Other-orientation, 166–167, 221
Outlines, 317–320
Overattribution, 63, 114

Panels, 246
Paralanguage, 135–137
Paraphrasing, 89, 155
Parent-Effectiveness-
        Training (P-E-T), 87–88
Passive listening, 82–83
Pauses, 328
Peaceful relations, 99
Percentiles, 357
Perception, 54–67, 184

attribution and, 61–63
checking, 67
defined, 54
guidelines for, 64–65
implicit personality theory and,
    57
primacy effect and, 60
process of, 54
recency effect and, 60
self-fulfilling prophecy and,
    57–59
stereotypes and, 60–61, 66,
    104–105, 109–114, 196
strategies for accurate, 63–64
Personality
    paralanguage and, 136
    perception and, 57
    small groups and, 267
Personal style, 309–310
Personification, 306
Persuasion interviews, 209
Persuasive speeches, 293, 294–297,
        298, 349, 367–389. See also
        Speeches
    credibility appeals in, 380–384
    example of, 384–388
    guidelines for, 368–369
    logical appeals in, 373–377
    psychological appeals in, 38–39,
        378–380
    types of, 369–373
Phatic communion, 153, 154
Pitch, 326
Plain folks, 374
Playfulness, 134
Polarization, 100
Politeness, 99
Positiveness, 134, 162–163, 171–172,
        195, 221, 310, 333–334
Posture, 329
Power, 9
    appeal to, 378
    coercive, 194
    compliance and, 238, 243
    in conversation, 157–158,
        170–171
    cooperation and, 171
    credibility as, 383
    expert, 288–289
    information, 349
    in interpersonal relationships,
        192, 194, 198
    language and, 97
    legitimate, 263
    nonverbal factors in, 125, 126,
        133, 136, 220

persuasion, 349
referent, 36
reward, 194
self-confidence and, 213, 220
in speeches, 288–289, 305
and strategic self-presentation,
    61
from task and dominance cues,
    264
through listening, 81
Primacy effect, 60
Privacy, 108, 127
Pro-and-con pattern, 297–298
Problem solving, 239–245
    group, 239–245
    speech organization based on,
        294–295
    steps in, 240–243
Pronunciation, 326, 327–328
Propositions
    development and support of,
        290–293
    previewing, 312
    restatement of, 311
Psychological appeals, 38–39,
        378–380
Psychological time, 138–140
Public speaking. See Speeches
Punctuation, 17
Pupils (eye), 127
Purpose, 20
    of speech, 281–282
Purr words, 97
Pygmalion effect, 58

Quality circles, 243–244
Questions
    from the audience, 317
    to the audience, 309–310, 311,
        312
    in conversation, 154, 160–161
    ethics and, 160–161, 223–225
    to focus audience attention, 359
    interview, 209, 211–212, 219–220,
        222–225
    in listening process, 89
    rhetorical, 306
    unlawful, 223–225
Quotations, 311, 358

Racism, 109–110, 309
Rapport, 212
Rate, 326
Receiving, in listening process,
        74–77
Recency effect, 60